The Case of
Stephen Lawrence

Brian Cathcart

VIKING

To my parents

VIKING

Published by the Penguin Group
Penguin Books Ltd, 27 Wrights Lane, London w8 5tz, England
Penguin Putnam Inc., 375 Hudson Street, New York, New York 10014, USA
Penguin Books Australia Ltd, Ringwood, Victoria, Australia
Penguin Books Canada Ltd, 10 Alcorn Avenue, Toronto, Ontario, Canada m4v 3b2
Penguin Books (NZ) Ltd, Private Bag 102902, NSMC, Auckland, New Zealand

Penguin Books Ltd, Registered Offices: Harmondsworth, Middlesex, England

First published 1999
10 9 8 7 6 5 4 3 2 1

Copyright © Brian Cathcart, 1999

Set in 11.25/13.25 pt Monotype Sabon
Typeset by Rowland Phototypesetting Ltd, Bury St Edmunds, Suffolk
Printed in Great Britain by Clays Ltd, St Ives plc

A CIP catalogue record for this book is available from the British Library

ISBN 0–670–88640–1

Contents

Contents

The Main Participants

The family, friends and advisers
Stephen Lawrence – the murder victim, aged eighteen
Neville Lawrence – Stephen's father
Doreen Lawrence – Stephen's mother
Cheryl Sloley – Doreen's sister
Imran Khan – solicitor
Michael Mansfield QC – barrister
Stephen Kamlish – barrister
Ros Howells OBE – race relations expert
Elvin Oduro, schoolfriend of Stephen

Witnesses, informants, and those believed to have knowledge of the crime
Duwayne Brooks – Stephen's friend and companion
Joey Shepherd – bus stop witness
Royston Westbrook – bus stop witness
Alexandra Marie – bus stop witness
Conor Taaffe – passer-by who helped comfort Stephen
Witness B – youth who said he saw group fleeing after crime
Witness K – man who visited Acourt house after crime
Emma Cook – girl who passed scene minutes before murder
Michelle Casserley – local girl who named suspects in her diary
EE – boyfriend of Emma Cook, suspected of knowing something
DD – mother of EE
FF – brother of EE
James Grant – pseudonym of key police informant
Stacey Benefield – alleged he was stabbed by Dave Norris
Mattie Farman – friend of Benefield
Darren Witham – alleged he was stabbed by Norris

The prime suspects, their families and friends
Neil Acourt – prime suspect for the murder
Jamie Acourt – prime suspect for the murder
Gary Dobson – prime suspect for the murder
Luke Knight – prime suspect for the murder

David Norris – prime suspect for the murder
Pat Acourt – mother of Neil and Jamie
Scott Lamb – half-brother to Acourts
Bradley Lamb – half-brother to Acourts
Clifford Norris – professional criminal, father of David
Tracey Norris – mother of David
Danny Caetano – friend of the suspects
Charlie Martin – friend of the suspects

Police officers at the murder scene
PC James Geddis – stopped to help Stephen while off-duty
PC Linda Bethel – questioned Duwayne Brooks at scene
PC Anthony Gleason – went from scene to hospital
PC Joanne Smith – present at scene
Inspector Steven Groves – took charge of murder scene
Acting Inspector Ian Little
Chief Superintendent Christopher Benn
Detective Inspector Philip Jeynes

Police officers involved in first investigation
Detective Superintendent Ian Crampton – first senior investigating officer (SIO)
Detective Superintendent Brian Weeden – second SIO
Detective Inspector Benjamin Bullock – deputy SIO
Detective Sergeant Peter Flook – office manager
Detective Sergeant John Davidson – in charge of 'outside' inquiries
Detective Sergeant John Bevan – liaison officer to Lawrences and Brooks
Detective Constable Linda Holden – liaison officer to Lawrences
Detective Constable Christopher Budgen
Detective Constable Mick Tomlin
Detective Constable Dennis Chase
Detective Chief Superintendent John Barker – conducted review

Other police officers
Detective Chief Superintendent William Ilsley (3 Area)
Chief Superintendent John Philpott (3 Area)
Commander Hugh Blenkin (3 Area)
Deputy Assistant Commissioner David Osland (3 Area)

Sir Paul Condon, Metropolitan Police Commissioner
Assistant Commissioner Ian Johnston
Commander Perry Nove
Detective Superintendent William Mellish – third SIO
Detective Chief Inspector John Carnt
Deputy Chief Constable Robert Ayling (Kent police)
Detective Chief Superintendent David Clapperton (Kent police)

The inquiry
Sir William Macpherson of Cluny – chairman
Tom Cook – adviser
Bishop John Sentamu – adviser
Richard Stone – adviser
Edmund Lawson QC – leading counsel to the inquiry
Jeremy Gompertz QC – counsel for the Metropolitan Police
Ian Macdonald QC – counsel for Duwayne Brooks
Jane Deighton – solicitor to Duwayne Brooks
Sonia Woodley QC – counsel for the superintendents

Others
Henry Milner – solicitor to Acourts and to Dave and Clifford Norris
Charles Conway – barrister for the prime suspects
David Cooper – magistrate
Mr Justice Curtis – judge at the Central Criminal Court
Sir Montague Levine – coroner
Howard Youngerwood – senior prosecutor, Crown Prosecution
   Service
Paul Dacre – editor, *Daily Mail*
Peter Bottomley – MP for Eltham, 1975–97
Palma Black – member, Anti-Racist Alliance (ARA)
Marc Wadsworth – leading figure in ARA
Rolan Adams – murder victim, 1991
Rohit Duggal – murder victim, 1992

Metropolitan Police Ranks

Commissioner
Assistant Commissioner
Deputy Assistant Commissioner (DAC)
Commander
Detective Chief Superintendent
Chief Superintendent
Detective Superintendent
Superintendent
Detective Chief Inspector
Chief Inspector
Detective Inspector
Inspector
Detective Sergeant
Police Sergeant
Detective Constable
Police Constable

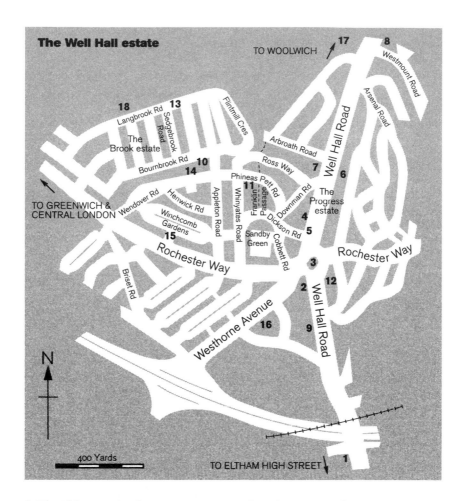

The Well Hall estate

TO WOOLWICH

17

8

Westmount Road

Arsenal Road

Well Hall Road

18 Langbrook Rd 13

Sedgebrook Road

The Brook estate

Flintmill Cres

Arbroath Road

Bournbrook Rd 10

Ross Way

7

14

6

Phineas Pett Rd

11

The Progress estate

TO GREENWICH & CENTRAL LONDON

Wendover Rd

Henwick Rd

Appleton Road

Whinyates Road

Franklin

Passage

Downman Rd

4

Winchcomb Gardens

Dickson Rd

5

15

Sandby Green

Cobbett Rd

Rochester Way

Rochester Way

Briset Rd

3

2

12

Westhorne Avenue

16

9

Well Hall Road

N

400 Yards

TO ELTHAM HIGH STREET

1

1 The Eltham station bus stop, where Stephen and Duwayne boarded the 286 bus
2 Coronet cinema
3 Well Hall Roundabout
4 The 161/122 bus stop, where Stephen, Duwayne and others waited
5 The mouth of Dickson Road, where Stephen was stabbed
6 Where Stephen fell, now marked by a plaque
7 Public telephone
8 Welcome Inn pub
9 The kebab shop on Tudor Parade
10 The Acourt home
11 The Dobson home
12 The Knight home
13 Where Stacey Benefield was stabbed
14 Where the Wendover Road knife was found
15 Where 'Hurry up J/Jamie' was heard
16 The Tyler home
17 Towards Brook Hospital
18 Samuel Montague Sports Club

Foreword

I first wrote about the Lawrence case for *Granta* in the spring of 1997, a narrative account based on what was then publicly known. It was obvious that there was more to come out and by the end of that year, with the PCA investigation complete and the public inquiry ready to begin work, it seemed likely that at last it would come out. This book was conceived and commissioned at that time. Such was the scale of revelation that the book has grown considerably beyond what was originally planned. I have, however, restricted its scope to the events of the case itself and have resisted the temptation to add context such as social history, comparison with other cases or commentary on the culture of the Metropolitan Police. This is partly because these subjects are undoubtedly books in their own right and partly because I feel that the case of Stephen Lawrence, in its detail and as a whole, is rich enough in meaning. Like others who attended the inquiry I was struck both by the depth of the emotions it stirred and by the inability of the media, mainly for understandable reasons of space, to convey more than a fraction of what emerged to those outside. I hope this book can help to fill that gap. I cannot pretend that it is objective, but nor is it intended to be a polemic; I hope that readers, armed with this information, will be able to discuss and argue about the case much as those who saw the inquiry unfold did during the breaks in the proceedings. The story is not a tidy or simple one and much about it remains unexplained and unresolved. We will all have our own views.

In this account I have observed the same guidelines relating to the protection of identity of witnesses and informants that were in force during the inquiry. As a result a few people are identified only by letters or, in one case, by a pseudonym. It will soon be apparent to the reader that the true names of most of these people have been known to the suspects in the case for years; none the less I see no reason to use the real names now.

No one – no group or individual – has authorized me to write this book; it has been an independent project. Many people, however, have helped me with information and advice since I first worked on the case for *Granta*. A number of them made clear that they would rather not be acknowledged by name; because their assistance was, in journalistic terms, off the record. The remainder, more or less close to the events described, I will not identify either, not to create a mystery but because the effect would be distorting and unfair. I would like to thank them all, while making clear that any opinions I express in the book and any mistakes I have made are entirely my own. I must also thank Ian Jack for setting me on this path and Ian Hargreaves and Peter Wilby at the *New Statesman* for their support and their commitment to the story. Some early passages owe something to my *Granta* article and others towards the end of the book draw from my *Statesman* column. Finally, I thank my family – Ruth, Thomas and Patrick – for putting up with it all.

London, 1999

Part One The Fish Pool

Chapter One **Murder**

It would be wrong to say that the morning of Thursday 22 April 1993 was a morning like any other for the Lawrence family, for on that day, unusually, Doreen Lawrence was not at home. At the age of forty, with the children in full-time education, Doreen had enrolled for a university degree and that week she was attending a course in Birmingham. In her absence the running of the household was in the hands of Neville, her husband of twenty years, who was becoming used to this domestic role since he now spent most of his time at home. Although he had enjoyed prosperity in the 1980s as a plasterer and decorator, the 1990s were proving tough and Neville had been unable to find steady work for more than a year – the longest spell of unemployment he had known. He was now fifty years old and, while he still took night classes to learn new skills and he still had ideas for the future, the resourcefulness and determination that had long been part of his character were wearing thin. Money was short and he was depressed.

Neville got breakfast for Stuart, aged sixteen, and Georgina, aged eleven, and then packed them off to school. Stephen got up a little later and had a cup of tea while his father went back upstairs. In the Lawrence home, a compact modern house in Plumstead, southeast London, the kitchen was on the ground floor while the living room and bedrooms occupied the two floors above. Stephen put on his anorak, fetched a bag of school things and then went up to say goodbye to his father. 'See you later,' he said. Neville's thoughts turned to the evening. 'Don't go anywhere because your mum's coming home later,' he replied. Stephen could see that his father was feeling low; for him this was the hardest part of the day. 'Are you OK?' he asked. 'Yes,' came the reply. Stephen went downstairs but quickly returned to check again. 'Are you sure you're all right, Dad?' Yes, again. Neville watched from the window as his oldest child, now a man of eighteen, walked off down the road with his black canvas bag over his shoulder.

He was a son of whom any father would be proud, an amiable, well-rounded and popular young man, not in the first flight academi-cally but still bright and capable. At 5' 8" tall and with a slim build he was no Hercules, but he was a gifted athlete, training and competing regularly as a sprinter with his club, Cambridge Harriers. He was also good-looking, albeit still with traces of adolescent gawkiness, and he had no trouble attracting girls. From his parents he had learned or inherited a certain seriousness about life, and classmates and teachers knew him for his calm and thoughtful nature. In short, he was good company, a good friend, a good son.

Most of us think we understand the world we live in and know what to expect of it, but we rarely do. The world that Stephen stepped out into that morning was the one he had known all his life: the Nightingale estate, the borough of Greenwich, the city of London, modern Britain. Being black gave him a particular perspective on these surroundings in which almost everybody who was powerful or important – from teachers and policemen to government ministers and company directors – was white. But he was used to that. He had his own plans and ambitions, his own networks, his own friends. Colour wasn't everything, he believed; black people like himself could usually do well and be happy if they were reasonably smart and avoided the obvious traps. And most of Britain, most of white Britain, was only too keen to agree with him and to believe that race and racism were diminishing concerns, and not nearly as bad, say, as in France or Germany. But Stephen was wrong. For him, on that day in southeast London, colour *was* everything. And because he was the sort of young man he was, and because Neville and Doreen were the sort of people they are, the case of Stephen Lawrence would eventually make the whole country stop and think. But that was for the future.

After a morning of classes, Stephen emerged at 12.40 p.m. to meet his friend Duwayne Brooks outside the gates of Blackheath Bluecoat School in Old Dover Road. This was Duwayne's day off – he attended a college in Lewisham but on Thursdays he had no classes – and he was in the habit of meeting Stephen at lunchtime. On this particular day they had made a vague agreement to meet some girls from the John Roan School, which was about half a mile away on the edge of Greenwich Park. The rendezvous was a chip shop close to a local junction called, after a pub that stands there, Blackheath Standard. It was five minutes' walk so they strolled down. When they arrived they didn't buy food but played a couple of video games before deciding to wander on in the direction of the girls' school to see if

4

there was any sign of them. At about 1 p.m. they accepted that they had been stood up and headed back to Old Dover Road, chatting at the school gates for the last few minutes before Stephen had to go in. On the face of it this was a dull way to pass a lunchtime, but they were happy enough with each other's company and as the bell rang for classes they arranged to meet again after school. This time they would go down to the Riverdale shopping centre in Lewisham to see who was around.

The friendship between Stephen and Duwayne was a strong one, perhaps unusually so for boys of their age. They had known each other since their first day at Blackheath Bluecoat, when they were eleven, but it was not until they were fourteen or fifteen that they started spending time together, and then they were notable as much for their differences as their similarities. Like Stephen, Duwayne was the oldest of three children, but in his case his parents had separated when he was nine. He was more outgoing and generally noisier than his friend, less conscientious and more streetwise, although he was no tearaway. Duwayne left school after his GCSE exams to enrol for an electrical engineering qualification at Woolwich College, and at the same time he also left home. It was the start of a difficult period; he was young to be on his own and he had difficulty keeping himself steady, so he drifted unhappily between bedsits and hostels, mostly in the Lewisham area, and began to skip classes. Soon he dropped out of college altogether.

Stephen, meanwhile, continued his studies. He had ambitions to be an architect and was working part of the time at school and part at Woolwich College in pursuit of the qualifications he needed to get into university. In most cases, two boys following such different paths would lose touch, particularly as it was a connection of which Stephen's parents disapproved. Neville and Doreen worried that this 'ragamuffin' boy Duwayne was distracting their son and they resented the way that, during the inevitable domestic arguments over curfew times, Stephen would often say: 'Duwayne doesn't have to be home, so why do I?' As a result, Duwayne rarely visited the Lawrence home in Llanover Road. But the two boys remained steady friends, meeting two or three times a week, and this bond proved something of an anchor for Duwayne. Doreen Lawrence was later to remark that Duwayne needed her son more than her son needed him, but for Stephen, who was never short of company, there must

5

also have been something valuable in the friendship. By the start of 1993, in any case, Duwayne was beginning to sort himself out, settling down in a hostel in Charlton and starting a course in electronic servicing at Lewisham College.

At 3.10 p.m., the school day over, the two friends duly caught the bus to Lewisham, Stephen with his bag over his shoulder and a baseball cap in the colours of the Jamaican flag tugged down over his close-cropped hair. With them were some other kids from the school: Stephen's cousin Karina, her friend Zerin and another boy, who was a relative of Duwayne's friend Leon. They changed buses at Blackheath Village, parting company with Zerin, and took the 54 to Lewisham, where Karina went her own way. That left the three boys. At the Riverdale centre they wandered around for a while, eventually bumping into Leon, who went off with his relation (whose name Duwayne had never quite remembered). Now they were two again, but not for long, for they spotted Anne, a friend of Duwayne's whom he had not seen for some time. Anne lived in Grove Park and the three of them decided to head off there together, catching another bus. Grove Park is about two miles from Lewisham, and some way to the south of where Stephen and Duwayne lived. It was now about 5.45 p.m.

The boys' plan was to go to the house of Stephen's uncle Martin, Doreen's younger half-brother, who lived close to Grove Park on the Chinbrook estate. Martin Lindo was friendly with both boys – he had known Duwayne's mother, who lived nearby, for some years – and such visits were common enough. Duwayne, however, had something he wanted to do before going to Martin's; he had taken a shine to Anne and wanted to see her home. So they split up, Stephen going directly to Martin's and Duwayne accompanying Anne part of the way to her home before jumping on another bus to Chinbrook and rejoining his friend at his uncle's at about 6.30 p.m. For the next three and a half hours Stephen and Duwayne chatted and played Nintendo games – a recent passion – and ate dinner with Martin and his wife, Millie.

Stephen probably forgot that his father had asked him to be home early, but he knew that his regular curfew hour was 10.30 p.m., so just before 10 p.m. he and Duwayne set out for home. The journey before them was not long – about three miles – but in a direction that London's transport system was not really designed to cater for. They were going north, along a line roughly parallel with the

Greenwich Meridian, while the main roads and rail services in that part of the city run mainly east–west, in and out of central London. It meant they would need more than one bus to get home, but they were used to this. They knew all the routes and had bus passes, so they could easily string together short hops to get where they wanted to go. Stephen was the one under pressure to get home and he knew that unless he had unusually bad luck he would be back in Plumstead soon after 10.30 p.m.

They walked from Martin Lindo's house to a stop in Dunkery Road and caught a number 126 bus to Eltham High Street, getting off near the McDonald's at around 10.15 p.m. They went around the corner into Well Hall Road to wait opposite Eltham police station for a number 161 that would take them to Woolwich. While they stood there a white man in his thirties whom they did not know arrived at the stop and waited close by. His name was Royston Westbrook and he was a hospital support worker on his way home after an evening shift. The three of them overheard a conversation among bus staff suggesting that the drivers on the 161 route might be on strike. Westbrook stayed where he was, but Stephen and Duwayne decided they would walk down to Well Hall Roundabout, where they knew there would be a better choice of buses. It was on their present route, so if anything came along as they walked they could run for it. Sure enough, they had not gone far before a 286 overtook them. They chased it to the next stop, opposite Eltham railway station, where by good fortune it was delayed and they were able to catch up and board. The delay was caused by a young woman who was asking the bus driver questions. This was Alexandra Marie, a French au pair on her way back from an evening in central London. She had come by train from Charing Cross and was asking how to get to Shooters Hill. The bus wasn't going all the way there, but eventually the driver told her to get on. Already on the bus was Royston Westbrook.

Duwayne now suggested to Stephen that they stay on the 286 all the way to Blackheath Standard and change there for a number 53, which would take him to his home in Charlton and Stephen on to Woolwich. Stephen thought differently. Instead of Duwayne's dogleg route he favoured an option that was far more direct, for him at least. This meant getting off in a couple of stops, at the Coronet cinema close to Well Hall Roundabout, then crossing over and taking either a 161 (if they were not on strike) or a 122 over the hill to Woolwich. Even though it did not suit him quite as well, Duwayne agreed to do this; after all, he wasn't the one in a hurry. So they got off at the cinema, as did Royston Westbrook. The bus pulled away and then stopped again at the edge of the roundabout, where Alexandra Marie alighted. There was no stop there; the driver was bending the rules a little to help the young Frenchwoman. He told her to cross the roundabout to a bus stop on the far side and wait there for a 122 or a 161, which would take her where she wanted to go. The boys and Westbrook were heading the same way with the same intention, and they walked behind her across the middle of the roundabout to the bus stop a little farther up Well Hall Road, just past the junction with Dickson Road. Marie got there first and looked at the timetable; one of the boys arrived and looked over her shoulder, remarking: 'A couple of minutes.' Duwayne checked his watch: it was 10.25 p.m.

Alexandra Marie sat on the ground with her back to the bus shelter and lit a cigarette while Duwayne and Stephen chatted nearby. To the French girl they seemed happy and full of life, and she thought she saw one of them practising a few dance steps. Westbrook heard the boys talking about football – Arsenal or West Ham. He saw the same foot movements but interpreted them in a different way; he thought one of them was kicking an imaginary ball. Two minutes passed, then three, then four, then five, but no bus came. The group at the bus stop – the two boys, the older man and the young Frenchwoman – were joined by a fifth person, a blond, white eighteen-year-old called Joseph Shepherd, who walked up, as they all had, from the direction of the roundabout. Joey, as he was known, lived on the same estate as Stephen and they knew each other by sight, but they were not friends and they did not exchange more than a glance. Duwayne did not know him.

Soon the two friends became restless. It was after 10.35 p.m. now, so they had waited more than ten minutes. Stephen was late and beginning to contemplate, without relish, the roasting he would get when he got home. The story about the strike on the 161 route seemed to be true, which meant his only hope at this stop was a number 122, which would come up from Westhorne Avenue. Duwayne wondered again about the dogleg route, which would mean going around the corner to catch the 286 in Rochester Way, but Stephen was reluctant. He was almost home; it was just a mile and a half over the hill. (In fact if he had walked instead of waiting for the bus he would have been nearly home by now.) If a bus came along, he could still be there in a few minutes. As they talked they drifted back towards the roundabout, to a point from which they would be able to see across and down Well Hall Road; that way they might know whether another 286 was on its way in time to get around the corner into Rochester Way. This decision, which took the two boys away from the company of the three people at the bus stop and left them on their own, was to prove fateful.

It was just fifty yards to the roundabout but their movements towards it betrayed their differing inclinations. While Stephen hung back Duwayne walked ahead, crossing Dickson Road. As he did so he noticed a group of youths – white youths – over to his left, crossing Rochester Way where it left the roundabout on the eastern side. He wondered fleetingly what they were doing. At the same moment, however, Duwayne spotted a bus coming up the lower part of Well Hall Road. 'Can you see the bus?' he asked, turning to Stephen. There was no reply. From this moment the relative positions of the two boys, and their different states of mind, are important. As Duwayne moved back towards the bus stop Stephen stayed where he was, perhaps trying to see the number of the bus in the distance, and so Stephen was now the nearer of the two to the roundabout. Duwayne looked back to see if the bus had reached the cinema stop where he and Stephen had got off earlier, and as he looked he realized that the group of white youths – there seemed to be six of them – had come much closer. They were twenty yards away on the opposite side of Well Hall Road, close to a zebra crossing.

Both black boys were now moving back towards the bus stop, with Stephen a few yards behind. Duwayne, having looked back, was aware of danger, but Stephen, although he was nearer to the white boys, was not. Perhaps he was preoccupied, worried about being late and juggling bus numbers and routes in his head. It may also be that his Walkman distracted him; he was wearing one, although nobody knows now whether it was switched on. Duwayne had asked once whether Stephen had seen the bus, and received no reply; now he called out more urgently: 'Can you see it?' Again, no answer. But if Stephen wasn't listening somebody else was, for Duwayne heard a shout from across the road: 'What? What? Nigger!'

9

Whipping around, he saw the white boys charging towards them. The one in front – Duwayne formed the impression that this was the boy who had shouted – was staring at him. 'Run! Run!' he called to Stephen, and took a few paces up the hill in the direction of the bus stop. He looked back and saw that Stephen, the trained sprinter who had won medals and certificates, had not moved. And then the white boys were upon him. Duwayne had seen the leading youth draw something long from inside his clothing as he crossed the road. Now he saw this object again as the boy raised his arm above his head and brought it down on Stephen.

What happened to Stephen in these moments is clearer than what happened to Duwayne. Only a few yards separated them at the moment the white youths charged, and two of the other witnesses at the bus stop later said that, in the first moment of contact, Duwayne was caught as well. Held only by an arm or a sleeve, he managed to shake free and run. Duwayne did not remember this, but some time later he recalled that one of the white boys had chased him briefly before turning back to join the attack on Stephen. What is certain is that Duwayne got away and ran a short distance – perhaps twenty yards – up Well Hall Road, repeatedly looking back to see what was happening to his friend.

The whole encounter took no more than a few seconds – seven seconds, it was later estimated. Stephen was struck and either fell or was pushed to the ground. Some of the witnesses said he was kicked and one saw him try to fend off the blows. Then it was over, and while the attackers disappeared down Dickson Road Stephen rolled over, got to his feet and ran in the opposite direction, across Well Hall Road. It was so sudden that none of the five people who had been waiting at the bus stop – not even Stephen himself – realized what had really happened. Royston Westbrook, Joey Shepherd and Alexandra Marie had been watching (although Marie had only a partial view), and they were all left with the impression of a fleeting attack, a flurry, a few blows, a man going down and then rolling free, his assailants fleeing. None of them saw a weapon.

But there was a weapon; at least one. In that brief moment Stephen was stabbed twice. One blow, to the chest, cut through two major nerves, a large vein and an artery before penetrating a lung. The other, gashing the left shoulder, also cut through an artery and a vein. As a result, Stephen lost all feeling in his right arm and his breathing was constricted, while he was losing blood from four major blood vessels. The shock of the attack had sent his heart rate sharply up, so the blood was pumping out into his clothing and on to the ground. At such moments, however, the body plays tricks. The nervous system reacts to mask the damage and natural painkillers flood the system, while fear and shock produce a rush of adrenalin. Stephen had no idea how terrible his injuries were; he knew he had been hit very hard, but that was all. He picked himself up and ran. By the time he reached the far side of the road, however, he realized something was wrong. His right arm was not working – it hung numb and limp at his side – and he felt the wetness of blood on his front. 'Duwayne!' he called out, but his friend, crossing over after him and leading the way uphill, insisted: 'Just run!'

Stephen managed to cover more than 200 yards up the hill behind Duwayne, but his body felt stranger and stranger. Progressively he was losing feeling and slowing down, and his head was swimming. He called out: 'Duwayne, look at me, tell me what's wrong.' His clothes were dark and it was night, but looking closely now Duwayne could see by the orange light of the streetlamps that his friend was soaked with blood and that it was actually gushing out through his clothing just below the neck. Duwayne was appalled, but he was also afraid that the white boys would come back for more. 'Just keep running,' he said, breathless. 'I can't,' protested Stephen, putting his hand to his chest. 'I can't.' And with those words he slumped to the ground.

Duwayne himself was terrified and in shock; now he looked down and saw blood trickling out on to the pavement from Stephen's body. He realized for the first time that his friend might die, and this realization all but overwhelmed him. Desperate though he was, he did not quite panic; he looked for help. It was no use going back to the bus stop; down the hill he could see the three other people who had waited with them boarding the 161. Directly across the road, however, Duwayne could see a public telephone tucked into the hedge beside the Roman Catholic church. He ran over and dialled 999. He was extremely frightened and agitated; Stephen was alone by the roadside and the boys might come back. Putting the receiver down on the shelf for a moment, he stepped back to check down the road. Just then he saw a couple on foot and called out or gestured to them for help, but they seemed just to hurry on. This made

Duwayne even more frantic. Remembering the phone, he went back and picked it up again. Shouting, he asked for an ambulance and said that his friend had been hit on the head with an iron bar. The operator asked who he was and he gave his name. Then she asked where he was calling from. He hesitated. The question came again. Where was he? Eltham, Well Hall, near the roundabout, he stammered. The operator asked Duwayne to look at the address given above the phone. Duwayne read a postal code, but as he did so he knew it was wrong, and he said so. The operator asked for more but Duwayne, speechless with frustration and shock, dropped the receiver, kicked the telephone stand and stumbled away.

He knew that Stephen was bleeding very badly, but he also knew that Brook Hospital, with its accident and emergency department, was less than a mile away, up Well Hall Road and to the left. By car it would take three or four minutes. Would that not be better than waiting for an ambulance? Duwayne ran into the road to flag down a passing car, but he soon found that there were not many drivers on the road – it was now 10.45 p.m. – and those who were did not want to stop. One car slowed to a halt, raising Duwayne's hopes, but then it suddenly accelerated off past him. Rage and despair flooded the young man's mind. First the couple on foot, now this. Why would no one help? What could he do to save Stephen? Should *he* be doing something to stop the bleeding? Then at last a light-coloured car pulled up on the far side of the road from where Stephen lay; Duwayne spoke to the driver, who turned his car and parked. The couple inside got out to help. When they reached Stephen they found another couple already there. They were Conor and Louise Taaffe, local people on their way home from a prayer meeting at the Roman Catholic church just beyond the public telephone on the other side of the road. It had been the Taaffes whom Duwayne had seen before he made his 999 call, and he thought they had simply walked away. In fact they had seen Stephen fall and sensed that something was seriously wrong, but they took a moment to dismiss a fear that this was a mugger's trap. Then they crossed and knelt beside Stephen.

For Duwayne, who had seen the blood flowing, getting Stephen to Brook Hospital had an overwhelming urgency. Every second that his friend lay on the pavement seemed to Duwayne like an hour. In fact all this had happened – the running, the collapse, the 999 call, the desperate waving down of cars – in just a few minutes, long enough for the 161 bus to reach the bus stop, pick up three people and cover the distance up the road and past Stephen's prone form. By the time Westbrook, Shepherd and Marie looked down from the bus window to see what had happened to the two black boys who had run away, a cluster of people had gathered around the one who was lying on the ground. The three on the bus were still under the impression that they had witnessed nothing more than a rumble between a group of lads, with no lasting harm done. 'He got a pasting, didn't he?' Shepherd had remarked as they boarded the bus. 'It was probably because he was black.' Marie had noticed that Stephen had abandoned his black bag at the spot where he was beaten, but seeing him run she assumed that he had suffered only slight injury. As for Westbrook, when he read and heard reports of the attack later in the media, he did not even connect them with the events he had witnessed.

The driver who stopped to help Duwayne was an off-duty police constable, James Geddis, who coincidentally was also returning from a prayer meeting. His wife Angela knelt beside Stephen, and Duwayne asked her: 'Is he still breathing?' She said he was. PC Geddis asked whether an ambulance was coming and Duwayne pointed to the telephone, saying he had tried but did not know if the message had got through. Geddis crossed the road, picked up the hanging receiver and spoke to the operator. He returned to say help was on its way. Stephen lay on his front, with his head turned to the side and a knee and an arm raised, approximately in what is called in first aid the recovery position. Geddis fetched a blanket from his car and stretched it over him. Duwayne kept asking the same question: 'Is he still breathing? Is he still breathing?' Stephen's breath was now faint and shallow. Three people were beside him: Mrs Geddis and the Taaffes. They thought he seemed peaceful and not in pain. Mrs Taaffe, feeling there was little else she could do, prayed.

Duwayne, meanwhile, was pacing up and down and wondering where the ambulance was. He was angry, angry at the whole situation, angry about the attack, angry at his own powerlessness, angry that the people who had turned up seemed to make no difference. He recognized the Taaffes as the couple he thought had ignored him a few moments earlier; that made him angrier. Then he heard a siren and saw a flashing light on the road. His hopes rose, but it turned out to be a police car. His feelings boiled over. 'Where's the fucking ambulance? I didn't call the police!' he screamed as two officers stepped out. The time was now 10.50 p.m.; about ten minutes had passed since the attack.

Duwayne was also angry with himself, because he was afraid that due to his own panic the first 999 call had not got through, and valuable time had been lost. He was wrong. The British Telecom operator received his call at 10.43 p.m. and despite the difficulties of the conversation she was able quickly to trace it to the public phone at the junction of Well Hall Road and Downman Road. She alerted the London Ambulance Service, advising them that a hysterical male had reported that another man had been assaulted with an iron bar and was injured at the scene. An ambulance was despatched from Greenwich Hospital. The operator passed the same message to Metropolitan Police Headquarters at Scotland Yard. Their radio alert had brought the police car from fairly close by.

In the car were two uniformed constables, Linda Bethel and Anthony Gleason. As he got out Gleason radioed for backup, then he made straight for Stephen, took his pulse and found it very faint. Without moving Stephen, he checked his head for signs of the reported head wound. Finding none, and still without moving the body, he had a quick look to see if there was any sign of a wound elsewhere. Through the several layers of clothing nothing was visible. Meanwhile Bethel, seeing the blood, radioed in to check that the ambulance was on its way and was told it would be three to four minutes. She also asked for another police car to be sent. Then she turned to Duwayne to find out what had happened. He was still pacing up and down, still asking whether Stephen was breathing, still looking distractedly along the road for signs of an ambulance. He was able to answer a few questions but soon broke off, demanding to know why they could not simply put Stephen into their police car and drive him to the hospital, since it was so close. They insisted that it would be wiser to wait for the ambulance.

A panicky atmosphere hung over the scene. Duwayne was shouting, angry and frantic, while Stephen's breathing, which a few moments earlier had been strong enough to cause a visible movement of the chest, had weakened. People were emerging from nearby houses, asking what was happening. For the police officers this was an unsettling situation; usually they would expect to reach an attack scene at much the same time as the ambulance – often after it. An anxious Gleason consulted Bethel about what to do and decided to drive towards Woolwich (from where he assumed it would come) to see if there was a problem on the road that might be causing a delay. As he left another police car arrived, bringing another woman officer, Joanne Smith. She and Bethel spoke to Duwayne, who managed to spill out the essential details. They had been attacked by six white men who used the word nigger; he had told Stephen to run but they had caught him and struck him with something that looked like an iron bar; the attackers had run off down the side road. Duwayne also supplied his own name and address and Stephen's name.

The Taaffes were still crouching beside Stephen, praying and offering comfort. 'You are loved, you are loved,' Mrs Taaffe whispered to him. He had moved his head a little once – Mr Taaffe thought this was in an effort to breathe more easily – but apart from that he seemed peaceful. Now the Taaffes were concerned that his breathing had ceased altogether, and they called Bethel over. She too crouched down and put a hand in front of Stephen's mouth. She thought there was a faint breath. She took his pulse, and once again thought she just detected something. Later she was to say that in the tension of the moment it might have been her own pulse that she felt.

At 10.54 p.m. – four minutes after the first police car – the ambulance arrived. It had come from four miles away in Greenwich, and although there might have been a very slight delay because of a confusion over the location, it had come as quickly as was possible. Geoffrey Mann, the paramedic on board, examined Stephen and found no vital signs at all: no pulse, no heartbeat and no respiration. Mann and his driver, with a little help from Mr Taaffe, put Stephen on a stretcher and loaded him into the ambulance. When they lifted him they saw with horror that the clothing that had been under his body as he lay, and the pavement beneath, were awash with blood. What kind of attack had this been, wondered Mr Taaffe. How was it possible to inflict such damage with an iron bar? There was an unopened ginger beer can on the ground – Stephen's. Duwayne stooped and picked it up. Later he took it home and kept it there, until one day it exploded.

The ambulance left the scene at 11.03 p.m., with Mann already working to restart Stephen's heart. Duwayne had wanted to accompany his friend but was persuaded to follow with Joanne Smith in the panda car, which was right behind. With his siren on and with Gleason driving ahead of him, ambulance driver Michael Salih headed straight up the hill in the direction of Woolwich and then, at the traffic lights at the crest of the rise, turned left into Shooters Hill Road. Another left took him into the forecourt of Brook Hospital and to the A&E department, where a trauma team, forewarned by radio, stood ready. The journey took three minutes. Stephen was swept into Resuscitation Room One, where many things happened at once: his blood-soaked clothes were cut away, a continuous effort was made to restart his heart by pressing down on his chest, a tube was passed into his windpipe to restore respiration and attempts were made to insert further tubes into the veins of his arms so that lost blood could be replaced. As they worked, briskly and efficiently, the medical team became aware of something: there was no head injury, which was what they had been warned to expect; instead the removal of the clothes revealed two large upper-body wounds. While the resuscitation efforts continued, a surgeon and a nurse, still in their green surgical attire, went to find out what had really happened to Stephen. Outside in the waiting area they found Duwayne, Gleason – and Doreen and Neville Lawrence.

It may have been only seconds after the ambulance turned left at the traffic lights that Stephen's parents reached the same junction from the opposite direction. By a remarkable chance they had found out very quickly that their son had been attacked. Like them, Joey Shepherd lived on the south side of the Nightingale estate – he was a neighbour. From the scene of the attack he had travelled on the 161 bus over the hill towards Woolwich. Alighting by Woolwich Common, he walked home and there told his father what he had seen. Father and son went promptly to the Lawrence home and knocked at the door.

Earlier in the evening Neville had expected to see Stephen for dinner with the rest of the family, as instructed. When the boy failed to turn up he simply assumed he was visiting a friend – not Duwayne, but Elvin Oduro – and put his plate in the oven alongside Doreen's. At about 9.30 p.m. Neville left Stuart and Georgina (who was in bed) and took the car down to Woolwich to pick up his wife from the coach. Doreen, tired, was disappointed to find that Stephen was not at home. She ate her meal and sat down to watch television. After *News at Ten* the local news began; it was past 10.30 p.m., past curfew. A little anxious, but mostly weary, Doreen went to the bathroom to get ready for bed, and while she was there she heard the knock on the door. Her first reaction was that Stephen was home, and she was pleased. Then she heard the voices of strangers. Going down to find out who it was, she heard Joey Shepherd explain that he had seen Stephen being attacked at a bus stop near the Welcome Inn on Well Hall Road. Was he badly hurt? Joey didn't know. For a moment the Lawrences just looked at each other, then Joey's father suggested they call the police. Doreen immediately dialled 999 and was put through to the police, who told her they had no report of such an incident. The call was logged at 10.56 p.m., which was just after Geoffrey Mann's ambulance had reached the scene on Well Hall Road.

Doreen threw on a coat and Stuart appeared with some shoes for her. He also had his coat on but she told him he had to stay with Georgina. Then she and Neville jumped in the car. Joey had mentioned the Welcome Inn so they drove there, stopping for the red light on Shooters Hill Road along the way. All was quiet near the pub; no police and no crowd. At the bus stop, too, nothing. This was because the Welcome Inn is higher up the road, so they were still some distance short of the scene of the stabbing. They did not carry on southwards but turned and headed for Brook Hospital to see whether they could learn anything there. It was just around the corner; while Neville parked, Doreen ran in. If her son was there she expected him to be in the casualty waiting area, and when she found that he was not she was relieved and ready to leave. But when Neville arrived he recognized Duwayne immediately and asked him what had happened. At that moment the surgeon and nurse, in their green robes, emerged from Resuscitation One asking questions.

Duwayne could only tell them what he thought he had seen: Stephen had been hit with something that looked like an iron bar. Neville and Doreen, now having their first inkling of the seriousness of their son's position, stammered out questions. Was it really Stephen in there? Yes, it was. What was happening? He was being worked on. Could they see him? No, not yet. They were ushered into a nearby room to wait. Doreen was unable to sit, and went off to telephone her sister Cheryl to let her know what had happened. Neville also called a cousin. Duwayne joined them in the room, but though they asked him questions he was too distressed to help. The Lawrences were in torment. Neville recalled later: 'We thought maybe Stephen had been stabbed in his arm or he had cut his hand or something. I was just praying that he was not dead. I thought it was just a fight in which he got cut badly . . . I don't remember if we talked to each other; we just sat there. All sorts of thoughts were going through my mind.' After about half an hour he looked up and saw the doctor and nurse approaching, still in their green garb. 'I was thinking, "Are they coming to tell me that Stephen is dead?"' They were.

The struggle in the resuscitation room had not continued for very long. Even at the time that Stephen was loaded into the ambulance, the paramedic, Geoffrey Mann, had thought there was very little hope, and the trauma doctors knew it as soon as they saw the wounds and established how much blood had been lost. They tried everything they could – medicine doesn't give up easily and it doesn't pay to assume anything until you know it – but to no avail. They could staunch the bleeding but they could not replace what had been lost; Stephen's veins had collapsed. Nor could they restart his breathing. When after ten minutes there had been no sign of pulse or electrical activity in the heart, they abandoned the struggle. Stephen's death certificate was signed at 11.17 p.m., but the real moment of death had come earlier. He had been stabbed just before 10.40 p.m. and his heart continued to beat for at most another fifteen minutes. We don't know exactly when it stopped, but it was probably some time between 10.50 p.m., when PC Gleason said he detected a faint pulse, and 10.54 p.m., when Geoffrey Mann found none. He died where he fell, on the cold pavement of Well Hall Road, in a pool of his own blood, a couple of feet away from the passing traffic.

Chapter Two **A Place, Some People**

These events occurred in the borough of Greenwich, but the thoughts usually conjured up by that name are in this case misleading. Greenwich, with its Meridian, its *Cutty Sark* and its noble architecture rising up from the bank of the Thames, occupies a lofty niche in the gallery of British heritage, but the districts of Plumstead and Eltham where Stephen Lawrence lived and died, while they fall within the same borough, belong in practice to another suburb. Their ties are to Woolwich, an altogether more workaday town a little farther downstream. Where Greenwich had the Royal Naval College, Woolwich had the Arsenal; where Greenwich had the Enlightenment, Woolwich had centuries of manual toil; where Greenwich had Georgian grandeur, Woolwich had many visits from the Luftwaffe. Tourists are in short supply here, and gentrification, for the most part, is still awaited.

If you turn your back on the Thames at Woolwich and head up the hill that becomes Shooters Hill, you soon pass a forbidding modern housing development on your left. Here, in the Nightingale estate, lived the Lawrence family. Carry on along the side of Woolwich Common to the lights near the crest of the hill and you pass close to the site of Brook Hospital, now closed. Continue south and you begin the gentle descent by Well Hall Road, past the place where Stephen died, past the roundabout across which he and Duwayne walked, and on down as far as Eltham railway station, where the line to London Bridge and Waterloo runs over your head. From here a final, steep climb takes you up to the corner of Eltham High Street, by St John's Church of England church. It is a three-mile journey, and a century ago much of it would have been made through open country, but then the trams came, and the First World War, and all was transformed.

Though it is not a Greenwich or even a Woolwich, Eltham can boast a little history of its own. From the fourteenth century to the sixteenth Eltham Palace, of which a rump remains, was a home to kings. It was then far beyond the edges of dirty, disease-ridden London and proved a happy royal refuge on the edge of Kent, with good hunting to hand. Here Richard II employed Geoffrey Chaucer as his clerk of works, and here the young Henry VIII received an educational visit from Erasmus of Rotterdam. When the kings moved on (to newer, smarter palaces at Greenwich and Hampton Court) the village on its hill remained, little more than a stopping place on the way to other places not much bigger. So it was for centuries, until in the 1860s the railway came by; a station opened a little to the south and suddenly Eltham was in easy reach of the metropolis. Houses filled the southern slopes down towards Mottingham and the population multiplied, with some residents grander than others: W. G. Grace set up home and so did E. Nesbit, and this was where Kitty O'Shea entertained Charles Stuart Parnell. At the same time a little light engineering took root in the area, attracting the working classes. Then a second railway line arrived, this time cutting through the valley to the north, and the Victorian streets swiftly worked their way out in that direction to meet it. The decisive northward shift in Eltham's centre of gravity came when tramlines were laid along Well Hall Road, linking the town with the new northern station and then running on over the wooded hill to Woolwich.

With the coming of war in 1914 the Arsenal in Woolwich sprang to life and the workforce turning out the howitzers for the Western Front became an army in its own right. They needed houses and so the fields beside Well Hall Road were ploughed up for homes and Eltham acquired battalions of new residents who took the tram north to work in Woolwich every day. This expansion began handsomely with the 1,298 family homes of the Progress estate, built in short order and opened in 1915. It was a Garden City development full of charm and space, the streets of pretty houses with steep roofs and dainty windows – no two homes the same – artfully wound around wide, green lawns and hedges to create the illusion of organic growth, of a jumbled English country village on the edge of London. Architecture students are still brought there to draw and admire. But after this the imperatives of war overtook aesthetics, and from the summer of 1916 the new accommodation thrown up along the southern slopes of Shooters Hill took the form of row upon row of wooden houses, known as 'hutments'. Inevitably this short-term solution became a long-term expedient, and the hutments stood for twenty years.

Well Hall Road remains the spine of the Progress estate, and this was where Stephen Lawrence died. Dickson Road, down which his killers escaped, plunges westward from the main road to meet Downman Road and Phineas Pett Road in a handsome, open junction, with little Cobbett Road to the left and the narrow Franklin Passage off to the right – all of these streets were to have a role in the police investigation that followed the murder. After Dickson Road the 1915 housing ends and you find yourself in streets of charmless concrete houses built decades later: Appleton Road, Winchcomb Gardens, Wendover Road. Beyond, there used to be the brook, the stream that ran down from a spring up near the hospital but has long since been relegated to a culvert. And beyond that, another estate, known as the Brook. Dating from the 1940s and 1950s, it is part of the second great overspill that brought people from inner London slums to new, modern housing in a district that had its own factories but was also in easy reach of town. Unlike the tangled layout of the Progress, the streets of the Brook form a simple grid, with Langbrook Road along the north side, Bournbrook Road on the south, and Crossbrook, Sedgebrook and the others cutting in between. The houses are for the most part solid and square, built in warm, dark brick and by no means cramped. This estate was to play a leading part in the case of Stephen Lawrence.

The new, urban Eltham acquired its own particular tone, a tone encapsulated in the list of its famous sons. This was now the birthplace of Bob Hope, the home town of Frankie Howerd and Denis Healey and the chosen residence, even when he was a Cabinet minister, of Herbert Morrison. It came to see itself as a place for improvers, for the upwardly mobile, for working-class people who intended to make something of themselves. And for years, housing policies based on kith-and-kin preference ensured that the character of that population did not change: sons and daughters lived around the corner from their mothers and fathers, while cousins were neighbours. Although today local industrial employment has all but disappeared and there are pockets of harsh deprivation among the patchwork of estates, people are still generally better off here than in most of the wider borough of Greenwich. They still have their green space; they are, very often, owner-occupiers; in the Thatcher years they returned a Conservative to Parliament.

An unprovoked, racist murder may not seem to belong in such a place, but this crime had a context. Eltham, Mottingham, Shooters Hill, Plumstead: these parts of London's outer city were no strangers to ethnic violence. In the borough as a whole, demographic conditions were apparently perfect for racism. The ethnic minority population, at around 13 per cent, was not particularly large; if it were larger there might have been strength in numbers, but at this level the black and Asian people were scattered and often isolated among the white majority. In economic terms the wider area was struggling: unemployment was far above the national average and in particular the number of jobs for men had slumped disastrously over the past twenty years. Most measures showed a high level of poverty; one household in five, for example, was seriously behind with utility bills.

Racial harassment of one sort or another was commonplace. In one recent year 440 incidents were reported to the police, one of the highest levels in the country, and by common consent this was a fraction of the total. Gacara (Greenwich Action Committee Against Racial Attacks), an independent group supported by the local council, logged 930 incidents in the same year, and even that figure certainly fell short of the true total. For one thing, an 'incident' was not always a single event. To take an example, Gacara recorded what had happened to one Asian woman over a period of three weeks: she was verbally abused and then punched in the arm; a boy deliberately rode his bicycle into her; she was verbally abused and threatened; another boy rode his bicycle into her; she was verbally abused ('Get back you black bitch'); four youths blocked her way as she tried to leave home by car and then abused and threatened her ('Paki bitch'). These six events were recorded as a single incident. For dozens, perhaps hundreds of families in the borough, racial abuse, threats and violence of this kind were so common as to be routine. At least one such family lived in the Brook estate: Asians, they were the target of constant harassment by local youths over many months but they were too afraid to take the matter to the police, even when one visitor to their house was so badly beaten he needed hospital treatment. And just as there were many victims there were many perpetrators, active racists who thought little or nothing of spitting or swearing at black and Asian people, or throwing eggs at them from passing cars, or pushing excrement or burning paper through their letter-boxes, or spraying slogans on their doors or walls, or kicking or punching them. Elected representatives, council officials and the police never tired of insisting that Greenwich had no problems that plenty of other districts in Britain did not have, that the vast majority of people were responsible and law-abiding, that the press and the anti-racist activists exaggerated. But there was no escaping it: this borough was at or close to the top of Britain's racism league, and Eltham played its part.

In the year after Stephen's death a research team led by Roger Hewitt of the Institute for Education at the University of London conducted a study in Eltham. They looked for racism – 'We went to certain neighbourhoods which black people experienced as especially threatening and got to know the young people there.' And they found it – 'We were surprised at the level and ubiquity of the racism we encountered . . . In some neighbourhoods it seemed that open and unapologetic racism was wall to wall amongst adolescents, with almost no gaps.' The team (whose report was called 'Routes of Racism') found few real gangs, but many loose, informal friendship groups with members drifting in and out. These groups tended to hang around on street corners or in any other space they could find, talking and arguing, drinking, sometimes taking drugs and occasionally indulging in petty theft or joyriding. Much of the time they simply moaned about how bored they were. 'There's nothing really,' one girl declared. 'You just wander around. Go in. Go to bed.' Bored kids are hardly unusual, but here the common currency of their conversation, and one of their main forms of entertainment, was racism. There were jokes. Question: how long does it take a nigger to shit? Answer: nine months. Also popular were lurid stories of black people attacking white people – rapes, muggings, burglaries – often with no more grounding in fact than urban legends. And there was current affairs: 'My aunt said AIDS only got over in this country 'cos a black man fucked a monkey, right, and then he fucked a white person, and then . . .'

This was not learned from parents, Hewitt found, but generated among the young people themselves. 'The racism of adolescents was a world of its own, policed from within through criticism of anyone who flirted with inter-racial friendships, and of those "wiggers" – "white niggers" – who came near to embracing black youth culture.' And this was happening in a district where there are very few black or Asian people, for Eltham is 95 per cent white. Hewitt explained: 'Perhaps one of the most important facts about the areas that we investigated was that, as well as being predominantly white, they had some proximity to ethnically more mixed areas while also opening out, to the south and east, on to the hinterlands of Kentish suburbia and the Kent countryside.' Thus Eltham, with its back to Kent and its face towards Lewisham, Greenwich and Woolwich, stood at the front line of the white hinterland. As the misspelt scrawl on the church gate declared: 'Watch out coons, your now entering Eltham.'

White children in these areas often encountered black people of their own age in any number only when they reached secondary school, and there they could find themselves under pressure to conform to strict anti-racist policies. Many came to feel, Hewitt says, that 'too much attention' was paid to the problems of black people, that black people were protected by special rules, that ethnic minority cultures were taken more seriously than their own, or even that they had no culture of their own. One boy complained: 'Say you 'ave a fight with a black person, I reckon the school itself is racist towards white people. Like, you see, they always take up a black kid's side and they don't wanna know what your version of the story is.' From here, said Hewitt, it was a short step towards group action. The white kids daubed graffiti, they made nuisances of themselves outside Asian-owned shops, they shouted abuse at black passers-by or they engaged in violence. 'Paki-bashing' was often talked of as Hewitt's group carried out their interviews. Some of this they did with the idea that they were defending their 'white area'. 'People who move [in] round here that are black, they get knocked off this estate 'cos they don't like 'em,' one girl said. And her friend added: 'And they go. They can't put up wiv no more so they 'ave to go.'

Worse could happen. In 1991 there had been two murders – of Rolan Adams and Orville Blair – elsewhere in the borough, which were widely thought to have a racial element, and then in July 1992 a young Asian man, Rohit Duggal, was killed by a local white boy on Well Hall Road, below the roundabout. Duggal died after trouble between him, his friends and a larger group of local white boys spilled over from a kebab shop into the road. Duggal and a youth called Peter Thompson fought and then Thompson produced a knife and stabbed Duggal. At the time of Stephen Lawrence's death this was a very fresh memory, for Thompson had been convicted at the Old Bailey only eight weeks earlier. In the week of Stephen's murder the front page of the *Eltham Times* was filled with the story of Thompson's aunt, who was campaigning locally to persuade young people not to carry knives.

Violence, of course, did not have to be racially motivated. Local boys might be the sons or grandsons of hard men or criminals from the old south London, and toughness and fighting were commonplace. Often low achievers at school, they tried to be high achievers when it came to muscle – if they played football almost every boy wanted to be Vinny Jones. They were tribal, causing trouble on the terraces at football matches or on the street, and when they hung around with too little to do in the evenings they would maintain their subtle pecking orders through almost absurd acts of violence – 'You starin' at me?' was often the prelude to a beating. And one popular way to enhance your status was to travel 'tooled up' or 'chivved up' – carrying knives or coshes in breach of the law. Most of this rivalry was between white youths, but the bottom line in status was a difference with black people. These young men might not have jobs or girlfriends or money, they might not be much good at anything and they might have got in trouble with the law, but one thing they did have was their whiteness. It would be easy to exaggerate this. Eltham was not the Bronx or the Gorbals and most people went about their lives without encountering trouble, but by London's standards it was a place with a distinctly ugly streak.

Two boys who were perfectly at home in this world, living all their lives on the Brook estate and embracing with enthusiasm the dangerous side of the local culture, were Neil and Jamie Acourt. Their names would become permanently linked to that of Stephen Lawrence.

With a half-sister and two half-brothers who were twins, the Acourt boys were brought up by their mother, Patricia, in a house in Langbrook Road. The twins, Scott and Bradley Lamb, were three years older than Neil and four years older than Jamie. Mr Lamb had left the scene before Mr Acourt married Patricia, and Mr Acourt in turn disappeared while his sons were still small. Pat herself was a strong character, with some pedigree. She was born Patricia Stuart and she had four brothers of whom three had criminal records and one, Terry Stuart, was a well-known figure in the Eltham area. Terry had a string of convictions for high-value burglaries and in 1990 he was arrested in France for large-scale drugs trafficking and spent several years in a Lyons prison.

Pat's sons grew up tough, too. Of the two Acourt boys Neil was the more obviously 'hard'. He was muscular but compact and his walk had a certain roll to it, while his brown hair was kept clear of a bony face which at rest seemed usually to fall into a smile. The effect was one of aggressive confidence. Jamie, though younger, was a little taller and if he was noticeable it was for different qualities – he was good-looking and, superficially at least, personable – but he was also strong and fond of a fight. With four sons in the house Pat always had a job on her hands and as they grew older her ability to control them naturally diminished, but with the Acourt boys this process was accelerated: as their older brothers, the Lambs, became adults Neil and Jamie assumed by right all the same freedoms, so that when they were respectively fifteen and fourteen they were striking the attitudes of eighteen-year-olds. They both went at first to the same school, Crown Woods, but at the end of 1989 Jamie transferred to another local school, Kidbrooke. The reason is not clear but it had something to do with discipline, and it seems most likely that both boys had been getting in trouble at Crown Woods and it was thought prudent to separate them.

It was not long before Jamie was in trouble again. Late in 1990 he was twice excluded temporarily from Kidbrooke, for abusive behaviour towards a teacher and for trespassing in the school out of hours and causing damage. Neil, too, was carrying on as before at Crown Woods, maintaining a record of disruptive behaviour and poor attendance. Nineteen ninety-one proved to be an important year, particularly for Jamie. He had been referred to an educational social worker and his head teacher was calling in Pat Acourt for discussions, but his conduct slipped from bad to worse. In February, when he was still fourteen, he was cautioned by police after being found in possession of cannabis, and four months later he was seen by police again after brandishing what appeared to be a handgun at another boy in the school playground. The gun was an air pistol, but in the shape of a Smith & Wesson revolver. The other boy was black.

Kidbrooke had a small minority of black pupils and at this time racial tension was increasing, largely, it was believed, because of the influence of the BNP (British National Party) in the area and because of feelings stirred up by the murder of Rolan Adams, a black teenager, a few miles away in Thamesmead. Jamie played a leading part in the trouble, along with close friends including a boy called Luke Knight. This was the time when Neil was leaving school; in July 1991, at the age of sixteen, he passed out of the educational system and into the adult world, where he was given a job as a drayman at a bottling and soft drinks firm run by two uncles in Woolwich. That left only Jamie in the family still at school – he had another year to go – but things did not long remain so. The autumn term of his final year had barely begun when Jamie once again became involved in fights with black boys. One local black youth called Sean Kalitsi was accused of 'giving the lip' to a friend of Jamie's, and in a scuffle on 11 September Jamie sent Sean tumbling down a flight of concrete stairs. Sean was left unconscious. He stayed away from school for several days, while Jamie was excluded for five days. During this period the temperature in the school rose, and a white girl was beaten up and called a 'nigger lover'. Then after school on 16 September Sean went to the gates with a group of black boys, mainly from other schools, and there they found an even larger group of white boys waiting for them. A fight followed, at the end of which the black youths fled. Police arrived too late to intervene. The next day the school was in a state of high alert and some pupils were searched on arrival; Jamie's school bag was found to contain a monkey wrench. His permanent exclusion was confirmed on 2 October and he was referred to another school called Fox Field, a specialist institution for problem boys. He never attended. Jamie Acourt's school career lasted very little longer than his brother's, which suited both of them. Three weeks after his expulsion he again came to the notice of police when he was cautioned for threatening a woman with a stick in a public place. He too went to work for his uncles.

By now the two boys had made a particular friend: David Norris. They had first met him when they were all children, at social events involving Terry Stuart and David's father, Clifford, another professional criminal in the drugs business. Slight and dark, Dave was a disturbed youth, the son of a man who, though known for his affability, was also, according to the police, capable of savage violence and fits of rage. For example, in 1983, when he was twenty-five, Cliff was driving along the New Kent Road in south London with Alex Norris, his brother and partner, when they were cut up by a passing van. Outraged, Cliff gave chase, forced the van to a halt and was belabouring it with a hammer when he heard the approach of police sirens. Realizing that he was carrying something incriminating, he threw his wallet away. It was found, and in it police discovered the key to a safe deposit box, which in turn proved to contain £17,000. Cliff denied any knowledge of the money and in court the link could not be proved. He was fined £150 for damaging the van, but his outbreak of road rage had cost him a small fortune. Another example came six years later when gossip circulated in south London about the state of Cliff's marriage to Dave's mother Tracey. When he became aware of it he decided to stamp it out. He marched into a shop where he believed the gossip originated and shot the woman behind the counter in the throat. Although she survived, she always declined to identify her attacker to the police.

Young Dave attended Coopers School near his home in Chislehurst until the end of 1989, when he was permanently excluded for persistent, uncontrollable disruptive behaviour. This was four months after his thirteenth birthday. Like Jamie, Dave was referred to a special educational unit but unlike Jamie he attended it, under his mother's watchful eye. It was football that brought him together again with the Acourts, probably in 1990. Dave began to attend the Samuel Montague Club, a stone's throw from the Brook estate, where Neil and Jamie also played, and before long they were on the same team. Here the friendship was consolidated as the three boys found that they complemented each other. Jamie was probably the brightest – teachers at Kidbrooke believed he could have done well if he had applied himself. He was also the best football player, and he was the best looking; he had a succession of girlfriends, including some steady relationships. Dave was the most violent and also the most unpredictable; for him, life had no rules. He had money and he made no secret of the fact that he had a powerful, almost glamorous criminal father. Cliff, at this time supposedly on the run from the police, would occasionally be seen dropping his son off for football training (perhaps in the Porsche which, according to legend, he had bought brand new with a bag of banknotes). Neil, for his part, longed to be the leader of this trio, and to dominate. He wanted to prove himself the hardest and the smartest and the most mature. This drive was all the stronger because it was not at all clear that he was. For a start he was the smallest of the three and he also seemed to have difficulty with girls, so he had something to prove.

This was, then, a complex triangle, with plenty of unacknowledged tensions. Of the three Dave, the rich boy with the murderous father, probably had the least chance of finding a normal life. Neil and Jamie, with a little luck, might have grown up and fitted in. Violent though they were, they were part of a youth culture which most local boys left behind as the business of work, money and girls pushed them into adulthood. But Neil and Jamie did not have that luck. In 1992 their mother began a romance with a married man, John Burke, and the liaison brought convulsion to the Acourt home. When Burke's wife found out about the affair she turned up in Langbrook Road and there followed a battle in the street. Each side subsequently blamed the other and there were contradictory complaints to the police, but it is clear that the two women exchanged blows and ended up on the ground, while their cars were battered and damaged. A baseball bat and a golf club were used, and Neil was said to have been involved. No charges were ever laid and the police did their best to calm things but the upshot was that Burke separated from his wife and Pat Acourt began spending time at his home in Rotherhithe. This meant she was spending less time in Eltham, and as her remaining influence over her younger sons faded away, so their behaviour became more extreme. At around this time they began dealing in drugs, small-time street-work supplying cannabis and Ecstasy to local kids. Although the Acourts had their own link to the drug world through their mother's family, it seems more likely that it was the Norris connection that furnished the supply.

In May 1992 Dave finally left his special school and was free to spend all the time he wished with the Acourts. With no adults around apart from the older half-brothers, who do not seem to have been a restraining influence, the three boys indulged themselves. They no longer played football at the Sammy Montague. Neil had been thrown out for threatening to stab a player – by some accounts a black player – and the others left in sympathy. Similarly they could no longer attend the Orchards youth club in the middle of the Brook estate: Neil and Dave were barred for daubing 'NF' (for National Front) on the walls in letters several feet high. Instead, some evenings they used to hang around outside the Orchards and intimidate the other kids. They were not the only tough teenagers in the area and every now and then there were fights. Occasionally, for example, there was conflict with a group of youths associated with the Tyler family, who lived to the south of the estate, and also with a family of four boys who, for their own safety, were later identified only by letters, the two youngest being 'EE' and 'FF'.

While the Acourt group were establishing themselves as among the hardest boys of their age group, they were also acquiring a reputation for being odd, for being 'nutters'. Local people would later say that in this period the youths developed a fascination for the Kray twins and began to style themselves the Eltham Krays. They also became fascinated with knives, and here Neil and Dave appear to have competed with each other, buying bigger and bigger knives and carrying them about. It is hardly surprising that there were tensions with the neighbours and that these came to the attention of housing officials. Towards the end of 1992, in an attempt to ease the problem, a house-swap was arranged between the Acourt/Lamb family and the residents of 102 Bournbrook Road on the other side of the estate. The switch took place around Christmas-time and the price the Acourt and Lamb boys paid was that their new house was one of the shabbiest in the Brook. This did not worry them in the least, and they swiftly made themselves at home. The last trace of parental control disappeared and visitors to the house at this time noticed knives everywhere and extremely violent films playing on the video.

Nutters or not, these youths had their followers and hangers-on. One was Gary Dobson, who lived on the Progress and had been at Crown Woods with Neil. Another was a younger boy, Luke Knight, who was Jamie's friend from Kidbrooke. Both were quieter and generally calmer than the others, but they were drawn in by the independent, assertive style of the Acourt household. There were also three boys from the estates who were related to each other: Charlie and Stephen Martin, who had, by remarkable coincidence, played the roles of the Kray twins as children in a film of their life, and their cousin, Danny Caetano, who was also related to Knight. And there were others. When Neil, Dave and Jamie wanted a bit of fun, they were not short of company. And by the early months of 1993 it was widely believed on the estates that their idea of fun included stabbing people.

*

The police investigation of the Stephen Lawrence murder, like all serious crime inquiries, was given a name: in this case Operation Fishpool. Why this unusual word was chosen or whether it was picked at random was not recorded, but it has a certain appropriateness. When the detectives got to work they found that they were dealing with a clearly defined area stretching from Well Hall Road in the east, across the Progress to the Brook estate in the west, and spilling southward just a little beyond Rochester Way. Rarely did the pursuit of the killers take them far beyond these limits. So this was their fish pool and those inside, particularly the Acourts and their friends, were the fish.

Chapter Three Twenty-four Hours

The streets of the Progress and the surrounding estates were quiet on the night of 22 April; many witnesses were to testify to that. Around 10.40 p.m., one of them would remark, it seemed more like the small hours of the morning. At the Coronet cinema business was so bad that patrons for the evening's features, *Body of Evidence* and *A River Runs Through It*, found themselves outnumbered by the staff. Nor was there any rush in the kebab shop, where those working behind the counter had plenty of time to chat with customers. But the streets were by no means deserted; in the days and weeks that followed a surprising number of people would say that they were out at some time between 10 p.m. and 11 p.m. – driving home, walking the dog, returning from a friend's house, picking up a takeaway. In the eyes of the police four of these people, three young men and a young woman, were to acquire paramount importance; it was thought that in different ways they could cast light on the murder. One of them was the youth called EE, one of those teenagers who in the past had fought with the Acourt group. He lived on Well Hall Road and spent some of that night on his doorstep watching the street, talking to passers-by and listening. Another of the four was EE's girlfriend, Emma Cook, who walked home from his house past the scene of the murder just before it occurred. The third was another youth, called Witness B, who at a critical moment was on a bus that travelled past the murder scene. And the fourth, a slightly older man, connects the other three but also has an importance all of his own, arising from what he was reported to have seen and said that night. He is called Witness K. (As with EE and B, Witness K acquired his pseudonym long afterwards; police investigating the murder in 1993 knew him by his real name.)

The story of these four people on this night is like a chain, a series of links, and the chain begins with Witness B. This was a young man, not long out of school and working at his first job. For some years he had lived to the south of Rochester Way and he knew the area and the local youth pretty well. He spent the evening of the murder with his girlfriend in Woolwich, leaving at about 10.30 p.m.

to return home. He caught a 121 bus and took a seat upstairs. This
meant that he was travelling in the opposite direction to the way in
which Stephen and Duwayne were hoping to go at that same time.
The bus brought him over the hill, down past the Welcome Inn and
on to the roundabout. He must have passed the murder scene very
close to the moment at which Stephen was stabbed. The bus then
went round the roundabout until it faced west before turning south
again along Westhorne Avenue, and there B alighted. In those final
stages of the journey he had seen something, and it was something
that he thought curious, even suspicious. It involved, he believed,
Dave Norris, Neil Acourt and two other boys, one of whom might
have been Jamie. These three were boys he knew, not least because
he had played football with them at the Sammy Montague Club.

Witness B was making his way home from the bus stop, thinking
all the while about what he had seen, when he connected with
Witness K, the second link in the chain. K was older – he was
twenty-two, an only son living with his mother and stepfather – but
he lived close by and he and B knew each other fairly well. In fact
K mixed a good deal with boys younger than he was, and there may
have been a reason for this, for he was of lower than average
intelligence. Police officers who had dealings with him later would
describe him variously as slow, immature and even simple, although
simple was too strong a word. It seems, however, that he was most
comfortable with younger people. He had lived in this area all his
life and like many young men on the estates he had been in trouble
with the police a few times, acquiring convictions for burglary and
shoplifting. He knew the local young hard cases, among them the
Acourts and their followers; in fact he was reasonably friendly with
them, although he was not a member of the gang. It may be that he
occasionally bought drugs from them.

That night, K was out walking somewhere on Briset Road, near
his home, when he bumped into Witness B and they had a conversation. The time was approximately 10.45 p.m., at which moment
Stephen was still lying unconscious on the pavement half a mile
away on Well Hall Road. We cannot be sure what was said. Much
later, B would deny that he mentioned to K what he had seen –
Norris and Neil Acourt acting suspiciously – but there are some
grounds to suspect that he did. After their conversation they parted;
B went home (he had to get up early for work the next morning)

33

while K wandered off. Where he went next is another thing we do not know, but about fifteen minutes later he was still on the street only a few hundred yards away and he had his second significant encounter of the night. Louise Kavanagh had been babysitting in Woolwich that night for her sister Kelly while Kelly took their mother to the bingo, and now Kelly was delivering Louise and her mother home. Their journey over the hill from Woolwich had been interrupted on Well Hall Road when they noticed the flashing hazard lights of a car parked by the roadside on the left. Slowing down, Kelly saw a cluster of people standing, and one person lying on the pavement. Thinking that there had been an accident, she stopped to offer help. As she got out she saw that the man on the ground was black, and there was blood. 'What happened?' she asked, and a man with a beard told her there had been a stabbing. A police car then arrived and Kelly decided she was not needed. She returned to her vehicle and finished the journey, telling her mother and Louise on the way what she had seen and heard.

So it was that Louise, catching sight of K just as she turned to go into her house, was able to tell him there had been a stabbing. Since it was still only about 11 p.m., this made K one of the first to know. Just how odd this is may be measured by the fact that at that moment not even Duwayne Brooks was aware that Stephen had been stabbed; he still believed his friend had been struck by an iron bar. The explanation was simple: K knew the truth because the bearded man to whom Kelly Kavanagh had spoken at the scene, almost alone of those present it seems, had guessed the true cause of Stephen's injury. He was Alan Massey, a computer engineer who lived on Well Hall Road and had stopped to help as he approached his door. Unlike others, he had not heard Duwayne say that the attacker used an iron bar, and from the blood on the ground he simply drew his own conclusion about the nature of the attack. Transmitted to K, Massey's assumption became a fact. There are two possibilities now about K's thoughts. If we believe that in the earlier conversation with B, K had indeed learned about what B had seen from the bus, then he was in possession of a very striking combination of facts. A young black man had been stabbed and at about the same time the Acourts and Dave Norris had been seen nearby behaving in a suspicious manner. K may not have been bright, but he was capable of drawing a conclusion from that. If, on the other hand, B had *not* spoken to him about what he had seen, K still knew about a stabbing, and that in itself was news. Whichever was the case, there is no mystery about what K did next.

Saying goodnight to Louise, he decided to pay a call on a family who kept late hours. Ron and Ann Tyler had five children in their teens or early twenties, of whom four – Ricky, Jane, Karen and David – still lived at home. To most parents this would have been a full house, but the Tylers' door on Westhorne Avenue, a little to the south of the Well Hall Roundabout, was always open to more. Karen's boyfriend Jamie Evans spent a lot of time there; they had a baby. Ricky's girlfriend Michelle Granger also often stayed over, as did another local girl, Michelle Casserley, who was a friend of Jane's, and a boy called Tony Francis. Other young people visited frequently, treating it almost as they would a pub or a club. When K got there that night it was business as usual: groups in every room and even some people spilling over on to the pavement. None of them had heard of the incident on Well Hall Road, although they were aware of police sirens, and K's news prompted a general drift to go and take a look.

By the time they reached the roundabout, however, cordons were in place and they could not get near the scene of the stabbing. A few went back to Westhorne Avenue straight away but the rest sat on a wall for a while, chatting, waiting and watching the passing police vehicles. At one stage a policeman asked if they had seen anything and they said no; he in turn would tell them nothing about what had happened. Eventually they gave up and followed the others back to the house, but by now they were without K. Somehow, probably by using side streets, K had got past the cordon to reach a point higher up Well Hall Road. There, near the place where Stephen collapsed, he found two more people he knew. One was a man called Gareth, a friend of about the same age who now lived in Plumstead, and the other was a younger boy. This was another link in the chain, for the boy was E E.

E E and two older brothers lived in a house on Well Hall Road with their mother, who is identified as Mrs D D. Over the months before the murder, as the Acourts and their friends grew wilder, the younger boys in the family had felt the consequences more than most. One, F F, had been stabbed in the arm, a slight injury which he did not report to police, but it was E E who had attracted particular attention from the Acourt group. The reason was probably a simple one: EE was now going out with Emma Cook, who had some time previously been Neil's girlfriend. One day not long before the murder, EE had been sitting in a car when the Acourts appeared. There was an altercation, which ended with a pickaxe being driven through the car roof while EE was still inside. The four brothers avenged this with an attack on 102 Bournbrook Road, but at the time of the murder EE was still reluctant to go out on his own for fear of whom he might meet.

If K brought two links of the chain to that meeting by the roadside – himself and B – then so did EE. Emma Cook had spent the evening with EE at his home, leaving at about 10.30 p.m. She lived with her parents on Rochester Way, just ten minutes' walk away, but EE decided not to accompany her beyond his garden gate. As they said goodnight they saw two friends, Greg and Lisa, across the road on the corner of Arbroath Road, and they exchanged greetings. Emma did not linger, however; perhaps because she too was worried about meeting the Acourts. She crossed the road and headed down towards the roundabout. As she passed the bus stop before Dickson Road she encountered two young black men laughing together; they stepped aside to let her by. She thought another man and a woman were also waiting there. Walking on to the roundabout, she turned right and a few minutes later she was home. In police parlance, Emma had 'walked through the plot'. She had passed Stephen and Duwayne at the most six or seven minutes before they were attacked and at the least one or two. More importantly, when she reached the roundabout she had a commanding view over the area from which, Duwayne said, the attackers were to come. Did she see them? If she saw the Acourts and their friends she would certainly have recognized them – not only had she been Neil's girlfriend, but she had virtually grown up with Neil and Jamie because her mother, who was friendly with Pat Acourt, had been child-minder to the boys for a time. The question of what, if anything, Emma saw when she looked across the roundabout was to become a matter of intense speculation and concern.

EE was not immediately aware that Emma had come so close to witnessing the murder, but after she left to go home things also happened at EE's house. Greg dropped his girlfriend Lisa home and then returned to visit his friend EE. By Greg's account, the boys went up to EE's bedroom and stayed there for a while, talking. Although EE's mother called up to them that there were a lot of police outside they did not surface again for about half an hour, by which time Greg was in a hurry – he had a job as a night security guard in central London and needed to get to work. As he left the house he saw a car parked with its hazard lights flashing. A woman in the car was crying, and on the ground there was a lot of blood.

'What's happened?' asked Greg.

'Just an accident,' the woman replied.

'What kind of accident? An assault? A fight?'

'Just an assault.'

Greg rushed on to catch his train. The woman was Angela Geddis, the wife of the off-duty police officer, who had been left alone to guard the scene of Stephen's collapse after the body was taken away in the ambulance. That means the time was probably 11.10 p.m. or a little later. As Greg left, EE had stepped outside again, but we do not know whether he heard the exchange with Mrs Geddis; he now stayed to watch the events unfold, and so was on the doorstep when Gareth came around the corner. Gareth was really a friend of FF, one of the older brothers, but he and EE knew each other well, and it was as they began to chat that K rolled up, having left the Tyler group down near the roundabout.

From that doorstep on Well Hall Road the three of them – Gareth, EE and K – watched the police at work, and while they watched they talked. Gareth explained that he had been visiting his mother, who lived a couple of streets away, and on leaving her had taken a short cut between the houses to Well Hall Road, where he emerged to find a policewoman, a lot of police tape and what seemed to him an enormous amount of blood on the ground. EE, for his part, said he had been watching for a while. He was concerned about Emma, and he broke off at one point to check with a police officer on guard near where Stephen fell whether a young blonde woman had been affected in any way. As for K, perhaps he merely listened, or perhaps he spoke about his conversation earlier in the evening with the youth on the bus, Witness B. If he did, and if he recounted the story that B had seen Norris and at least one of the Acourts behaving suspiciously near the roundabout, that would be one possible explanation for EE's subsequent behaviour. For like K, young EE would have no difficulty drawing conclusions from such a story. But even if K did not speak about Witness B, it is safe to assume that these three young men well acquainted with the youth of the estates would have speculated that night about who might have been responsible for a street stabbing. And it is also safe to assume that the Acourts and Norris – well-known 'nutters' with knives – would have been among the names to come up.

After a little while K and Gareth left E E behind and made their way down the road, eventually sitting on a wall near the roundabout. They watched and talked a little more and then Gareth moved off, leaving K alone. It was after 11.30 p.m., and by now K knew that the stabbing victim was dead. How he knew we do not know – perhaps the news coming through on the police radios from Brook Hospital reached the bystanders at the scene, or perhaps it was just rumour founded on the intensity of police activity – but what matters is that K was sure the stabbing had become a murder. The Acourt group, it was widely believed in the area, had stabbed a number of people, but they had never murdered anyone. Were they capable of it? Could this have been their work? K made up his mind to act. He liked to bring news – it was he who had reported the stabbing to the Tyler household – and if the Acourts *had* done it, they would probably not know yet that the boy had died. K would be the one to tell them. He knew where they lived and he also knew that, whatever had happened, there would be no problem going to that particular house at such a late hour. So he set off for the Brook estate, heading along Rochester Way, then turning right up Appleton Road and left at the top into Bournbrook Road. Number 102 was a few houses down on the left. He insisted later that he arrived there at 11.30 p.m., but it is more likely that it was 11.45 p.m. or a little later, and that more than an hour had elapsed since the stabbing. He knocked on the door and it opened.

Whatever it was that happened next, we know one thing: when K walked away from Bournbrook Road a little later he believed that his suspicions had been well-founded and that the Acourt group *was* responsible for the murder. It seems that he had seen or heard things which convinced him. Exactly what those things were, however, has never been established beyond doubt. Many accounts were subsequently supplied by other people and they are all subtly differ-ent, some of them perhaps edited by the tellers, leaving out details or names because of fear or discretion, and some of them probably embellished and altered by the normal, natural process of youthful story-telling and Chinese whispers. As far as the police were concerned, however, the only version that had any value, the only version that could ever be used in court, was K's, and they were later convinced that he had not provided it to them in full. But things had not yet become so complicated; on leaving the Acourt house K was electrified by his discovery, and as quickly as he could he made his way back to the Tyler house on Westhorne Avenue. For the fourth time that night he would be the bringer of news.

The chain was complete. In time police would come to believe that these four young people held the key to the crime – they saw something; they had been well placed to see something; they were said by others to have seen something; they behaved as though they had seen something. Whichever was the case, for years the evening of 22 April would cast a long and chilly shadow over the lives of the four. But first the police had to find them.

The police presence in Well Hall Road built up rapidly after Stephen was taken to the hospital. A vanload of officers from the Territorial Support Group (TSG) – a roving reserve who served a large area of south London – arrived while the ambulance was still there and they drove off to tour surrounding streets. PC Linda Bethel and the off-duty officer, James Geddis, meanwhile, left Angela Geddis to guard the scene where Stephen collapsed and followed the trail of blood down to Dickson Road, where they found a pool of blood and, beside it, Stephen's abandoned bag. More TSG vans arrived over the next hour, while from Plumstead station came local officers and detectives, some summoned from home. In time both locations – where Stephen was stabbed and where he collapsed – were formally preserved with rings of scene-of-crime tape and the cordons were progressively extended until eventually Well Hall Road was sealed off from near the Welcome Inn down to the roundabout. Searches were conducted in Dickson Road, at first a quick check and then at greater length when dogs and powerful lamps were brought in to assist.

For much of this time Duwayne remained at the hospital, still overwhelmed by his friend's death. He was taken to see the body and he spent some time with the Lawrences, but he seemed to be unable to communicate with them. In time P C Gleason persuaded him to talk and for a while they remained together by the reception counter going over what had happened, Gleason scribbling in his notebook as Duwayne tried to concentrate. He was subject to floods of emotion and occasionally he would have to break off and walk away. Soon another police officer turned up: Acting Inspector Ian Little. He told Duwayne that he must go to Plumstead police station to make a full statement, but not before Little had done a few jobs at the hospital. Duwayne, who was more than ready to leave, was taken to an unmarked car in the car park and left there alone for a while. When Little was ready they drove down to Plumstead, where Duwayne waited again in an interview room. The inactivity seems to have helped and a transformation slowly came over the young man, his overt distress and anger giving way to calm and quiet, his memory growing clearer. Soon he was talking without strain to D C David Cooper, and they were ready to begin work on the statement when Detective Superintendent Ian Crampton appeared.

Crampton was now in charge; he was the S I O, or Senior Investigating Officer, the detective who would lead and direct this inquiry and would make the important decisions. He had been selected for the job by the rota: serious crime was the responsibility of a body called the Area Major Investigations Pool (Amip), and on this night Crampton was the Amip duty officer, deputed to turn out in response to emergency calls and take charge. Roused from his bed at 12.30 a.m., he initially intended to go straight to the scene at Well Hall Road but he had diverted to Plumstead after hearing that the prime witness was there. He now listened while Duwayne described to him what had happened, saying that there had been six white attackers and he didn't know any of them personally, and that one of them had hit Stephen with what he thought was an iron bar. There had been no provocation; the white men had used the word nigger, and after the attack they had run away down a side road. Crampton asked a few questions and then left, instructing Cooper to take the fullest statement possible.

At Well Hall Road Crampton was brought up to date by Detective Inspector Philip Jeynes with the results so far of activities at the scene, and the pickings were slim. One local man, a postman by the name of Barry Nugent, had come forward to say that from his living-room window he had seen a group of three or four men running down Dickson Road, and his statement had been taken. Unfortunately he had seen them only from behind and could not really describe any of them. Another man, a bus driver on his way home, had stopped at the police cordon to report that one of his colleagues at the depot said he had seen some commotion earlier that evening by the roundabout. The police searchers, for all their lights and dogs, had not found much: apart from Stephen's schoolbag and its strap, which had been ripped off, there was a telephone card, a small battery, a pair of dark blue woollen gloves and the remains of a kebab. It was the usual random detritus of street life and it did not include a weapon. Crampton walked the scene, had a look at the bus stop, Dickson Road and the roundabout, asked about the local pubs, late-night shops and fast-food joints and generally satisfied himself that proper routine had been followed. Then he set in motion the arrangements for a much fuller search of the area in daylight, including examination of local drains, and for a full-blown house-to-house inquiry likely to last at least two days. He asked about Stephen's family and was told that the Lawrences had already been to the hospital to see the body and had left instructions as they went home that they did not want to see anybody until the morning.

Crampton was concerned about the cause of death. Duwayne, the prime witness, had described an iron bar, but everyone else was talking about a stabbing and there was certainly a lot of blood on the ground, both in Dickson Road and at the spot where Stephen fell. All doubt could be removed by an immediate post mortem, but Crampton was told the pathologist would not be available until 9.30 a.m. He did the next best thing. An officer was on his way to the hospital to take charge of Stephen's belongings and he was told to get details of the wounds from the staff at casualty and phone in. That would have to do for the moment. It was 3 a.m.; one last look around and Crampton gave orders for the road to be reopened to traffic.

When he got back to Plumstead station he found Duwayne still there, still dictating his statement. And there was some good news: Duwayne had provided an outline description of one of the attackers and was sure he would recognize him if he saw him again. When questioned, Duwayne remained confident that the weapon he had seen was a bar or bat made of wood or steel, and when asked about the number of attackers (Nugent, the postman who looked out of his window, had said he had seen only four men running) Duwayne stuck to six. Pressed again on the shout he had heard, he was adamant that the word nigger had been used. Importantly, moreover, he revealed that there had been other witnesses to the attack: the woman and two men at the bus stop. These people must be traced as a matter of urgency. In fact, as always at this stage of a murder investigation, there was a lot of work to do. For the next few hours Crampton wrestled with the red tape of setting up searches and house-to-house inquiries and laying other routine groundwork.

Aged forty-nine, Ian Crampton was regarded by colleagues and subordinates as a good detective and something of a copper's copper. A tall, fit-looking man with grey, wiry hair and a ruddy complexion, he dressed smartly but soberly, as senior detectives must, and wore spectacles. He was a Londoner by birth and became a policeman at the age of twenty-one and a detective at twenty-three, rising steadily through the ranks thereafter. A superintendent since 1991, he now held the highest rank for officers still directly engaged in investigations and this was, he knew, the farthest he would go, since he was due to retire in 1995 on completing his thirty years with the Met. His record at this level, dominated by a single, very complicated case involving the murder of a paid police informer, was thought to be good. It was a delicate and important affair – curiously, the victim's name was David Norris – and he later received a commendation for his handling of it. Although he could be a man of action, Ian Crampton was also a worrier, as the lines on his face suggested, and in the early hours of Friday 23 April he was worried. Towards dawn he was given Duwayne's completed statement to read: ten pages setting out his background and Stephen's, what they had done during the day, how they came to be at Well Hall Road and everything he remembered about the attack. It was impressive, but as Crampton pondered the case after reading it, he found it hard to be optimistic.

What had happened in those few moments on Well Hall Road? By Duwayne's account, which Crampton was inclined to accept, the two black boys offered no provocation; they never even spoke to their assailants. The attack simply came out of the blue. Yet it was surely premeditated, in the sense that the perpetrators must have agreed among themselves that they would attack, and the use of the weapon or weapons was hardly accidental. The white boys may well have seen Stephen and Duwayne some minutes earlier and then discussed and agreed what they would do. Or they may have been watching casually from a distance and decided to strike only after they saw the two black youths separate themselves from the others at the bus stop. Either way, when they reached Well Hall Road and faced Duwayne and Stephen across the traffic, it is clear that they knew they were going to attack. They had strength in numbers, and at least one of them was armed. (The word from the hospital was that a knife had definitely been used.) By approaching from the direction they did, they gave themselves the best chance of preventing their prey from rejoining the group at the bus stop. Then, once Stephen was down, they did not linger.

Why did they run down Dickson Road? They had other options, but Dickson Road was the obvious choice for flight. It was right before them, darker and quieter than any other escape route, and it forked just fifty yards away, so that they would be out of sight in seconds. But a getaway route has to lead somewhere; they would hardly have run down it if it led directly away from their ultimate place of safety. So what was down there? Did they have a car parked in that area to which they were returning? Unlikely: in Eltham parking is not so difficult that you need to tuck your car away in residential side streets. Perhaps they were cutting through with the intention of rejoining Rochester Way farther down, escaping thereafter by car or bus. Or were they locals, running home? The field was a broad one, in fact every young white man for miles around would be a potential suspect, which meant that many witnesses would have to be traced and interviewed, many alibis established and confirmed. In the end, Crampton thought, unless the investigators struck lucky with eyewitnesses or some sort of confession, the case would probably hinge on identification, a notoriously tricky area in stranger attacks. Would Duwayne, or the others at the bus stop, be able to pick the killers out of a line-up, and if so would those identifications stand up in court?

At 6.30 a.m. Crampton rang his boss, Detective Chief Superintendent Bill Ilsley, to let him know what had happened and arrange an early meeting. If Crampton as a superintendent was still a working detective, Ilsley at the next rank up was a full-time manager. He ran the Amip, overseeing major crime detection throughout Metropolitan Police 3 Area in southeast London, and his job took him also into the political sphere. As he listened to Crampton's account of

43

the crime he could see that this might not only be a difficult case but also a very sensitive one. He knew southeast London well; he knew about other race killings in recent years, that they had provoked varying degrees of outrage in the black community, and with it fierce criticism of the police. And he knew there would be close media and political scrutiny of the handling of this murder: the Met must be seen to do a good job.

Another matter of mutual concern hung over this early morning conversation: however important this investigation might be, Crampton could not stay on it for long. His other big case, involving the murdered informant Norris, was finally coming to trial the following week at the Old Bailey and because of the complexity and sensitivity of the evidence he would need to be on hand. Consequently he would not be able to remain as SIO on the Lawrence murder beyond Monday and Ilsley would have to find a replacement. This was not ideal but neither was it unusual: Amip did not have the manpower to run a duty roster comprising only officers who had no other commitments. In those days London's 3 Area had more murders to deal with than any other police region in the country with the exception of Strathclyde and Northern Ireland, so an officer of superintendent rank who was not heavily engaged was a rarity. As it happened, Ilsley had a man who should be available for the Lawrence case, for another Amip superintendent, who had been off sick, was due back some time the following week and he had no other cases on his plate. With a little persuasion he might be able to take over the investigation on Monday and release Crampton. Such thoughts were probably only beginning to form in Ilsley's mind at this early hour, but the relevant decisions had been taken by noon that day.

The priority was to lay the foundations of a full murder investigation and in conversations that morning Crampton stressed to Ilsley his fears about the difficulty of the case and the likelihood of it 'widening', as he put it later, to embrace many witnesses, suspects and lines of inquiry. There was no ready-made CID team standing by to begin work that morning. Crampton had only one officer permanently attached to him, Detective Sergeant Philip Sheridan, who performed the role graphically known as superintendent's 'bag carrier'. Beyond that, staff had to be assembled by drawing in officers from wherever they could be spared. This was a task for Ilsley, who had the clout to move staff around within the Amip. He first chose Detective Inspector Ben Bullock to act as deputy to the SIO, and then he rounded up a relatively large team for the investigation. There were official Met guidelines for staffing a murder and this team came closer to meeting them than most. Although everybody did not arrive immediately, Crampton was pleasantly surprised by the resources he was given.

Together, Ilsley and Crampton made another important decision that morning: the Lawrence investigation would make use of the Holmes system. This was computer database software designed and introduced after the Yorkshire Ripper fiasco in the 1980s, when card-index chaos was found to have contributed to the long delay in catching the culprit. Its full name was Home Office Large Major Enquiry System (an acronym contrived in honour of Sherlock) and its use was steadily creeping into Metropolitan Police operations. With Holmes, all information coming into the incident room, whether it be statements, telephone messages or door-to-door reports, is entered in the system and marked in special ways for easy cross-referencing. The database is then used to instigate and monitor the progress of particular inquiries arising out of that information. For Crampton it would be the first time he had used the system. As for offices, no permanent Holmes-equipped incident room existed in 3 Area in 1993, but another previous Holmes-based inquiry had recently operated in makeshift fashion from the conference room on the first floor of Eltham police station and that equipment was still up, if not running. It would be a squeeze for a full murder case of this kind but it was the best that could be done; the embryonic incident room was transferred there from Plumstead as rapidly as possible.

Crampton was occupied out of the office most of the day, so a heavy load fell on Bullock and Sheridan and that Friday they presided over an incident room often near to chaos. In part this was normal for the first day of an investigation, with staff arriving from various directions, being introduced and briefed, finding desks and pigeon-holes and letting others know their whereabouts. This, too, was an improvised incident room, so that tables and chairs, telephones and notice-boards, safes and filing cabinets were either in short supply or in a muddle. And to compound the confusion, the computer network had to be reconnected and enlarged, cleared of the data from the previous investigation and made to work. This last, unsurprisingly, proved problematic, and although the first 'action' was recorded in the system a little before noon, the investigation remained for some time uncomfortably poised between computer and paper.

Crampton attended a lengthy post mortem that morning, starting at 9 a.m. It was conducted by Dr Richard Shepherd at Greenwich Public Mortuary. The victim, Shepherd recorded, was a slim, young Afro-Caribbean male whose body bore a number of marks. Besides minor scars from old injuries there were numerous fresh needle-marks in the skin, consistent with the trauma team's efforts the previous night to find a route to replace all that lost blood. There were also signs of abrasion on the right side of Stephen's face, and on the back of his right hand. On his chin there was a small cut, perhaps a nick made by a knife. Then there were the two serious injuries, quite different from one another. One was a small, neat wound high up on the right side of the chest, about 1.5 inches in length – a knife-wound. The blade penetrated vertically down from just in front of the collarbone, severing the axillary artery, which supplies blood to the arm, and the subclavian vein, running beneath the collarbone. Both these blood vessels are almost as thick as an adult's little finger. The knife also cut through two nerve trunks, which was why Stephen had immediately lost feeling in his arm. From there it passed between the ribs and entered the lung to a depth of one inch, causing partial collapse. In all, Shepherd calculated, the blade travelled slightly more than five inches into the body before it was withdrawn. While that wound was neat, conveying little outward hint of the inward damage, the other was an angry L-shaped gash about five inches in length, running around from the outer aspect of Stephen's left shoulder towards his chest. It was none the less very similar in its effect, in that the same two blood vessels, axillary and subclavian, were severed on the left as on the right, and another nerve trunk was damaged. Given such injuries – to the blood system, the nervous system and the lung – it was remarkable that Stephen managed to run as far as he did, proof both of his physical fitness and of the power of the body's natural opiates.

The cause of death was formally recorded as haemorrhage resulting from stab wounds. Either both wounds were caused by the same knife, Dr Shepherd concluded, or they were caused by knives with very similar blades – at least five inches long and about 1.5 inches across, tapering towards a point and with a cutting edge on one side only, like a kitchen knife. From the angle of the wounds, it was likely that the chest wound was struck first, downward, while Stephen was standing, and that the shoulder wound followed when he was on the ground. Everything else about Stephen's body was normal, although various samples were taken for further tests and analysis.

After the post mortem, Crampton made his way to Woolwich police station where there was to be a press conference in early afternoon with Ilsley in charge. At Woolwich he met Neville Lawrence, and in the time available – half an hour or more – they sat together in the canteen and Crampton went over with him what he could say about the case and how he expected the investigation to proceed. Then they went into the press conference. This had been called for a number of reasons: first, as a response to inquiries from journalists; second, to appeal for witnesses to come forward (Crampton was particularly keen to trace the remaining bus stop witnesses) and third, to confront the issue of race. Given the borough's record of racial harassment and racial violence, and in particular the history of murders regarded as racially motivated, black people were outraged that morning when they heard the news of Stephen Lawrence's death. Ilsley was conscious of a need to offer reassurance and to demonstrate publicly the determination of the police to solve this latest killing. His senior uniformed colleague in the district, Chief Superintendent John Philpott, who had put some effort into improving relations between the police and the black community, also believed there was a danger that black anger might erupt into violence. And both men were conscious of concern in high places.

The new Metropolitan Police Commissioner, Paul Condon, had been in office for just a couple of months and had made an early statement of his determination to improve relations between the police and the black community. This brought him into contact with the chairman of the Commission for Racial Equality, Herman Ouseley, and they had discussed among other things the need for the police to acknowledge swiftly and openly when a crime was racially motivated. Strict national guidelines already existed stating that a crime must be classed as racially motivated if the victim, the officer dealing with it, or anybody else stated that it was. Experience showed that police hesitation in putting this on the record enraged

47

black people, so when he heard of the Lawrence killing first thing that Friday morning, Ouseley rang Condon to say that here was a test case. Condon had the message passed to 3 Area.

Ilsley, Crampton, Philpott and Neville Lawrence faced a crowded room at 2.30 p.m. and Ilsley made no bones about it. 'It appears to be a racial murder, considering the remark that was made to one of the boys,' he added. It was, he added, 'outrageous and senseless'. The basic details of the crime were spelled out, although the precise words used by the attackers were not quoted. The presence of a friend of Stephen at the scene was mentioned, but again his name was not given. And Neville Lawrence spoke movingly of Stephen as a good boy, with an ambition to be an architect, who had never been in any kind of trouble in his life. 'I would bring back hanging for something like this,' he said. 'This is an obscene, senseless murder of a decent young boy who worked hard to try and get his grades to go to college. My son has been killed for no reason. I appeal to anyone who saw this horrific crime to call the police . . . This murder has been devastating to my family. My wife is under sedation.' It was Philpott who added an appeal to the public to remain calm: 'I would not deny that we have a racial problem in this area, and I am certainly concerned at the possibility of a backlash. We would ask young people to be sensible.'

For the press this was a strong story, not only because straight-forward race murders are rare, but also because of some of its incidental characteristics. Stephen's appeal as a bright, conscientious young man (rapidly confirmed by his headmaster) and his father's powerful words heightened the sense of tragedy. The location also gave the crime a sense of crisis. The Labour MP for Woolwich, John Austin-Walker, said he was seeking meetings with government ministers: 'This is the third racist stabbing in the area and the community needs to be reassured that effective action will be taken to combat racial harassment and prevent further attacks.' There was a specific political angle too, for the British National Party had offices in Welling, a couple of miles from Well Hall Road and just outside the Greenwich borough boundary, and this had long been a focus of anti-racist protest. The BNP was accused of fomenting race hatred from this building – 'the Nazi bunker', as it came to be labelled – and the Lawrence murder brought intensified demands for it to be closed down. The story was well covered: in all its elements – race murder, witness appeal, father's grief, local anger, calls for calm and anger towards the BNP – it appeared in late editions of the *Evening Standard* that Friday, and in radio bulletins and London-wide television news broadcasts. The following morning every national newspaper reported it, some of them at length. It was not front-page or top-of-the-bulletin news, but it was an important event.

After parting with Neville Lawrence at the end of the press conference, Crampton, Ilsley and Philpott went round the corner together to face a stormy and emotional emergency meeting of the Greenwich council police consultative group in Woolwich Town Hall. Present were councillors and council workers as well as race relations officials, representatives of various ethnic minority groups and two MPs, Austin-Walker and the Conservative MP for Eltham, Peter Bottomley. Here all the issues of friction between the police and the black community were aired and the three policemen were left in no doubt about the depth of public concern; they struggled to provide reassurance. The pressure for successful action, from a gathering of people who could hardly be described as hot-headed, was enormous.

Crampton made it back to Eltham station in time to preside over the first daily staff meeting in the incident room, an event that began at 5 p.m. and took well over an hour. Bullock's notes identify some of the topics covered: an outline of events to date, the appeal for witnesses, an update on the house-to-house inquiries under way, mention of the Welcome Inn pub on Well Hall Road as a possible venue for suspects, efforts to track bus crews, a report of a fight in Wendover Road. Afterwards Crampton and Bullock got down to work, turning the grindstone of routine police procedures. Orders, known as 'actions', were issued for statements to be taken from many of those involved in the events after the stabbing the previous night: ambulance men, police officers, 999 operators and casualty staff. The Taaffes – the couple who came to Stephen's assistance – were to be seen, as were a couple of other local people who had called in to say they had been at the scene. One action issued just after 7 p.m. required the tracing of a red Vauxhall Astra car. This had been seen the previous night on Well Hall Road in the interval between the departure of the ambulance and the closing of the road. It passed twice, once in each direction, and there appeared to be five young white men on board who, in the words of one officer, 'seemed to think something was humorous'. Although a request went out on radio to stop the car, it had got away, but the officer had a partial record of the registration number, so it might prove possible to track it down.

Joey Shepherd's statement was now to hand. He had been quickly traced thanks to the assistance of the Lawrences, and in the early evening had provided his account of the events of the night. Broadly, it confirmed what Duwayne Brooks had said, but there were differences, some minor and some important. Shepherd saw no weapon at all, not even the long object reported by Duwayne, but he said that the attackers kicked and punched Stephen, which Duwayne had not mentioned. And while Duwayne spoke of six youths in the attacking group, Shepherd said there were four or five, putting his recollection closer to that of Barry Nugent, the local man who had seen something from his window. More important than the anomalies, however, Shepherd was able to provide descriptions of four youths, two of them quite detailed, and felt he would probably recognize at least two if he saw them again. He spoke of three males aged between eighteen and twenty-one, one with light brown and two with dark brown hair, and one taller than the others. A fourth man, he said, was eighteen or nineteen, 5' 10" tall, with medium build and medium-length frizzy fair hair, and a jacket coloured in dull browns and greens and cut like a donkey jacket. Duwayne had only been able to describe one youth, but the description in his statement had features in common with this fourth man. Duwayne had spoken of a man of eighteen to twenty-two, of medium build, 5' 8" tall with an oval face and frizzy hair over his ears. He was wearing a grey bomber jacket, possibly with a white strip on either side of the zip.

The time was now after 7 p.m. Crampton had been on duty more than eighteen hours and had had no sleep the previous night. He went home, leaving Bullock to struggle on with the job of getting the incident room shipshape and the paperwork up to date.

Out in the fish pool things had been stirring, and some there wanted to make the job of the police easier. By the morning everyone knew it was a murder; it was on the radio. In their home on Well Hall Road, the young man called EE discussed the crime with FF, one of his brothers. They were both convinced that the Acourt group was responsible and they believed that this time they had gone too far. At lunchtime the brothers listened to the radio news again and there was no word of arrests, so F F rang Eltham police station. The call – the first important tip-off to reach the police – was logged at 1.50 p.m.:

> There is a group of youths on the Kidbrooke Estate who always carry large knives and threaten people; they may have been involved in last night's stabbing. Two of them are Neil Acall and Dave Norris, both of 102 Bournbrook Close, Kidbrooke Estate.

The record states that the caller refused to identify himself. The boys felt they had done enough.

And things were soon moving elsewhere. More than once at the Tyler house on Thursday night and on Friday, K recounted the story of his visit to Bournbrook Road. There was no love lost between the Tyler family and the Acourt group, and the wider Tyler circle also shared the general local view that they were over the top. The notion that Neil, Dave and Jamie might have had something to do with this stabbing had surely occurred to most of them at some time on Thursday evening, but idle suspicion is one thing and inside knowledge is quite another. K's story sent a frisson of excitement through the whole house. One person who heard it was a young man who was later given the pseudonym 'James Grant' by the police. He too had reason to dislike and fear the Acourt group – he and his friends had had dealings with them that proved very unpleasant – so the story struck him with some force. On Friday evening Grant was at home with his family when he saw the report of the murder on the local television news, complete with Neville Lawrence's appeal for help. Grant told his father that he had heard who was responsible, they discussed what he knew and Grant agreed that he ought to share his information with the police.

An hour later he presented himself at the front desk of Eltham police station and said he could help with the Lawrence murder. Soon a tall young detective came downstairs and introduced himself as Detective Constable Christopher Budgen. Grant explained that he had information to give, on condition that his name was kept out of it. He was prepared to identify himself to Budgen but he did not want anyone in the Eltham area to find out that he had informed.

Budgen assured him that this was possible; he said that arrangements could be made so that only two or three police officers on the inquiry team would know his true identity. Reassured, Grant gave his details and started to talk.

Most of what he said did not concern the Lawrence murder; it was background on the Acourt group – who they were, where they lived and what they looked like. He described their enthusiasm for knives and he repeated something that was widely believed in the area: that new recruits to the gang were required to stab someone. He said he knew of three attacks they had carried out. The first involved a boy called Stacey Benefield, who had been knifed by David Norris a few weeks earlier and had to be taken to hospital, but who had refused to identify his attackers to the police. Grant knew that Benefield would be re-interviewed as a result of this, and he stressed that they should on no account let slip his name. Budgen reassured him again. Grant then linked the gang to the killing of Rohit Duggal. Although Peter Thompson had been convicted for this, the verdict was wrong, Grant said. Thompson was there all right, but he had not struck the fatal blow; that was one of the Acourt boys. They had also stabbed a boy called Lee in Woolwich – he did not know his full name – putting a bag over his head and jabbing him in the arms and legs with a knife, by way of torture.

As far as the Lawrence attack was concerned, Grant seems to have been sparing with detail: the Acourts and David Norris were responsible, along with two other youths whom he did not know. That was it. There would subsequently be a dispute about how much more Grant was asked. Did Budgen press him, or simply record what he was saying? Did he ask where Grant had discovered this information about the murder? Did Grant tell him? The answers have been contradictory, but it seems most likely that at this stage at least the source was not identified. The interview complete, Grant was told to stay in touch, but he insisted that the police must never call him or visit his home; that would give him away. So Budgen provided his pager number and said Grant should call him on it every day, stressing that he must ring the following day without fail. Grant agreed, secured one last guarantee of his anonymity, and left. The time was about 8.30 p.m. and twenty-two hours had passed since the murder.

FF had called the police with his tip-off at 1.50 p.m., but on the local television news that evening he and his brother were disappointed to see there was still no word of arrests, and instead what seemed to them a great deal of foolish speculation about the possible involvement of the British National Party. By now it may be that the EE family had also learned more about the murder, and they were quite convinced of the guilt of the Acourt group, so they decided to go a little farther. They wrote a letter, a very full letter which, they thought, would leave the police in no doubt about whom they should be investigating. It was scribbled on both sides of a lined sheet torn from a reporter's spiral-back note-pad, and it went like this:

The people involved in last night's stabbing are 1. Neil Acourt, 2. David Norris, 3. Jamie Acourt, 4. Gary Dobson.

Names 1 and 2 are also <u>rumoured</u> with Wimpy bar stabbing (Eltham).

Name 1 was <u>definitely</u> seen in the area prior to stabbing.

Names 2 and 1 are ringleaders and are positive knife users.

Names 1, 2, 3 share house in Bourne Brook Rd, Kidbrooke.

Name 4 lives in Phineas Pett Rd.

One of these names stabbed that poor lad.

The names 1 and 2 are very dangerous knife users who <u>always</u> carry knives and quite like using them.

Names 1 and 2 have stabbed before. Stacey Benefield was their victim about 6 weeks ago. He lives in Purneys Road off Rochester Way.

These bastards were definitely involved and must be stopped because they keep getting away with it.

This is <u>not a BNP related incident</u>. (You must stress this.)

Approach these shits with care. Do us all a favour and prove it. Good luck.

FF and EE put this message, unsigned, into an envelope marked with the words: 'Plumstead police. For eyes officer in charge only. (Eltham stabbing)'. Then they left the envelope in a telephone box near their home. Surely, they thought, that would be enough to get the Acourts arrested.

And there was somebody else out in the estates who was intent on helping the police with their inquiries. A woman who became known as Female Anon rang at 9 p.m. 'I think I may know the boys that committed the murder to the black boy,' she said. 'I don't know their names but I may be able to find out. They are two white boys who hang around Eltham and think they are the Krays. They stabbed a boy called Stacey in Mottingham or New Eltham. I will try to find out more and call you back.' Thirty-five minutes later, she did call back. 'I phoned earlier and the boy that got stabbed was Stacey Benefield. He was stabbed by two boys that call themselves the Krays, one of them possibly Andy Goodchild.'

FF and EE, James Grant and now the Female Anon: what results did their efforts produce? First, the lunchtime phone call: that this was anonymous impaired its value to the police – an informant who does not give a name cannot be further questioned and may have something to hide or be engaged in mischief. That the caller used the words 'may have been involved' was also cause for scepticism, for it showed that even he was not sure. But still there were reasons to take the call seriously. First, it came quickly. The shorter the lapse of time, the less likely it is that tip-offs of this kind will be based on mere rumour or will have been distorted by repetition. Second, it contained the statement that the named youths carried *large* knives. There had already been radio coverage of the Lawrence murder, but none of it contained the information, revealed by the post mortem, that the killing was done with one or two relatively large knives. Third, it contained names and an address not far from the murder scene, which could be checked. The mistake in the spelling of the Acourt name was not FF's, for he knew it all too well, but it may reflect his haste and nervousness during the call – the officer on the other end did not have a chance to check the spelling.

The task of 'researching' the two names given by the caller, Neil 'Acall' and David Norris, was allocated to Detective Constable Dennis Chase. This did not mean that he was told to knock on the door of 102 Bournbrook Road (there is no Bournbrook Close) and ask questions, but that he was expected to run the names through a variety of computer databases and other indexes to see if Neil Acall and Dave Norris were known to police. This check did not happen immediately. Although the relevant 'actions' were raised in the Holmes system just after 3.10 p.m., they were not allocated to Chase until 3.43 p.m., by which time he was on his way to Plumstead police station to take Joey Shepherd's statement. In his absence, the message was probably left in a tray for him, but since he was kept occupied on other tasks until late in the evening – he and Budgen were sent to sit in a car at the murder scene for an hour and a half around 10.40 p.m. – it probably did not reach him until last thing at night or even the following morning. In the meantime it seems that neither Bullock nor Crampton was told about the call that day or the next; indeed by their account four years were to pass before they were told of it. As for the anonymous letter left in the telephone box by FF and EE, it also went astray. It was found by a twelve-year-old girl at 8.30 p.m., but despite the words on the envelope she did not immediately recognize its importance and she simply took it home. It did not reach the police that night.

If FF and EE were unlucky in their efforts, they were not alone. Grant's visit to Eltham station did not produce the effect he hoped for, and the reason for this was later to become a matter of dispute. Christopher Budgen had joined the investigating team that afternoon and when the call had come from the front desk he volunteered to go down and see to it. Budgen realized very soon that this was an important informant – supplying names of suspects with descriptions, an address near the murder scene and details of allegedly related stabbings – so he left Grant downstairs, under instructions to stay where he was, and returned to the incident room to inform Bullock. By Budgen's later account Bullock took little interest, and merely told him to put the man's information on a green sheet and get it entered in the Holmes system. To Budgen this reaction was no surprise; he felt that Bullock, with whom he had worked before, disliked him and grudged him credit for good work – 'I could have recovered the Crown Jewels, it would not have made any difference.' Bullock told a quite different story. He accepted that at that time he was extremely busy and possibly preoccupied with other matters, but he denied that he fobbed Budgen off. He insisted instead that Budgen told him about Grant's information only after Grant had left the station, when it was too late for him to speak to the young man personally. Whichever was the case, Budgen wrote an account of Grant's information, marking the form 'male: particulars refused' and adding at the bottom 'believed identity of informant established'. Then he left it for the indexers to enter in the computer system. There was no immediate action.

And the Female Anon was no luckier. This woman, who called back after checking her information, obviously had access to someone with knowledge, and what she reported was consistent in two important respects with Grant's information: he had mentioned the Krays and Stacey Benefield, so did she. And she added another name: Andy Goodchild. By the time she called, however, the incident room was winding down for the night. This investigation might be generously staffed by the standards of 3 Area, but it did not have the luxury of a night shift; most officers had done a long day's work and they were heading home. Bullock did not hear of the woman's call before he left that night, so of the three important leads, from FF and EE, from Grant and from the Anon Female, he was only aware of Grant. Ian Crampton, the senior investigating officer, went to bed that night knowing nothing of any of them.

Chapter Four The Weekend

Friday's gentle but significant flow of information swelled to a flood over the weekend of 24 and 25 April. This no doubt reflected the impact of Saturday morning's press coverage, with its appeals for assistance, and the effectiveness of the house-to-house inquiries set in motion by Crampton. But another factor was also at work. Information moved easily within the estates around Well Hall, and among the young there was a particular closeness; there were only a handful of schools and not many places to go afterwards. Gossip travelled fast. When Witness K recounted what he knew at the Tyler house he dropped a stone into the pool, and the ripples moved quickly and strongly outwards. On Friday classrooms and school corridors were alive with speculation about the black boy's murder, and the same was true of family conversations at mealtimes or in front of the television later in the day. Teenagers are rarely good at keeping secrets, no matter how fiercely they are sworn to silence, and some of those who had heard K's story seem to have been unable to resist repeating it. Before long, versions of it, fragmented and distorted in the usual ways, had reached more ears than K ever intended. Among those who heard it were the Acourts and their friends. They had answered the door to K on the night and they knew exactly what he had seen and heard; now they knew what interpretation was being put on it. Within forty-eight hours of the stabbing K had an encounter with Dave Norris that left him unhurt but very frightened. When he bumped into Witness B again that weekend B noticed that he was very jumpy, and that he was carrying a knife. K said it was for his own protection, because he was having trouble with Dave. From now on he would be very careful, but it was a little late for discretion.

Even without the assistance of rumour, many people on these estates were quick to make a connection between the Acourts and the stabbing, and as police officers knocked on door after door over the weekend the boys reaped the harvest of their unpopularity. The name of Acourt and the address of 102 Bournbrook repeatedly 'cropped up', as one constable put it, and this was not only on doorsteps but also in telephone calls, anonymous and otherwise, to

Eltham station. In particular a schoolgirl, two mothers and two anonymous male callers tried to point the police towards the group, some suggesting in so many words that they were the killers and some restricting themselves to the heavy hint that these were known knife carriers.

Ian Crampton was briefed about Grant and the Female Anon soon after his arrival at Eltham station on the Saturday, and if he had any doubts about the importance of the information they were soon dispelled. At 11.50 a.m. the phone rang in the incident room and Detective Sergeant Peter Flook took the call.

'About the murder, there is a letter in the bin outside the Welcome Inn in Westmount Road about it.'

'Would you like to tell me your name?'

'No.'

'Can you tell me more?'

'No. The letter is in the bin. It's about the murder.'

Then the line went dead. Two officers, Sheridan and DC Peter Canavan, set out immediately for the pub in separate cars. The idea was that the person who delivered the letter might be at the scene to ensure it was collected and that a second officer, watching from a distance, might spot him. So it proved. Canavan drove into the pub car park, got out and made for the bins, of which there were several, while Sheridan parked outside in a residential street behind the pub. He was still manoeuvring when he caught sight of a white youth by Canavan's car. Before Sheridan could reach him, the youth had made off at a run. Canavan had also spotted him, and they were later able to record a description. Under the rear windscreen wiper of Canavan's car was a note written on both sides of a single page of lined paper torn from a reporter's pad. It read as follows:

1. Neil Acourt
2. Dave Norris
3. Jamie Acourt
4. Gary Dobson
were involved in stabbing in Well Hall Rd.
Names 1 and 2 are also rumoured for Wimpy Bar stabbing (Eltham).
Also the same two stabbed Stacey Benefield in Purneys Rd off Rochester Way.

1,2,3 live in Bournbrook Rd Kidbrook. 4 lives Phineas Pett Rd Eltham.
All know to use + carry knives openly. These must be stopped as are
very dangerous beings.
This is not a BNP related incident.
Approach with care.
It's down to you to prove it, you will come up trumps.
Name one was seen in area of stabbing, plus other lads not quite
identified as was dark. Not sure what one stabbed that poor lad. Will
find killer if you arrest these.
Good luck.

Crampton and Bullock were still digesting this when word came
from Shooters Hill police station that a woman had come in with
another letter about the case. She reported that her twelve-year-old
daughter had found the envelope the previous evening at 8.30 p.m.
in a telephone box at the junction of Westmount Road and
Heatherbank, barely fifty yards from the Welcome Inn car park.
The envelope was swiftly fetched; both the writing and the paper
matched the other letter, and the content was almost identical. For
Crampton these letters offered strong corroboration of the other
information provided the previous night. The Acourts and Norris,
Bournbrook Road and the carrying of knives: all of these were
repeated, as was the Stacey Benefield story, with some extra detail.
The name of Gary Dobson was added, with an approximate address,
while Neil Acourt and Dave Norris were linked to yet another
stabbing incident, at a Wimpy restaurant. Almost as striking as the
allegations was the imploring, fearful tone of the letters: 'These must
be stopped as are very dangerous beings', 'It's down to you to prove
it' and 'Approach these shits with care'. Most important of all, the
writer appeared to be or to know a witness. 'Name one [Neil Acourt]
was seen in area of stabbing . . .' This was the first explicit claim to
police by anyone that evidence existed which could link one of these
named youths to the Lawrence killing. The telephone box letter,
recovered second but presumably written first, said Neil Acourt 'was
<u>definitely</u> seen in the area prior to stabbing'. The word underlined
suggested that as far as the writer was concerned this was no rumour;
he *knew*. Somewhere out there in Eltham, it seemed, there was at least
one witness who could link one of these boys to the murder scene.
  The second letter was, like the first, the work of FF and EE, who

had decided that the telephone-box message must have gone astray, and this family had not finished in its efforts to point police towards the Acourts. The boys were out on Saturday afternoon when their mother answered the door to PC Wendy Bennett, engaged on house-to-house inquiries with her clipboard and forms. Mrs DD was well aware that something had been going on in her house and she had a good idea of what it was. Like the boys, she was outraged by the conduct of the Acourt group and their ability to get away with whatever they did. She was also concerned for the safety of her sons, particularly EE, her youngest. So when Bennett presented herself at the door Mrs DD was ready to tell what she knew. It was her belief, she told the policewoman, that at some stage on Thursday night EE had looked out of his window and seen the Acourt brothers 'walking around the corner'. She also recounted what she had heard about EE's girlfriend Emma: that she had walked past the two black boys at the bus stop and might have seen something. Mrs DD was nervous and she stressed that she did not want EE to know that she had been talking to the police about the Acourts. PC Bennett, having been supplied with the names of two possible witnesses, gave her assurances of discretion and departed.

Emma Cook was high in someone else's thoughts that day. Just below the Coronet cinema was a row of shops known as Tudor Parade, and the owner of one of these was a responsible and concerned citizen. First thing on Saturday morning, after reading about the murder in the papers, she had telephoned the police to report that the window of an empty shop in the parade had been broken on Thursday night and that an empty whisky bottle lay on the ground outside. Perhaps it had something to do with the murder, she suggested. A police officer duly came and inspected the scene, concluded that it was not relevant, thanked her and left. But in the early afternoon, the shopkeeper had cause to call again, and what she said was recorded in the Holmes system as message 69:

> A young girl who comes into my shop has just told me that she saw
> the two boys as she was passing the bus stop and that there was also a
> man and a woman at the stop. She carried on walking and as she
> passed the Well Hall Odeon [the Coronet's previous name] saw a
> group of three to four youths kicking the fire door. She does not know

if they were the same youths involved in the stabbing and would not contact you herself.

The girl in question was Emma Cook, and she was not a casual visitor to the shop but an employee, working there every Saturday.

These leads – from the shopkeeper and Mrs DD – were provided to the police voluntarily and openly. Mrs DD went so far as to supply Emma Cook's address. By Saturday evening, therefore, the police had in their hands, from two separate sources, the means to find and question two potential witnesses – they were not to know it, but two people closely linked to the anonymous letters. But that is not what happened. The content of PC Bennett's interview with Mrs DD was recorded on the appropriate form that evening and timed at 5.30 p.m., but nobody in the investigating team could later recall having seen it that night. Crampton was to say that, as with the very first anonymous telephone message from FF, he never saw it during his time as SIO. The Holmes records imply that it was not entered into the database for another twenty-four hours, although this does not necessarily mean that it lay unnoticed all that time. Certainly there is no record of any follow-up action that weekend, and when Mrs DD received another visit from the police on Monday it was from an officer who knew nothing about her previous interview. As for the shopkeeper's information, recorded in message 69, it fared little better, for she was not seen that weekend either. What was going on?

In the course of Saturday the chaos that had reigned in the incident room the previous day had been largely tamed. Desks, chairs, terminals and so forth were in place, the Holmes system was hooked up and functioning and the investigating team was almost up to the staffing level agreed by Ilsley. Although there was too much to do and too little time and manpower to do it, this was normal for the early stages of an investigation, when everyone works long hours and it falls to senior officers to ensure that the most urgent tasks are identified and dealt with first. But Bullock, the deputy SIO, was aware of a problem. Like Crampton, he had not run an investigation on the Holmes system before, and they both had received minimal 'read-only' training for it. This in itself was not a grave handicap; properly supported, they could have functioned perfectly well on that basis. But they were not properly supported.

In the first place, they were short of the proper complement of 'indexers', the Holmes operators whose job was to type documents into the system and format them for easy cross-reference between names, places and other key points of information. Even with a full staff of indexers it would be a struggle to cope with the flow of information in these early days (in an ideal world, beyond the dreams of 3 Area, there would be a night shift of indexers to clear backlogs), and so the trays of documents awaiting processing were permanently piled high. As if that were not bad enough, hardly a single detective on the 'outside', or investigating team, could operate the Holmes machines, which meant that they were unable to exploit the system properly. This created a communication gap. Bullock investigated what training was available and found that the formal procedure would have required him to send his officers on a short full-time course, which was impossible, so he improvised some on-the-job instruction for the detectives. The drawback with this was that it had to be provided by the indexers, whose full in-trays were all the fuller in consequence. And there was another problem.

Holmes was supposed to work like this: as items of information arrived they would first be assessed and sorted by a 'receiver', who would consider how urgent the document was and what distribution it should have – whether a copy should go directly to the SIO, for example. Then the receiver would 'mark up' the item for the indexers by underlining or making notes in the margin to identify facts and names which should be available in the system for cross-referencing. He or she might also specify 'actions' which should be initiated. For example, if a message referred to a car, the receiver would write, 'Action: trace car; interview owner/driver', and this action would be entered separately in the system and numbered. With complex documents the task of marking up would be performed by a second figure, the 'statement reader', who was supposed to master the detail and potential of witness evidence. A third officer performed the role of 'action allocator', assigning the actions – always very specific tasks – to detectives and chasing them until they were completed and a 'result' was filed. Finally there was the office manager, whose task was to oversee all this work, double-check where appropriate and catch errors and omissions. According to Amip guidelines each of these four jobs was to be performed by a different officer of the rank of detective sergeant, and in a murder investigation it would be the SIO's 'bag carrier' who acted as office manager. Rarely, if ever outside a major Scotland Yard inquiry, was there sufficient staff in the Metropolitan Police to fill all these posts, particularly with detective sergeants, and this was not one of the exceptions. In Operation Fishpool the jobs of receiver, statement reader, action allocator and office manager were all done by one man. At first it was DS Sheridan, Crampton's bag carrier, but by Saturday lunchtime he was passing the responsibility to DS Flook. Flook was bag carrier to Detective Superintendent Brian Weeden, the man who, it had now been agreed, would take over from Crampton as SIO on Monday morning on his return from sick leave. The effect of these shortages of 'inside' staff – indexers and more senior ranks – compounded by a general lack of Holmes skills, was significant. The natural muddle of the first day, when personnel, chairs and screens had to be mustered and arranged, gave way to a less visible and less acknowledged confusion. With the Holmes indexers lagging badly behind events, an office ostensibly organized around computers was functioning on a combination of paper and word of mouth. As the trays of documents piled up, some copied to senior officers and some not, some marked up and some not, it is little wonder that leads were being missed.

All the time, fresh information flowed in, and where someone had a message of importance to convey they had to compete with a cacophony of background noise. A woman called to say there was a knife in her front garden; it proved too small to be the murder weapon, and it was unstained. Several people reported seeing speeding cars on Well Hall Road just after the murder; the cars had to be traced, if possible. A caller said she had seen a group of Rastafarians on Well Hall Road before the murder; a statement was taken. The hunt for bus drivers on routes passing the scene continued; did they remember any passengers boarding, or had they seen anything? The cinema, kebab shop, off-licence and garage on Well Hall Road were all open late; who was on duty, had they seen any white youths, did they have security videotapes? And so on.

There were some items that caught the eye. A man rang in to say that a few days before the murder he had been working on his car in Whinyates Road when he saw a youth battering the inside of the telephone box on the corner of Wendover Road, as if attempting to steal the money. The man told the youth to stop, whereupon he swore, produced a knife with a nine-inch blade and said: 'Do you want some of this?' At this point a neighbour appeared and threatened to call the police, so the young man walked off. He was described as white, smallish, seventeen to eighteen years old with collar-length black hair and a leather jacket. A father living in the area told the house-to-house team that his teenage daughter, Samantha, might know who was responsible for the attack. Another local householder reported that at about 9.30 p.m. on the night of the murder he heard raised voices by his garden fence. A group of boisterous young men were heading for Phineas Pett Road in the direction of Well Hall Road, and one of them had amused the others by dragging a 'hard object' along the slatted fence to create a loud rattling noise. The householder, however, had not seen the men.

Two schoolgirls, Sarah and Kelly-Ann, were walking home through the Progress estate after 10.30 p.m. They had crossed Dickson Road and were heading up Franklin Passage when they heard something. Sarah thought it sounded like a fight: 'It was very loud ... It sounded like boys' voices, but I couldn't make out what was being said.' Kelly-Ann recalled 'a lot of screaming and shouting and what sounded like a load of yobs'. Frightened, they ran home. At that same moment a young mother was walking with her son in Sandby Green when she heard loud, male voices which seemed very angry coming from the direction of Dickson Road or Downman Road. She too was frightened and she grabbed her son and turned for home. A plumber whose house had a view over the roundabout recalled seeing a group of between four and six youths running across the roundabout from the direction of the cinema towards the scene of the murder. He was able to pinpoint the time fairly closely: he had watched snooker on television until 10.30 p.m., and then switched off when a Liberal Democrat party political broadcast began. He went into the kitchen for a smoke and very soon after he had lit up he saw the group running. They were, he thought, about seventeen or eighteen years old and one was wearing a white top, but he could not describe them any further than that.

The telephones rang and rang. One anonymous caller said that someone named Fox had committed the murder as a result of an argument. Another said that a boy called Alex had either been involved or knew who did it. Then on Saturday afternoon the Female

Anon of the previous evening rang again, and this time she had more to say:

> The boys who did your murder, there are five of them not six like the paper says. One is called Gary Dobson of 13 Phineas Pett Road, Eltham SE9. The two main boys are Neil Acourt and Jamie Acourt, they call themselves the Krays. They are real nutters. Be careful when you go and arrest them. Their house is full of knives. They live at 102 Bournbrook Road. They stabbed Stacey Benefield who is white, and about two months ago they stabbed another white boy and were taunting them – they stabbed him in the legs and side – he was taken to the Brook. I don't want to give you his name.

Important progress was made in tracing the remaining bus stop witnesses. Joey Shepherd had been found easily but the other man and woman took a little longer. Royston Westbrook read about the case in the newspapers on Saturday morning and did not at first associate it with the events he had seen. Then the penny dropped and in the afternoon he called the police. He didn't know if he could be any help – 'Basically all I saw was what looked like the young man being punched and then him legging it' – but he would come in to make a full statement. His recollections confirmed much of what Duwayne and Shepherd had described and cast up no significant anomalies. Like Shepherd, Westbrook saw no weapon; he didn't even see any blows. Stephen, he said, 'was surrounded by them and he went down. I can't say precisely what it was that made him fall to the ground', just 'weight of numbers'. He could describe only one of the attackers, a man aged about twenty, 5' 7" to 5' 8" tall, of stocky build, with 'dirty fair-coloured hair' that may have been wavy and was generally short. He was wearing a light-blue jumper with a marble-effect pattern, tucked into his jeans. Westbrook was confident that he would recognize him if he saw him again. Considerable efforts were made to trace Alexandra Marie – it was thought that a young Frenchwoman staying or living around Shooters Hill would not be too hard to find – but it turned out that she had gone away for the weekend. Late on Sunday the English family who employed her telephoned to say that they had just returned with her and made the connection with the murder. Like Westbrook she had not realized the seriousness of the attack but she was keen to help and would

65

make a full statement if a translator could be provided. Marie, it seemed, believed she had seen one of the attackers boarding the bus. An appointment was made for the next morning.

The man called James Grant was not forgotten. When, true to his word, he rang in on Saturday to renew his contact with Budgen, he was asked to return to the station that afternoon to go over the ground again. He turned up at 4.30 p.m. and was interviewed by Budgen and a more senior officer, Detective Sergeant John Davidson, who had joined the team that lunchtime on his return from a golfing holiday. Davidson was a tall, red-faced, middle-aged Scot of generous girth who rejoiced in the nickname 'OJ'. This had no connection with O. J. Simpson but was short for Obnoxious Jock, a name which appears to have been affectionately bestowed since the initials were used to his face even by superior officers.

Davidson had the reputation, and wore the air, of a 'can-do' detective, a man who had little time for niceties and got results his own way. He was a big personality to have in the team and he was to play an important part. By the time he and Budgen met Grant they had confirmed the informant's identity by checking his record on the Police National Computer. The encounter that followed does not seem to have added much to what had been said the night before. Davidson said later that he pressed Grant to reveal his source, but to no avail. Grant, for his part, asked why the people he had named had not been arrested. Davidson recalled: 'I gave him a hard time . . . I am talking about a skinhead turning up at a police station when a black has been murdered and wanting to know what is happening. I had to treat him on both fronts: whether he was a genuine informant, whether he was somebody in that perhaps his mates were involved and he wasn't really going to tell us.' There was also the matter of confirming what Budgen had reported. As Davidson said, 'perhaps it was thought that his [Budgen's] mouth ran away with himself occasionally and therefore everything had to be checked as regards informants'. The encounter lasted half an hour, finishing at 5 p.m. on Saturday.

The investigation by then had its prime suspects: Neil and Jamie Acourt, Dave Norris and Gary Dobson. The anonymous letters mentioned all four, while Grant had named the first three and the Female Anon the Acourts and Dobson. A few other names were in the air – the Female Anon had spoken of an Andy Goodchild in her second call; there were also 'Alex' and the man called Fox, while the house-to-house inquiries had linked the Acourts with a boy called Caetano – but these were secondary. Police had addresses for the Acourts and Dobson and basic descriptions and approximate ages for the Acourts and Norris, while by popular local assent it was clear that some or all were knife carriers. Crampton, however, wanted to know more, and given what was alleged about these boys it seemed more than likely that the information he needed would exist somewhere in police files. The job of 'researching' the Acourts and Norris was still in the hands of Dennis Chase, and his first inquiries showed that none of them figured on the National Police Computer, which meant that they had no serious convictions. Nor were they on Scotland Yard's criminal intelligence files. They did not even appear in Department of Health and Social Services records as claiming welfare benefits. If the police had anything on them it would be minor offences, arrests, cautions or complaints, and these records were not computerized but held in the crime collators' files in local police stations. Chase spent much of the weekend trailing from station to station around southeast London sifting through card indexes.

Another possible way of learning more about the boys was surveillance, and Crampton first considered having the Bournbrook Road house watched on the Saturday, when he sent an officer to have a look. On Sunday Crampton made up his mind. Surveillance was a job for specialists and these were provided from a central pool known as the Force Intelligence Bureau (FIB), based in Dulwich. For budgetary reasons the FIB was not usually staffed on a Sunday, so an officer was contacted at home and advised that the Lawrence murder squad wanted help. The surveillance team was booked for a theft case on Monday morning, it seems, but would be available after that. In the meantime, Crampton and Bullock went to take a look at Bournbrook Road themselves; it was, they found, difficult terrain for observation, since a car or van would soon be spotted. A vacant house, or one with a cooperative owner, would be the best bet. At the same time Crampton also extended the house-to-house inquiries to embrace almost all of the Brook estate and he gave special orders for dealing with the two addresses linked to the suspects: 102 Bournbrook Road and 13 Phineas Pett Road. These would be visited simultaneously, and by detectives rather than uniformed officers. No hint was to be given that it was anything other than a routine inquiry.

What else could be done? It is not clear whether the possibility was aired at the staff meeting on Saturday, but Crampton, Bullock and Ilsley (who looked in on the incident room in the evening) would later say that they discussed the merits of simply picking up the named boys, or at least those whom they could get hold of, searching their homes for forensic evidence, interviewing them and putting them in line-ups to see whether Brooks, Shepherd and Westbrook would pick them out. Arrests are usually made first thing in the morning, so a swoop at first light on Sunday might well bring in the Acourts and Dobson. Against this, according to the three senior officers, weighed a number of factors. First, they hardly knew anything about the suspects. The addresses for the Acourts and Dobson were correct, but there it ended. They had no photographs, no firm ages and no idea whether the boys were at home. Second, the suspects were believed to be juveniles, which always made arrests and questioning more complicated and sensitive – rushing the process might mean having to release them in short order without making any real progress. Third, identification parades involving a number of suspects and a number of witnesses are a logistical nightmare, and the chances of arranging a full series at a weekend were slim. Fourth, there was no hard evidence to throw at the suspects during questioning. This in itself was not legally an obstacle to arresting – 'reasonable grounds for suspicion' are sufficient – but evidence of some sort, rather than anonymous or confidential tip-offs, would clearly make it easier to put the suspects under pressure during interviews.

By their later account the three men took a conscious decision to wait. Crampton said later that he knew this meant the suspects would have more time to destroy forensic evidence, by disposing of or washing bloodstained clothes, shoes or knives for example, but he felt this was a gamble worth taking. He had never been optimistic that blood would have found its way on to the attackers' clothing in the first place and now, after nearly forty-eight hours had passed, he suspected that any traces there might have been had probably already been washed away. Ilsley and Bullock apparently concurred and a delay was agreed. No record was made of this decision, which proved to be one of the most important of the whole investigation.

At 6.10 p.m. on Sunday evening, having visited a number of neighbouring houses by way of cover, two plainclothes officers duly knocked at the door of the Acourt home. It was answered by a dark-haired woman in her forties who identified herself as Patricia Acourt and invited them in. She had obviously been decorating, and excused herself for a moment to wash Polyfilla off her hands. A man could be seen in another room, also decorating. When Mrs Acourt returned, she explained frankly that the whole house needed to be painted and papered and that she had only moved there recently with her sons from Langbrook Road after problems with neighbours arising from her relationship with John Burke, the man in the other room. The two detectives then went to work, one filling out a form and the other asking general questions. Had she heard rumours about the murder? She only knew what she had seen on television, and maybe her sons had spoken of it. Who were the sons? She had two older boys, Bradley and Scott Lamb, who were twins aged twenty, and two younger ones, Neil and Jamie Acourt, seventeen and sixteen. And where was she on the night of the murder? At this she stumbled, became vague and even, one of the officers said later, evasive. At first she couldn't remember but when one of the officers suggested she think about what she had watched on television she said yes, she had been at home that night because she had seen *EastEnders*. In fact, she went on, she spent the whole evening at home, going to bed at around 11.30 p.m. And the boys? Bradley was at home that night with flu, or perhaps not; perhaps he went out later on, she couldn't remember. Scott was at home, or at least he came in around 10 p.m. And a friend of the boys, called Luke, who lived in Well Hall Road, had come round. She couldn't be certain what they did but she thought Jamie was at home all night. John Burke's memory was even worse. When questioned, he was able to explain that he was Mrs Acourt's boyfriend, was fifty years old, lived in Rotherhithe, worked as a security guard and drove a Datsun Cherry. But as for Thursday night, which was just four days earlier, he was unable or unwilling to say anything more than that he had been at the Bournbrook Road house between 7.30 and 9 p.m. and had driven home afterwards.

As alibis go, these were feeble in the extreme. Burke said nothing about the Acourt boys and removed himself from the scene nearly two hours before the murder. Pat Acourt could scarcely account for her own movements, let alone those of her sons. It was to Jamie, her youngest, that she gave the best cover, and even then she only 'thought' he was at home on the night of the murder. The boys themselves were not in to account for their movements, so the two police officers said thank you and left.

A couple of streets away in Phineas Pett Road, Gary Dobson was at home when the police called. Officers noted that he was 5' 9" tall, seventeen years old, with short, straight, dark-brown hair and a spotty face. He wore a green shirt and army-style trousers, and all he knew about the murder was what he had read in the papers. As to his movements on the night, he said he had been indoors all evening. He explained that he had just started a computer course at a college in Covent Garden and had got back at about 5.30 p.m., after which he had spent the evening studying. On the house-to-house form there is a line marked: 'Interviewing officer's observations.' Beside this the detective who spoke to Gary wrote: 'Nervous.' As for Gary's parents, Stephen and Pauline Dobson explained that they too had been in all night, watching television with a couple of friends who had been visiting. That, it seemed, was that, so the two detectives left.

A few minutes later, however, they saw Gary on the street with a girl and they followed them. The young couple walked west along Phineas Pett Road, turned right into Appleton Road and then left into Bournbrook Road, where they entered number 102. Five minutes later Gary and the girl emerged (the Acourt boys, as we know, were not at home) and police followed them as they walked down to Rochester Way, across to Well Hall Road, and then south to Eltham High Street, where they entered the McDonald's. This banal episode had its significance. Why did Gary visit the Acourt house? Was he perhaps hoping to report to the boys that he had been visited? Was he going to ask whether they too had seen the police? If asked about it, he would probably say he was merely calling on friends, but that in itself was important, for this short visit provided proof of association between Gary Dobson and the Acourt family. Up to now the connection was based on hearsay or anonymous information – in particular the anonymous letters – but this was cast-iron observation.

*

70

Every Monday morning at 8 a.m. the senior detectives of the 3 Area
Amip squad held a meeting, usually at their headquarters in Catford
police station. With their boss, Detective Chief Superintendent Bill
Ilsley, in the chair, these five or six superintendents each accounted
for the progress of their various investigations, brought themselves
up to date on policy matters and swapped notes on problems, budgets
and other developments. The meeting of Monday 26 April saw the
return to duty from illness of Detective Superintendent Brian Weeden.
As soon as it was over, he and Ian Crampton sat down to begin the
handover of the Lawrence case, which would install him as SIO
and free the other man to attend his big trial at the Old Bailey.
Crampton, with Bullock's help, had established a team and an
incident room. Further than that, he had identified some prime
suspects and, it seems, made the decision to investigate them rather
than make early arrests. Now he was to hand over the reins to another
detective. This was another moment of considerable importance in
the case of Stephen Lawrence: the change of command marked the
end of the first period of the investigation, but it also raised a
possibility of interruption and even confusion. Would Weeden hit
the ground running?

As Crampton summed up the case, Weeden listened and took
notes. The outgoing SIO described the murder, with Stephen's
movements on the night, the wait at the bus stop and the call of
'What? What? Nigger!', and then he ran through the details of the
post mortem. Turning to the suspects, he said that information had
been coming in from three or four different angles – he explained
about the Female Anon, Grant and the anonymous letters – but in
his opinion it probably originated at the same source. Who this was
he could not say. As to the boys themselves, he described to Weeden
the events of the previous night, with the two house-to-house visits
and Gary's movements afterwards, and he explained that he had
commissioned a surveillance operation to establish proof of association and find out if there was somebody in the group who matched
Duwayne's description of the lead attacker.

The case – Weeden scarcely needed to be told – had another
dimension. Crampton spoke of the Duggal, Blair and Adams murders, the suggestion of a possible BNP link, the interest of MPs and
of Greenwich Council and the angry meeting at the town hall in
Woolwich on Friday. There were also plans for marches, including

one the following Sunday. It was all very sensitive, he said, and he had stressed this to the officers. As for the Lawrence family, they were nice people, although it appeared the mother was (Weeden noted the words) 'a bit excitable'. Crampton had appointed two officers to liaise with them while another specialist officer had been attached to the investigation temporarily from the small Racial Incident Unit at Woolwich. The family, for their part, had appointed a solicitor to act for them.

Summing up, Crampton was less than sanguine. Although there were four known witnesses to this murder, he said, his experience suggested that it was unlikely that any of them would be able to identify any of the attackers. The best hope was to secure a confession from one of the group – there was always a weak link – and then to make the rest of them 'roll over'. This would require simultaneous arrests and interviews and he had already given orders for the information given by the witnesses about the attackers' clothing to be collated so that officers searching the suspects' homes after arrests would know what to look for. One other matter he mentioned: Davidson was supposed to be interviewing Stacey Benefield, who was said to have been the victim of another knife attack by the gang. If he cooperated, then they would have something to throw at these boys. This briefing was long and detailed and Crampton felt that, where he had left gaps, Bullock and Flook could fill them in. When it was over his involvement in the investigation came to an end, although he returned to the incident room briefly around lunchtime to sign some papers. He felt he had done what he could.

Chapter Five **Eleven Days (I)**

Eleven more days were to pass before anyone was arrested for the murder of Stephen Lawrence. Brian Weeden chose at first to continue the policy adopted by Crampton of seeking more information about the suspects, finding out who they really were and what their background was. As time passed, however, his investigation acquired a different emphasis, for gradually the Operation Fishpool team became convinced that hard evidence was almost within their grasp. There was, they thought, at least one person who knew enough to secure convictions or at least enough to put pressure on one or more of the killers to confess. The anonymous letters implied this, as did the strength of the other information coming in. There had to be somebody at the source of these strong ripples of accusation emanating from the estates and that person seemed tantalizingly near. So it was that the search for the decisive witness came to be placed before confrontation with the suspects.

Twice on Saturday, by Mrs DD and the woman shopkeeper, the police had been told about someone who might well be this vital person and on both occasions the opportunity was lost. It required a third tip-off before the trail to Emma Cook was picked up. On the Monday morning, while Crampton was talking to Weeden at Catford station, out in the estates a local woman was telling house-to-house officers that a family called Acourt were thought to carry knives and to use them on people. Such reports were by this time commonplace but an action was raised that day and allocated to Detective Constable Steve Wilkinson to interview the woman. When Wilkinson came to question her on Wednesday she proved to be passing on information she had picked up from the girl called Lisa, but when the detective spoke to Lisa the following day she told him that she had merely been repeating rumours. It might well have been a dead end, and one among many, except that they talked a little more. Lisa told Wilkinson what else the rumour mill was saying – she knew about the Benefield case, for example – and then she said something that was more than rumour. She described how she and her boyfriend, Greg, had been on Well Hall Road on the night of the 22nd at about 10.30 p.m. when they saw Emma Cook leaving

EE's house and heading south towards the spot where the murder was committed. Emma, she informed Wilkinson, had seen nothing unusual or relevant on her journey home. And incidentally, she added, EE was terrified of the Acourt boys because there had been trouble between them in the past.

At about the same time on the Wednesday that this conversation took place, DC Canavan visited the woman shopkeeper, who repeated to him what Emma had told her the previous Saturday about the group at the cinema kicking the fire doors. He also learned, presumably from the same source, that Emma had once been the girlfriend of one of the Acourt boys. That afternoon Wilkinson and Canavan reported what they had discovered to Weeden and the other detectives in the team and everyone could immediately see the importance Emma might have. It was 28 April and the investigation was six days old; at last they had identified the first link in the chain. No time was wasted. Wilkinson visited Emma at home that night and she agreed to talk the following day to Wilkinson and Canavan together. Because Emma was still sixteen and a juvenile she could not be interviewed on her own, so her father sat in while they talked. Although the interview was long the result was disappointing. Emma confirmed that she had left EE's house at around 10.30 p.m. and she confirmed that she had gone home via the roundabout, passing the two black youths and a white man and woman at the bus stop on the way. She also told the detectives that as she walked along the side of the roundabout she had heard banging by the cinema. But despite persistent questioning she insisted that she had not seen who was responsible for the noise, nor had she seen anyone else near the roundabout whom she recognized.

Adamant though Emma was, there were grounds to doubt her. She was the ex-girlfriend of one of the Acourts and the current girlfriend of a boy who was known to be afraid of them. If she still had contact with the Acourts she had a motive to protect them from the police, and if she did not (which was more likely) she may have had reason to fear them, just as EE apparently did. Furthermore, the detectives felt strongly that this girl was under the influence of her father, who was reluctant for his daughter to get involved or give a formal statement. If Emma knew more than she had said, police believed she would be more likely to talk if her father was not there. It was not as though she had been entirely unhelpful. On the evening after the second visit to the Cook house, Wilkinson filed in the Holmes system a report based on information from Emma: 'The Acourt brothers (Jamie and Neil) associate with Lukey Knight (who lives in a house in Well Hall Road near the cinema). David Norris address not known. Danny Catona (spelling unknown) who is believed to be in custody for stabbing somebody at a caravan site somewhere in Kent around Easter time.' This is far from being a direct allegation against these boys – it does not link them with the murder – but it identifies them as youths who associate. It was fresh information from a valuable source and it might also be an indication that, deep down, this sixteen-year-old girl wanted to cooperate.

Emma had also confirmed something of practical importance: there was a disturbance at the cinema shortly before the murder. Stephen Lawrence's attackers had to have come from that general direction; perhaps it was them that she had heard, high or drunk or bored, and throwing their weight around. And if she had heard them, surely somebody had seen them? It was another line of inquiry, and one that was already in hand. A couple of days earlier the house-to-house team knocked on a local door and found themselves talking to the manager of the Coronet. He explained that, because trade was so slow on the night of the murder, the cinema had emptied quickly after the final credits and staff were able to lock up and leave very soon after 10.30 p.m. As they left, he remembered seeing some youths larking about in the road, down towards the kebab shop. There seemed to be two groups, one of three boys and the other of two. A boy who he thought was about fifteen years old chased another, who might have been younger, and there was laughing. The manager heard the words 'fucking wanker'. He believed that stones were thrown and as he left the scene he had the impression the youths were moving in the direction of the roundabout. The manager told the officers that if they wanted to know more they ought to talk to the cinema doorman, because he had had a better look at the boys.

The doorman, it turned out, had not only seen the commotion but was able to give the police a good lead on who these youths were. He described the shouting and chasing in similar terms to the manager, although he said the boys were older: between seventeen and twenty. He had taken a good look, he said, because he thought their behaviour was threatening, and he had waited and watched from the other side of the road until all the cinema staff were safely clear. While watching, he realized he knew some of the faces: these boys were patrons of the Coronet. Once his colleagues were safely on their way he too went home. By an odd chance, however, that was not the end of it. The next evening, his night off, the cinema doorman went out to dinner with a woman friend at the Harvester restaurant a mile or so away in Falconwood, and there he found himself sitting at the next table to some of the youths he had seen outside the cinema. He went over and spoke to them. 'I told them to be careful as there had been a group of coloured people driving about and asking questions about the murder,' he said later. One of the group, a tall, dark boy whom he recognized as the chaser-kicker from the previous night, said, 'Fair enough,' and the doorman returned to his seat. This meeting was a bizarre coincidence, but potentially a very useful one. For the police, the next step would be to check whether the staff at the Harvester had any record of who these young people were.

Meanwhile, the name of the young man we call EE – a second link in the chain – was finally registering in the Fishpool incident room. Lisa had mentioned him to Wilkinson, but only as Emma's boyfriend; it was another young woman who raised the possibility that EE might be a crucial witness. The house-to-house officers spoke to the woman as part of their routine inquiries and she said that, while she would put nothing in writing, she had heard that the EE and FF brothers saw the Acourts in the street at the time of the murder. So shortly afterwards, and for the third time, the mother of those two young men, Mrs DD, found herself answering the door to the police. Once again she explained that EE was very frightened and did not want to talk, that he was sure the Acourts were responsible and 'apparently' saw them on the night, and that Emma had walked past the two black boys by the bus stop and 'may have seen more'. She also added two items that she had not mentioned to PC Bennett on the Saturday, items which she may have picked up since then: a boy called Gary Robson was supposed to be involved, and the Acourts had recently stabbed somebody called Stacey.

The following morning two officers, DC Hughes and DC Andrews, returned to the house and spoke at length to EE. It was evident, Hughes reported later that day, that EE was frightened of the Acourts. 'He denied he saw anything that night, although he contradicted this by saying continually that they were responsible for the stabbing.' EE described seeing Emma off and insisted that she saw the two black youths but nothing else. Hughes continued:

> He was very nervous throughout our visit. He had trouble holding a piece of paper that we had given him. He tended to talk around whether he had seen anything and both Paula and I felt that he knew a lot more than he was saying. He admitted previous run-ins with the Acourts . . . His mother believes he knows more than he is telling us and I am sure she is pushing him towards telling the police. We both feel that a gentle approach when he is seen again would be the appropriate method of extracting information from him. He may be responsible for the two notes to the incident room.

So by 30 April, the eighth day after the murder, Emma and EE were at last at the heart of the investigation. Both had been spoken to, both had said they had seen nothing that could help, but in both cases rumour in the estates suggested that they *had* seen something and the police suspected that they were holding something back. In terms of witnessing the crime itself, or the build-up to it, it was clear that Emma had been well placed and might easily have seen something she was reluctant to speak about, but EE's behaviour was less easy to understand because he had been at home, nowhere near the scene of the murder. Not only that, but given what was known of the attackers' movements he was not in a position to see them immediately before or immediately after they struck. So why was he so nervous? Was he worried for Emma or for himself?

By now detectives were on the trail of their third potential witness, a third link in the chain. On Tuesday 27 April Witness K's story, which had travelled through the estates with such rapidity, finally reached police ears, albeit only as a faint echo. Again it was the house-to-house team, simple but relentless, who first heard it. First, some remarks by a woman householder aroused the interest of the officers knocking on doors and they suggested that a detective should call on her for a chat. She then told DC Graham Cooke that she had picked up some rumours about the murder from two local girls, Tara and Michelle Casserley. When Cooke knocked on the door of the Casserley home to check this he found the girls' mother on her own. As he questioned her it emerged that both her daughters were friendly with the Acourts and that she had heard from them that the Acourts and Gary Dobson were said to be involved in the murder. Where had this come from? Michelle, Mrs Casserley said, had been spending a lot of time at the Tyler house lately and was there on the night of the stabbing with a lot of other young people. Pressed by Cooke, she told the story she had heard, which he later summarized as follows:

> One of the youths her daughter was with, name unknown at present, went out and saw lots of police activity and he went up to 102 Bournbrook Road SE9, knocked on the door and went in, saw Neil and Jamie Acourt and Gary Dobson and two others unknown. He stated that they were very edgy and nervous. The boy was suspicious and told the group that there was a lot of police about and someone had been stabbed. The Acourts replied: 'It's got nothing to do with us.' The youth noticed that the five boys had wet hair and the five gave the reason as they all just had a bath.

Here, for the first time, was a version of the story of K's visit to the Acourt house that night.

Cooke had no difficulty in seeing the potential importance of this. Merely to find a witness who could place Neil, Jamie, Gary and two others in that house together shortly after the murder would be extremely valuable, but to find one who would say that they were edgy and nervous and all had *wet hair* might well prove the turning point of the investigation. But who was this witness with the vital knowledge? Mrs Casserley did not know. Cooke returned immediately to the incident room, filed his green message and reported what he had found in person to Weeden and others. It was very promising but there was a hitch, he explained, for Mrs Casserley had said the police should on no account approach her daughters directly. If confronted, she said, 'they will go back to their friends and inform them'. She agreed to talk to Michelle herself to see if she would help. So the police waited.

These were the days when the hopes raised by tracing Emma Cook and EE were at their highest, and the attention of most of the squad was on those two. DC Cooke, however, stayed on the trail of K, turning his attention to the Tyler household. That was where

Michelle Casserley had picked up her story and Cooke calculated that the source of that story – the youth who had knocked on the door of 102 Bournbrook Road – might be found there without waiting for Michelle to speak. Interest in the Tylers intensified when Detective Sergeant 'OJ' Davidson picked up a rumour that Dave Norris had admitted committing the murder to Ricky Tyler, possibly during a visit to the Westhorne Avenue house, and that Norris had boasted that he was safe because he had found himself an alibi. But there was some dismay when the liberty hall character of the Tyler establishment became evident – half the neighbourhood, it seemed, went in and out of those doors – and matters were further complicated when Cooke discovered that the house was already under police surveillance. The local crime squad, pursuing inquiries into drug and cheque offences, were actually preparing a raid, but they agreed to consult with the Fishpool incident room before moving in. It was all very untidy; if the third link was to be identified, Michelle Casserley might prove vital after all.

Brian Weeden scarcely realized it when he became SIO, but he was taking charge of the investigation of more than one crime, for Grant, the anonymous letters and the Female Anon had all alleged that some of the boys they named were responsible for stabbing others besides Stephen Lawrence. Establishing the truth about these other incidents, as background to the Lawrence murder and as offences in their own right, proved to be a lengthy business and an astonishing one.

All three of the key sources mentioned Stacey Benefield. The name came up a few times in the conversation as Crampton briefed Weeden, and the latter jotted down: 'Need to int. Benefield and his group; is the info true.' In fact Benefield had been seen the previous night and he had taken a decision which was, in the long run, to have the most unexpected consequences. Aged twenty at this time, Stacey was a member of a large family with many connections in Eltham – the Casserleys, for example, were cousins. He had attended Crown Woods School but left without qualifications and had never had a permanent job. The Fishpool detectives had no difficulty in finding him, for his stabbing had come to the attention of the police on the day it happened, Thursday 18 March 1993, and the file was still open with his details in it. What the file said was this. Some time after 7 p.m. on that day, somewhere in the Brook estate, Stacey was stabbed. An ambulance was called and he was taken to Brook Hospital, where casualty staff administered sixteen stitches under local anaesthetic to a gaping wound across the upper part of his chest. The police were called but Stacey refused to say who had attacked him. He was worried, however, about a friend called Mattie Farman who lived in the Brook estate, so he asked the police to find out if his friend was all right. Farman proved to be unhurt but he too refused to help the police. It was clear that the boys were both frightened.

As the information provided by the likes of Grant and the Anon Female later showed, the local community soon came to know a good deal more than the police. Stacey was released from hospital late on the night of the attack and his story travelled rapidly round the estates – not just that he had been stabbed plum in the middle of the Brook and that the wound required sixteen stitches, but also that the ambulance man who attended to him said he was lucky to be alive. The grapevine named two culprits: Dave Norris and Neil Acourt. This caused little surprise but a good deal of anger, and the Benefield family in particular put Stacey under pressure to talk to the police and have these boys brought to account, but he refused. When Stephen Lawrence was stabbed, exactly five weeks later, this local anger had still not subsided, and it clearly contributed to a widespread desire to ensure that the Acourt group was caught this time. As one of the anonymous letters put it: 'Stacey Benefield was their victim about six weeks ago . . . These bastards must be stopped because they keep getting away with it.'

It was O. J. Davidson who turned up at Stacey's home that Sunday night hoping to persuade the young man to break his silence, but it seems that the job had been largely done for him by the Benefield family. Stacey was obviously terrified, but following the murder he was ready to help and he provided a short, clear statement, setting out his version of what had happened to him. He and Mattie Farman, he said, had been walking towards Mattie's house in the Brook estate when they bumped into Neil Acourt and Dave Norris in Langbrook Road. Neil had also been to Crown Woods and the boys knew him of old, while Norris they had got to know only in recent months. There was an immediate altercation. Neil said to Mattie something like: 'Did you call me a wanker?' When Mattie said he hadn't, Norris pulled out 'what looked like a miniature sword with about a nine-inch blade' and Mattie took to his heels. Neil and Dave pursued him round a corner but soon reappeared, whereupon Stacey asked what was going on. Dave replied: 'Shut up you cunt', stabbed him and ran off with Neil. Stacey, bleeding profusely, stumbled to the house of a family friend who summoned the ambulance. His statement, recorded by Davidson, ended: 'I am willing to assist police in this matter and attend court if necessary.'

This was a milestone: the first hard evidence to suggest that any of the prime suspects had committed a crime of violence – a crime, moreover, that involved a large knife, as in the case of Stephen Lawrence. It transformed the character of the investigation. The time was 9 p.m. on Sunday and Davidson quickly reported his success to the incident room, but Crampton and Bullock had gone home and no one thought of calling them to let them know. So it was that Crampton remained unaware of the Benefield statement when he briefed Weeden first thing on the Monday morning, and that Weeden found out about it only at lunchtime that day.

The next step was to question Mattie Farman. By Stacey's account he was not a witness to the attack itself – he had run away – but he would be in a position to provide important supporting evidence. Davidson reached him on Wednesday and found him if anything more frightened than his friend, but Mattie was also prepared to give a statement. He had known Neil Acourt for a couple of years, he said, but David for only a couple of weeks, and he had not previously known David's second name. By his account the encounter in Langbrook Road began with Neil asking him: 'What have you been saying about me?' He replied: 'Nothing, you idiot.' Then he saw David pulling out a large knife and he ran. David chased him, but Mattie dodged past and made his way home. It did not occur to him at the time that Stacey might subsequently have been attacked and it was only an hour or so later that he heard his friend was in hospital.

This evidence was helpful, confirming that 'David' had pulled out a large knife at the relevant time and place and when Mattie left the scene seemed prepared to use it. Any doubt about whether this boy was indeed David Norris could presumably be removed by allowing Mattie to pick him out in an identification parade. In short, there was now a good prosecution case for the stabbing of Stacey Benefield.

However, although, like Stacey, Mattie had declared in his statement that he was willing to attend court if necessary, in conversation with Davidson he had laid down a condition. Only if this case was pursued in conjunction with other, more serious offences would he be prepared to give evidence. If he was going to finger Neil Acourt and Dave Norris he wanted others to be in the same position; he wanted safety in numbers.

Besides the Benefield case, the anonymous letters had mentioned another attack: Neil Acourt and Dave Norris, they said, were 'rumoured' to be responsible for a stabbing in a Wimpy burger restaurant in Eltham. As with the Benefield case this proved to be a real incident and two officers at Eltham station were investigating it. On Thursday 11 March 1993, one week before the Benefield attack, a man called Gurdeep Bhangal had been knifed in the stomach immediately outside the Wimpy in the High Street. He was rushed to Brook Hospital where he underwent an emergency operation, thereafter making a full recovery. Bhangal was the son of the manager of the restaurant and worked there himself. From his evidence and other sources the Eltham officers had established what had happened.

That evening at about 8 p.m. two white men thought to be aged between nineteen and twenty-one appeared outside the restaurant and the taller one of them entered, bought a Coke, and left. Moments later he returned and complained to Bhangal's father that the drink he had been served was an ordinary Coke and not the 'floater' he had requested. A short argument followed as the elder Mr Bhangal denied there had been a mistake, and while this was going on the smaller of the white men also entered the restaurant for the first time. Gurdeep spoke to him, saying he should not interfere because the matter was being sorted out. Sure enough, the cost of the original drink was refunded and the two men left. But the matter did not end there, for they remained outside, making faces and shouting at the staff through the window. Eventually Gurdeep and his father went outside too and Gurdeep took hold of the taller white man, intending, he said later, to restrain him until the police could be called. There was a struggle involving Gurdeep and both white men, during which Gurdeep felt something being withdrawn from his stomach. Looking down, he saw blood pouring out, and the smaller man was holding a large kitchen knife. Helped by his father, Gurdeep

Bhangal staggered back into the restaurant while the two white men ran away.

There were a good many witnesses to these events: the victim, his father, another member of the restaurant staff, at least one customer and two women who were waiting at a bus stop outside. Although none saw the knife going in, one of the women at the bus stop saw the smaller man draw back his arm at his side during the struggle and then thrust it forward. She and her companion also recalled him saying 'Paki bastard' at the same time (although no one else remembered this). But by the time, six weeks after the stabbing, that the Fishpool squad contacted them the investigating officers on this case had made no connection with the Acourt group and were pursuing other suspects. In the event these other suspects were eliminated, while it was found that the descriptions of the two white men, and particularly of the smaller one, could be said to fit more than one of the Acourt group. Superintendent Weeden brought the Bhangal stabbing into the ambit of his own investigation.

Crampton had spoken of the likelihood of the Lawrence case 'widening' and his prediction was being proved right, although perhaps not in the way he had expected. This was not only an expanding search for witnesses and other evidence relating to the murder, it was becoming an inquiry into a whole series of stabbings and knife crimes. And the list did not end with Benefield and Bhangal, as Detective Constable Chase found when he finally unearthed a reference to the suspects in police records. First assigned the task of 'researching' the suspects on Friday afternoon, Chase spent a very long time looking through police and other official files without success, a matter that caused Crampton some frustration. Crampton, in fact, had already moved on before anything turned up. It was in the local card indexes at Chislehurst police station, two miles to the south of Eltham, that Chase found the record of yet another stabbing. David Alan Norris and James Arthur Acourt had both been arrested in relation to an assault that took place in the street in Chislehurst on 30 May the previous year, 1992.

The details of this case were as follows. Two youths, Darren and Terrence Witham, presented themselves at Chislehurst police station that day claiming that they had been the victims of an attack. Darren had a two-inch knife-wound in his left arm and Terrence had suffered bruising and two cuts to the head. They told the police they were

83

on the High Street when Darren saw and greeted David Norris, whom he had known as a fellow-pupil at Coopers School. Darren entered an off-licence to buy a can of Pepsi and a few moments later a boy who was with Norris approached Terrence and, without provocation, struck him twice on the head with a wooden truncheon. Darren emerged from the shop in time to see this, and he threw the contents of his drink over the boy. At this Norris produced a knife, Darren kicked him and as they fell to the ground, fighting, the boy with the truncheon joined in, striking Darren on the shoulder. As soon as they could, the Witham brothers ran off. Darren realized he had been stabbed when he saw a cut in his coat sleeve and felt a painful lump on his arm. That was when they decided to go to the police. Norris and two other boys were stopped behind the local branch of Sainsbury's very soon afterwards by a uniformed sergeant. They tried to make off but he soon caught them, whereupon one of the youths slipped away again and was seen to throw something over a fence. This boy was once again caught, while a woman called out from behind the fence to say something had just landed in her garden. It was the truncheon, and the boy identified himself as Jamie Acourt.

At subsequent identification parades Darren Witham picked out Norris as his attacker, but failed to identify Jamie. Terrence Witham was unable to attend the parades because, he said later, he was on holiday. Norris at first refused to say anything but eventually provided his own account of the events, and it was a very different one. Terrence Witham had stared at Jamie and then punched him, Norris said, after which there had been a fight and Jamie had taken the truncheon from the Withams – this was why he had it when he was stopped. As for the knife, Norris knew nothing about it at all. The other friend of Norris who was present, Luke Knight, was also questioned, but he shed no light on matters. After a long delay Norris was charged in November with wounding and threatening unlawful violence, and Jamie with possession of an offensive weapon. In January, however, the Crown Prosecution Service dropped the case against Jamie on the grounds that it was 'stale' and incomplete, and the following month it came to the conclusion that the same should be done with the Norris case. The evidence, said the CPS, was not strong enough to overcome a plea of self-defence, while the accused was just fifteen at the time of the incident and 'of good character' (this was not an assessment of his personality, but a lawyer's way of saying he had no previous convictions). Chislehurst police disagreed strongly with this view and wanted the case pressed, but the CPS had their way. On 12 March 1993 David Norris appeared at Bromley Youth Court to be informed that both charges against him had been dropped.

Besides the Witham stabbing, Chase had also turned up another, lesser, case involving Jamie Acourt, which had a similar ending. On 24 January 1993 Jamie was stopped while driving along Philippa Gardens in Eltham, about half a mile from his home – the police officer thought he might be drunk. Jamie was sober, but he was sixteen years old and had no licence or insurance, and he gave false particulars. To make matters worse, when he was taken to the police station he was found to be in possession of a folding knife. The knife was in the car and Jamie claimed that he had merely been using it to repair the car stereo. He was charged with various vehicle offences and with possession of a pointed instrument. Unlike Norris in the Witham case, Jamie could not claim to be of good character, for he had two juvenile cautions on his record from 1991, one for possession of drugs and the other for possession of an offensive weapon. But at Camberwell Youth Court on 1 April 1993, this latest weapon charge was dropped and he was given a conditional discharge for the other offences.

The list was now Lawrence, Benefield, Bhangal and Witham, and still the file was growing. It was the man known as James Grant, in his first visit to police on the Friday, who had mentioned a boy named Lee. 'They also stabbed a young lad at Woolwich town centre called Lee,' Grant told Budgen. 'He had a bag placed over his head and was stabbed in his legs and arms in order to torture him.' On the face of it, finding the right lad called Lee in southeast London was a tall order, but fortune intervened in the shape of the girl called Samantha. Her father, a local man, had advised officers on Friday that she seemed to know something about the killing and when Davidson saw her on Wednesday 28 April he found that, although she had no information about the Lawrence murder, she was able to tell him who Lee was. Two days later Davidson and Budgen interviewed Lee Pearson.

The events that he described took place on New Year's Eve in 1991, and they bore little relation to Grant's account. Pearson said he was in Well Hall Road that night with a group of friends including one called Alex. They had just bought some cigarettes, beer and cider when they bumped into another group of boys. One boy in this other group, with whom Alex had had a fight in the past, pulled a knife so Lee, Alex and their friends ran off. But Alex was not prepared to let things lie. Arming himself with a pickaxe handle he led the group back to the scene in search of his enemy, only to find he had disappeared. Instead they came across one of the Acourt boys – Lee was not sure which – who had been in the other group, and they asked him where his friend with the knife was. When the Acourt boy refused to answer, Lee called him a wanker. Jamie or Neil, whichever it was, responded by throwing a bottle at Lee, who ducked. 'He then came at me and went to pull something out of his pocket,' recalled Lee. 'I didn't know what it was so I hit him on the head with the bottle of cider I was carrying. He then backed off and threw another bottle at me, so I chased him and he ran away.' That was before 9 p.m. An hour or so later Lee was on his own near the garage on Well Hall Road, 'a little bit drunk', when he was set upon by a crowd of youths. He was struck on the head with a piece of wood, punched and kicked, but in the midst of this, he said, he recognized Jamie and Neil Acourt among his assailants, and he 'knew they were the ringleaders'. He saw an opening and ran, ducking into an alleyway where he collapsed. Later he was taken to Brook Hospital, where he was found to have been stabbed twice in the left leg. He did not know which of his attackers stabbed him.

All of this Budgen recorded in a statement but when he presented it to Pearson to sign the young man had second thoughts. He refused, and no amount of persuasion that day could induce him to change his mind. Pearson also recounted a sequel to the New Year's Eve attack, which for some reason Budgen did not put in the statement but which Davidson reported to the incident room later. In April 1992, four months after he was stabbed, Pearson met Neil Acourt again. Acourt was with a friend, and Pearson said they threatened him with a knife and Neil head-butted him. Pearson's story of the New Year's Eve stabbing did not have the makings of a prosecution. Even by his own account he was scarcely blameless in the affair and he admitted he was drunk and had been struck on the head at the time he recognized the Acourts during the later attack. Moreover, he was unable to say whether it was one of them who stabbed him. A defence lawyer would make hay with all this.

Lawrence, Benefield, Bhangal, Witham and Pearson: it was a catalogue of crime, with not a single conviction to date. And there were more allegations and suspicions involving lesser crimes. For example, there was that story of the young man who was interrupted while trying to rob a telephone box and who then threatened someone with a large knife. The description of the young man, it turned out, was strikingly similar to the descriptions of Dave Norris given by Benefield and Farman, and the telephone box in question was just around the corner from 102 Bournbrook Road. There was also a report from a local seventeen-year-old who said that four weeks before the murder he had been standing in Well Hall Road when a passing youth called him a cunt. When he asked him why he had said this the boy – a friend later told him it might have been Neil Acourt – 'slapped him on the head'. And there was the story of Kevin London, a black youth who said that Gary Dobson had once threatened him with a knife. Another informant came forward a little later to say that four days after the Lawrence murder Dobson had again approached London and said: 'You are next.' Even if only half this information was correct the Acourt group, and particularly it seemed Dave Norris, were extremely dangerous and out of control. But who were they? Where did they spring from and what were they up to? Why all this violence? It was remarkable that such a group had so slight and peripheral a presence in police records.

The desire for information had prompted Crampton to commission some surveillance. It had not begun when he handed over to Weeden but preparations were in hand, and according to the action which Crampton signed that day the objective was to 'establish address and association' of the leading suspects. Crampton said later that these were merely the formal grounds and that what he intended was a more general fishing expedition. With the intelligence cupboard apparently so bare, whatever the surveillance turned up would be a bonus. Arrangements had been made on Sunday afternoon for the FIB to send a team and since then a little more had been learned about the suspects. The house-to-house visits to the two addresses confirmed that the two Acourt boys lived at 102 Bournbrook and Gary Dobson at 13 Phineas Pett Road, while Gary's call at 102 showed that he did indeed associate with the Acourts. But this was not thought sufficient and there was still nothing at all about Norris, so the surveillance plan went ahead. And it proceeded as Weeden felt his way in his first couple of days, even though by Monday night the Fishpool team knew about the Witham stabbing and had a statement from Stacey Benefield. They had also discovered by then a little more about Norris's background, because Chase had established from the Chislehurst files that Dave was the son of a professional criminal, Clifford Norris, and that his address in 1992 had been 7 Berryfield Close, Bickley, a district close to Chislehurst that was notably more upmarket than the Eltham estates.

The surveillance was a modest affair, scarcely worthy of the word 'operation'. An FIB officer, PC Victor Smith, turned up on Monday for a briefing and set off for Bournbrook Road with a civilian photographer in late afternoon. Ten minutes after they arrived at the observation point they saw a white male emerge from number 102 carrying what appeared to be clothes on a hanger, covered with a black plastic bag. He got into a silver Sierra Sapphire car and drove off. The photographer had not set up his camera, so this event was not photographed. They could not follow the vehicle since they might betray their position, and in any case one vehicle is rarely sufficient for pursuit. And they could not report it to Eltham station because neither man had a mobile telephone. So the dry cleaning, which is what they believed to be on the hanger, left the scene unimpeded. Once his equipment was set up the photographer spent that evening, the following morning and part of Wednesday on his own at the observation post taking pictures of the comings and goings at number 102. At 8.16 a.m. on Tuesday, for example, another white male (it proved to be Neil Acourt) got into a car carrying another black bag thought to contain clothes. Several other people, including Gary Dobson, arrived and left, as well as two or three vehicles, and all were photographed. On Thursday the photographer transferred to Berryfield Close to observe movements at the Norris family home. It proved a difficult spot because this was a group of detached houses in their own grounds. Number 7 was protected by high hedges and fences and a nine-foot gate; in fact, the house itself, which newspapers were later to value at £700,000, could not be watched from the road. The best that could be had from two days' work there was a handful of car movements with registration numbers, which proved to be of little interest. At the end of five days, therefore, the modest operation had produced modest results: a few photographs of the Acourts, Dobson and some unidentified men, and a few car registration numbers. The latter were traced and threw up some names, one of which, Darren Davies, was to prove of interest, although not until a later date.

Norris was still causing frustration. Did he live at the Bournbrook Road house, as several informants had suggested, or in the big house at Berryfield Close, or somewhere else entirely? Without a photograph of him it was impossible to say whether he figured in the surveillance pictures and all efforts to find a photograph, through Chislehurst station and the passport office, had been in vain. Yet Norris seemed to be at the heart of matters. In both the Benefield and Witham cases he was alleged to have been the stabber, and he was most frequently identified by rumour as the stabber of Stephen Lawrence – several informants even said he had been bragging about it. Norris, moreover, was the one with a known criminal connection – his father, Clifford.

Chapter Six Eleven Days (II)

Police murder investigations – it may be obvious – can be confusing things. Unlike the plots of most murder novels they do not usually proceed in a linear fashion towards solution, but instead they advance on a broad front, sweeping up masses of information most of which is certain to prove irrelevant. Usually, there is no single development or revelation that constitutes a solution, but rather a series of discoveries which turn into items of evidence that may together add up to a case to be used in court. In pursuit of this evidence dozens of lines of inquiry will be in hand at any moment and again most of them are likely to be red herrings. While fiction lionizes the lone detective, it is rare for a single person to crack a case. Modern police thinking suggests that the only way in which such large volumes of information can be turned into results is by dealing with detail systematically. Anomalies and conflicts of evidence have to be hunted down and probed. Rigorous standards have to be applied when deciding that such problems have been solved and, for example, suspects can be eliminated. Every thread, every 'result' from the field must be analysed and digested; every last fact and recollection must be squeezed from witnesses. Such thoroughness will prevent opportunities from being missed and lies from going undetected. Senior detectives must have an overview and must be able to identify priorities, but if those priorities fail to bear fruit then they should be able to fall back for their evidence on the painstaking, almost mechanical process of elimination. Such, at least, is the ideal.

As the Lawrence investigation broadened and acquired new dimensions in the last days of April, strains and difficulties in the incident room were growing. The team that Brian Weeden inherited consisted of about twenty-five people. Besides Detective Inspector Bullock, the deputy SIO, there were half a dozen detective sergeants, eight detective constables, half a dozen uniformed police constables, a few trainee investigators and two or three civilian support staff. For a time Weeden also had the assistance of a number of uniformed officers from the Territorial Support Group who carried out house-to-house inquiries, but they were withdrawn after a week to be deployed on the investigation of the I R A bomb attack at Bishopsgate in the City of London, which took place two days after the Lawrence murder. Of the core team, roughly half were engaged in 'outside' investigation work while the remainder, predominantly junior officers and civilians, staffed the incident room, where the Holmes terminals were located.

The operation of the Holmes system remained a problem, as the documents it generated demonstrate. Every Holmes message had a date showing when it was written by the officer who originated it, and a number, indicating where it stood in the sequence of entries into the database. If the system had been running smoothly the two sequences would have existed roughly in parallel, with some variation for urgent messages jumping the queue. In other words, groups of numbers would roughly correspond to the days of the investigation. In Operation Fishpool, however, they were seriously out of kilter. To take one series as an example: a numbered item among the hundreds in the system was originated on 30 April while the item that followed it was written on 24 April, and the item that followed *that* was dated 1 May. A few items later a whole batch began that were dated 26 April. None of these messages, in other words, was entered until 1 May or later, although at least one was dated six days earlier. The order in which actions flowed from the messages was almost as haphazard, while the 'results' – in which detectives recorded the outcome of their inquiries – were often dated a week or two weeks later. This does not necessarily mean that actual inquiries were in a similar state of chaos, or were tangled up in the Holmes schedule at all. On the contrary, it seems that the investigation was proceeding as best it could almost independently of Holmes, with information exchanged verbally or on pieces of paper. Most of the coordination took place at the daily briefings, held in the incident room usually around 5 p.m. So, for example, a detective would not wait for an action to be raised and allocated in the computer before taking action but would report his findings at the briefing and receive instructions straight away. The whole procedure up to the result might be complete before anything was recorded in the system.

This dislocation, however, had consequences. If the investigation in this period was not in practice a Holmes inquiry at all, it was not a card-based inquiry either, so it was proceeding largely without any reference or cross-reference system other than the individual memories of busy officers. This may have been one explanation for the twenty-four-hour and forty-eight-hour delays that sometimes occurred in following up leads, and for the sluggish way in which some connections were made. In these circumstances, moreover, it was particularly unhelpful that the SIO should have changed at such a delicate moment in the investigation. Crampton bowed out with three long days of work behind him and a reasonable mastery of the information gathered so far (with a few notable exceptions). Weeden started from scratch, having to read the background and oversee current operations at the same time, and by his own subsequent admission a week had passed before he was comfortable with the detail of the case. Weeden's character also played its part. A tall, soft-spoken, polite man who wore large-framed spectacles that seemed to screen most of his face, he had an owlish nature, and his style was to immerse himself in the paperwork of a case and leave fieldwork to subordinates. Though he had a good record as a detective, he seemed to some to be more a managerial figure than an investigator. He presided over the daily team briefings and made decisions, but he did not, for example, personally interview Emma Cook or EE when they became important to the case. He left that to subordinates. Nor did he speak personally to the bus stop witnesses, or Duwayne Brooks, or the Casserleys; that was not his style. All this was in contrast to Crampton, who was brisk, open, sharp and very hands-on. And if Weeden was a low-key presence, Bullock was scarcely a counterweight. Thickset but quiet, he too seemed to prefer the office to the field and the paperwork to the people. Together they made a cautious partnership.

The officers operating in the field were undoubtedly stretched. Two of the dozen found their time largely taken up with the task of maintaining liaison with the Lawrence family and Duwayne Brooks, while the rest were constantly juggling a large and varied workload. Here the Holmes system is eloquent: cumbersome though the process was, by the time Crampton signed off on Monday morning more than 100 actions had been raised. Besides routine or extraneous matters such as organizing the search of drains and finding the owner of a woman's purse discovered during the searches, there were a great many important lines of inquiry: researching the prime suspects, tracing the bus stop witnesses, checking the kebab shop and the Harvester group, investigating the Benefield and Bhangal stabbings, tracing and interviewing Emma Cook, EE, K, the Tyler group and others, following up leads from the house-to-house team and many, many more. Weeden was to say much later that the workload for each individual officer in the Lawrence investigation was far heavier than in any case he had previously handled. All this, of course, made the absence of an effective reference and collation system the more worrying, and Weeden acknowledged this when he took an officer off outside investigation for a time to speed up statement-reading, and when he applied for an extra experienced Holmes operator to be added to the team.

The flow of information was relentless. On the Monday after the murder Alexandra Marie, the last of the bus stop witnesses, gave her statement through an interpreter and proved to have seen little of the attack itself. She could add nothing about the event, and since her view was obscured, nothing about the appearance of the attackers, but she reported a curious incident after the stabbing. Before long the 161 bus drew up and the three – Westbrook, Shepherd and Marie – all boarded and soon afterwards glimpsed Stephen lying on the ground on the other side of the road. Soon after that, Marie said, the bus pulled up at the next bus stop. Two men boarded, one of them out of breath, and as they got on one seemed to hand the other a ticket. But if they knew each other they did not show it, for they sat in separate seats, which Marie found strange. She told police she believed one or both might have been among the attackers, so an action was raised to 'T.I.E.' – trace, interview, eliminate – these two men. Eventually, after considerable effort, the incident was explained: the men did not know each other and nor could they have been in the attacking group, but one had boarded the bus and found himself with a spare ticket, which he simply gave away to the other man.

In the fortnight that followed 22 April the police received about twenty-five anonymous telephone calls about the Lawrence murder, almost all of them naming members of the group of prime suspects: Neil and Jamie Acourt, Dave Norris and Gary Dobson. The name of Acourt came up most frequently, although it was spelt in a great variety of ways: Acall, Acorn, Alcott, Haycourt, Almond and Arnold. Half a dozen callers mentioned Norris and three or four Dobson.

One or two more gave relatively vague information, such as that the killers were brothers who had older twin brothers, which pointed towards the Acourts, while a few linked the prime suspects with other names previously unheard. Only four of these calls named completely different people. And the anonymous informants were vastly outnumbered by the people prepared to give their names. Whether on the doorsteps to the house-to-house officers or in calls to Eltham station or in conversation with detectives from the Fishpool team, these people overwhelmingly pointed the finger at the Acourt group. Most often, it seems, their information represented the ripples spreading out from K, and as they spread these ripples usually became weaker and more confusing. Very often detectives following up leads found themselves in a wild goose chase of rumour: a mother would report something her son said; the son would say he heard it from his girlfriend; the girlfriend would say it came from a school-friend; the schoolfriend would say she overheard it in a shop. One trail led from a policeman's wife through a cook in a pub to a conversation in a hairdresser's and, not surprisingly, proved in the end to be quite irrelevant.

Of the false information, one persistent category concerned Stephen's movements before the murder and the possibility that there had been some history behind the crime or at least some form of provocation on the night. One man said that Stephen and Duwayne had been in the kebab shop by the cinema before the murder at the same time as some white boys, while another informant said the two black youths had walked past the kebab shop and shouted a remark about 'honkeys' at those inside. Both of these could be shown to be false, since not only had Duwayne provided a clear account of his movements with Stephen that night, but Royston Westbrook had confirmed it. Westbrook first saw the boys when they were at Eltham High Street, saw them again when they boarded the 286 bus he was travelling on, disembarked with them near the cinema and walked a little ahead of them, in earshot, all the way to the scene of the murder. If there had been an incident he would have seen or heard it. In the same way, other reports and rumours could be shown to be false, including one suggesting the murder was part of a school gang dispute between white boys and black boys and another which said that the murder was an act of revenge for the rape of a white girl. Although both of these stories were widely repeated in Eltham and beyond, they were demonstrably groundless.

The weekend that began on 1 May was a bank holiday weekend, and so lasted three days. The Fishpool team had worked through the initial period when the budget allowed everyone to do a maximum of overtime, and now the hours were beginning to contract to more normal levels, indeed over the long weekend itself a surprising number of them were given one or two days off. The feeling among the detectives was that the investigation was running out of steam. Emma Cook and EE appeared to be dead ends, while there was still no sign that Michelle Casserley was going to come across with the name of the youth who had supposedly witnessed scenes of panic and wet hair in 102 Bournbrook. As for the Benefield case, though it seemed to provide a breakthrough the SIO was reluctant to move on that alone. Some detectives were wondering why he didn't just arrest the four prime suspects and see what they had to say for themselves, and so were some people out in the estates. One anonymous caller asked simply: 'When are you going to pick up the Acourt brothers? If you don't bring them in soon they will be done.' Exactly what 'done' meant was not clear.

But things had not quite come to a halt and the police were about to pick up the next link in that chain of important young people. On the Saturday the decision was taken to approach Michelle Casserley, a move prompted by classroom rumours. Michelle was a fifth-year student at Eltham Hill secondary school, and a report came in that a classmate had been overheard saying that Michelle had told her the murder was the work of the two Acourt boys and 'Gary Gibson'. Traced and questioned by Davidson, the classmate confirmed the story, adding that since then Michelle had been threatened by the youths. Davidson's interest was aroused. Perhaps Michelle had been given enough time to make up her mind, and perhaps, if the story about a threat was true, time was working against the police and not for them. The following morning he called at the Casserley home. Mrs Casserley had feared her daughter would not want to talk to the police and she was proved right. When Michelle saw the detective she exploded, using, Davidson said later, 'venomous language' towards him in front of her mother. Somehow, however, calm was restored, possibly through the intervention of Tara, who at twenty-one was by nearly five years the older girl. Then things improved and by the time he left the Casserley house Davidson had more than one valuable lead in his notebook. Chief among them was the name and address of the man we call K.

It was a couple of days before Davidson saw K, and it proved another difficult interview. The young man was by now very frightened and very reluctant to speak, but he was encouraged by his mother and stepfather. Grudgingly, he confirmed that he had gone to the Acourt house on the night of the murder and that he had seen Neil, Jamie and Gary Dobson there, among others. One of them had his T-shirt off, but K insisted he could not remember which. He said nothing about wet hair and nor did he name Dave Norris. When Davidson asked him to record what he had said in a formal statement he panicked and ran out of the house. Davidson's note on the encounter ended: 'He, although 22 yrs, appears to behave as a 12/13 yr old (his mother will endeavour to find the truth).' Now they knew who he was, it wasn't long before the police encountered K again. On Thursday 6 May the crime squad raided the Tyler house – no charges followed – and DC Martin Hughes visited soon afterwards. There he found David Tyler, his brother Ricky and K, and he appears to have had a surprisingly relaxed conversation with them. Although K still refused to make a statement he repeated his story for Hughes and this time added the detail that when he asked the group inside 102 why they seemed to be undressing they said they were having an early night. Hughes thought it a promising encounter.

Weeden, meanwhile, was not giving up on Emma Cook and EE. He felt at last that he had caught up with the mass of information in the case and he was ready to adopt, as he put it later, a more pro-active role. He asked for another round of interviews to fill in as many gaps in the stories of these two young people as possible. Canavan was to go back to the woman shopkeeper to see if she remembered anything more about Emma's words or demeanour. Wilkinson was to get a statement from the boy called Greg, who was supposedly with EE at the time of the murder, and from Lisa, Greg's girlfriend. Duwayne Brooks and the bus stop witnesses – Westbrook, Shepherd and Marie – should be asked if they remembered a blonde girl walking past them. And when these inquiries were complete, both Emma and EE should be seen again.

DS Davidson – the experienced, forthright and bullish 'OJ' – would be in overall charge.

The woman shopkeeper duly went over the ground again and came up with some further small details. There had been two conversations with Emma on the Saturday. In the first the girl had mentioned passing the boys at the bus stop and seeing a man and a woman waiting there too. Then later in the day she referred to the banging at the cinema and said she had seen boys there. 'Were they small boys?' the older woman had asked.

'No,' said Emma.

'You ought to go to the police.'

'Why? I haven't seen anything.'

Emma had gone on to explain that she walked on the north side of Rochester Way and that she tried to ignore people. As to the question of whether Emma might know more than she was saying, DC Canavan picked up a curious piece of gossip. Emma, he reported, had discussed the murder with a local schoolgirl called Kelly-Ann, and had apparently stated: 'It wasn't the Acourts.'

Greg could not help much. At first he suggested that he left his home with Lisa at 10.15 p.m., which would have meant that they saw Emma leave EE's house rather earlier than 10.30 p.m. When Lisa was questioned about this, however, she was sure she left Greg's at 10.25 p.m. and Greg subsequently accepted that this was the correct time, so the anomaly disappeared. As for his dealings with EE, he said that after saying goodnight to Lisa (and after Emma had set off down the road), he went to talk to EE and they went up to his bedroom and stayed there about half an hour. By his guess he returned home at 11 p.m., leaving EE standing on his doorstep. If EE saw the Acourts, Greg knew nothing about it. The bus stop witnesses, for their part, offered nothing more. Only Duwayne seems to have been asked about Emma, and he said he had no memory of a blonde girl passing.

After the bank holiday weekend the whole position was reviewed and it seems that both Emma and EE were seen again, but without success. Emma said she knew the Acourts, Lambs, Norris and Dobson but saw none of these people during her journey home. Weeden grumbled in his notes about Emma's 'stroppy dad, can't see relevance of it. Doesn't want police there again. We'll go back when dad not there' – Emma would be seventeen the following week and perhaps she could be seen then on her own. As for EE, he refused to say anything more than he had, which was to deny any knowledge about the murder.

Attempts to track down those responsible for the commotion near the cinema resumed on Tuesday 4 May, the twelfth day of the investigation, when an officer went to Falconwood to interview staff at the Harvester restaurant. The table occupied by the young group on the night of 23 April had been booked by telephone for ten people but only six had turned up. By good fortune the staff remembered them. First, they had argued about their bill and second, one member of staff had reported on the night that he had seen one of the group steal a steak knife before they left. This had been reported, by way of a warning, to the taxi firm across the road. There the story was quickly confirmed: a group of young people had asked for a taxi to Eltham and left in one almost immediately; then the warning about the knife had come from the restaurant. The radio operator contacted the cab driver and, after instructing him to close the glass partition so that his passengers could not hear, explained the danger. The driver continued to Eltham and stopped, as requested by his passengers, at Well Hall Roundabout, but when one of the group asked to be taken on a little further he refused, demanded his fare and drove off.

This was intriguing. It was now established beyond doubt that there had indeed been a commotion by the cinema in the minutes after 10.30 p.m., the minutes immediately before Stephen Lawrence was killed. The cinema doorman had connected those responsible to the group in the Harvester, and now the restaurant staff had linked the group to the theft of a knife. These young people, moreover, were almost certainly local: the taxi had dropped them by the roundabout on the Friday night; they had been at the same spot the previous night and the doorman knew them as customers of the Coronet. So who were they? The police had a good lead, because the caller who booked the table at the restaurant had given a name and left a telephone number. It was a young woman and she could be traced.

And there were other important leads, although different in character. Maureen George, who lived in Winchcomb Gardens, was in bed in her front bedroom after 10 p.m. on the night of the murder, but not asleep. She was in dispute with a neighbour, who blamed Mrs George's son for noise in the street, so she was particularly alert that night when she heard footsteps outside. Between three and six people, she thought, were running hard from the direction of Dickson Road towards Wendover Road. As she listened, one person slowed down and she heard the words: 'Hurry up!' This was followed by a name which she did not hear clearly, but which was either 'J' or 'Jamie'. All this was consistent with the Acourt group leaving the scene of the murder, except that Mrs George insisted she had looked at her clock and the time was 10.28 p.m. An action was raised to establish whether Mrs George's bedside clock was running slow.

Another local woman, Eileen Gooch, reported a conversation she overheard in Wendover Road on the Tuesday following the murder. A scruffy, blond youth aged nineteen or twenty said to another youth: 'They have walked past me and driven past me loads of times.'

'Aren't you scared?' asked his companion.

'I'm not fucking well scared of anyone,' said the first youth.

Then the pair noticed the presence of Mrs Gooch and the scruffy one said to her in what she took as a threatening manner: 'You didn't hear any of that, did you?'

Mrs Gooch said this youth was 5' 5" tall, had blond collar-length hair with a quiff at the front and was wearing a jacket with the logo NAFNAF on the back.

The third woman to come forward with first-hand evidence was Linda Williams, a nurse who was driving home from work around the time of the murder. Her route brought her to Well Hall Round-about from the south, then around the west side and up Well Hall Road, past Dickson Road and the bus stop, in the direction of Woolwich. As she turned off the roundabout shortly before 10.40 p.m. she saw four white boys walking on the pavement on the east side of the road. She was sure there were four. One of these youths had mousy, wavy, collar-length hair and was wearing a greenish jacket with a large white 'V' motif on the back. This was extremely important, for it seemed that Williams had glimpsed the attacking group moments before they struck, when they were still on the opposite side of the road to Stephen and Duwayne. She had seen them all from behind so she could not identify anyone, but the 'V' jacket could be a vital clue.

On Tuesday 4 May, a teacher (again a woman) rang the incident room from a local primary school to say that two pupils had come forward to report that they had seen a knife in a front garden in

Wendover Road. By this time the police had found several knives in various places but none of them corresponded to the pathologist's description of the likely murder weapon. This knife was different. It had a black wooden handle and a blade nine inches long but with a cutting edge on only one side, like a kitchen knife. It was clearly, in legal terms, 'consistent' with the wounds on Stephen's body. It had apparently not been carefully concealed but lay close to a hedge only half-hidden from passers-by using the pavement four feet away. And it had been found in a very interesting location: the back of the Wendover Road house, which was unoccupied at that time, faced the back of 102 Bournbrook Road.

One more witness trail remained to be discovered, one remaining link in the chain, and that was the trail that ultimately led to Witness B. By the end of April the Fishpool team were aware of suggestions that somebody from the estates – not Emma Cook – might have seen the attack and recognized one or more of the culprits. The trail began with the informant known as James Grant, who had a further meeting with Davidson and Budgen on Tuesday 27 April in a pub some distance from Eltham. After the meeting Grant rang in to add something he had apparently just discovered, which Davidson recorded in a message:

> He thinks he may have found a witness who stated to him that Neil stabbed him [Stephen Lawrence] in the bottom part and David stabbed him in the top part. He said that this witness was on a bus. He is going to firm up the info and contact us on 28th April.

Detail about Stephen's wounds was not in the public domain, although it was known that he had been stabbed twice. These details – that he was stabbed 'in the bottom part' and 'in the top part' – are hardly accurate, since Stephen's wounds were both at roughly the same level, but they could be seen as implying knowledge. It was possible, for example, that Grant had garbled what a genuine eyewitness had seen from a bus, so this was an important lead. It is very unlikely, however, that Grant got back in touch with the police about this as promptly as he promised – a delay of two or three days seems to have followed – but in the meantime DC Keith Hughes had picked up a similar titbit from another source.

This time the informant was a man, another member of the family who had originally helped point the police in the direction of EE. On 28 April he made contact with detectives to say he had some information. DC Keith Hughes saw him the next day and afterwards wrote:

> Saw subject who declined to make statement. However, stated that the 'word on the street' was that the Acourts (the two youngest) had been responsible and that the youngest probably did the stabbing. Went on to say that he had heard that the victim had been stabbed in the arm prior to being stabbed in the chest. Refused to name his source but promised he would speak to him and contact me if his source was prepared to assist . . .

Once again, here was some information about the wounds – more accurate than Grant's – which suggested that someone out on the estates might really have seen what happened. Unlike Grant, the man who passed this titbit to the police appeared to know his source at first hand. Like Grant, however, he was not quick to get in touch again.

The Casserleys provided the next connection, on 2 May, when Davidson had his fractious meeting with Michelle. While Michelle provided K's name, her older sister also had something to contribute. 'Tara stated that an 11-year-old child had witnessed the assault from a bus,' wrote Davidson afterwards. 'Tara will endeavour to get the name of this boy.' Grant, the informant and Tara: three leads to a possible eyewitness and once again all the police could do was wait. It seems that it was Grant who provided the identity in the end. Much later, Davidson recalled that Grant got back to him with a first name and a street name and that he had traced the witness from those. By whatever means he found out, Davidson had acquired the real name of Witness B, or something approximating to it, by the afternoon of 6 May and was expecting to see him that evening. (B was not, as Tara had suggested, eleven years old.) Before that, Davidson visited the Tyler house and mentioned the name casually during a conversation with the Tyler boys and K, only to receive a dismissive response. Weeden's notes that evening include the words, based on Davidson's report: 'Tylers say he is a liar.'

*

On Thursday 6 May – a fortnight after the murder – Superintendent Brian Weeden was beginning to think the time had come for a change of strategy. They had fished in the pool for the decisive witness and they had found several young people who might fit the bill, but so far none of them was ready to cooperate. The police could not wait for ever. So at 1.30 p.m. he called Bullock, Flook and Davidson, the three most senior men on his team, to a meeting. The purpose was to address a single question: two weeks on, what evidence and information had been turned up that could be used against the Acourts, Norris and Dobson? As they talked Weeden made a list, and the first item on it was a photofit which Joey Shepherd had helped to provide, which was thought to be very close in appearance to the Acourt boys. The second item was that the Acourts and Norris had a history of carrying out knife attacks. Then came two items ranked as 'information': the unsubstantiated story that Norris had admitted the killing to Ricky Tyler and the story which K had told, but refused to put in statement form, about what he had seen at 102 Bournbrook. After these, the group discussed the question of identification and reached the conclusion that, on the basis of the statements, only one of the bus stop witnesses was likely to be able to pick any of the attackers out of a line-up, and that was Shepherd. He had provided the best description and appeared to have had the best view. The next item on the list was in the form of a speculation: 'If there, those arrested: possibly one of them might talk?' Then Weeden noted that it might be difficult to trace Norris, and finally two simple matters: the Wendover Road knife and the overheard name, 'J' or 'Jamie'.

It was a fair summary. There were some pending matters, such as the Harvester group and the possible new witness, B, and the detectives had by no means given up hope of getting more out of EE, Cook and K, but in terms of hard evidence in hand this was a generous account of what had been learned in the Lawrence investigation. Duwayne Brooks had remembered almost nothing more about the attackers, and when it came to making an E-fit picture he had been able to describe only the hair and head-shape of one person and no facial features. Westbrook and Marie recalled even less. They had, however, identified some clothes, while Linda Williams had added the 'V' jacket, so if arrests were made these items could be looked for. And it is clear that Brian Weeden, hitherto so cautious, now had arrests in mind, because out of this meeting came two decisions. The first was noted as: 'Put pressure on – charge with Benefield case.' And the second was to put one or more of the suspects in identification parades before the witnesses in the Bhangal case. On Thursday afternoon, then, it seems that Weeden intended to defer making arrests for the Lawrence murder but to bring in some of the suspects – presumably Norris and Neil Acourt – for the other stabbings. At the very least it would rattle their cages, and getting them off the street might even encourage some of the reluctant witnesses to talk. It was a new strategy, but it was not one that Weeden was given the opportunity to implement.

Chapter Seven **The Lawrences**

While Weeden conducted his review of the evidence that Thursday afternoon, 6 May, across London the Lawrences were paying a call on Nelson Mandela. The president of the African National Congress was making only his second visit to Britain since his release from prison, and space had been found in his schedule for a meeting with Neville and Doreen. The encounter, which took place in Mandela's suite in the Athenaeum Hotel in Piccadilly, lasted about twenty minutes, during which the Lawrences told their story and the South African leader listened and expressed sympathy. Afterwards Mandela posed with the couple for the cameras and made a few remarks for the press. 'The Lawrences' tragedy is our tragedy,' he said. 'I am deeply touched by the brutality of the murder – brutality that we are all used to in South Africa, where black lives are cheap.' Backed as they were by Mandela's unique moral authority, these were strong words: he was drawing a parallel between race relations in Britain and life under apartheid. Still stronger words followed from Doreen, who flayed the police for their failure to catch Stephen's killers. 'I'm sure they know who these people are and they haven't arrested them,' she said. 'They are walking, eating and drinking and my son is lying on some slab.' What was more, she and her family had been treated shamefully by police officers: 'They are patronizing us and when they do that to me I get very angry. They're not dealing with illiterate blacks. We're educated. It's time they woke up to our people.' And then she asked: 'Why is it that the leader of a foreign country shows us sympathy while our own government has expressed no interest at all?'

As its organizers and participants intended, this event made the evening local news bulletins in London and was reported in the national broadsheet press. The message was clear: the family had not only lost confidence in the police, it was in open conflict with them. How had this come about?

Anger was always present in the response of the Lawrences to the murder of their son, but some time passed before it came to be directed at the Metropolitan Police. The first night, naturally, was one of grief. At Brook Hospital they were taken to see their son's body and they prayed and wept beside him and then, conscious that Stuart and Georgina were alone at home, they drove back to Llanover Road. Neither could afterwards recall anything about the journey, but soon they were at home breaking the news to Stuart, who had remained awake. He cried and cried. When he was finally settled Doreen went to bed and tried to sleep, but she was too distressed. Neville stayed up all night; a cousin of his and her husband, whom he had called from the hospital, came round to console him and keep him company. For the whole of the following day he remained outwardly calm, and several people who spoke to him formed the view that the loss he had suffered sank in only slowly.

Georgina woke at 7 a.m. 'What's wrong?' she asked Doreen, and when she was told she 'went mad', as her mother later put it – running, screaming, wailing. It was a terrible moment, as was the visit in those early hours of Duwayne Brooks's mother, who had called by after going to see her son in Plumstead station while he was making his long statement. There was no meeting of hearts; the Lawrences were angry with Duwayne and were not ready for his mother's sympathy; indeed the visit only deepened their grief. Afterwards, Neville began to phone friends and relatives to break the news. Elvin Oduro, Stephen's friend, was among them. 'You're joking,' he said at first. Another call was to Jamaica, where a relative collapsed at the news. A third was to an old friend of Neville's who was a local councillor in north London. As he talked, Neville began to realize how little he knew of what had happened. Stephen had been stabbed near a bus stop when he was with Duwayne; the killers were white and they escaped, and the attack was racist (Duwayne's mother had told them the word 'nigger' had been used). That was it. When his friends asked for an explanation of what had happened, Neville found he could not begin to give one.

He got hold of some of that morning's newspapers but there was nothing about the murder; not a single word. His son was dead, Neville thought with horror, and the tabloids were still peddling their trivial nonsense. In fact the news of the killing had broken too late to be included in the morning papers, but Neville did not know that. He telephoned a reporter he knew on the *Independent*, Nick Schoon – Neville had done plastering work in the homes of several journalists – and told him what had happened. Schoon, still having his breakfast, said he would come round straight away. By the time he got there an hour or so later, things had moved on. Stuart and Georgina insisted on going to school, despite their mother's reservations. She agreed to let them go only when a group of her oldest friends – women she had been to school with – turned up and two of them offered to act as escorts. Among these friends was Clara Marrett, who had taken time off from work to help, and she began to take some control of the situation. It was she who answered the door at 8.45 a.m., when the police called. Detective Inspector Philip Jeynes and Police Constable Alan Fisher were led upstairs, where they found Doreen in some distress on the sofa, being comforted by friends, including a white woman who was the next-door neighbour. Neville gave up his seat for Jeynes and eventually sat on the floor, and the conversation was largely between these two. Jeynes set out some practical facts: there would be a murder inquiry based at Eltham police station, with Superintendent Crampton in charge; there would be a post mortem examination of the body, which would take place that day, and within a few days there would be an inquest, although that was likely to be quickly adjourned. It was probably also at this meeting that Neville was told there would be a press conference later in the day, and was invited to attend and issue a public appeal for witnesses. Neville, for his part, told Jeynes about the role of Joey Shepherd and provided his address so that the police could speak to him. He also asked about the murder and Jeynes – who had not at this time seen Duwayne's statement – gave him a brief account of what little he knew. It seems that the racist element was not discussed.

For the Lawrences at this stage, even stronger than the desire to know more about the circumstances of the murder was the need to see their son. They had seen the body only briefly at the hospital during the first crisis of their grief and they wanted to touch him again and spend time with him. Like all grieving people they were aware of the void in their midst and held out the hope that seeing and touching the body might in some way help to fill it. They were also conscious that their son was lying in a cold, impersonal institution far from those who loved him, and they wanted to get him out of there as soon as possible, and bury him. These were complex matters. An early visit to the mortuary was impossible – the post mortem that morning would take a matter of hours – but after that, something could be arranged. As for burial, Jeynes had to explain that this could not happen for weeks and possibly even months. Stephen was a murder victim and when eventually charges were laid the defendants would be entitled to commission a second post mortem; only then could the body legally be released to the family. It was distressing news.

When Nick Schoon, the reporter from the *Independent*, reached the house at about 10 a.m. the police had left but numbers inside had been swelled by the arrival of more relatives, and a doctor had called to prescribe some sedatives for Doreen. Like Jeynes, Schoon spoke mainly to Neville, who went over a story he was to repeat at the press conference and many times after that in the days that followed. Stephen, he said, was a popular young man with high hopes of becoming an architect; he had never been in trouble; the family was law-abiding and unpolitical and had nothing to do with gangs or race matters. In short, neither Stephen nor his parents had ever done anything to deserve this. Schoon, who had grown to like Neville when he had worked on his house, found the interview moving and upsetting. After the reporter left to pursue his story elsewhere, others called at Llanover Road: someone from the Social Services, people from black community groups, young people who had known Stephen and, eventually, other reporters. The phone, too, was ringing. It was becoming clear to everyone in the house that however deeply they felt their loss, this was not a private tragedy but a public and in some ways a political event. In their shock, Neville and Doreen were probably among the last to recognize the implications. As Neville had told Schoon, they were not the sort to draw attention to themselves.

Palma Black was a young activist with the Anti-Racist Alliance (ARA), a black-led umbrella group which aimed, among other things, to provide help to people such as the Lawrences by tapping into a network of black experts and professionals. Late that morning she took a call at the ARA's Islington office from a community activist in southeast London, who told her about the murder and said she had been contacted by someone in the family seeking help. She had recommended the ARA, she said, and Black should expect a call shortly. Moments later the phone rang again; a cousin of Stephen Lawrence was calling from Llanover Road. The ARA was needed; could they come as soon as possible? Black and a colleague, Anne Kane, agreed a plan of action. Kane would go directly to the police press conference and introduce herself to Neville there, while Black would go to the Lawrence home via Greenwich, picking up on her way a prominent black local councillor, Vicki Morse, who was an ARA supporter. Before she left the office, Black made a call intended to set in motion the process of finding a sympathetic lawyer who could advise the Lawrences.

At the house, she and Morse introduced themselves and offered their help. At first, neither they nor any of the relatives and friends in the house had a clear idea of what their role should be, except that their advice was needed on how to handle the public aspects of the murder. Various community groups had been in touch and there was talk of marches, for example, while the press kept calling and knocking at the door; what should they do? One practical first step involved security, something few in the house had thought about. Morse said she would arrange for the council to fit a secure letter-box to prevent arson attacks, while Black discussed with the family arrangements for screening mail and phone calls to ensure the Lawrences did not personally receive racist abuse or threats. They also spoke of arranging regular escorts for the children on the way to school and back. It was a beginning; in the days that followed, Black found herself working full-time at the Lawrence house, and often very long hours.

Anne Kane, meanwhile, was at the press conference to hear the police acknowledge that it was a racist killing and to hear Neville say that he would like his son's killers to be hanged. She also heard Chief Superintendent Philpott's appeal for calm: 'I am very concerned that some may want to take the law into their own hands, which will not help the situation. I would appeal to the good sense of the young people. In the long run, retaliation will do no good.' Afterwards, outside the station, Kane was able to brief journalists on the history of racial violence in the area, including the Blair, Adams and Duggal murders, and to point to the presence of the BNP in the area as a serious problem. (Neville had been asked at the press conference if he blamed the BNP. 'What's that?' he replied.) The public face of the Lawrence murder was taking shape. Emotions were running very high among the black population of southeast London and people were looking for something they could do, somewhere they could direct their energy and their anger. At this stage the lightning rod was the BNP building in Welling. As the

ARA said, Greenwich had had one of the lower levels of racist violence before that office was established and now it had one of the highest. By leafleting and recruiting in the area, the BNP was encouraging racist attacks, and the hub of this activity was the sinister, anonymous 'shop' in Upper Wickham Lane. As it happened, the BNP building lay in the borough of Bexley. Councillors there, while expressing revulsion at the BNP message, insisted that they had no legal grounds to close the office, but opinion in Greenwich saw this as spineless. A few days after Stephen's murder the Labour MP for Woolwich, John Austin-Walker, led a demonstration outside Bexley civic offices demanding action against the BNP.

This was not all. The murder prompted calls by Austin-Walker and Peter Bottomley, the Eltham MP, for government action on racist violence and it added fuel to an argument then being aired that Parliament should create a new offence of racial harassment. It also brought pressure to bear on the police, as Ilsley and Crampton found at the Woolwich Town Hall meeting on the Friday afternoon. There was anger that another murder should have been allowed to happen and there were demands that the police should make a proper job of this investigation. But in these early days the police were not the principal focus of anger; for those demanding that 'something must be done', forcing Bexley to close the BNP office was the priority.

That Friday, Ian Crampton chose two detectives from his team to act as 'victim liaison officers', charged with maintaining the links to the Lawrence family and to Duwayne Brooks. One was DC Linda Holden, who had performed the role before, and the other was DS John Bevan, a burly officer with no experience of the task, but who was thought to have the necessary personal skills. Both were expected to combine the liaison role with detective work on the investigation. Their first job was to sort out a family visit to the mortuary, and it went badly. In the early evening Holden made contact with the coroner's office and explained that because of the post mortem and the press conference it had not been possible to fix a visit for that day. Could the family see their son's body over the weekend? The reply, as noted by Holden, ran: 'No, I'm sorry but the mortuary cannot be opened until Monday morning, when a time can be arranged. Please note that this will only be a one-off opportunity so everyone who needs to attend should be included.' When this was communicated to the Lawrences that evening, they were outraged and extremely upset. They made contact with a Greenwich councillor, who got in touch with Chief Superintendent Philpott. He in turn made representations to the coroner's office, which ultimately relented and gave permission for the mortuary to be opened for the family the following day, Saturday, at noon. But damage had been done and when the visit took place the relationship between the Lawrences and the police officers, Bevan and Holden, was less than cordial. There was an awkward delay on arrival at the mortuary and some sour exchanges as the visit began. Neville and Doreen had come with four or five friends and relatives and at first they viewed the body through glass panels.

'I wanted to touch him,' Doreen recalled later.

> At first the coroner's officer or the police said no we couldn't. I think I wanted to see the wounds and everything because someone else had told us that they had arrived later at the hospital [on Thursday night], that they had been in to see him [Stephen] and that he had pin-pricks all over his arm. I didn't know what this was suggesting, but this concerned me because I wanted to know what had been done to him. I didn't tell them why I wanted to see them, but eventually they allowed only Neville and myself in. Neville asked then if his friend could come in because we wanted things explained to us and his friend knew about medical things; he had worked in hospitals and we trusted him. We hoped he could explain what these pin-pricks were because we didn't trust anyone else to tell us the truth.

In fact there was nothing sinister about the marks – they had been made as the trauma team at the Brook attempted to find a blood vessel in the arm – but the Lawrences' concerns, and their decision to bring an adviser of their own, are eloquent.

It was a shocking and highly emotional visit. They saw Stephen's wounds, which they had not seen on the night of the murder, and of necessity they also saw the long incision marks and stitches left by the post mortem. The body was of course very cold, and it may have been at this stage that they realized that until someone was in custody for the killing it would be kept in a deep-freeze. As before, they wept and prayed, and Neville later recalled being uncomfortable at the presence of a police officer and asking him to leave them alone. Afterwards Bevan and Holden drove the Lawrences to Well Hall Road and showed them the two scenes, explaining how Stephen had fallen, got to his feet and run before collapsing on the pavement. Neville was amazed at the distance his son had covered, while Doreen longed to know about Stephen's final moments. Was he conscious? Was he in pain? Was anyone there to comfort him? Did he know he was dying? What did he say? Did he ask for her? Another question – how long did it take before the police and the ambulance arrived? – was also beginning to worry both of them.

Bevan and Holden gave what reassurance they could, though at this stage it was not much, while in response to Neville's inquiries about the hunt for the killers they stressed that a vigorous investigation was under way at Eltham station, with many detectives and a large house-to-house team at work. Highly experienced officers were in charge; everything that could be done was being done and as soon as there were any developments they would be told. In the meantime the Lawrences were given the telephone number of the incident room at Eltham and DC Holden provided her own mobile telephone number in case the family had anything to ask or report. All this, and the visit to the scene, went a little way towards repairing the damage done by the mortuary affair.

Meanwhile, efforts were still under way to find someone to advise the Lawrences on legal matters. Palma Black's early call had been to the Black Lawyers' Society, which recommended a particular member. He visited the Lawrences on the Saturday morning and gave some advice but was unable to commit himself to the case, so the ARA returned to the Society and received another recommendation: Imran Khan. On the face of it he was hardly ideal: the ARA did not know him, he had been qualified only a couple of years and he was based in Ealing, far away on the other side of London. But the need was thought to be urgent and he was prepared to see the Lawrences on Sunday, so he was urged to come. In fact Khan's name and contact details were given to Bevan on the Saturday, before he had even visited. When he did turn up the Lawrences were impressed by him, and although he himself had reservations about committing himself to clients so far from his professional base, he agreed to advise them. Khan had some experience of such situations, since before qualifying as a solicitor he had for several years been a support worker for victims of racial violence and discrimination. His relationship with the Lawrences, begun that day, was to prove a long one. While Khan was at the house Bevan and Holden visited and he introduced himself, saying he would be in touch with the incident room. They talked, and this was a good meeting for all involved: the police officers were supportive and the Lawrences were able to respond. On his return to the station that day Bevan delivered a message for entry in the Holmes system:

> From the Lawrence family 250493: We are most grateful for your interest and daily attendance. Please note that we wish to be left alone today – the Sabbath – and do not require or want contact from anyone . . .

A similar request followed the next day.

Neville and Doreen at this stage wanted to withdraw and grieve with their family. Neville had attended the press conference and spoken to Crampton; they had identified their son's body; they had passed on what information they had. Having found a lawyer they liked, they were content to leave any remaining police or legal matters to him. As for the public side of the case, that had calmed significantly. There had been no riots and police fears of black retaliation over the weekend proved unfounded. Meanwhile, the IRA bomb at Bishopsgate on Saturday had swamped the news bulletins and newspapers, so press interest in the murder virtually evaporated. Once again Neville found this shocking, but Marc Wadsworth, a leading ARA figure who was visiting the house, had ideas about drawing attention back. A well-known television journalist, Wadsworth had some flair in these matters: it was he, for example, who coined the phrase that Greenwich was 'the race murder capital of Britain', which had already appeared in many press reports.

On Sunday morning the Lawrences attended Trinity Methodist Church in Plumstead, where Stephen had been a cub and a scout and the family was well known. Later the minister, David Cruise, visited Llanover Road and was able to pass on some information he had learned about the involvement of the Taaffes in Stephen's last moments. Doreen was comforted to learn that he had been calm and at peace, and that there had been people with him, talking to him and trying to help. Some of her fears were allayed. But this was the time when Imran Khan, Bevan and Holden were also in the house, so that the conversation with Cruise had to take place in a bedroom. The pressure on the family was barely tolerable. As the new week began, they were hoping for some peace, some time with their closest friends and relatives and no strangers at the door.

Back in his office in Ealing on Monday, Imran Khan dictated a letter to Weeden. He explained that he had been asked by the family to advise them on legal matters, 'particularly in relation to the investigation of Stephen's murder', and then he asked for answers to a series of questions 'in writing as a matter of urgency'. Six questions related to the progress of inquiries: had any suspects been identified, arrested or interviewed; were charges imminent; had all the important witnesses been traced, and so on. He also asked whether the police still took the view, expressed at the press conference, that this was a racial crime, and he asked for the post mortem report and any clothing or effects of Stephen's that could be returned at this stage. Then Khan explained:

> You will of course appreciate that the Lawrence family has suffered a
> tragic loss which cannot be compensated for. It can, however, be
> mitigated to some extent by the knowledge that every attempt is being
> made to find and successfully prosecute Stephen's murderers.

The letter concluded by expressing the hope that the police would reply by return of fax. Although dictated on the Monday, however, this communication was not faxed from Khan's firm, J. R. Jones, to the incident room in Eltham until 8.44 a.m. the next morning. Three hours and thirty minutes later another fax dictated by Khan travelled the same route. It asked for a response to the first letter 'as a matter of urgency' and then it reported a 'rather disturbing rumour' which had reached the family, to the effect that Duwayne Brooks was regarded as a suspect. 'Clearly that is untenable to the Lawrence family and has caused them great concern,' Khan wrote. Would the police either confirm that it was false or explain what evidence they had for suspecting Duwayne? Again, the letter ended with a request for a swift reply.

Two hours and twenty-one minutes later, at 2.35 p.m. on Tuesday, an assistant at J. R. Jones rang the incident room at Eltham to say:

113

'We have sent you two faxes and are concerned we have received no reply.' He was assured that the faxes were being dealt with. That afternoon Brian Weeden, on his second day with Operation Fishpool, wrote a reply acknowledging the two letters and stating that the questions raised in the first had already been addressed by the liaison officers in discussion with the family. He understood that the Lawrences were happy with the liaison system and he hoped it would continue to prove useful both to them and to Khan. 'I wish to assure the Lawrence family and yourselves,' he added, 'that the police are conducting a vigorous and thorough investigation into this grave and tragic case to ensure that those responsible are identified and apprehended at the earliest opportunity.'

This letter, though written on the Tuesday, did not reach Imran Khan until the morning of Thursday 29 April, two days later, and by that time he had written again. He began: 'This is now the third letter within a period of three days we have sent you regarding the murder of Stephen Lawrence. Regrettably we have had no communication from your office at all . . .' Khan explained that he understood that Weeden must be busy but he made no apology for pressing for information, since the liaison officers were providing none. He was particularly concerned, he wrote, because the family had received a number of complaints from young people who knew Stephen that the police were harassing them and asking questions which suggested that Stephen had been a member of a gang. 'As you might expect,' he wrote, 'the Lawrence family have been greatly upset by this course of action and consider that you should be concentrating your efforts on finding the racist perpetrators of the murder.' As a parting shot he warned that if he did not receive a timely reply he would have 'no alternative but to raise this matter with the Commissioner's office directly'.

On the same day, an assistant from J. R. Jones spoke directly to Weeden, who assured him a letter was already on its way. Weeden also said that he had never before received such requests for information in writing and that besides the letters he had heard nothing to suggest there was any problem with the normal family liaison procedures. If Khan was still not happy, Weeden suggested, then he should speak to a more senior officer, Commander Ray Adams. Khan, indeed, was not happy with Weeden's letter when he received it on the Thursday, and he replied on the same day. The letter did not answer his questions, and neither had the family received the information they wanted from the liaison officers, he said. 'We have confirmed this position with the family, who state that whenever information is requested about the investigation the usual response normally provided by Detective Sergeant Bevan is to give an account of the number of officers presently investigating the matter.' He accepted that the liaison had been helpful to the family but insisted that on this matter of information he had clear instructions from his clients to get answers in writing. This eventually brought a letter of response signed by Commander Adams, effectively the second-in-command of 3 Area. It was dated 30 April, the Friday, but it did not arrive until after the long weekend.

Adams adopted a tone of dismay. The normal procedure for dealing with victims' families, he explained, was through liaison officers and it was most unusual to find a solicitor acting for a family 'since there is no conflict of interest or purpose'. Many of the questions contained in Khan's letters sought information that was routinely provided through liaison officers, but some went farther – in particular the requests relating to suspects, witnesses and possible arrests embraced 'material that is not normally released'. As for the reported difficulties with the liaison officers, Adams had spoken to Weeden to ensure that they were properly briefed. 'We shall also be talking to both Mr and Mrs Lawrence to satisfy them of our earnest wish to do everything to keep them properly informed.' In the meantime, Adams asked Khan not to press his inquiries with Weeden, who was already under a lot of pressure, but to raise any further matters with either himself or Chief Superintendent Philpott. This marked the end of the exchange.

Six letters and as many phone calls in one week left nerves and tempers frayed on both sides. At the core of the dispute – for that was what it was – lay the family's desire for concrete information about the progress of the investigation. As Khan had said in the first letter, their loss might be mitigated 'by the knowledge that every attempt is being made to find and successfully prosecute Stephen's murderers'. The police believed they were doing what they could and they were annoyed by Khan's tone and his persistence. In the Fishpool incident room the solicitor was beginning to be seen as a disruptive interloper in the case.

*

Doreen was to say much later that she had never trusted the police, even before the murder, but this was not the impression the family gave at the time. Then, Neville was usually the spokesman and during the days immediately after Stephen's death he never associated himself with any of the criticisms of police performance in race cases that were aired by others, or with any of the calls for protest and action. Instead the family urged people to help the investigation: at a candlelit vigil on Well Hall Road on Thursday 29 April, a week after Stephen's death, both Neville and Doreen made emotional appeals. 'I call upon parents, children, friends who are aware and know of the people who did this horrific thing to Stephen, please come forward, don't shield them. You are not just going to help the black community but the white community as well,' said Doreen. ARA activists and others who visited the house were surprised at the Lawrences' apparent lack of scepticism about the police, but then they were people routinely dealing with cases which involved claims of injustice, while Neville and Doreen had no experience of such matters. Neville told one interviewer: 'Before, we'd hear about these racial things happening, but we'd never think it could happen to us. We tried to bring our kids up in the right way, to obey the law.' And to another he said: 'I suppose we have been walking around with our eyes closed, not realizing what had been happening in the community until now.' It may well be that Doreen's views differed from her husband's, but there was nothing about her life before the murder to suggest any particularly strong feelings.

From the morning after the murder, however, both of them heard the police criticized many times. The people from the ARA were not confident that Stephen's murder would be thoroughly investigated and one of their strategies from the outset was to raise the public profile of the case explicitly in order to put pressure on the police to do a good job. Stephen's young friends who called at the house also had little faith in the police; unlike Doreen and Neville, as young people who spent time on the street they had first-hand experience, for example, of the way that stop-and-search and the 'sus' law had been applied disproportionately to black people. And the idea that the police were irredeemably racist was simply assumed by such groups as the Anti-Nazi League and Panther UK, which both sent representatives to knock on the door of the Llanover Road house. But the Lawrences gave no public hint that they shared such views: the police, whatever their shortcomings might be, offered the only hope of bringing their son's killers to justice and they were prepared to give them the benefit of the doubt.

Slowly, their position changed. Ian Crampton's initial assessment of the murder was that as a 'group stranger attack' it would probably take some time to solve, but many black people took a different view. The murder was carried out by a racist gang in Eltham; how many of those could there be? The police must have some intelligence about such groups, while local people would surely know who the likely culprits were. It should not take long, this argument went, to pick the killers up. On the Friday in school playgrounds black boys began asking questions about white gangs, and that evening and over the weekend that followed more than one group of black youths ventured into Eltham to do their own investigating – reports of their activities reached the police. Very early on, word got back to the Lawrence house that there were indeed known gangs of knife-carrying racists there, boys who had stabbed people before. Rumours circulated about who might know their names. The effect of this was to raise the hopes of the family, who naturally sought confirmation from the police liaison officers. They were not satisfied with the response and when they discussed this with Imran Khan he said he would put their questions to Weeden in writing, as he did in his first letter.

As the exchange of letters shows, matters escalated from there, not least because of delays in communication. Weeden was plainly rattled by Khan's abruptness and persistence, to such a degree that he passed responsibility for dealing with him up the command line. Not only were the police unaccustomed to dealing with a solicitor representing a bereaved family, they were also, as the letters show, extremely cautious about committing to paper any discussion of the case. The official line on providing information was clear: nothing that could identify suspects or lines of inquiry should be divulged. The Lawrences were not asking for that but for more general material, yet even here the police were reluctant, and they were adamant that if they were to share any knowledge then it must not be in writing. The burden thus rested upon Detective Sergeant Bevan and Detective Constable Holden, the liaison officers.

Theirs was not an easy task, and was never likely to be. A study carried out by Liverpool University in 1990 had found that the great majority of families of murder victims were left with feelings of grievance towards the police, and at least some of the reasons for this were inevitable. Most families complained that they were not given enough information about the murder, many were angered by delays in the release of the victim's belongings and body and many thought identifications were insensitively handled and officers were insufficiently patient. Family liaison officers were supposed to overcome these problems but there was no escaping the unwelcome character of some of the information they were required to pass on and some of the questions they were required to ask. In the case of the Lawrences, Bevan and Holden were always uncomfortable in the Llanover Road house, mainly because it was usually so full of people whose role or relationship to the family they did not understand, and their discomfort was increased by the early problems over the mortuary visit. Although they established some rapport with Neville Lawrence in the early days the problem of information steadily broke it down, for whatever Bevan and Holden were prepared to tell the Lawrences about the progress of the investigation, it was not nearly enough.

Day by day, scraps of information were coming into the Llanover Road house from local black youngsters, friends and other callers. It was by no means equivalent to the flow of tip-offs that the police were receiving but it was enough to feed the growing conviction that there were people in and around Eltham whom the police should be interviewing or even arresting. This information was noted down in a log book for visits and calls that had been started by Clara Marrett on the morning after the murder, and most of it seems to have been passed on to the Eltham incident room for investigation. For example, Elvin Oduro reported that another friend of Stephen's, Dean Simpson, had been approached in Woolwich by a white girl who named someone called Danny as one of the killers. The full name was given to Bevan, although it turned out that Simpson was reluctant to speak to police.

It was on Thursday 29 April that the most shocking and remarkable piece of information came to the Lawrences. It was late in the evening, after the vigil at Well Hall Road, when the doorbell rang and Cheryl Sloley, Doreen's sister, went to answer it. Outside she found a white woman aged about thirty who said that she had just heard some information about the murder. Five boys had apparently been seen in a flat shortly after the stabbing and they had no tops on, were holding knives and acting suspiciously. The woman said that the attack had apparently happened when some boys went out to commit a robbery in Lovelace Gardens, close to the bus stop where Stephen was waiting. And she went on to give the names of three young men, none of whom was on the police's list of prime suspects. Two of these named men, she said, were infatuated with the Kray twins. Having passed this information on, the woman refused to give her name and address and left on foot. While some of what she said was obscure, it was without doubt based on the K story, and what he was said to have seen at 102 Bournbrook Road. The detail was too close for coincidence. So just a day after the police first heard of it, the Lawrences learned of the possibility that there was a witness to the aftermath of the murder. Cheryl Sloley called Imran Khan straight away and he phoned Linda Holden on her mobile number. The time was ten minutes past midnight. When he began to talk about youths setting out to commit a robbery Holden thought at first he meant they were doing so that night, but then he explained that he was talking about the night of the murder. At this she said there was nothing she could do immediately – the incident room was closed – but that she would put the names he had given her in the system in the morning. She was irritated at being disturbed so late with information she did not regard as urgent, and she remarked: 'Do you know what time it is?' Khan replied: 'Well, yes, but I get phone calls late at night as well.' When she reached the station the next morning Holden entered the two names in the system as she had promised, and actions were raised to trace and interview them.

The following night saw another uncomfortable telephone conversation between the Lawrence home and the police. Clara Marrett wanted to report another piece of information that had come in, giving another new name, and she telephoned Scotland Yard, asking them to pass the message to the Eltham incident room. A few minutes later, when she had not been called back, she rang the incident room herself and although it was shortly after midnight she found DC Bob Crane still there. Crane's note records the exchange:

The caller was concerned that there had been no response from police. I explained that the information would be logged in the system and followed up. I had to explain to caller that no immediate action would be taken re the information which was by the nature anonymous. Caller was concerned that information had not been forwarded from NSY [New Scotland Yard]. I explained that information would in all probability have been sent for station to deal.

It is easy to see how such events were construed by the family, and how they increased the Lawrences' desire for proof that the investigation was being properly pursued and that their information in particular was being followed up. They were hearing a great many reports and rumours and they could safely assume that the police were hearing far more, so every day that passed without arrests increased their sense of frustration.

Other events fed those feelings. When Stephen's young friends complained that the police were implying that Stephen or Duwayne might be members of a gang the Lawrences were annoyed, and subsequent attempts by the police to question Neville and Doreen about Stephen's background met with a very frosty response. Neville took exception to being asked whether Stephen owned the dark blue gloves found at the murder scene because he thought the implication was that his son had been a burglar.

On the night of Wednesday the 28th the Lawrences had experienced a scare. A relative left the house quite late that evening and saw two white boys walking towards her as she approached her car. Frightened, she leapt in, closed the door and drove off quickly, but she noticed as she left that there were other white boys standing behind a van, also close to the Lawrence home. She was now concerned about the safety of the family so she drove to a police station – not Eltham – and reported what she had seen. The officer on the desk, however, knew nothing at all about the Lawrence case and she formed the impression that he did not grasp the urgency of the matter. When she got home a little later she called the Lawrences to tell them what she had seen and find out whether anything had been done. Neville had heard nothing. Now he was alarmed – it was not the first scare at the house – and he rang Holden, who in turn alerted Eltham station, which sent a police car. The following morning Cheryl Sloley was again in contact with

Holden saying the incident showed the Lawrences needed full-time protection.

Doreen Lawrence's first response to the death of her son was emotional collapse but as the days passed and her strength returned the grief was supplemented by anger. She was angry about the killers and the families who seemed to be sheltering them – what sort of depraved people could they be? She was angry about the press and the way they seemed to have dropped the story. She was angry that the country had not taken notice – when she met her MP, Peter Bottomley, she asked him whether the Prime Minister knew about Stephen's murder, because, she said, he *should* have been told. And over time she became angry towards the police. Neville followed a different path. He had been angry from the outset about many of the same things, but just as his grief was more muted, so was his outrage. It was the grinding force of events that wore down his patience and caused him eventually to snap.

By the second weekend – the bank holiday weekend – the family's views on the police had largely been shaped. They had talked to Imran Khan, to the ARA people and to others such as Vicki Morse and Ros Howells, a local race relations professional who was to become close to the family. More importantly they had talked to friends such as Clara and to close relatives such as Cheryl, and among them all there was little dissent. No one could suggest a good reason why, given the amount of information that seemed to be circulating about the murder, there had been no arrests. On the other hand there was a feeling that the police were wasting time investigating Stephen, his parents and his friends. There was also a strong sense that the family was not being treated with respect and that its assistance and its concerns were being dismissed as unimportant. Neville and Doreen were beginning to see incidents that had happened soon after the murder in a new light. That night in the car, before turning back to go to the hospital they had looked down Well Hall Road; why did they see no police activity there? Why did it take so much time to get Stephen to hospital? Why was he left bleeding on the pavement for so long? And why did no police officer visit the Lawrence home until ten hours after the murder?

On the Saturday Doreen had an experience that might have been calculated to plunge her deeper into despair and rage. Eight days had passed and apart from visiting the mortuary and going to church she had scarcely been out of the house. There was, however, a need to replenish stocks, so she set out with her sisters Cheryl Sloley and Lorna Graham, and a cousin, Vivien Leslie, to do some shopping in Woolwich. As they drove into Sainsbury's car park in the middle of town they saw two white women (a mother in her fifties and her adult daughter) returning to their car with a full shopping trolley. Doreen, who was behind the wheel, said later that she stopped the car to let the women pass, but they did not move. The gap was small so Doreen manoeuvred to make more room, but a misunderstanding developed and Doreen eventually made a gesture of impatience, saying inside the car: 'What are you doing?' The younger of the two white women became angry and called Doreen a 'fucking nigger'. Doreen parked, but her passengers were furious and as soon as they could they ran over to the white women to remonstrate. There followed a very angry exchange. One of the white women was said to have used the words 'black cunt', while either Cheryl or Lorna said: 'It was one of you bastards that killed my nephew.' According to Cheryl this received the answer: 'If he hadn't been here [in this country], he'd still be alive', after which the younger white woman took a brick out of the boot of her car, held it up and said: 'If you come anywhere near me, this is what you'll get.' With that the incident ended, but it was reported to Imran Khan, who alerted the police. An investigation was opened and placed in the hands of PC Alan Fisher, a racial incidents specialist.

The Lawrences, so much in need of a break, went away on the Sunday and stayed overnight with relatives, returning on the bank holiday Monday afternoon when plans were laid for a family press conference the following day in Woolwich Town Hall. They were still waiting at this stage for the reply from Commander Adams to Khan's fourth letter, and there were tetchy telephone exchanges between J. R. Jones and Adams's office before it arrived on Tuesday morning. There was also a very unhappy scene that morning at the Lawrence home, when Bevan and Fisher paid a visit and were confronted by an angry Georgina. 'When are you going to catch the people who killed Stephen?' screamed the eleven-year-old before being led away in tears.

The press conference marks a watershed in the relationship between the Lawrences and the police, for there the family made public for the first time their dissatisfaction with the investigation. 'The police are not really concerned about arresting anyone,' declared Neville. 'They are just going through the motions.' Doreen used even more uncompromising language, arguing that a form of ethnic cleansing was taking place in south London: 'If it was the other way round and a white boy had been killed by a gang of black men, they would have arrested half the black community in the area. But nothing has been done and there have been no arrests and the police won't tell us what is happening ... The black community and I cannot stand for this any longer. The killers are still out there and other black kids can't feel safe on the streets.' Despite the strong language the public effect of this was slow to build. Reports appeared on the local television news bulletins that night and in two national newspapers the next morning – 'Parents of stabbed youth attack police,' said the *Times* headline. The reports were short and gave very little vent to the family's complaints. On the surface it seemed that no one was paying much attention, but this was not the case. The story caught the eye of a number of editors, on the *Daily Telegraph*, the *Daily Mail* and BBC2's *Newsnight*, among others, and reporters were sent down to Plumstead and Eltham to investigate what was going wrong in the Lawrence case. The news that the family was to meet Nelson Mandela gave added interest to the story.

For the police, now under pressure to respond to the family's accusations, these were uncomfortable days. Deputy Assistant Commissioner David Osland, the police officer in overall command of 3 Area, lent his name to the official response, which ran: 'The inquiry continues with a dedicated team of officers pursuing the task diligently and with total professionalism. We refute any suggestion that it is not so.' The buck had been passed up to him partly because Adams, who had supposedly taken over responsibility for this side of the case from Weeden, suddenly disappeared from the scene. On the Tuesday morning, with his letter to Khan still unsigned, he reported to Osland that he had received medical advice to stop working because of persistent back problems, and from that afternoon, once he had put his name to the letter, he was listed as long-term sick, ultimately retiring from the police without returning to work. Osland's other senior subordinates were fully involved, including Chief Superintendent Philpott, a leading uniformed officer, and Chief Superintendent Ilsley, the top detective in 3 Area.

Weeden, too, did not escape, and his desk notes for these days show him increasingly beset by requests for press interviews. At one point, before seeing a *Newsnight* journalist, he jotted down a 'brief thought' on the subject of arrests:

> I quite understand that people, especially the Lawrence family, want the case to be cleared up as quickly as possible. However, police are not going to be pressurized into any quick-fix solution. We've had one tragedy with Stephen's senseless murder and we're not going to compound matters with a second disaster. Police actions will be determined by evidence, not emotion and expediency.

Weeden also wanted to repair relations with the family and with that in mind he invited the Lawrences to visit the incident room at Eltham, but his gesture backfired when Doreen and Neville asked if they could bring Imran Khan. The answer was no and the family, offended, decided that they would not go without him. Seeing matters deteriorating, Bill Ilsley stepped in. He invited the family, and Khan, to meet him for a discussion about their complaints and the progress of the investigation. This invitation was accepted and the meeting was set for Thursday afternoon.

That was the day of the Mandela meeting and the day when Weeden conducted his review of the evidence at Eltham station with Bullock, Flook and Davidson. That review concluded, Weeden's notes indicated, with a decision to put pressure on the prime suspects by arresting Neil Acourt and Dave Norris for the Benefield stabbing. Afterwards Weeden presided over the daily meeting of his squad in the incident room. At the same time, 4 p.m., the Lawrences, having left Nelson Mandela early in the afternoon, arrived at Ilsley's office in Catford station in company with Imran Khan, Clara Marrett and an ARA member called Carl Booth. As Ilsley greeted them, he was almost certainly aware that the press office was being asked for police reaction to the remarks made by Mandela and Doreen a little earlier, and the meeting started with the police clearly on the defensive. But before they began, Doreen handed to Ilsley a sheet of paper torn from a notebook on which she had written six names, including 'Dobson' and 'Arecourts'. These were the names that had come into the Lawrence home in one way or another over the previous fortnight and that had been recorded in Clara Marrett's log book. Ilsley took the note, looked at it briefly and then opened the meeting.

Imran Khan was the first to speak and he expressed the family's anxiety that two weeks should have passed without arrests. Restating Doreen's view, he said that if the victim had been white and the attackers black a great many people would have been detained for questioning in a very short time. There followed a general airing of the family's grievances, from the failure to provide them with information about the investigation to the specific difficulties over family liaison. Ilsley, for his part, explained that there were clear reasons, some of them legal, for the police reluctance to hand over information about suspects, and on this subject it seems that a certain amount of common ground was discovered. The family, Khan made clear, had never wanted the names of suspects or other such details; they merely wished to know whether any suspects were in view and particularly whether the police were acting on the information they were providing and whether it was proving useful. The question of the late-night phone calls to Linda Holden was aired, and Ilsley asked the Lawrences to call at night only if they had urgent information. He also suggested that, for as long as it was necessary, the Lawrences and Khan should come and meet him once a week to discuss the investigation and any difficulties they might have. This discussion lasted more than an hour and proved to be a politer encounter than might have been expected, although Ilsley never escaped the feeling that he was under pressure.

One person present played little part. With Khan doing most of the talking, Doreen sat and watched Ilsley. As she watched, she saw him toying with the piece of paper she had given him, a sheet from a reporter's pad. He folded it once and then twice until it was small enough to fit in a wallet. Then, while he listened and answered questions, he folded it again, and then again and again until it was little bigger than a postage stamp. Doreen was not really listening now to what was being said. For days she had wanted to know what the police did with the information they were receiving about her son's murder and now she watched as a detective chief superintendent fiddled with the lump of paper that had been her list of six names. She grew steadily more certain of where the list would end up if she did not say something, so when the meeting ended she went to Ilsley, pointed at the paper still in his hand and asked: 'You are not going to put that in the bin now?' He assured her that he would not, and that all information was taken seriously. In fact he went directly to the incident room at Eltham and had the list entered into the Holmes system.

That was not all he did, for while he was there Ilsley had a long conversation with Brian Weeden which ended with a decision that was formally recorded by Weeden in what is called the SIO's 'policy file', the record of his most important decisions. It read as follows:

> Decision: arrest, search for evidence and interview the following suspects in connection with the murder – this to be done on 7/5/93. 1. Jamie Acourt. 2. Neil Acourt. 3. David Norris. 4. Gary Dobson. Reasons: sufficient grounds exist for proposed action based on: 1. All are known associates. 2. Artist's impression similar to Acourts. 3. Information from numerous sources re their involvement. 4. Norris and possibly others thought to possess a knife. 5. Strong possibility they were in the area around the time of the murder.

Weeden, then, had changed his mind. He would not just arrest two boys for the Benefield attack, but four boys for the Lawrence murder. And although he had not suggested this at the earlier staff briefing he was now proposing to make these arrests at the earliest opportunity, the very next morning at first light. That meant a frantic evening of planning and preparation, including a visit to a magistrate at his home at 8.45 p.m. to have the warrants signed. Such forthright action was a dramatic departure for the cautious Weeden, but it was one for which he did not bear sole responsibility. The record in the policy file shows that this entry, decision number 25, unlike all those which preceded it, was signed not just by the senior investigating officer but by Detective Chief Superintendent Ilsley as well.

Chapter Eight **Arrests**

At 6.32 a.m. on Friday 7 May a squad of twenty police officers under Detective Sergeant Kirkpatrick smashed through the side door of 102 Bournbrook Road. Immediately the house was filled with shouting, running feet and an air of suffused violence. Bursting into the downstairs front room D C Canavan and D C Budgen found a young man in bed.

'What's your name?' asked Canavan, according to his subsequent note.

'Jamie Acourt.'

'Are you awake?'

'Yeah.'

'You are under arrest on suspicion of the murder of Stephen Lawrence in Well Hall Road, Eltham on the night of Thursday 22 April 1993,' said Canavan, who then read the routine caution.

'I haven't done anything. That's the honest truth,' said Jamie.

Canavan then read from a piece of paper: 'My grounds for arresting you are as follows. One, you fit the description of the youths involved. Two, you with others have a history of being involved in recent stabbings in the area. Three, we have information from various sources that you were involved in this. Do you understand?'

Jamie rose from his bed and began to dress, saying: 'I was in all night with Neil, my mum and her boyfriend John. I was playing Nintendo.'

In the room above a similar scene was played out as Kirkpatrick confronted Neil. 'I am Detective Sergeant Kirkpatrick from the 3 Area Major Incident Room. I have a warrant to search the premises for bloodstained clothing and knives.'

'What's all this about? Give us a minute, will you?'

'Now listen to this. It's very important,' said Kirkpatrick, going on to caution Neil and list the same three grounds for arrest. Asked if he wanted to say anything, Neil said simply: 'No reply.'

As the atmosphere grew calmer both boys, and Bradley Lamb, who was also in the house, were allowed time to dress and then kept separately under guard for a short while as the search of the house began. Then Jamie was taken to Lewisham police station and Neil to Catford station.

Near by in Phineas Pett Road, Gary Dobson's arrest was a little more gentlemanly. D S Davidson and his team of nine officers were greeted at the front door by Gary's mother. 'I have a warrant to search these premises,' said Davidson, showing it. 'Is Gary in?'

'Yes, why?'

'I intend arresting him. Could you show me where he is?'

At this Gary's father appeared and asked: 'Why are you arresting Gary?'

'If you come with me, I'll explain to Gary.'

In an upstairs room they found Gary in bed, and his father said: 'You'd better get up, Gary, the police are here to arrest you.'

'Sit up,' said Davidson. 'Are you awake?'

'Yeah.'

'You are under arrest on suspicion of the murder of Stephen Lawrence.' Davidson cautioned him and read the grounds for arrest, to which Dobson offered no reply, although his mother protested that Gary had been at home throughout the evening of the murder. He was then taken to Bromley police station.

At number 7 Berryfield Close things went less smoothly. D S Bevan turned up with thirteen other officers including a dog team, but these were not premises that could be taken by storm. Bevan rang the bell at the electronic gates and a blonde woman leant out of an upstairs window. He called out that they were police officers and she pushed the button to let them in. The woman turned out to be Tracey Norris, but while her two younger sons were at home, Dave was not. After some discussion she said she would try to get in touch with him and bring him to a police station, and in the meantime the search team set about executing their warrant.

The searches produced a variety of samples for the forensic scientists. Jackets, jeans and trainers were taken from all three homes to be examined for bloodstains and other traces. A CS gas canister was found in Gary's bedroom and a knife in a drawer beneath his bed – 'It's one of the kitchen knives I use for dinner,' he said. The drawers in Dave Norris's bedroom yielded a photograph of him – the first that police had seen – and also something stranger and uglier: the head of a claw-hammer with a thin circular strap about three feet long strung through it. This was clearly a weapon to be swung at an adversary. But it was 102 Bournbrook that produced the real harvest of hardware. Under the cushions of a sofa officers found a two-foot-long sword with a scabbard, while in an upstairs room – probably belonging to one of the Lamb brothers – they discovered a tiger-lock knife and a Gurkha knife. Jamie's air pistol, the replica Smith & Wesson with which he was said to have threatened a black pupil at school, was also uncovered, with its holster, while in Jamie's bedroom two more knives were found in a toolbag and another one was found behind a television set.

With three of the four prime suspects in custody, the next step was to question them. It was lunchtime before the interviews with the Acourt boys began – on the police side the morning was taken up by searches, while the suspects for their part had to summon solicitors. At Catford it fell to Kirkpatrick to question Neil, with DC Lee Doel assisting. Neil was represented by a solicitor from Henry Milner and Co., a firm with which most experienced officers in south London had had dealings. Milner acted for a number of notable criminals, including Kenneth Noye, and also for Clifford Norris. Once its representatives were on the spot, the firm's advice to both Acourt boys was to exercise their right to silence, which in 1993 they were free to do without risk of prejudicing a future jury against them.

Kirkpatrick soon saw the lie of the land. After repeating the formal caution – 'You do not have to say anything unless you wish to do so, but what you say may be given in evidence' – he asked Neil to confirm for the record that the cassette tapes being used had been unsealed in his presence.

'You told me I ain't got to say nothing and I don't want to say nothing yet.'

Kirkpatrick explained that he was investigating the Lawrence murder and he made plain that he believed Neil was involved in the attack. He then asked the direct question: 'Did you kill Stephen Lawrence?'

'No comment.'

'Where were you on the 22nd April 1993?'

'No comment.'

'Do you deny the offence?'

'No comment.'

For the next half an hour Neil repeated those two words at every opportunity while Kirkpatrick and Doel made a variety of vain attempts to shake him. They tried to coax him – this was his chance to clear his name if he was innocent – and to unsettle him – his silence gave the impression he was hiding something – but to no effect. They also tried to provoke him: 'So you don't deny being involved in this murder?' And: 'Doesn't it bother you that a life has just been taken?' But only once did they get a reaction, to a question from Kirkpatrick: 'It's OK for people just to go around stabbing people to death?'

'No comment.'

'Do you think it's funny?'

'No comment.'

'Why do you smile?'

'No comment.'

At Lewisham station Canavan and Budgen had a similar experience with Jamie. 'This is your opportunity to give your side of the story, to say what you know and what your involvement was,' suggested Canavan. 'Do you understand that?'

'No comment.'

Moments later he asked Jamie: 'Are you nervous?'

'No comment.'

'You'd probably feel better if you spoke to me about it.'

At this the solicitor intervened to complain that the proposition was inappropriate. After seven minutes of being stonewalled, Canavan called a halt to the interview.

Gary Dobson, by contrast, had a good deal to say, and this conformed to expectation. One of the titbits that the man known as James Grant had told Davidson and Budgen during their second meeting was that 'the Acourts and Norris would probably say nothing and Dobson would crack up and probably tell all'. It was on this basis that Weeden assigned Davidson, his most experienced interviewer, to deal with Dobson's arrest and his subsequent questioning at Southwark station. Dobson, moreover, was not represented by Henry Milner and Co., but by another solicitor. So when Davidson asked him whether he took part in the murder of Stephen Lawrence he replied in plain terms: 'No, I had no involvement in that.' Then he suddenly volunteered some information about his movements on the night. He had spent the evening in, he said, but at 11.45 p.m. he had 'popped out' to the Acourt house to borrow a CD (Bob Marley's *The Legend*) from Jamie. He spent fifteen minutes with the Acourts; as well as Jamie, Neil was at home with Bradley Lamb and their mother. It was while he was paying this short visit that K knocked at the door and brought the news of the murder on Well Hall Road. After this, Dobson said, he went straight home and went to bed.

This was rather different from the story he had told the house-to-house officers who questioned him at home on Sunday 25 April, and it was also different from what Dobson's mother had told Davidson that morning. Why had he previously failed to mention this trip to 102 Bournbrook? 'I didn't find it necessary,' he said, weakly. And why had his own mother said he was at home all evening? She was probably unaware that he had slipped out. Davidson and Hughes drew their own conclusion about why the story had changed, as they explained to him: 'Before you came here you knew that [K] had spoken to us and you knew exactly what he'd said.' He had thus been obliged to admit visiting the Acourt house. Since he was now acknowledging that he was in the house when K called, they asked him about K's description of what he had seen and heard, but Dobson was evasive, saying he hadn't heard anything apart from the news of the murder. What about the suggestion that the boys had their tops off? 'I know my friends were ready for bed 'cos they had to get up for work,' he replied. Then came the question which was to dominate the interview: which friends?

Dobson was happy to say that the Acourt boys were there, but nothing would induce him to include David Norris in the group, indeed nothing would induce him to say he had ever met or ever seen anyone called David Norris. Other associates he would identify, such as Luke Knight, Danny Caetano and Charlie Martin, but not Norris. For some time the detectives also declined to use the name, asking questions such as: 'What's the other boy that knocks about and makes a foursome [with you and the Acourts]?' But eventually they began to press him about 'Dave', insisting that they had any number of informants on the estates who linked the boys with this 'Dave'. 'We've done a lot of homework on the ground and we know that you've got one main associate that you're not talking about now,' they said, but still the answer was a stubborn ignorance. 'I don't know who Dave is,' said Dobson. Finally an exasperated

Davidson declared: 'The Dave we're talking about – and I think we've messed around long enough – is Dave Norris.'

'I've heard the name, but I don't know who he is,' said Dobson.

'You've been seen with him time and time and time again. He's Neil's best mate, isn't he?'

Still nothing. 'I know of a David Norris . . . I've heard the name mentioned once or twice . . . I've not actually met him.'

'Why are you refusing to name that boy?' asked Davidson. 'Is it because you're frightened of him?'

'No.'

Asked about the many people who were saying he was involved in the murder, Dobson said it was just malicious gossip. When Davidson went over some of the information given by K, EE, people at the Tyler house and others, Dobson replied that those people were all 'part of the same mob' and they were hostile to the Acourts. Why weren't the police investigating *them*? He also claimed to be a stranger to knives. The knife found in his bedroom, he said, was a kitchen knife he had used to change a plug, while another knife he was asked about had been bought for work at a time when he was doing a bricklaying course. As for the Acourts, he was not aware that they were interested in knives and had never seen them carrying knives or threatening people with them. He had heard about the attack on Staccy Benefield, but had been told that the stabber was a girl.

Throughout all this, Dobson was cooperative, talkative and generally calm; it was only when Davidson mentioned the incident involving a black boy called Kevin London that Dobson became agitated. Was it true that soon after the Lawrence murder Dobson had approached London with a knife and said, 'You're next'?

'Well that is a lie,' declared Dobson, clearly outraged.

Davidson picked up the change of mood. 'You mean the other things aren't lies?' he asked, and Dobson was flustered. In the course of three interview sessions that day the two detectives returned several times to Dobson's reaction to the London allegation, asking why he should have been so indignant about a relatively minor matter when the suggestion that he was a murderer did not seem to upset him at all. Could it be, they asked, that the London story was genuinely untrue while the Lawrence charge was founded in fact? Dobson denied this. One explanation he gave for his strong objection to the London story was: 'That makes me look like a racist.' Which received the obvious answer: 'And the murder of Stephen Lawrence doesn't?'

This opened a new line of discussion. Dobson insisted: 'Yeah, well, I ain't racist, I ain't murdered him and I've not threatened Kevin London. I've got nothing against blacks. I don't know why you're trying to accuse me of being racist.'

'Nobody's accused you of being racist . . . Nobody's even mentioned Stephen's colour.'

'Yeah, well, it's obvious that I knew he was black anyway and it's obvious that, it says in the papers that it's a racist attack. And it's obvious that if I've said to Kevin London that you're next . . .'

'Have we suggested that? Have we suggested that it was a racist attack?'

'No, but that's what the papers say, innit?'

'Forget what's in the papers,' said Hughes.

And Davidson continued: 'Personally I don't think it was particularly a racist attack. From what I've found out, with you and your gang the bloke could have been yellow, green, blue, black or white, he just happened to be there at the wrong time when a gang of thugs – you and your mates, one of them seems to be a bampot with a knife – decides to plunge a knife into somebody. The fact that there was a comment about him being a nigger or being a black bastard or something in that line, which is regarded as a racist comment by everybody – and it is pretty racist – the comment put it into a context, but I think it's incidental because there are a number of stabbings that we believe that you lot have been involved in, have been black, white, green and blue. I don't think your little gang are racist; I just think you like stabbing people.'

The effect of this speech, made to steady murmurs of agreement from Hughes, was to calm Dobson, who soon almost apologized for 'getting the hump' over the Kevin London accusation.

His manner for the most part was pained but helpful; there was no insolence and no overt obstruction, yet he could not be shifted from his story about the night of the killing and he persisted in the contention that he did not personally know David Norris. Though he was obviously an unhappy young man, he did not 'crack up' as predicted. With the Acourt brothers remaining silent and Norris not yet in custody, progress was disappointing, but the police had other avenues of attack. A number of garments and shoes taken from 102 Bournbrook showed stains that might be blood, so forensic examination might yet produce a breakthrough, and then there was the possibility that some of the witnesses might recognize the boys.

Identification parades must conform to strict procedures if they are to have any standing in court, for the obvious reason that if defence lawyers can show that the process is tainted in any way then the identification becomes questionable. So it is that parades are an elaborate ritual in the police world. Designated police stations have identification suites with their own entrances and exits, carefully laid out to ensure that people flow through them in a manner which prevents contamination by accidental encounter. The parade rooms themselves have one-way viewing windows, so that witnesses are not seen by suspects, and there are formal procedures intended to satisfy suspects that the process is fair. They or their solicitors may object to individual 'stooges' – the ordinary members of the public in the line-up – if they believe there is no superficial resemblance. Parades are usually conducted with the line-up sitting down to minimize disparities in height and stooges or suspects may change their clothes to conform more closely to the norm. In short, everything should be done to ensure that the people in the line are broadly similar in appearance and that there is nothing to make the suspect stand out. All this requires a good deal of work. Not only do witness, suspect and stooges have to be brought together in one place and defence lawyers satisfied, but arrivals and departures must be choreographed and the whole business must be religiously recorded in statements and forms. In the case of multiple parades, when there is more than one suspect and more than one witness, the complexities are correspondingly multiplied. Add to this the fact that in 1993 London was short of identification suites and they were in constant heavy demand, and you have a picture of what was involved in the Lawrence case.

Weeden was fortunate, considering that the decision to arrest had only been made the previous night, to have the use of the identification suite at Southwark station the following evening. Ideally Neil, Jamie and Gary would all stand in parades to be viewed by all three potential identification witnesses in the Lawrence case: Duwayne Brooks and two of the bus stop witnesses, Joey Shepherd and Royston Westbrook (the third, Alexandra Marie, having ruled herself out by saying that she did not see any faces). But inevitably circumstances were not ideal: Royston Westbrook could not be reached that day and there were difficulties finding a sufficient number of stooges for evening parades. Dobson's parade had to be abandoned altogether for want of similar stooges, but there were just enough for Jamie and Neil. Just enough, that was, until the two boys and their solicitor, from Henry Milner and Co., were asked if they objected to anyone. In each case they picked out three people whom they thought unsuitable and these had to be replaced. This searching for new stooges took time: Duwayne and Joey Shepherd were brought to the identification suite between 5 p.m. and 6 p.m., but they had still not seen a line-up three hours later. Finally at 9 p.m. Shepherd was brought to the viewing room. 'Joseph Shepherd,' read the supervising officer, 'you have been asked here today to see if you can identify the person you saw on 22 April 1993 at Well Hall Road in Eltham . . .' Shepherd listened and said: 'Yeah.' Then he moved slowly up and down the row of windows, looking at the ten seated figures. Jamie Acourt was in position number two. After a short while Shepherd was asked if he had seen a man he recognized from the attack and he said simply: 'No.' Moments later Duwayne was brought in and the same procedure was followed. He too said: 'No.' After this, the two witnesses waited another hour while frantic efforts were made to find enough stooges for Neil's parade and to persuade the existing stooges, who were growing impatient, to remain. At about 10 p.m. those efforts were abandoned. 'Neil Acourt parade aborted due to lateness of hour and insufficient participants,' the record states. So ended a frustrating day for the police. At midnight all three boys were freed on police bail until mid-July, to return as required for identification parades.

The arrest of David Norris did little to ease the frustration. On Monday morning he presented himself at Southwark station in company with his mother and Henry Milner in person, and to no one's surprise he answered 'no comment' throughout his interview. He too was freed on bail, with instructions to return for identification parades which were being prepared for Thursday.

On Saturday 8 May, the day after the arrests, the Lawrence case finally spilled over into violent protest. The occasion was a march, organized by a group called Youth Against Racism In Europe, which had originally been planned for central London but was switched to the Woolwich area after the murder. The route ran from Woolwich to the BNP building in Welling; several thousand people took part and there was a large police presence. As the marchers approached their destination the police, intending to prevent them from getting close to the building, blocked off the road and tried to divert them. Some of the marchers, believing that police promises had been broken and that they were caught in a bottleneck, became angry and trouble began. Sticks, stones and punches were thrown, a BMW car was overturned and a number of shop windows were smashed. In the mêlée nineteen police officers and demonstrators were injured, some shops were looted and several arrests were made. It was very far from being another Brixton '81, which some senior police officers had feared, but it was ugly enough.

The Welling riot had an important part in a two-page spread that appeared two days later in the *Daily Mail*, under the headline: 'How race militants hijacked a tragedy'. The report began with a short account of the murder and spoke of the Lawrence family's devastation on learning the news of Stephen's death. It continued:

> Even then the first moves were being made behind the scenes to sweep the 18-year-old's death into a whirlwind of high-profile publicity – organised largely by anti-racist groups who would later bring in Nelson Mandela on the short path towards the making of a cause. Yesterday, as police continued to search for Stephen's murderers, senior officers accused outsiders of using the murder to further political motives – and warned that their involvement could seriously hamper attempts to bring the killers to justice. In the words of one of them, Stephen's death had been hijacked.

Who were these outsiders? The *Mail* article mentioned the Anti-Nazi League, the Greenwich Commission for Racial Equality, Gacara and the ARA. Such groups, it said, were right to be outraged by a killing of this kind, but questions were being asked about their motives. These questions were apparently coming from the police, who the *Mail* said had been 'locked in a behind-the-scenes dispute with anti-racist organisations involved in the case'. One officer was quoted at some length:

At the beginning we were very close to the family and had a good rapport. But later we had to go through several representatives before we could speak to them. We often only knew about the family's concerns after they had appeared on the television. We believe that the family are being used as pawns in a far wider game. Our inquiries are, in fact, being hampered by these people.

The *Daily Mail* is and was a conservative paper with no great interest in crimes against black people and a long track record as a defender and supporter of the police, so no one can have been very surprised when it took this line. The identity of the quoted officer was not revealed, and although Weeden's notes suggest that he spoke to the *Mail,* so apparently did at least two other officers, so the source remains opaque. Whoever it was, he undoubtedly voiced the opinion of many of the detectives on the case, who resented the involvement of the A R A and Imran Khan. The message was simple: if there are problems with the Lawrence case it is not the fault of the police but of politically motivated black radicals.

Neville and Doreen had also been shocked by the events in Welling and were scarcely less outraged than the *Daily Mail* at the activities of some of the black groups. They gave an interview to the paper in which Neville condemned Panther UK and the ANL and stressed that the family wanted no violence. 'When the Panther UK people came to me I was really frightened of them. We told them to back off. We do not want to know; this is a private thing. They came to the door unsolicited, saying they wanted to offer help. Next thing, they had our names on their leaflets. We feel we are being used.' He also said: 'We have got no control over those groups who try to use us for their political purposes. I wish we did, because we do not want Stephen's name associated with the violence we saw on Saturday ... We are going to send them legal letters this week asking them again to refrain from using our names.' Such letters were duly written to a variety of organizations.

What was not apparent to readers of the *Mail* interview was the great difference of view that existed between the police and the Lawrences. Not for one moment did the family accept, as the unnamed officer had suggested, that outsiders were hindering the police investigation. Nor did they believe that the A R A and Imran Khan were obstacles to communication with the police – the letters to black groups were actually written by Khan on their behalf, while the ARA was not one of the groups to receive them. Palma Black, Marc Wadsworth and others from the ARA continued to visit the Lawrence home and occasionally to speak for the family in public. While the Lawrences were keen to distance themselves from the Welling riot and from those they saw as hot-headed and radical, they still believed that the police alone bore responsibility for the slow pace of inquiries and for treating them in a high-handed fashion.

The *Mail* interview set another ball rolling, for while he was speaking to the reporter Neville mentioned that he knew a journalist on the paper, somebody senior who was another former client of his. The reporter recognized this as the paper's editor, Paul Dacre, and he promptly rang Dacre's office and got the two men speaking to each other. Dacre, for his part, remembered Neville well; he had liked him, as most people do. The editor's interest in the case sharpened just a little.

The second round of identification parades, on 13 May, brought the breakthrough that the police had been looking for. The additional time for preparation made it possible to put all four suspects on parade before a good number of witnesses, although it proved a long day. Henry Milner was acting for Norris, and as the day wore on he took over the handling of the two Acourt boys as well. His efforts to ensure fairness for his clients proved exhaustive, with a great deal of picking and choosing among stooges, which once again caused delays as others had to be sought. He also wanted to take photographs of his clients, and of whole line-ups, and this led to some dispute with the police, who felt he was pushing proper concern for fairness to its limits. When Milner attempted to make a video recording of both line-up and witnesses a bitter argument erupted which later resulted in formal complaints being made on both sides. Despite all this, between 10 a.m. and 7.15 p.m. ten parades were held. First, Gary Dobson was seen, but not picked out, by Duwayne Brooks and Royston Westbrook -- they both picked out the same stooge. Then it was Neil Acourt's turn. He sat at number nine, and Duwayne identified him. 'It's him,' he said firmly. Westbrook, however, did not recognize Neil. One of the witnesses to the Bhangal stabbing saw Dobson and Neil without picking out either. Then

Duwayne saw Norris without result. By now it was early evening and Westbrook had gone home. He was nursing a terminally ill friend, which was why he had been unavailable the previous Friday, and he felt he could spare no more time that day, so he did not see the Norris line-up. Two other people, however, did: Staccy Benefield and Mattie Farman picked out Norris without difficulty as the youth who had stabbed Stacey back in March. At 7.15 p.m., with all parties exhausted, the parades were brought to a close.

The day had produced substantial progress. Following Duwayne Brooks's identification, Neil Acourt was charged that night with the murder of Stephen Lawrence. Neil and David Norris were also charged with the attempted murder of Stacey Benefield. And it did not end there, for the police were also hoping to reopen the Darren Witham case from the previous year – this was the stabbing incident on Chislehurst High Street involving Norris and Jamie. Darren himself had identified Norris as one of his assailants during the original investigation, but later that week Norris appeared again in an identification parade for Darren's brother Terrence, and was picked out. On the basis of this additional evidence, Weeden's team began to press the Crown Prosecution Service, which had earlier discontinued the case, to consider charging Norris again. Twenty-four days after the murder of Stephen Lawrence, it seemed that justice was beginning to catch up on his attackers. And there was still some unfinished business for the identification suites – Westbrook had yet to see Norris and Jamie, which he did without result towards the end of May, while Joey Shepherd had not viewed Neil Acourt, Norris or Dobson. Shepherd was still regarded, on the basis of his statement, as the most promising identification witness, with the clearest memory for faces, but a problem had arisen.

Joey appeared willingly at the first set of identification parades on the evening of the arrests, but something happened there which changed his attitude. When he was called to view the parade that included Jamie, the officer in charge addressed him formally by name. Joey believed that these words were said within earshot of the line-up, or at least of the suspect's solicitor, and he was alarmed by this. By the following week he had become so concerned that he declined to attend the parades at which the other suspects appeared, and he never again took part in the identification process. His family complained about his name being read out, although the police later insisted that this was normal and that no unauthorized person would have heard it. Joey, for his part, came to insist that he 'only had a brief glimpse' of the attack and did not remember enough to be of any help to the investigation. If the true reason for his sudden reluctance to help was a fear that he had been identified by the killers and was now in danger, he may have had more than one reason to be afraid. His girlfriend lived in Eltham and worked in a shop near the estates – he had been visiting her on the night of the murder. A few days after the murder a young man whom she did not know called into the shop and asked her in a manner she found aggressive and frightening what she knew about the Lawrence case. She reported this to Joey, who told the police. Her visitor was never identified, but it is clear that at the time Joey saw this as a possible act of intimidation. He always subsequently denied, however, that he had been frightened off. Whatever had happened, the police had lost the cooperation of a very important witness.

Meanwhile, the investigation continued. On the one hand, detectives were pursuing witnesses and potential witnesses, and on the other they were examining further possible suspects besides the four who had been arrested. On the eve of the arrests 'OJ' Davidson had been on the point of making contact with a boy who might have seen the attack from the top of a bus. It was 12 May before he finally spoke to Witness B and the result, once again, was acutely disappointing. Despite having told a number of people that he had seen the murder from the top of a bus, when confronted by the police B described something completely different: a fight 500 yards away outside the Welcome Inn. The police knew that there had been no such fight, so why was he making something up? By repute – even his mother said this – the young man was something of a fantasist, so it was possible that he was simply trying to draw attention to himself. And yet the incident he described bore some resemblance to the attack on Stephen Lawrence, and it included the stabbing of a black boy. On the evidence of Grant and one other informant, moreover, it seemed that B might have some knowledge of Stephen's wounds. Detectives returned to question him several times, and DS Kirk-patrick took him to Well Hall Road in an attempt to straighten out the location of the events he was describing, but still he talked of the Welcome Inn. Davidson, meanwhile, was asking around about the boy, and Mattie Farman told him that B had changed his story 'because he doesn't want to be involved'. Whatever the explanation, B at this stage was useless as a witness and on 19 May Davidson filed a result in the Holmes system: B, he wrote,

> is undoubtedly a Walter Mitty. I saw him twice, once with DC Canavan and a second time with DC Hughes, and because of other info I then asked DS Kirkpatrick to see him. He tells a story of a fight he saw. The circumstances are such that he only thinks he saw this. He told people that he saw the murder but completely gets the venue wrong. No statement taken.

Davidson and other detectives were also working on K, trying to persuade him to tell the whole story of what he had seen on 102 Bournbrook Road just before midnight on 22 April. Here was another example of a young man who said one thing when questioned by detectives and, it seemed, quite another thing to his friends. Again and again local people had recounted to police the story that the Acourts, Dobson and Norris were seen at the house in a state of panic soon after the murder, some or all of them with wet hair, some or all with their tops off, as if desperately trying to wash away the evidence of bloodshed. It was repeated in one form or another by informants both known and anonymous and it had been repeated by the white woman who called at the door of the Lawrence home a week after the murder. Some variants of the story even said that the boys were seen with one or more bloodstained knives and that they had admitted responsibility for the killing. The original source for all this was undoubtedly K, yet he, like Dobson, refused to implicate Dave Norris in his story and he was extremely vague on the subject of wet hair and tops that had been removed. The Fishpool team discussed him many times and they were certain that he knew a great deal more than he was saying. Again, a number of detectives met him in the effort to win his confidence, but although he was relaxed enough to talk about street life and events on the estates, he would not elaborate on his own story. As the police persisted he became nervous, on one occasion rushing out of a back door as soon as he heard the knock on the front. On 17 May, however, Davidson persuaded him to make a statement. This is what it said:

I am a single man and live with my mother at the address shown overleaf. I have lived in this area all my life, that is the Eltham area. I know a family on the estate called the Acourts, Neil and Jamie. I have known [them] a few years and they hang about in a group with Gary Dobson and Danny Caetano. Recently they have also got a mate called David Norris. On Thursday 22nd April 1993 I was with my friends the Tylers when I was told that there had been a stabbing up Well Hall. I went up to Well Hall and saw a lot of police around. I went down to 102 Bournbrook Road, the Acourts' home address, and by that time it must have been about 2330. I went there because I thought it must have been them. Jamie, Neil and Gary Dobson came to the door and I said, 'Someone's been killed, stabbed up Well Hall.' And they said, 'It weren't us.' One of them had his T-shirt off.

As a piece of evidence this statement had very little value. It placed Jamie, Neil and Dobson in the same house about an hour after the attack, but Dobson's new story about going round there to borrow a CD late at night was consistent with this. Although K was now prepared to link Norris with the Acourts he still did not place him in the house after the murder, and as for the T-shirt observation, it was hopelessly vague. There was no mention at all of wet hair, panic or knives, and there was an explicit denial of involvement from one of the boys. Even if K could be persuaded to repeat all this during a future trial of Neil or any of the others, which was very much in doubt, it would be as likely to assist the defence as the prosecution.

The frustration at this impasse increased when a youth in the Tyler circle was arrested in mid-July for an offence unconnected with the Lawrence case. Once in custody he announced that he had something to say about the murder and D S Bevan was summoned from the Fishpool incident room to take a statement. The boy said that he had been at the Tyler house late on the evening of the murder, with about a dozen others, when K arrived. This was K's second visit and he said he had news of the stabbing. The youth went on:

[K] then said that he had gone to the Acourts' address on the Brook estate and he asked them if they had done anything that night. He said they were acting paranoid and all had their tops off. He said that at their address he saw Neil and Jamie Acourt and David Norris. I think there was one other that he mentioned, but I cannot remember.

As far as I can remember he said that they had come from the kitchen and that all of them had no tops on, which he thought unusual. When [K] asked them if they had done anything that night one of them answered, 'Why do you think it was us?' . . . [K] then said to them that he thought that the person had died (he didn't say how he knew that). He said that they all looked pale and were quiet. As far as I can remember, [K] said something about them washing clothes although I'm afraid I cannot be more specific. [K] then left the Acourts' address . . . I think he may have had the door slammed in his face.

Once again, this was not usable evidence; it was hearsay. But if K himself could have been persuaded to repeat all of this in a statement (assuming it was true) it would have been a powerful weapon in the hands of the prosecution. He would do no such thing.

EE and his girlfriend Emma Cook were no more forthcoming. Hopes that, now that she was seventeen years old, Emma would be prepared to speak to police without having her parents present proved to be unfounded; although she was visited several times, she continued to insist that she had seen no one she recognized as she walked past the bus stop and along the side of the roundabout on the night of the murder. With EE, another person said by local gossip to know something of importance, the story was the same: repeated visits seemed to make him less, rather than more, cooperative. Detectives were marching up a series of dead ends. The Tylers, also revisited, had nothing to add. A story that came in, that a local girl had seen the boys both before and after the killing and they had changed clothes in between, proved on examination to be untrue. Yet the police were still certain that there were people on the estates who knew enough to convict some or all of the prime suspects, but who were not ready to help. Why?

Could this have been a case of local solidarity? This was, after all, a close-knit community with a larger than average criminal presence, in which cooperating with the police, particularly over the murder of a black youth, was scarcely part of the culture. Yet everything suggested the reverse was the case in this instance, for many local people – albeit not eyewitnesses – had come forward to help the investigation. The contribution of women, both on their doorsteps and on the telephone, had been especially important, and there was no doubting the strong revulsion felt about the murder

143

and about the Benefield stabbing. These young men were hated by many in their community. They were also feared, and it was surely fear that was blocking the path to the evidence. Again and again rumours and second-hand reports came into the incident room of people being threatened – K, the Tylers, the Casserleys, EE – just as there were persistent rumours of the suspects, usually Norris, bragging that they had killed Stephen Lawrence. Police still believed that Norris was indeed the most likely stabber of the group and was probably the most feared of the boys. K refused to say that Norris was at 102 Bournbrook on the night, and Gary Dobson was even ready to make himself look a fool by claiming he did not know Norris. Although from 13 May onwards Norris and Neil Acourt were both off the streets and in custody, their power to intimidate seemed undiminished. The likely explanation for this was to emerge in time, through the story of Stacey Benefield.

The process of tracing and eliminating other youths who might have been involved absorbed rather less energy in this period than the pursuit of key figures – the Acourts, Norris and Dobson. Now that one of the prime suspects had been identified and charged with the Lawrence murder, it probably seemed safe to assume that no other, distinct group of youths were involved. And yet there were loose ends. One of these concerned the red Astra car which had been seen twice by the police on Well Hall Road, very soon after the murder. It drove down and later up the road with a number of young men inside who were laughing and jeering at what they saw. The Astra was not stopped on the night but a partial registration number was taken and by chance, a week later, an officer spotted the car again, stopped it and took the details of those inside. When they were questioned by detectives a remarkable fact emerged: two of the youths who were in the vehicle on the night Stephen Lawrence was murdered, Daniel Copley and Jason Goatley, had been convicted in connection with the killing of Rolan Adams two years earlier, albeit of relatively minor offences. A third, Kieran Hyland, was a leading light in a gang with racist tendencies, known as the Nutty or Nazi Turnout. All three were based in the Thamesmead area, a couple of miles away, where the Adams murder took place. When they were interviewed their story was that they had been drinking that evening at the Wildfowler public house in Thamesmead – a pub well known to police as a haunt of racists and extreme right-wingers – and at about 10.30 p.m. had left to take Goatley's girlfriend home to Eltham. They denied laughing at the police, whom they passed on the way to the girl's house and on the way back. Although there were contradictions between the accounts they gave, and although the presence of such people at the scene of a racist murder just minutes after it had taken place amounted at the very least to a surprising coincidence, the matter was not pursued.

Another group who were investigated were the youths seen around the kebab shop and the cinema shortly before the murder, who may well have been responsible for the commotion witnessed or heard by Emma Cook. They had been seen throwing their weight around that night by cinema staff, one of whom bumped into some of them the following evening at a Harvester restaurant, where one member of the group was said to have stolen a steak knife. They were all eventually traced and interviewed. On the night of the murder, they said, six of them, five boys and one girl aged between sixteen and eighteen, had been drinking at the Park Tavern off Eltham High Street, which they left at or just after 10 p.m. They walked down to the kebab shop, where they knew the staff and where one of them liked to play the fruit machine. After half an hour of eating and chatting there, they left for home, heading not north past the scene of the murder, but west. Most of them had eaten at the restaurant the following night, but they all denied stealing a knife.

It was while police were investigating a third group, the known associates of the Acourts and Norris, that they added a fifth name to their list of prime suspects. Several boys had been identified by informants as members of the gang or hangers-on, and two of the most frequently named, Danny Caetano and Charlie Martin, had been eliminated from inquiries because they were in custody at the time of the Lawrence stabbing for a separate knife attack. This was a horrific crime, of which both boys, with others, were subsequently convicted. They had been spending the Easter weekend of 8–9 April at a caravan park near the Medway estuary in Kent and during the Saturday evening they came into conflict with another group of men. After midnight Charlie Martin and his friends found one of these men, David Spurdle, alone and they accused him of staring at them during the evening. When he denied it they attacked him with knives, inflicting terrible injuries before someone appeared and they ran off.

At the trial a surgeon who treated Spurdle said he had never seen such wounds and there were suggestions that an attempt had been made to skin Spurdle alive. Caetano and Martin were arrested within forty-eight hours of the attack, and so it was certain that they could not have been in Eltham on the night of 22 April.

Other associates were identified, some of them names from the list given to Chief Superintendent Ilsley by Doreen Lawrence. There were two cousins of the Acourts and two other friends, but detectives could see no strong reason to link them to the murder. But one name that kept coming up was Luke Knight. It was Pat Acourt, mother of Neil and Jamie, who first mentioned him when she was answering questions from the house-to-house officers. On the night of the murder, she had said, her sons had been visited by a friend called Luke who lived in Well Hall Road. D C Chase also came across the name of Luke Knight in the papers of the Witham case: he was with Jamie and Norris when that stabbing occurred. Luke Knight was one of those named by Emma Cook as an associate of the gang, and his name appeared in lists of friends of the Acourts in a 1991 diary that had been kept by, and seized from, Gary Dobson. All this might have been enough to arouse curiosity, but there was still no information or evidence to connect Luke to the murder. On the contrary, house-to-house officers had twice questioned him and on each occasion both he and his parents had insisted he spent the evening of the murder at home. But in the last few days of May Luke became the subject of particularly close attention, and that was thanks to Michelle Casserley.

Of all the young people who came into contact with the police in Operation Fishpool, few demonstrated more clearly than Michelle the lattice of relationships that existed within the estates. She was a cousin to Stacey Benefield; she had been the girlfriend both of Gary Dobson and of Jamie Acourt (who once punched her in the face); her best friend was Jane Tyler and her sister Tara was the mother of David Tyler's child. Also in her circle were Lisa, the girl who saw Emma Cook on the night of the murder, and Kelly-Ann, one of the two girls who heard the voices of the attackers that night as they fled down Dickson Road. Michelle, moreover, was in the fifth year at Eltham Hill School, where one of her closer friends was a girl called Katie, and Katie's boyfriend Kevin London was the black youth said to have been threatened by Gary Dobson. Of all these connections, this last was the one that led detectives back to Michelle. As they followed up the story about Dobson's threat to London they took a statement from Katie, and she repeated the tale police had heard before about a conversation at school in which Michelle said she knew who had murdered Stephen Lawrence – directly or indirectly, Michelle had picked up K's story at the Tyler house on the night of the killing or the next day. But Katie added some striking new information to this tale of gossip in the science class. First, she said that Michelle had named 'Luke' as one of the perpetrators, and second she reported that Michelle had shown her her diary and that Michelle had listed in it the names of all the boys who were in the attacking group. This diary would clearly be an interesting document.

Detectives traced and interviewed the other girls said by Katie to have been present when the school conversation took place. Though they gave varying accounts, the core of the story was roughly consistent: Michelle had identified several boys as the culprits, had voiced strong disapproval of them and had indicated that she was frightened or had been threatened. Police then acquired a search warrant, visited the house where Michelle was staying and confiscated a *Just Seventeen* diary. It was a small affair, allowing a page for each week, and in it Michelle recorded the broad facts of her social life – where she went, whom she saw and where she spent the night (mostly at the Tyler house with Jane). The entry for 22 April contained a four-line note of no interest to police, but at the foot of the page, jotted down in an awkwardly shaped white space and linked to the 22 by a long line and an arrow, was the entry Katie had spoken of. It said: 'Acourts stabbed black boy up Well Hall Rd. Jamie, Neil, Gary, David and Lukey.' When she was questioned about this Michelle said that she had merely written down what everybody on the estates was assuming: these boys must be responsible 'because they go round stabbing people'. The entry, she thought, had been written on Tuesday 27 April, when she had updated the diary. As for the classroom conversation, she had never told anybody she knew who the killers were because she did not know, and when she was asked about a story that she had spoken to Gary Dobson about the murder on the telephone she confirmed it – she had asked him if he had done it, she said, and he had replied that he had not.

The diary was not evidence and could not be used in a prosecution; it was pure hearsay. But it stirred a much stronger police interest in

Luke Knight, and he was investigated. The son of a market trader and a cousin of Danny Caetano, he had attended Kidbrooke School with Jamie Acourt. He remained there after Jamie's expulsion and had just left school for the last time a few weeks before the murder. His address was particularly interesting: Emma Cook had mentioned that Luke lived in Well Hall Road near the cinema, but this did not do justice to the location. The Knight home turned out to be directly opposite the Coronet, near the southeast side of the roundabout. This was close to the point where Duwayne Brooks said the attackers were when he first caught sight of them. Luke had no criminal record, although just a week before the Lawrence murder he had come to the attention of police as a result of a dispute involving his mother and another woman. The other woman had alleged to police that Luke struck her, but Mrs Knight insisted that her son had merely intervened in an argument to protect her. Luke was questioned and released with a warning that charges might follow (the matter was formally dropped in June). From what was being said about Luke he sounded like a follower in the Acourt group rather than a leader; perhaps, the police thought, he would prove to be the weak link they so desperately needed.

At 7.05 a.m. on 3 June, Detective Sergeant Davidson knocked at the door of 252 Well Hall Road, Luke Knight's home. Luke was in, as were his parents. Davidson informed the boy that he was under arrest. 'We have information that you were involved, with others' in the murder of Stephen Lawrence, he said. Interviewed later in the morning at Plumstead station, Luke answered questions freely but without admitting anything. He continued to insist that he had been in his bedroom all evening on 22 April, playing Nintendo and then in bed, indeed he said he had been at home all day, as were his mother, father and younger sister. When it was suggested that his sister probably went to school he accepted that. His mother was present during the interview as the 'appropriate adult', and she confirmed that she was sure Luke had spent the evening in, although she admitted she had gone to bed early and had not actually seen him. Both she and Luke said it would have been impossible for him to leave the house without his parents hearing. The front door, Luke insisted, was stiff and noisy. Of the murder, Luke knew nothing and he had deliberately not listened to gossip because he did not want to become involved. Yes, he knew Neil and Jamie Acourt well, but they were no longer in contact – 'I used to go about with them like, I dunno about three, four months ago, but I stopped really going about with them.' He also knew Gary Dobson, although less well, and there was a boy he knew as 'Dave': 'I don't know his second name.' So far as he was aware they didn't carry or own knives, had never stabbed anyone and were not involved in the Lawrence murder. When it was put to him that people on the estates were saying he was one of the killers, he replied: 'Well it's a lie.'

If the interview was another dead end, however, the identification parade was not. Luke was taken that afternoon to the Southwark identification suite and placed in a line-up. This time there was no shortage of stooges and when Luke, his solicitor and his mother took exception to some of them, others were on hand to take their place. In a very short time, Luke acknowledged that he had no further objections and took his place in a line of ten seated males. Behind glass through which the men in the line could not see, Inspector McIlgrew once again explained the procedure to Duwayne Brooks. 'I will ask you in a moment to walk along the line at least twice, taking as much care and time as you wish. I want to make it clear to you that the person you saw may or may not be here and if you can't make a positive identification you should say so. Please indicate the person by calling out his number. Do you understand?' 'Yes,' came the reply. The time was 3.55 p.m. Duwayne walked slowly along the line of four windows. He stopped at the third window, moved on to the fourth, back to the third and then to the second. Then he spoke: 'Number eight.' The person sitting at position number eight was Luke Knight.

Neil Acourt and now Luke Knight: both picked out by Duwayne Brooks and by no one else. A great deal depended on young Duwayne.

Chapter Nine Duwayne

After the murder Duwayne Brooks entered a sort of hell. Stephen had been not only his best friend but a rock-like presence in his sometimes unsteady life, and Duwayne could hardly have lost him in more traumatic circumstances. Should he have stood and faced the murderers at Stephen's side? Was it cowardly or disloyal of him to run? And when Stephen was bleeding to death, did he panic? Did he make a mess of the 999 call? Was his lack of coherence the reason why the ambulance took so long? Could he, should he have done anything to help Stephen? Other questions were even more unsettling: would this have happened if Stephen had been out with someone else? Was he the cause of their being late that night, the reason for their being in Eltham? Would another friend have stood by Stephen? Anyone would have asked themselves such questions, and Duwayne was not well equipped to answer them. He knew, for one, that the Lawrences were angry that Stephen had been with him on the night of the murder. He had been too distraught to communicate with them at the hospital and his mother's visit to their home early the following morning had not been a success. Nor was his own visit. Invited to Llanover Road by Neville and Doreen, who wanted to hear what he had to say and what he could tell them about the murder, he once again sat in silence, unable to speak. The Lawrences did not press him and eventually he left.

He was feeling not only guilt but fear. He was, he knew, the key witness, and Eltham, where the killers doubtless lived, was just over the hill. There were people there who knew him, just as there were some who had known Stephen, and it was soon common knowledge at Blackheath Bluecoat School that Stephen had been with Duwayne Brooks when he died. Rumour reached him that white boys had been asking for his address and it did not take much imagination to see that killers who had stabbed Stephen for no reason might very well be prepared to kill him to ensure his silence. In the mind of a young man already terrified by his own narrow escape from death such thoughts became at times overwhelming. Others were concerned for his safety, too: the police logged worried messages about him from Doreen Lawrence and from a Greenwich Council officer.

One of the liaison officers assigned to the Lawrences, Detective Sergeant Bevan, was also given the task of maintaining contact with Duwayne and he offered the young man some form of protection, but it seems the offer was rejected.

Duwayne spent some of this time at his mother's home but most of it at his hostel, a halfway house before being allocated a housing association flat of his own. There were six young men there, each with his own bedsit, and Duwayne passed the days in his room alone playing Nintendo. The police were often in touch and on the whole he enjoyed a better relationship with them than the Lawrences did, although there were one or two experiences he found worrying. When he gave his statement at Plumstead on the night of the murder, for example, he was asked to surrender his trainers so that a foot print could be taken. He thought: 'What do you want them for? I haven't committed any burglaries.' And later Bevan asked him to supply a photograph of himself. He could not understand and nor could Bevan explain, why such a photograph was necessary and he became suspicious and frightened, so he refused. By and large, however, he got on well with Bevan, who visited him fairly frequently to check that he was all right and to seek further help with the investigation. Had he seen Emma Cook walk past the bus stop? Could he identify this hat? More than once they went over the events of the night again in the hope that further details would come up, but Duwayne could add very little.

And Bevan was not the only one asking questions. It was presumably at the suggestion of the Lawrences, who were concerned for his well-being and still eager to hear what he had to say, that Duwayne made contact with Imran Khan. On Sunday 2 May – ten days after the murder and five days before the first arrests – Khan visited Duwayne at the hostel, bringing with him Ahmed Ratip, an assistant solicitor from his firm. Ratip took notes of the conversation, which was largely devoted to reconstructing the events on Well Hall Road. As he had in his main statement to police, Duwayne explained to Khan how he had met Stephen after school, spent time in Lewisham and at the Lindo house and then set off for home. He gave the numbers of buses and the approximate times and he described the attack in terms very similar to those he had used in his statement. It is clear that Khan was using the visit to gather information about the crime, the sort of information which the Lawrences were desperate to know and which by this time they believed the police were withholding from them. But Ratip's notes contain two items which were not mere repetitions of Duwayne's earlier statement. One passage concerned the attacking group: 'First time I saw the boys was when we got off the bus and walked across the roundabout. They were just looking. I didn't think anything of it.' Duwayne was saying here that he had seen the attackers at about 10.25 p.m., before he and Stephen had even reached the bus stop. This implied that they were out in the open somewhere near the roundabout fully fifteen minutes before the stabbing, and if this was true then many people should have seen them, including anybody leaving the cinema who turned north, and perhaps those hanging around at the kebab shop. It also raises further questions about what Emma Cook did or did not see. For some reason, however, the police were not aware that Duwayne was saying this and they were operating on the premise that the attackers first appeared in the open just moments before they struck.

The other matter of interest in Ratip's notes was not to acquire significance until much later. Early in the discussion, Imran Khan asked Duwayne if he wanted to be interviewed for a *Newsnight* item then being prepared and Duwayne replied that he was worried about being identified afterwards. Then came the following: 'There were other people at the bus stop – police said one of them said he saw the fight with Stephen and other 6 boys. I've seen his statement.' It appears, but is not explicit, that these were Duwayne's words, and they are consistent with Khan's desire to find out as much as possible about the crime and the investigation. The witness who 'saw the fight' is either Joey Shepherd or Royston Westbrook. The words 'I've seen his statement', apparently underlined by Ratip, are surprising, because it is not usual for one witness who may take part in identification parades to read the statement of another, particularly if that statement contains descriptions of offenders, as Shepherd's and Westbrook's did. The effect, as would be pointed out in court three years later, is to bring into question any subsequent identifi-cations.

Khan gave Duwayne some advice. He was always entitled, the solicitor pointed out, to have someone present when he was spoken to by police, even if the police did not make this clear. Khan did not volunteer for this role himself, but suggested that Duwayne might have a friend who would do this for him. And they talked about identification parades. The notes say: 'Advised as to rights. That when people caught they will be put on ID parade – and you will have to look at them – you have to be careful – there will be pressure on you but if you choose the wrong person . . . suspect will be released.'

The following Friday Duwayne found himself in just that position for the first time. By now he was sliding into an acutely distressed state and his friends were noting changes in his behaviour. Feelings of fear and alienation had been heightened by the reports of a racist gang in Eltham, by the delay in making arrests and in particular by the rumour that he himself might be regarded by police as a suspect. The stress of attending the identification parades only made things worse. The first of these took place at Southwark on the evening of the first arrests, when he saw but did not pick out Jamie Acourt. Because of the haggling over stooges the proceedings were very slow, and he was bored and anxious. Twice he rang Imran Khan to report progress. The same problem dogged the parades on 13 May, when Duwayne saw but did not recognize Gary Dobson and David Norris, but successfully picked out Neil Acourt. On this day several witnesses – Duwayne, Royston Westbrook, Stacey Benefield, Mattie Farman and a woman who had seen the Bhangal stabbing – were kept together in one waiting room for up to nine hours. The delay made Duwayne nervous and at one stage he rang someone he described as his solicitor. Afterwards he came back into the room and began to ask the others for their names and addresses, an inquiry they did not welcome. But Duwayne talked to the two white boys, who, he said later, told him stories of other identification parades.

The third round at Southwark was short and sweet by comparison. He was the only witness, since Westbrook was again out of touch and Shepherd refused to attend, and Luke Knight was the only suspect. It took Duwayne less than a minute to decide that he recognized number eight, and that should have been that. But it was not. In fact the events which followed the parade proved to be among the most important to occur in the whole of the Stephen Lawrence case besides the killing itself. Duwayne had been brought from home to Southwark by Detective Sergeant Christopher Crowley, who sat with him in the waiting room and would also take him home. It is one of the rules of the parade procedure that no officer attached to the investigation of the crime should be involved in the identifications, so Crowley was not a member of the Fishpool team but was responding to a request for an officer at Plumstead station who had a couple of hours to spare. What took place between Crowley and Duwayne Brooks after the identification parade has been the subject of dispute between the two men ever since and can best be described by giving the two accounts separately.

Crowley, who made a written statement later that day, told it as follows. After the parade he saw the supervising officer, who told him to take a short formal statement from the witness recording the fact that he had picked out the person in position number eight. This he did. When it was done, according to Crowley, Duwayne began to talk. First he asked whether he had picked out the right person, observing that if it was the wrong person he would be released. Then he said that he had been told the Acourt brothers were responsible for the murder and he believed that the two men he had identified in parades were brothers. Once he had started talking, the words flowed out. Duwayne spoke frankly and at some length about his involvement in the case, saying that he did not see the faces of Stephen's attackers, only their physical build and hair, but that a friend had tipped him off that he should recognize the Acourt brothers because they had attended the same school as he had. And Duwayne said that on the first occasion when he picked someone out, he had known whom to choose because that person was dressed differently from the others in the line-up, wearing tracksuit bottoms, and gave the appearance of having spent time in a police cell. Before this parade, moreover, he had been told by friends of the physical characteristics of the Acourts, so that he would be able to recognize them.

Crowley's statement added:

> From the general conversation with Duwayne Brooks he admitted he was totally anti-police and that on the night of the murder of Stephen Lawrence he only called the ambulance service and had no intention of calling the police, his intention being to seek revenge in his own way for the stabbing of his friend.

After listening to this, Crowley wrote, he drove Duwayne to Rotherhithe police station, where they had stopped off earlier in the day and where Duwayne had left something. While they were there, Crowley contacted the Fishpool incident room and told them what had happened, asking the officer there to tell the senior investigating officer. Then he took Duwayne home and drove to Eltham station, where he spoke to Weeden and wrote his statement.

The following day Duwayne was interviewed about the encounter and he gave a statement. By this account, Crowley spoke to the supervising officer immediately after the parade and then returned to the waiting room saying: 'Do you think you picked the right person?'

'Yes, I have,' replied Duwayne.

'Well, them next door seem to think you have.'

Duwayne then told Crowley that he had heard that the Acourt brothers were responsible for the murder and that the person he had just picked out was either the brother of the person he had identified two weeks earlier or the same person. He then went on to talk about the murder and said that although he had only previously been able to describe the attackers' hair and general appearances, at the parade he had recognized them both from those characteristics and from their faces, which he remembered on seeing them. He had not been coached by friends about what the Acourts looked like, but he had described to them the first man he had picked out and they had said he was probably one of the Acourts. As for picking out somebody on the basis of their clothing, Duwayne did tell Crowley such a story but it came not from his own experience but from one of the other witnesses he had spoken to at a previous parade. Finally, Duwayne said that he did say to Crowley that he was anti-police and wanted revenge, and that he had deliberately not called the police on the night of the murder.

Much of what was said in these two accounts was complementary, or could be reconciled without difficulty. There was a conversation about whether Duwayne had picked out the suspect and Duwayne, who was aware of rumours about the Acourts, speculated about whether the two youths he had picked out in separate parades were brothers or even the same man. He acknowledged that he had recognized them in spite of the fact that he had previously been able to describe only hair and general appearance – something which was evident to anybody who had read his previous statement. And he admitted being anti-police. None of this was in dispute between the two men, and none of it was particularly damaging in itself to Duwayne's standing as an identification witness. Other differences could be readily put down to misunderstanding: the suggestion in Crowley's account that Duwayne would know the Acourts because he had been to school with them could be discounted because it was wrong, while the story about the tracksuit bottoms was not only explained plausibly by Duwayne but was scarcely credible anyway – neither the police nor the suspects or solicitors involved in the previous line-ups would have allowed such a thing to happen. What was damaging, however, was the notion that Duwayne had admitted being coached by friends about the appearance of the Acourts in advance of parades. This single point, asserted by Crowley and denied by Duwayne, was the nub of the dispute. And equally damaging was the overall effect of Crowley's words, which might be challenged in court and placed in a more benign context, but which would inevitably sow doubts in the minds of a jury about Duwayne's reliability.

By the beginning of June, when these events occurred, the official initiative in the Lawrence case was passing from the Metropolitan Police and its detectives to the lawyers of the Crown Prosecution Service (CPS). This was the body whose job was to review the evidence, decide whether the case was strong enough to take to trial and, if it was, to ensure it was presented to best advantage before the court. In fact, when word first reached him that Duwayne Brooks had identified Luke Knight, Brian Weeden was in a meeting with CPS officials, briefing them on the evidence gathered to date. He was able to tell them that a second suspect had been picked out, but he did not hear until later about the complications with Crowley. At the meeting, Weeden asked the lawyers whether he should charge Knight straight away and was advised to wait until Westbrook, and if possible Shepherd, had had a chance to identify him at further parades.

Weeden, with his twenty-nine years' experience in the police, was aware in these discussions that the case against Neil Acourt was not particularly strong, for besides Duwayne Brooks's identification there was very little evidence. None of the hearsay information that had found its way to the incident room was admissible in court, and neither were the anonymous letters or the entry in Michelle Casserley's diary. None of the other suspects had said anything at interview to implicate Neil, and neither had any of the potential witnesses such as K and Emma Cook. Forensic examinations on clothes seized from 102 Bournbrook Road had not shown anything useful, although the tests were still incomplete, and it was clear that none of the knives taken from the house was the murder weapon. On that front, however, there was a small ray of hope, for the pathologist had stated his view that the knife found in Wendover Road, behind the Acourt home, was consistent with Stephen's wounds. Fingerprint tests were under way. As for Neil Acourt himself, he had given nothing away under questioning. His mother was not prepared to give a statement but on the basis of her comments to house-to-house officers three days after the murder, Neil did not have a strong alibi. Taken together, all this did not add up to much.

The key to this case, then, was identification, which in law is a more complex matter than many might suppose. If a man is suspected of robbing a woman in the street and she picks him out of an identification parade on the basis that she recognizes him as the robber, most people would accept that as conclusive proof of the man's guilt. Not so the courts, which have to reckon with human fallibility. All law students learn about the case of Adolf Beck, who was tried a century ago for a series of frauds. The case against Beck rested on identification – no fewer than fifteen people said that they recognized him as the fraudster – and he was convicted. This proved, however, to be a miscarriage of justice, for the true culprit was eventually found and it had to be accepted then that all fifteen witnesses had identified the wrong man. The case taught the lesson that identification evidence had to be approached with caution. This lesson, however, has never been learned by juries, who still tend to be easily convinced when they hear a witness say he recognizes the man in the dock as the guilty party. To remedy this, and to prevent further cases like Beck's, judges developed the practice of withholding such evidence from juries altogether if they felt the identifications were unsafe. Over the years since 1905 judges established principles for determining what was safe and what was unsafe, and the definitive statement of these was made in 1977 in a ruling given during a case called *R. v Turnbull*. The quality of an identification was good, the ruling laid down, when it was 'made after a long period of observation, or in satisfactory conditions by a relative, a neighbour, a close friend, a workmate and the like . . .' Quality was poor, by contrast, 'when it depends solely on a fleeting glance or on a longer observation made in difficult conditions'. In other words, the critical test is: did the witness get a good, clear look at the offender, in decent light and in reasonably stable circumstances? If not, his recollection is not likely to be reliable, and when that is the case the Turnbull guidelines leave no room for discretion: 'The judge should then withdraw the case from the jury and direct an acquittal, unless there is other evidence which goes to support the correctness of the identification.'

The file on the Lawrence case was dealt with during the second half of May by a middle-ranking lawyer at the CPS, Philip Medwynter, who quickly took the view that the identification of Neil Acourt by Duwayne Brooks ran a high risk of being judged poor quality. Duwayne saw the attackers at night as he ran from them, and any halfway competent defence barrister would argue with force that this was a classic case of a 'fleeting glance'. But equally, Medwynter could see that the police investigation was not complete. The results of some of the forensic tests were still awaited, possible witnesses were being seen and some identification parades remained to be held. So, as was usual in such circumstances, he kept the file open while the Fishpool team continued their work. The time available to the police, however, was limited, for Acourt had been charged and was being held at Feltham Young Offenders' Institution in west London. On the one hand, the legal process must run its course and sooner or later the case must come to committal, the first judicial test of the prosecution evidence. And on the other, a defendant could not be held in custody long if the evidence against him was weak.

The pressure was beginning to build two weeks later, when the CPS drew up its first internal assessment of the case. Matters had not moved forward. Luke Knight, having been identified by Duwayne Brooks, had still not been charged; the CPS still wanted further identification parades but the police were having difficulty organizing them. Nor had Joey Shepherd been persuaded to change his mind and attend a line-up for Neil Acourt. The Lawrence file was now in the hands of Medwynter's immediate superior at the CPS, Graham Grant-Whyte, and on 15 June he drafted a gloomy report. 'This is,' he wrote, 'a case fraught with difficulties.' Duwayne

Brooks's evidence was crucial, but as a witness he had become 'suspect', even 'tainted' as a result of the Crowley affair. As matters stood, Grant-Whyte believed that the evidence was 'not sufficient to ensure a realistic prospect of conviction of Neil Acourt, Luke Knight or any other person', and consequently he recommended that, unless the police came up with new evidence, the case should be discontinued.

Three weeks later, on 9 July, when the CPS next met the police, the position was still unchanged, except that Luke Knight had been charged, even though Westbrook had still not seen him and Shepherd was maintaining his refusal to attend parades. The police investigation was stalled: forensic scientists examining clothes, shoes and knives were drawing a blank and there were no new witnesses. Time, moreover, was running out, since committal proceedings against Acourt and Knight had been fixed for the beginning of August. The CPS team, now led by the Branch Crown Prosecutor, Howard Youngerwood, was blunt: unless Westbrook identified Knight in a line-up, or unless some forensic evidence emerged, the case would have to be discontinued. The deadline was the last week in July. Weeden was present and he did not dispute this conclusion, although he took a more positive view of Duwayne Brooks's credibility than the CPS – he believed that Crowley had simply misunderstood Duwayne's remarks. But the case as a whole, he conceded, would have very little chance in court. He explained to the lawyers that he wanted to make one further attempt to arrange a line-up involving Westbrook and that there would also be a new television appeal for witnesses on ITV's *Crime Monthly*. If those failed, he conceded, a discontinuance was inevitable. Weeden warned, however, that the effect of such a decision among the public, and particularly among south London's black population, would be 'dynamite'.

The Lawrence family, the black population and the wider British public were at this time completely unaware that the Lawrence prosecution had run into such difficulties, for it remained shrouded throughout in the dark blanket of legal silence. From the moment that Neil Acourt was charged on 13 May, all discussion of the case in the media ceased. Since the defendant was under eighteen he could not even be named, so all the public could be told was that a seventeen-year-old youth had been charged with the murder. Single paragraphs to that effect appeared in the press on 14 May, tucked into the columns of brief news items, and on 24 June, after Knight was charged, when they referred to a second boy, aged sixteen. Further reporting on the case was not permitted. The Lawrences knew a little more, since they were aware that Duwayne had picked out two boys and that their names were Neil Acourt and Luke Knight, but they had no idea of the weakness of the case and no idea that Duwayne's identifications constituted the only evidence. So far as they were concerned there would be a trial and probably convictions, and one or two of their son's killers would go to jail. This was less than satisfactory to them, since it meant that at least two of the attacking group would get away scot free, but it was something.

There was some relief for the family during these weeks, because Stephen could finally be buried. His body had remained in Greenwich mortuary throughout the period leading to the arrests and when Neil Acourt was charged his defence had ordered a second post mortem. After that the family asked if they could have the body but were told they must wait as the arrest of Luke Knight raised the possibility of a third post mortem. Amid the delays in charging Knight the coroner, Sir Montague Levine, eventually lost patience and ordered the body to be released. A few days later, on Friday 18 June, a cortège of some 600 mourners walked behind the coffin from Llanover Road through the streets of Plumstead to the funeral service. Shops on the route drew down their shutters and people stood in silence as they passed. At Trinity Methodist Church a congregation including the MPs Diane Abbott, Paul Boateng and Peter Bottomley heard the Reverend David Cruise declare that 'many of us feel ashamed to be white'. Stephen, he said, was a popular boy, full of enthusiasm and charm, and those who knew him would always picture him with a smile on his face. He was conscious of, and confident in, his blackness, but he was incapable of aggression. He saw the best in everyone, and this may have been his undoing; it may have been the reason why he did not run from his attackers. 'On that night in April this country witnessed one of the worst forms of human evil,' Cruise said from the pulpit. 'Racial hatred is in our midst and we ignore it at our peril.' At the end of the service the congregation, many of them weeping, filed past the coffin. Later,

Neville Lawrence issued a statement whose final words were more prophetic than he could have known:

> We are finally able to put Stephen to rest. We, however, will not rest until all of Stephen's murderers are caught, convicted and punished appropriately. We will also continue to demand the closure of the BNP headquarters in Welling and call for a public inquiry into the number of racial attacks in the area. The racists must be told that the burial of Stephen is not the burial of our campaign for justice. It is only the beginning.

Stephen Lawrence was not buried in London but in Jamaica. Doreen and Neville had reached this decision, so rich in symbolism, after some anxious deliberation. Had he been buried in England it would have been in a cemetery in Charlton very near the home of his friend Elvin Oduro. Since this was a place Stephen had known well this might be appropriate, but it also had drawbacks. For one, the Lawrences feared that the grave might become the target of vandalism and this was a thought that they could not bear. They were also feeling bitter towards Britain and Neville in particular was contemplating a return to the country of his birth. A further consideration was the possibility that if there were more arrests there might be more requests for post mortems, and the family could not contemplate the notion of exhumation. If Stephen was in Jamaica that would be impossible. It so happened that Doreen owned, with an aunt, a plot of land in Clarendon, west of Kingston, which contained the grave of the grandmother who had brought her up in her early years. It was a quiet, shady spot where Stephen could rest in peace. So the decision was taken. The family flew out to Jamaica at the end of the month and Stephen was buried on 4 July with the British High Commissioner among the congregation. The Lawrences, with Stuart and Georgina, had decided to take a break and stay on for a month, relaxing and seeing relatives. The worst of their ordeal was over, they believed, and this was a time to mourn Stephen among friends and to start coming to terms with a life without him. For Neville and Doreen, who had been dealing with their loss in different ways over the previous two months, it was a chance to be together. More and more, Neville was attracted by the idea of settling in Jamaica and he began discussing this with his somewhat sceptical wife. They had no idea at all of what was happening more than 4,000 miles away in London.

The second half of July saw all hopes of additional evidence against Neil Acourt and Luke Knight evaporate. Westbrook was once again available to view identification parades but Knight's solicitors, perhaps sensing the police difficulties, had withdrawn cooperation and said that for the moment their client would not take part. Meanwhile the results of the remaining forensic examinations came in, and all were negative. With committal proceedings due to begin on 3 August, the CPS had already instructed a barrister to conduct the case and it seems that the last straw fell when he saw the papers and offered his opinion. So far as he could judge, he told Medwynter in a telephone conversation, the police had got the right boys, but on the evidence available there was 'not a cat in hell's chance' of convicting them. There was now no time left, and on 28 July formal notices went out to the relevant parties announcing that the case was being discontinued; there would be no committal and no trial. Weeden had spoken of dynamite; when this became public the following day the explosion came.

It was as if the murder had happened all over again. All the anger and frustration about racial killings, about police shortcomings and about the criminal justice system, which had been held back since mid-May in the hope that the killers would be convicted, now burst forth. Black groups denounced the CPS, with the ARA declaring that there was 'something rotten' at the heart of the service when it came to dealing with racial violence. Paul Boateng and Peter Bottomley demanded a meeting with the Attorney General, although Bottomley also called for calm. Newspaper editorials denounced the CPS, declaring that the Lawrence case conformed to a pattern of excessive caution in its decisions. In the effort to maintain a high conviction rate, it was said, the CPS was dropping far too many cases which had a chance of success. This formed part of a wider debate about the service, which was relatively new and had had rather more than its share of teething troubles – everybody but the criminals themselves was complaining about it in 1993, and its record on race cases in particular had recently been criticized by a House of Commons select committee.

The CPS responded to all this by insisting that its decision, however unwelcome, was in full accordance with its publicly stated criteria for assessing criminal cases. A case had to have a better-than-even chance of success in the courts before prosecution could be authorized, and it also had to be in the public interest to pursue it. The cases against Acourt and Knight, said the CPS spokesmen, simply did not pass the first test. But they stressed that this was not the end of the road for the Lawrence case; the door had not been closed. The police investigation was still under way and if it uncovered more evidence then the file would be reviewed and a new prosecution might be authorized. Moreover, they pointed out that if the case had been allowed to go to trial on the basis of the present evidence and if, as they believed likely, it had ended in acquittals, those defendants would thereafter have been immune from further action. All this did very little to calm the anger. On behalf of the police, Chief Superintendent Philpott issued a statement: 'I am disappointed. This is certainly not the end of our efforts. They will be redoubled and we still hope to bring Stephen's killers to justice.'

Neville and Doreen Lawrence were still in Jamaica when they received the telephone call. They were appalled and furious, and the main focus of their anger, significantly, was not the CPS but the police. In London later that day Imran Khan and Cheryl Sloley gave a press conference on their behalf. 'It is quite unbelievable that the police have been unable to secure the evidence required to bring these youths to trial after three months,' said Khan. 'What we need now is a full explanation from the police as to what kind of investigation they carried out.' Cheryl Sloley was more bitter: 'We were constantly told by the police to trust them and that they were doing all they could. It obviously wasn't enough. As Nelson Mandela told us, black lives are cheap.'

The events of that early summer in southeast London, from the murder to the discontinuance of the prosecution, provide the foundation of the case of Stephen Lawrence. Years would pass before it became a true *cause célèbre*, the stuff of newspaper front pages and television documentaries, but in the end everything would hinge on what happened and what did not happen, what was done and not done, in the ninety-eight days that followed 22 April 1993. Although both the police and the Lawrences tried to, they could never escape the consequences of those days. The 'first investigation', as it came to be called, was the best chance to solve the crime, punish the killers and reassure those who doubted the will of white Britain to deal with racism. Was that chance wasted? If so, why? The questions remained in the air, prompting speculation, suspicion and worse. A great deal had to happen before the answers were given.

Part Two Calvary

Chapter Ten A Sense of Betrayal

Any family would be shaken to the core by the violent death of a son, but for the Lawrence family the murder of Stephen was an especially acute shock. Neville and Doreen learned of the death in the most dreadful circumstances – the late-night knock on the door, the frantic search of the streets and the helpless, uncomprehending wait in hospital. That it was a murder, that Stephen took so long to die, that it was racially motivated, that the killers escaped and might be living only a mile or so away, all this could only compound their grief. What followed – the breakdown of relations with the police and the shattering blow of the CPS decision – heaped woe upon woe. But there was another sense in which Stephen's death fell unusually heavily on his parents: it destroyed their view of the world. As a couple and as individuals they had, like everyone else, their own way of seeing life, work, religion, society and family, and their own understanding of how they fitted in. To an extraordinary degree the murder of their beloved eldest child challenged and shattered these views, which had been shaped over many years.

They had been married on 4 November 1972, at Lewisham Register Office in south London: Neville Lawrence, a jobbing tailor living in nearby Brockley, and Doreen Graham, known to friends and family as Joy, a bank clerk whose home was in Greenwich, to the east. They made, as the saying goes, a lovely couple, for he was tall, slim, broad-shouldered and handsome while she was petite without being doll-like, and beautiful. Some in the bride's family, however, disapproved of the match, and her mother did not attend. There was a considerable age difference – Neville was thirty and Doreen just twenty – and there may have been a feeling that she should have waited. But the couple themselves were very happy and they settled together in Neville's home in Aspinall Road, alongside one of the surface railway lines that criss-cross that part of south London.

It had been through the bride's mother that they had met. Neville made his living doing piecework tailoring at home, collecting the materials from a local company and returning the finished garments. It is a tough business but he was at the top end of the market and doing well; clothes that he sewed were sold in fashionable West End shops. Doreen's mother was a dressmaker, and sometimes on his trips Neville would collect and deliver cloth for her as well. Early in 1970 he went to an open-air concert in company with Doreen and some friends and they fell in love. Despite the disparity in age (and height), they had important things in common. They were, for example, both eldest children, of the kind who learned to take on responsibility at an early age, and perhaps as a result they both took a serious view of life, sharing a strong work ethic and believing in self-reliance and self-improvement. Also, they had both been born in Jamaica.

Neville was from Kingston; his father was a leather tanner in a factory and his mother ran the cafeteria in the offices of the *Daily Gleaner* newspaper. As is common in Jamaica it was not his parents who took charge of his upbringing, and his early years were spent mainly in the care of an aunt. She moved to London when he was about ten years old but Neville stayed, finished school and took an apprenticeship with an upholsterer, embarking for England only when he had learned his trade. That was in 1960, the peak year for West Indian immigration to Britain, when the total touched 50,000. Like so many others, Neville had high expectations. 'From what I read and heard it was the Mother Country and the streets were paved with gold,' Neville recalled much later. 'It was completely different to what I expected. It was not as advanced. Maybe some people won't agree, but it was not as advanced as Jamaica.' Settling first in Kentish Town, in north London, he found that he could not get work in his chosen trade and to make ends meet he took an unskilled factory job. Determined to do better, he enrolled for night-classes in tool-making. It was a three-year City & Guilds course and he duly passed, but again he was unable to find employment to match the qualification. Eventually he took a job with a friend who had a leather goods factory, and there he remained for some years.

Neville's difficulties in finding the sort of job he was qualified to do were related to his race. He recalled: 'Just after I came here I went to the job centre ... The morning when I was supposed to start work, the people who had offered this job realized I was black and then all of a sudden the job disappeared ...' The same thing happened after he passed his City & Guilds exam: 'When it came to getting a job, all the other white students got places in factories but I did not. I had wasted three years of training.' It was the time of the colour bar, a form of apartheid that was not blessed by law but was not discouraged or prevented by it either. It was common and perfectly legal, for example, for pubs and clubs to display notices banning black people. Many companies openly operated 'last in, first out' employment policies, which in this context meant they hired black workers only as a last resort and fired them first if there was any downturn in business. Private landlords, too, frequently put signs in the windows stating, 'No blacks. No Irish.' In the street and workplace racism was commonplace; a man could call you a 'coon' and there was no redress. Neville recalls: 'I thought to myself that this was not my country, so I had to put up with certain things.' He got on with his life, settled and established a network of close friends – almost all of them black. He had expected to stay only five years, but he was putting down roots.

In the meantime Doreen had arrived in Britain. She was born in Clarendon, west of Kingston, in 1952; her parents split up when she was an infant and she spent her early years with her maternal grandmother. When she was nine her mother, who had remarried and settled in southeast London, asked her to come to England. Her first impressions were even less auspicious than Neville's: 'When I arrived in London I found it very frightening. The houses were close together and smoke would come out of the chimneys and all was generally dark and gloomy.' She attended primary school and then the Christopher Marlowe all-girls secondary school in New Cross, next to Lewisham. She does not remember experiencing racial hostility from white girls or teachers there, although she made no close white friends.

By now her mother had three children from her second marriage and young Doreen was sharing the burden of looking after them. Perhaps it was because of this responsibility at home that, although she was bright, she did not do as well at school as she might have. Still, she finished with respectable enough qualifications and then had to think of a career. 'I remember clearly when it was time to leave school,' she recalled later. 'I didn't go into further education because in those days, where black children were concerned, you weren't really encouraged at school . . . I think I told them I wanted to go into banking or something like that and the teacher said, no, you must go and do something with your hands, like working in a factory.' She was certain that this was not for her. 'I went on then and looked for my own job. I just applied for things through the papers. I had quite a few interviews, all in banking, and I went to NatWest Bank. You did the normal entrance tests and I passed that. About three of us from school went and worked at the same bank.'

After their marriage, Doreen and Neville continued to get on with their lives in the same businesslike fashion. They were not active in community relations or black politics and by a mixture of care and good fortune they did not encounter much in the way of racism. While Doreen continued her job at the bank, Neville gave up his tailoring work and switched to painting and decorating, which he had dabbled in as a youth in Jamaica. Seeing plasterers at work he soon realized that they were better paid, so he learned their trade – the third he had mastered. From then on, with the odd interval when work was scarce, he remained a decorator and plasterer. Meanwhile Doreen and he had formed a company with some friends, each putting up £1,000, and bought a small, run-down house with a shop below and a flat above. This they renovated, letting the shop and living for a time in the flat. Soon they sold up and moved on, taking a flat in Whitworth Road, Plumstead, and that was where they lived when their first child was born.

Neville was present for the birth, albeit reluctantly. The baby arrived on the day he was due, 13 September 1974, at 9.30 p.m., at Greenwich District Hospital. And the new arrival was just what both parents wanted, a healthy boy, given the names Stephen Adrian (Adrian was Neville's father's name). Doreen resigned from the bank to look after him and the task proved to be the usual mixture of joy and anxiety. A good-natured baby who slept at night, young Stephen was none the less capable of bouts of temper and tears which could drive his mother near to distraction. As a toddler he was inquisitive. 'He learned very quickly,' Doreen recalled later. 'He was the type of child that, whatever you taught him, he always wanted to go one further.' From the earliest days he loved to paint and draw and as soon as he could he was making birthday cards, Christmas cards and Mother's Day cards.

Soon there was another son, Stuart, and five years later a little girl, Georgina. Needing a bigger home, the Lawrences bought a former council house with a garden just around the corner in Llanover Road. It stood on the edge of the Nightingale estate, a grim place dominated by a tall tower block, but the Lawrence home was one of the nicer properties in the area – Neville had helped to build it –

and they were happy there. The family next door, who were white, had children of roughly the same age, so a friendly, sometimes noisy neighbourliness developed. The nursery and primary schools which the children attended were just around the corner.

Even when Stephen was a small boy his parents – as parents will – saw themselves in their firstborn. They knew what it was like to be the oldest and they saw Stephen in the same role. Stuart, two years younger, suffered from eczema and asthma and had to spend spells in hospital with his parents going backwards and forwards to see him. Stephen played the grown-up, showing concern for his brother and insisting on going along on the hospital visits when possible. With Georgina, seven years his junior, he proved proud and possessive, and pictures of the three children together show him cuddling her while attempting to elbow Stuart out of the frame. He also displayed some of the determination that marked his parents' approach to life. For his sixth birthday, he decided some time in advance, he wanted a watch. Doreen recalls: 'I said, "Only if you can tell the time," and he said, "When I am six I will be able to tell the time." And of course he got his watch.'

Stephen thrived at primary school, and when any difficulty arose Doreen was quick to respond. Once, she was called by Stephen's head teacher to be told that he had been getting into fights with a classmate, a white boy who had previously been a friend. She questioned Stephen when he came home, to be told that the boy had been calling him racist names. The following day she went to the school and told the head what she had learned, saying that in the circumstances her son was justified in sticking up for himself. That was the end of it. Doreen herself was back at work, although only part-time. Neville was working very hard: in the mid-1980s the building industry was thriving so he would often leave home at 6 a.m. and not return until after 9 p.m. They were comfortable, with their own house and car, but Doreen was not the kind to take it easy at home. She did a variety of things at first – working in a bookshop, office cleaning, care assistant – until she settled into a job at Stephen's primary school helping children with special needs.

At eleven, Stephen started at Blackheath Bluecoat School, selected by his parents because they thought it a hard-working establishment, and again he did well. He was no genius, but he could cope with the work and was popular. Doreen and Neville continued to push and encourage him, never missing a school parents' night, driving him around the country to attend athletics meetings, checking that homework was done. When Doreen thought he was not getting enough attention from coaches at his sports club, she switched him to another. And when the school suggested that Stephen do some work experience, Neville promptly arranged an assignment with an architect he had met through his work. Besides the close attention of his father and mother, Stephen's wider background was also rock-solid, with a large extended family of uncles, aunts and cousins, and a close-knit church community. He had every advantage that his family could provide. Teenagers, however, are programmed to cause trouble and Stephen was no exception; there were occasional feuds with Stuart, with whom he shared a bedroom; despite an early enthusiasm Stephen eventually lost interest in going to church; and at school in later years Doreen felt he did not do as well as he could. This last, she thought, was largely the result of being too bright, rather than not bright enough: he seemed to cruise, getting by on his wits and his charm. She also thought that some of his friends might be leading him astray.

Although his parents never made an issue of being black, Stephen was conscious of his race. No amount of parental protection could conceal from him the stresses of black life in Britain in the 1980s; right on his doorstep, for example, the Nightingale estate had a long record of racist incidents. Stephen himself had been called names at primary school and he was once spat upon by a local boy as he cycled in the street. As he grew older his experience broadened and his opinions developed; at school he once complained, for example, that a disproportionate number of exclusions seemed to involve black boys. Much worse was happening in the districts around where he lived, where the British National Party was now active, and Stephen was aware of it. He knew Rolan Adams, the black fifteen-year-old who was chased and stabbed to death by white youths in Thamesmead. That affair became notorious not only because of its intrinsic viciousness – black families soon began moving out for their own safety – but because it raised issues of policing and justice. The BNP congratulated the white people of Thamesmead for 'defending their estate', while the police were reluctant to accept that the murder was racially motivated. In the end, only one of the attacking gang was convicted of murder.

Stephen was concerned about the case and wanted to become involved. Much later, Doreen described what happened: 'They were having a march or something and he wanted to be there. I was very worried for him because Thamesmead is an area you always hear about with racism connected to it; it is always happening down there. I remember saying, "I don't want you to go", because he would be a stranger to the area and if anything happened they would pick them up quite easily. He had a strong conviction where that was concerned – because it was his friend – and he told me no, and in fact he actually went.' He was sixteen at the time.

Doreen feared for her son. 'I used to talk to Stephen about the dangers of being out and the dangers of the police as well, because of stories that you hear that used to frighten me. The stories that you would hear would be about walking on the street on your own, with your friends or whatever, and the police would stop you and bundle you into the back of the van and beat up the kids.' She told Stephen to be careful: if he was walking he should face the oncoming traffic so as not to be taken by surprise, and if he was in a train he should sit in an open carriage where there were other people. The son's feelings, however, were different from the mother's, more assertive, perhaps reflecting the change between generations: 'Stephen's attitude to the police was always, "Well, if I'm not doing anything wrong how could they do that to me?" I used to say to him, "From what I am hearing you don't have to." I didn't trust the police.' Neither view was tested; Stephen had no brushes with the law.

The year of the Rolan Adams killing, 1991, saw Stephen decide on the future he wanted for himself. He had spoken for years of becoming an architect and his ambition was confirmed by the fortnight of work experience at the architects' firm of Timothy Associates, in offices just south of Tower Bridge. When both parents looked back on that period later it was with a glow of pride. 'We soon realized how gifted Stephen was,' said Neville, 'because at the end of two weeks Arthur Timothy told us that Stephen was so good at his work and so punctual that he had been allowed to stay in his office in charge. Normally, work experience students do not get paid and yet Arthur Timothy paid Stephen for the two weeks he was there and asked him to return to work for him once he had finished his training.' Doreen remembers: 'When Stephen came home he would talk about it a lot and show us the work that he had produced. I was very impressed with it, I remember, because I used to talk to my colleagues about it and I thought it looked very professional.' With architecture in mind, by 1993 Stephen was dividing his education between Blackheath Bluecoat, where he studied for a design technology A-level and prepared to re-sit his GCSE physics (he would need a better grade to get into university) and Woolwich College, where he was taking A-level English language and literature. It was a busy schedule, but he kept up.

On the eve of their calamity, then, the Lawrences were a family of distinctive character. Stephen was set on a path that, if all went well, would move him decisively up the professional and social ladder. Neville and Doreen had not had his opportunities – neither had stayed on at school and neither had had the career they felt they might have had – so he was in a position to fulfil their dreams as well as his own. Nowhere in Stephen's make-up was there the young black male so familiar in white stereotype: disaffected, lazy, loud and under-educated, from a broken home, casual in relationships, prone to crime and drug abuse, angry and aggressive towards the white establishment and the police. He was the opposite. The Lawrences, in fact, fitted a quite different stereotype: the model of the worthy, earnest, working-class family, God-fearing and law-abiding, who bettered themselves by hard work and advanced their children in life by strict, though loving, supervision and the best the state education system could give. These children, the model dictated, should rise from their surroundings to become the middle classes of tomorrow. But for Stephen it was not to be. The Lawrences saw their son's rise brutally halted at the age of eighteen.

Chapter Eleven **Adrift**

After the CPS decision Doreen and Neville Lawrence rushed back from Jamaica. They were afraid that, if they did not act while public outrage was at its height, the case would inexorably slide down the list of police and political priorities until it was simply forgotten. Imran Khan pressed their concerns urgently on several fronts. He wrote to the CPS and the Home Office seeking meetings to discuss what had gone wrong and what should be done next. He also made contact with Michael Mansfield QC, the radical barrister, and secured his promise of help. At the same time Peter Bottomley, the MP for Eltham, was raising the case in various corners of Whitehall and Westminster, and all parties were aware that some time in the coming months there would be an inquest at which the issues surrounding the murder would inevitably be aired. The family's view could be briefly stated: they believed that the police investigation had been bungled. They had little specific knowledge of the Fishpool team's work but they could draw on their own experience of the police and they felt this showed a suspicious or even hostile attitude towards black people and a general sluggishness about pursuing the white killers. They also remembered the information that had come to them about the murder, including names, and they now knew that these were at least similar to the names of some of the prime suspects. Why, they wondered, did the police not make arrests more promptly once they had these names? Surely the long delay had meant that the chance of finding forensic evidence on the attackers or their clothes was reduced? Surely, if there was a violent racist gang in Eltham, the police should have known about them already? And on the night of the killing, did the police make any effort to pursue the attackers down Dickson Road, or to search the area?

The Lawrences knew that it would not be easy to extract the answers to these questions and they knew that marches and press conferences would not be enough. Indeed by now they were thoroughly disillusioned with campaigning and with the various protest organizations with which they had contact. Their patience snapped not long after their return when a dispute broke out between two leading bodies, the Anti-Racist Alliance and the Anti-Nazi

League, over the site of a march planned for October – the ARA wanted to challenge the government in central London while the ANL wanted to confront the BNP in Welling. Neville and Doreen, who had been relying less and less on the ARA for assistance, and who felt that such organizations were trying to exploit Stephen's name for their own advantage, declared a plague on both houses and dissociated themselves from the march, whatever its route. They also now broke permanently with the ARA. By this time they had a settled circle of advisers, of whom Imran Khan was already established as the most important. Ros Howells, the race relations expert who made contact after the murder, was also becoming a trusted friend, while within the family Cheryl Sloley had emerged as their principal confidante. This group, supported increasingly over time by Michael Mansfield, defined the strategies that were pursued by the family, and they looked for solutions mainly in the law. As early as mid-August the possibility that the family might mount a private prosecution of the prime suspects was first raised in public. Such prosecutions were virtually unknown in murder cases and the idea was dismissed by most lawyers as hopeless, but as a last resort it had some attractions, chief of which was that the CPS and the police would come under pressure to assist the family by releasing evidence. Another legal possibility was to ask the High Court to review the CPS decision, which again might yield some information. Imran Khan also spoke publicly of suing the police for negligence, and he repeatedly demanded a public inquiry into the affair. These were all things that the various official bodies and individuals involved – the Home Office, the CPS, the Metropolitan Police, the Attorney General's office – were anxious to avoid, so the Lawrences were able to exert a little pressure.

The various meetings were none the less frustrating. At the CPS Khan and Cheryl Sloley met Gordon Etherington, the Chief Crown Prosecutor, and his emphasis on the weakness of the evidence served only to harden their suspicion that the police had been asleep on the job. Khan referred to the CPS's unfortunate reputation, especially in race matters, and said that the Lawrences might be reassured by an independent opinion. He proposed that a leading barrister of the family's choice (it would have been Mansfield) should look through the CPS papers on the case. This would have killed two birds with one stone, enabling Mansfield both to determine whether there were grounds for challenging the CPS decision in the courts and to decide whether there was enough evidence to justify a private prosecution. Etherington, however, consulted Barbara Mills, the Director of Public Prosecutions, and returned the answer that no such outside scrutiny could be allowed because it would impinge on the confidentiality of evidence and would set a precedent. Rebuffed on that front, Khan took a different request to a meeting with Peter Lloyd MP, the Minister of State at the Home Office. There he asked for a public inquiry into the police handling of the case, saying the family suspected incompetence or worse. To this Lloyd replied that he would need evidence, and when Khan explained in writing about the information passed on by the family which they believed had not been acted upon, Lloyd replied that this was not enough. The Lawrences appeared to be in a Catch-22: they could not have an inquiry without evidence, and they could not have evidence without an inquiry. Although they may have felt powerless, however, behind the scenes their activities were causing a good deal of disquiet.

The first response from the police in southeast London to the public outcry over the case was a show of industry. The Community Action Trust, the charity which funded the Crimestoppers organization, was persuaded to offer a £5,000 reward for further information on the case, and this was publicized in Eltham and Plumstead through a leafleting campaign supported by Greenwich Council. In addition there were fresh appeals through the local press for anyone with knowledge of the crime to come forward, and for the first time these were made specific. For example: did anyone see a youth that night wearing a jacket with a large 'V' on the back? At the same time, senior officers in 3 Area defended the investigation. Chief Superintendent Philpott told a local paper he found the suggestion of police failure 'insulting', and declared: 'I don't think more work could have been put into this investigation than has been.' Deputy Assistant Commissioner David Osland, the top officer in the area, also struck an indignant tone: 'Our investigation followed a normal pattern, covering every possible avenue of inquiry. Suggestions to the contrary are grossly offensive to my officers.' A similar message was passed up the line, in forceful tones. Osland wrote to Paul Condon, the Met Commissioner: 'Our patience is wearing thin on 3 Area, not only with the Lawrence family and their representatives, but also with self-appointed public and media commentators.' He complained, among other things, that while his senior officers frequently made themselves available for meetings with the family, the Lawrences were usually late or they cancelled at the last moment. As for their complaints about the investigation and about family liaison, Osland was firm: 'I am totally satisfied that the Lawrence family have received a professional, sensitive and sympathetic service from police.' Condon, however, was under pressure from elsewhere: Peter Lloyd from the Home Office, Herman Ouseley from the Commission for Racial Equality, Peter Bottomley and others had been in contact seeking reassurances about the case, and both Lloyd and Bottomley had passed on specific questions from the Lawrences. If he was to continue reassuring such people the Commissioner would need some reassurance of his own from 3 Area that there had not been a dreadful cock-up. This Osland was eager to provide, and so he took what was to prove an important decision: he commissioned a review of the Lawrence investigation by an officer from another part of the Metropolitan Police. A fresh pair of eyes would examine the conduct of the case and decide whether there was any substance to the Lawrences' complaints.

In principle, and for public consumption, this was a routine matter: police rules at the time required all murder inquiries to be reviewed if they remained unsolved after ten weeks, and the Lawrence case was some way past that time limit. In practice this requirement was honoured almost exclusively in the breach, since only one murder had ever been reviewed before in the history of the Metropolitan Police. Osland was breaking new ground with his initiative, but he was confident that it would produce evidence justifying his faith in his officers and would allow him to placate public critics and satisfy official concerns. His number two, Commander Hugh Blenkin, drew up the terms of reference while Bill Ilsley looked for a suitable officer to do the job. After a series of rebuffs elsewhere, Ilsley recruited Detective Chief Superintendent John Barker. Barker was ideal: a slim and youthful forty-six, he was regarded as one of the Met's high-flyers, having been Head of Major Crime in northwest London and commander of the Flying Squad before taking over a policy department at Scotland Yard. Unusually, he had joined the Met at a senior rank after serving well over twenty years in another force, Bedfordshire, and this underlined his 'new broom' credentials. He had some other commitments, so he could not concentrate exclusively on the review, and he lived out in the northern suburbs of London, a long way from Eltham, but these were regarded as minor drawbacks. Osland told him he wanted results by November, so Barker, assisted by two detectives and a Holmes system expert, quickly got to work.

In mid-September, meanwhile, Paul Condon wrote to Imran Khan declaring that he had taken 'a close personal interest' in the case from the outset and expressing his determination that everything should be done to bring the killers to justice. Referring to the many representations he had had about the case, he went on:

> I think you are already aware that a review of the entire inquiry is being carried out by a senior officer who has had no previous dealings with the case. This is in accordance with nationally agreed policy, and any suggestion that it implies lack of faith in the Senior Investigating Officer [Weeden] or the conduct of the inquiry is entirely misplaced. I would not wish to comment on specific aspects of the investigation in advance of the review being completed, and even then we must of course be careful not to prejudice any future proceedings. In general terms I would like to take this opportunity to refute the allegations that have been made that the Metropolitan Police view this case with anything other than the utmost seriousness. Any impartial view of events since 22nd April shows that this is simply not true. I fully understand the grief and despair of Mr and Mrs Lawrence, but I am disappointed that there are others who seem to have chosen to take a less than objective view of our commitment to this inquiry.

Concluding, he said that he did not think that anything would be gained by a meeting between himself and the Lawrences, which Khan had proposed, since Khan and Bottomley were already relaying to them what he had to say. This was a grim communication: not only did Condon decline to meet the Lawrences but he was adopting in large measure the tone and attitudes of the senior officers in 3 Area, stubbornly defending his subordinates and insinuating that unidentified 'others' were exploiting the case to discredit the police. As for his remarks about the Barker review, they were scarcely designed to give the impression that it would be either rigorous or open. It seemed as though a heavy door was closing in the Lawrences' faces.

*

Operation Fishpool, meanwhile, remained active, although here too this was a disheartening time, for detectives had been genuinely disappointed by the CPS decision and were offended by the fierce public criticism of their work that followed. Worse, out in the estates opinion appears to have hardened against the police and the reward and the leaflets produced no significant results. August and September were spent either chasing hares – more wild stories about sightings of the suspects on the night, and hearsay accounts of them confessing to the killing – or revisiting people who were less inclined than ever to cooperate. Emma Cook, still speaking only in the presence of her father, had nothing to add to her original story. Joey Shepherd wanted nothing to do with the police. The Casserleys had had enough. And Witness K, the man who had visited the Acourt house on the night, was as elusive as ever. One day in August when 'OJ' Davidson was trying to trace K, his stepfather rang to complain. Davidson's note ran:

> He said he was concerned that I was harassing [K] as it was all over the estate that he was wanted by me. I explained that I had to further interview him, but [his stepfather] requests that all future contact is made by appointment through his solicitor . . . He states that [K] is afraid and does not want to become involved in view of the fact that we couldn't keep the suspects locked up. He says that it is also about the estate that the Acourts are after [him].

In fact K was seen, and despite his fears he went a little farther than he had before, confirming that Dave Norris was at the Acourt house when he called that night and saying that Norris had his top off. But he would not put this in a statement.

As for EE and his family, they endured a grim autumn as both the police and, it seems, the Acourt group kept them under pressure. At least two of the boys were rumoured to have been threatened and their mother expressed concern to police about their safety. EE, her youngest, had been frightened of the Acourts before the murder; now he was terrified. Detectives visited again and again, asking EE to go over the events of the night of 22 April and to explain why it seemed he knew more than he was saying. Although his family appeared keen that he should help the police, the young man remained extremely reluctant, until one day in September when DC Mick

Tomlin and DC Martin Hughes called at the house for yet another chat. This time, for reasons that are not clear, EE had something to say. He repeated that he saw Emma Cook off at about 10.30 p.m. that evening and went inside afterwards with his friend Greg for half an hour. Then at about 11 p.m. he went out to see what was the cause of all the police activity and he spoke to two officers because he was concerned about Emma. While he was talking to them, EE now said, he saw both Acourt brothers and another boy walk into Well Hall Road from Downman Road and then make their way down to the roundabout.

This story was consistent with what his mother, Mrs DD, had told police less than forty-eight hours after the murder – that her son had seen the Acourts walking round the corner – but it was none the less baffling. Less than half an hour after the stabbing and just minutes after the ambulance had left, EE was saying, the Acourts and a friend entered Well Hall Road and walked past the scene of the crime in full view of at least two police officers and a youth with whom they had a dispute. It was not impossible, but even if it was true it did not seem to be sufficient reason for EE's apparent certainty that they were guilty, indeed a defence lawyer might well invoke it as evidence of innocence (would they have done such a thing if they had just committed the stabbing?). Moreover, it hardly tallied with those versions of the K story that suggested the Acourts and friends were at home half an hour or so later in a state of panic and changing their clothes. If their clothes had been stained with blood, would they have appeared in Well Hall Road? All in all it was information that had to be treated seriously, but the police had to reckon with the possibility that EE was saying it in the hope that it would finally get them off his back. And he was never prepared to put any of this in writing.

While EE, Emma Cook and K caused little but frustration and headaches, the fourth of the key potential witnesses provided an unexpected breakthrough. Witness B was the young man who was returning from Woolwich by bus at the time of the murder and alighted in Westhorne Avenue shortly afterwards. He bumped into, and spoke to, Witness K in the street that night and subsequent rumour suggested that he had seen the attack. When detectives traced him in the second half of May, however, he claimed that what he had seen was a fight by the Welcome Inn, about 500 yards from the scene of the Lawrence murder. Police were sure there was no such fight, but he stood by his story and was eventually written off by 'OJ' Davidson as a Walter Mitty character. After the discontinuance in July, B was questioned again on Weeden's orders and he repeated the same implausible answers to the point where officers became irritated with him. But when in October D C Mick Tomlin and D C Bob Crane heard a report that B was still privately claiming he had seen something important, they confronted him again. They spoke to him at length, and to his mother, and his attitude began to change. On 5 November he presented himself at Eltham station, saying he was ready to make a statement.

On the night of the murder, B now said, he visited his girlfriend in Woolwich and caught a 122 bus home at about 10.30 p.m. He went upstairs, where he found himself alone, and took a seat on the left about five rows from the front. The bus went down Well Hall Road and followed its route around the roundabout, past the entrance to the eastern side of Rochester Way and the southern part of Well Hall Road, before turning left and south into Westhorne Avenue. At the point where it leaves the roundabout the bus faces the western part of Rochester Way for a moment, and there B said he saw something. Four boys were running out of Cobbett Road by St Barnabas Church, heading west. One had already turned in to Rochester Way and B did not see his face, but he had a good side view of the next two. One of these, he said, was Dave Norris, while behind him was Neil Acourt. B did not take much notice of the last boy, he said, because he was wondering why Neil and Dave were running, and because the group was passing out of sight as the bus swung left into Westhorne Avenue. Soon afterwards he got off to walk to his house, meeting K on the way. K then told him there had been a stabbing and asked if he would like to go up and have a look, but he said he had to work the next morning and went home.

This was evidence of the highest importance. B insisted that he knew Norris and Neil Acourt personally, so the identifications were likely to be reliable, and the scene he described was of compelling interest. Cobbett Road, from which the boys were said to have emerged, led out of the Progress estate. At its other end it met Dickson Road just at the point where Stephen Lawrence's fleeing attackers would have had to choose which direction to take. It was at that very junction that several witnesses heard shouting and running around the time of the killing. This information, in other words, was consistent with an account of events that ran as follows: the killers, four, five or six in number, escaped down Dickson Road and by the time they reached the first crossroads they were shouting to each other, possibly celebrating, possibly arguing about what had happened, and possibly throwing out ideas about what to do next. Four youths then turned left and ran down the short length of Cobbett Road, emerging into Rochester Way and heading westward. And B said two of them were Dave Norris and Neil Acourt.

The story raised a number of awkward questions. Why would the attackers have run out into Rochester Way, a relatively busy road where they might be seen? If it *was* the Acourt group who committed the murder, then the quickest way to their base at 102 Bournbrook Road was in the opposite direction, up through the shadows of Franklin Passage and then left, through quieter streets. Also, how did this appearance on Rochester Way fit in with the evidence of Mrs George, the woman who said she had heard running feet in Winchcomb Gardens, followed by the words 'Hurry up J!' or 'Hurry up Jamie!' All of these might be explained by panic – perhaps the attackers did not know what to do and zigzagged through the streets without thinking – but they remained complicating factors.

Another such factor was B's account of his encounter with Witness K. If he saw what he said he saw, then got off the bus at the next stop and bumped into K just two streets away, then it is impossible that K already knew there had been a stabbing. At most four or five minutes could have passed since the attack, and although K found out very quickly from Louise Kavanagh that someone had been stabbed, it was not so quick as that. B was certainly mistaken about what K said, and it is surely more likely that it was B who had something to report – he had just seen Norris and Acourt, mutual acquaintances, behaving very strangely.

More pressing than any of these difficulties was the familiar issue of credibility. A defence lawyer would be certain to cast doubt on B's ability to identify anyone from the top of a moving bus at night, and from the far side of the bus at that, but the lawyer would first make an even simpler point: B was a liar. He had a local reputation as a fantasist and an attention-seeker, and he had already spun one false tale to the police; was there any reason to believe him now? A second statement was taken, in which B explained that he had not previously told the truth because of 'fear for the safety of myself and my family'. A couple of days after the killing, he said, K had told him he had been threatened by Norris, and this frightened him. 'I knew it was wrong to lie, but because of what [K] had said about Norris and because of the reputation for violence the Acourts had, I lied because at the time I thought it was the best thing to do.'

B's change of heart was not the only development in the case. In early September the Fishpool incident room received an anonymous call giving information about a young Eltham man called Darren Davies, and the following day an unsigned letter arrived, conveying the same information but with more detail. At the time of the murder, the letter said, Davies worked in a shop called Coles Menswear in Oxford Street, and one day he claimed to colleagues there that on the night of the Lawrence killing his cousin came to his house and gave him a bloodstained knife to look after. The cousin was not named but the letter said that Davies often spoke of him and that he seemed to be a 'nutter'. This was an intriguing lead, and all the more so because the name of Darren Davies was already in the Holmes system: he was the owner of one of the cars that was photographed outside 102 Bournbrook Road in the week after the murder. Further investigation revealed, moreover, that his mother was the sister of Clifford Norris – in other words, the cousin in question was Dave Norris.

The Davies house, in one of Eltham's posher streets, was searched and a black-handled knife was removed from the garden shed (it was later judged unlikely to have been the murder weapon). Meanwhile detectives tried to confirm the story of Davies's claim about a knife. Coles Menswear had gone out of business but a number of employees were traced and when they were interviewed they corroborated, in general terms, the contents of the letter. Davies was apparently in the habit of bragging about the exploits of his violent cousin and three of his colleagues remembered him saying that this cousin had stabbed Stephen Lawrence and that he, Davies, had looked after a bloody knife. The date on which he said this could not be established exactly, but it had to have been within three weeks of the murder because the shop closed down for good on 10 May. In early December, once statements were in hand from the three colleagues, D C Tomlin confronted Davies. The young man admitted telling the staff at

Coles that his cousin David had stabbed Stephen Lawrence, but he insisted that the claim was based on guesswork and not on anything Norris had told him. He had heard a report of the murder on the television news and simply assumed that his cousin had done it. As for the story of the knife, he denied it outright: Dave Norris had not given him a bloodstained knife after the murder or at any other time.

By now police had seized another knife, this time from the home of Gaynor Cullen, the girlfriend of Gary Dobson. Dobson, the supposed weak link in the suspect group and the one who had talked most freely after his arrest, continued to intrigue the Fishpool team. His alibi in particular was in a curious state. He originally told house-to-house officers he was at home all night on 22 April and his mother confirmed this, but once he was in custody Gary announced that he had 'popped out' to the Acourt house at 11.45 p.m., for fifteen minutes. Asked by Davidson to explain why his mother had not mentioned this, Gary said she probably did not realize he had gone out. His father, when questioned, admitted that he too had not known about the late-night visit to the Acourts, and added: 'He's always popping in and out, but he usually tells us.' The matter did not end there. Gary's parents had visitors that night, a couple who shared an Indian takeaway and watched television with them, and these visitors went some way towards confirming Gary's story. Gary had been in a different room from them for most of the evening, they said, but they believed he was in the house until they left at 11.10 p.m.; he 'put his head round the door' several times and he came downstairs to say goodbye. It was an alibi, but it was not cast-iron; a prosecution lawyer would dwell on Gary's ability to 'pop out' unnoticed.

It was in September that the police received a tip-off about the Cullen household, where Gary Dobson spent a good deal of his time. They were told that Gaynor's mother, Beryl, had found a machete hidden under the mattress of her daughter's bed. Officers promptly visited the house with a warrant, but Gaynor saved them the trouble of searching: from a drawer in the hall she produced a battered-looking knife with a curved, eighteen-inch blade and a red plastic handle. Mother and daughter then explained how it came to be in their home. Some time in March, Gaynor said, Gary arrived at the house with the knife, saying he had found it on his way there. He gave it to her and she hid it under her mattress because she was worried that her mother would not like it being in the house. Soon afterwards Gaynor went into hospital for an operation and while she was away Beryl decided to decorate her daughter's bedroom. On moving the bed, she discovered the knife. When Gaynor returned she explained its provenance and they put it away in the kitchen. There it lay until July, when the Cullens, with a little help from Gary, were clearing up their garden and they used it to cut back a privet hedge. After that, Gaynor put it away in the drawer of the telephone table in the hall. Gary, she insisted, had never spoken of the knife since the day he gave it to her. It was all perfectly innocent, provided that the knife really had been in the house since March, as both mother and daughter insisted. What did Gary have to say? His account of the red-handled knife would be a matter for a later day.

Besides Darren Davies, the Cullens and Witness B, one other person occupied a great deal of police time during the latter months of 1993: Duwayne Brooks. Much later it would be said that after the murder Duwayne became caught up in 'a sequence of truly extraordinary events'; the encounter with DS Crowley after the Luke Knight identification parade was perhaps the first of these, but others followed in short order as Duwayne, at the heart of the case, found himself under pressure from all sides. After the Crowley affair he was subjected to very close police scrutiny. John Bevan and later Mick Tomlin visited him several times to go over what he knew and they even took him out to Well Hall to walk the ground again. Tomlin, a bull-necked, bald-headed Mussolini lookalike, seems to have adopted in this period the role previously played by 'OJ' Davidson, who left the team during the autumn. Just as Davidson was involved in almost all the main lines of inquiry, so Tomlin now chased up many of the best leads. When it came to Duwayne, he reached a straightforward conclusion that was shared by Bevan: this was a good, honest witness who had provided a full and very valuable statement at the outset, to which he could add very little. One thing Duwayne did add in this later period was something he had mentioned in his conversation with Imran Khan back in May, that he thought he may have seen the attackers on the other side of the road just after Stephen and he got off the 286 bus. Although he could not be certain this was not another group of boys, this detail was recorded in an additional statement.

Duwayne's emotional state remained parlous. He was frightened, angry about the Crowley affair and still oppressed by natural guilt and anxiety over his friend's death. Necessary or not, the police questioning made matters worse. He felt, as the Lawrences had felt, that despite all his efforts to help he and his friends were being investigated and his word was doubted. As his frustration grew, his relationship with Bevan deteriorated. He was receiving some help from Greenwich Council, which arranged for him to see a counsellor, but it was not enough. During this time he had two particularly disturbing experiences. One day in September he was on a bus passing through Greenwich towards Woolwich when the traffic came to a halt. He was sitting upstairs and he heard the sound of car horns, so he got to his feet to see what was causing the obstruction. A car was trying to turn right. As he watched, his attention was caught by a group of white boys standing on the pavement outside a Starburger restaurant. Among them were two with short, black hair who looked very alike, as if they were brothers or even twins. One of them he recognized as a boy he had picked out of an identification parade and the other, he was sure, had also been a member of the group that attacked Stephen. Seeing them, as he subsequently explained, had jogged his memory. Moments later the traffic cleared and the bus moved off, with Duwayne still on board feeling frightened.

The second incident was more dramatic. By November a television company was researching a programme on the Lawrence case for ITV and a journalist called Heenan Bhatti was in contact with Duwayne. On the evening of 6 November they went out together to the Plough pub in Lewisham. Bhatti bought a couple of pints of Guinness and they decided to play pool. They had played a few games of doubles against other drinkers when two youths, one with black hair and the other fair, walked in and sat at the bar. Duwayne recognized the dark youth as one of the boys he had seen outside the Starburger, one of the two who appeared to be brothers and were, he thought, among Stephen's killers. As he watched, they put their money down on the pool table for a game. Duwayne said quietly to Bhatti: 'You know who that is, don't you?'

'Who?'

'Who do you think it is?'

'I don't know, tell me. Go on, go on,' said Bhatti, intrigued.

'He was one of those who was there at the murder of my friend.'

'You're joking. Really?'

'Yeah,' said Duwayne, adding sarcastically: 'Can I beat him up then?'

By Duwayne's later account, Bhatti then suggested: 'No, no. Let's play pool with them, so I can speak to them.'

The four young men played pool and Bhatti exchanged a few words with the dark-haired youth. When the game was over Duwayne, now feeling very uncomfortable, wanted to leave, so he and Bhatti went outside and discussed what had happened. Bhatti was keen to talk to the dark boy a little more and suggested that Duwayne should go home, but Duwayne said he was going nowhere on his own. At this moment Duwayne saw a friend of his and all three of them went back into the pub, where Bhatti once again spoke to the dark-haired youth, asking him his name. He looked at Duwayne and then at the floor before answering that he was called Keith. Duwayne thought this was a lie, because he believed he had earlier heard the youth addressed by another name. Soon afterwards Duwayne and Bhatti left.

A few weeks later, in early December, Duwayne mentioned these two incidents to Detective Sergeant Bevan, who was extremely interested and took a long statement. Asked about the dark youth in the pub, Duwayne said he believed this was the larger of the two boys he had seen outside the Starburger, and that he was not the one whom he had picked out of an identification parade. The implication seemed to be clear. Duwayne had previously identified two youths: Neil Acourt and Luke Knight. Of these two, Neil had a brother who resembled him in some respects but was taller: Jamie. Duwayne had seen Jamie in a line-up on 7 May and failed to pick him out, but now, it seemed, he might have recognized him and come face to face with him in the pub. Although the police made a determined attempt to trace the dark-haired youth, interviewing as many patrons and staff of the Plough pub as they could find, it was fruitless. Time would tell whether these sightings were important.

In the closing months of 1993 Duwayne found he had something far more worrying to contend with, for early in October he was arrested and charged for alleged involvement in a riot. The riot in question was at the Welling demonstration of 8 May, a march on the BNP office. This was just a fortnight after Stephen's murder and it was the day after Duwayne attended his first identification parade. The police treated the trouble very seriously and mounted an investigation, entitled Operation Fewston, to identify those responsible. They had some video and still photography evidence of their own but they also took legal steps to seize pictures and film from newspapers and television companies which covered the march. None of this was needed to establish that Duwayne was present during the trouble, for an officer who had met Duwayne at the Southwark identification suite recognized him in Welling and reported this to the Fewston team. In late June, with the photographic and film evidence in hand, the officer was asked to view it and see if Duwayne was one of those pictured breaking the law. For some reason the officer did not do so until late September. In the meantime, in July, another officer who knew Duwayne identified him from the pictures. How far these showed Duwayne taking part in violence would be disputed, but he was certainly very close to it and at one period he held a piece of wood in his hand. After the second identification Duwayne was charged with two serious offences: criminal damage to motor vehicles and violent disorder.

Duwayne needed a solicitor and he turned not to Imran Khan but to Jane Deighton, a campaigning lawyer who had been involved in the Rolan Adams case and had acted with considerable success in a number of race cases referred to her by Gacara. She soon began to prepare a defence for Duwayne founded on the argument that he was suffering from post traumatic stress disorder and in consequence was not responsible for his actions. Duwayne was obviously disturbed and over the summer there had been a number of incidents that caused concern to his friends – on one occasion, in June, he was stopped by a police officer as he walked down the street alone, shouting about the night of the murder. Deighton commissioned a psychiatric evaluation of her client and she also began to search for contemporaneous evidence of his condition – proof that he was acutely distressed at the time of the demonstration. It wasn't long before she was asking for papers relating to Duwayne from the Fishpool investigation.

All of this was nothing short of a disaster for the Lawrence case. Despite Witness B's change of heart, Duwayne remained the key witness for any future prosecution. His identifications of Neil Acourt and Luke Knight were the best evidence available so his credibility was crucial. Already he was vulnerable to the suggestion that he had had only a 'fleeting glance' of the attackers and to the argument that Detective Sergeant Crowley's statement showed him to be a tainted witness. Now there was a possibility that he would be convicted of grave public order offences. If so, he might have to be brought from prison to testify in a Lawrence trial, something defence lawyers would be certain to exploit. Even worse, Deighton was assembling evidence intended to prove that on 8 May, five days before he picked Neil Acourt out of a line-up, Duwayne was seriously psychologically disturbed. This might save Duwayne from prison – which was Deighton's natural and legitimate objective – but it would render him almost useless as an identification witness against Acourt and Knight. By December it was beginning to look as though this case against Duwayne, which had been so slow to emerge, would wreck any hope of a future prosecution in the Lawrence case, whether it was brought by the CPS or by the family. Another door was closing against the Lawrences.

In October, after about seven weeks' work, Chief Superintendent John Barker produced an interim report on his review of the initial investigation, and a month later he delivered a final verdict. Sixteen pages in length, the Barker review covered a broad canvas, including the quality of the investigation itself, the resources devoted to it, the quality of victim liaison and the role of black organizations and the media, but its most important findings occupied a single paragraph on page one. 'My observations are,' Barker wrote:

> The investigation has been progressed satisfactorily and all lines of inquiry correctly pursued.
>
> Liaison between the victim's family and the investigation team deteriorated at an early stage. This affected communication and confidence between the two parties.
>
> Press and media relations were hampered by the involvement of active, politically motivated groups.

Senior 3 Area officers believed that they and their detectives had been vindicated and most who read it at the time agreed, yet the review was something less than a whitewash. Unevenly written and sometimes internally inconsistent, it none the less identified problems that could not be laid at the door of the family or their politically motivated allies. For example, Barker noted that the change of SIO after the first weekend, from Ian Crampton to Brian Weeden, came at a critical moment for the investigation and may have delayed some urgent decisions. He also saw that the Holmes system was inadequately staffed, causing some backlogs. And he stated that forensic evidence against the Acourts might have turned up if their home had been searched earlier. Yet these observations were couched in such muted terms and mingled so thoroughly with praise that they had almost no impact. What readers noticed were those three opening points and another prominent sentence on page one:

> This has been and remains an investigation undertaken with professionalism and dedication by a team who have experienced pressures and outside influences on an unprecedented scale.

Barker was particularly critical of these outside influences and of the family solicitor. 'Mr Khan required all dealings with them [the family] to be through him. This requirement effectively cut police off from personal contact. It also allowed those with political objectives to use the Lawrence family to their own ends . . .' And there were direct criticisms of the Lawrence family, who were accused of repeating confidential information to the press and of making 'inappropriate calls' to the liaison officers in the early hours. These views reflected closely those of the senior 3 Area officers who had commissioned the report, and particularly those of Deputy Assistant Commissioner Osland. Perhaps surprisingly, Barker's findings were not made public. There was no press conference, not even the briefest summary leaked out and the Lawrences were not given any information about the review until some months later. The importance of the Barker review was primarily internal, and it was to influence police decisions and statements for years.

The inquest into the death of Stephen Lawrence opened at Southwark Coroners Court on Tuesday 21 December, eight months almost to the day after the murder. Postponed many times, it had come to be viewed by the family and their advisers as an important moment in their struggle for justice and it was clear from the outset that it would be no ordinary inquest. Presiding was Sir Montague 'Monty' Levine, by some margin the country's best-known coroner. Lacking the robes and hauteur of judges, coroners are usually functionary in style and little noticed as individuals, but in a long career on the bench Sir Monty had acquired a particular standing. With a handlebar moustache and a flower always in his lapel he cut a raffish figure, while his experience and authority enabled him to conduct affairs in a manner quite his own. For this inquest he had agreed to a request from the Lawrences that there should be a jury – this was unusual in such cases, but the family, Khan and Mansfield were convinced that they could command the sympathy of jurymen. They were hoping that, besides its formal purpose of identifying the circumstances of death, the inquest would accomplish other things. It might, for example, bring into the open more information about the case, and about the police investigation, and it might provide an opportunity to question the suspects. From the family's point of view, it might also revive public interest and anger. Others were aware of this potential and no fewer than six parties were represented by barristers, which again was unusual for an inquest. Besides Michael Mansfield for the Lawrences, counsel appeared for the Metropolitan Police, for the borough of Greenwich, for Duwayne Brooks, for Luke Knight and for the Acourts and David Norris together. The proceedings were expected to last a few days, but they were over more quickly than that.

After some opening remarks from Sir Monty, the jury was sent out to allow counsel to raise legal arguments. Mansfield was the first to rise and he surprised everyone by immediately asking for an adjournment. Speaking in terms that were vague to the point of obscurity – partly, it seemed, to protect witnesses, partly to avoid compromising possible lines of inquiry – he stated that fresh information had become available in recent weeks and recent days. Some of it involved new identifications, some involved changes of evidence by a witness, and some involved a witness who had disappeared. The latest of this information had been passed to police the previous day but, said Mansfield, it seemed they had not yet done anything about it. He explained that he was asking for an adjournment because it appeared that the CPS did not intend to mount a prosecution and so the family planned to make use of this new information in a private prosecution. In such circumstances, he said, it would not be appropriate for the inquest to continue since its proceedings might prejudice such a prosecution.

There followed half an hour of near farce, as Sir Monty, Mansfield and the police counsel, Sam Wiggs, tried to establish without openly going into detail whether this new information was being investigated and whether it was substantial enough to justify an adjournment. For much of this time they were never quite sure whether they were talking about the same information, so elusive was it. And throughout the exchanges Mansfield made it plain that he did not trust either the police or the CPS to deal properly with new leads:

CORONER: This information you say is very dramatic, has that been told to the police?

MANSFIELD: Well, I do not know whether the authority that has it has told the police, but we are not the authority that originally had it.

CORONER: Will you be in a position to notify the police about this authority?

MANSFIELD: I am very happy on behalf of the family to communicate anything to the police that is of a dramatic kind, provided – I say this at once – provided it is taken seriously and it is pursued. Provided there is that undertaking by the police, the family would much prefer the prosecuting authorities to do it, rather than having to engage in this themselves.

Sir Monty's ruling was thus a diplomatic affair: he granted an adjournment, at the same time appealing to the public to help the police solve the crime: 'I would ask anyone with any information, no matter how tenuous, or possibly trivial, to come forward . . . The police cannot act when confronted with a possible wall of silence.' He also urged the press, 'in the interests of all concerned', to show restraint in its reporting.

This last request was extravagantly ignored. The sudden adjournment, the involvement of a famous campaigning QC, the mystery about the new information and the accusation that the police and the CPS were dragging their feet – it was too much for the media to resist. 'New evidence halts inquest on youth knifed at bus stop', declared the headlines, while reporters dwelt on the prospect that the 'dramatic new information' might lead to the identification of up to three of the killers. Imran Khan, interviewed on LBC radio, accused the police of failing to listen to criticism and of systematically ignoring or misreading information that was supplied to them. If they had acted on the names the family had given them back in April, he said, there might very well have been convictions by now. Later in the day Detective Superintendent Brian Weeden was offered a chance to reply and he shed some light on the mystery of the evidence. The police had indeed received some new information on the day before the inquest and they had since interviewed those involved. Unfortunately, this did not take matters much further. As for the 'dramatic' information, his officers were informed about it by the borough of Greenwich very late in the day and they had only just made contact with the man concerned. On the wider questions raised by Imran Khan, Weeden was polite but firm. He sympathized with the Lawrence family and took very seriously any information they gave him, but there was a world of difference between information that was based on rumour and evidence that could be presented in court. He could not arrest people on the basis of rumour.

The 'dramatic' information, in fact, was a report that Luke Knight had confessed to the murder. A senior official at Greenwich Council had heard through a family connection that Knight had spoken of his involvement in the crime to a social worker at the institution where he had been held while on remand during the summer. The council reported this to the police and to Mansfield just before the inquest, and for the Lawrence team it appeared to be the last straw. They had already heard that an important new identifying witness had come forward – this was Witness B, although they had no idea who he was and very little knowledge of his evidence – and they knew about the sightings by Duwayne Brooks of suspects he said he recognized. Taking these together with the material already in hand, notably Duwayne's earlier identifications, Mansfield, Khan and the Lawrences believed there *had* to be sufficient evidence now to mount a prosecution. They could not understand what, if it was not malice, racism or incompetence, was holding the police and the CPS back. At the last minute, therefore, they had decided to ask for an adjournment – a desperate course, but it might just shame the authorities into action. There was a price to pay: though effective in terms of publicity, the change of plan meant that the evidence they wanted to hear was not aired and so they were thus left without any additional knowledge of the detail of the case.

The Metropolitan Police and the Crown Prosecution Service were indeed acutely embarrassed by the publicity the inquest generated, and correspondingly angry with the Lawrences and their legal team. Their discomfort was all the greater because they had been in close touch about the progress of the investigation, and both parties were aware that the case was still weak. The two most important new items to come to hand before the inquest were Duwayne Brooks's sightings at the Starburger and the Plough pub and B's account of seeing Norris and Neil Acourt running in Rochester Way. Neither was thought likely to withstand much scrutiny in court. And when the 'dramatic new evidence' was investigated, it proved to be another case of Chinese whispers. When traced, the social worker reputed to be its source said that he had barely spoken to Luke Knight while he was in custody and there had certainly been no confession of any kind. Other social workers were questioned in case there had been a mistake, but it was a dead end. More minor leads were pursued, with a similar lack of success. As weeks dragged on it became clear that the trail was cold, and when Brian Weeden eventually met Howard Youngerwood of the CPS in early April to review the case the mood was gloomy. On balance it seemed to them that the case was actually weaker now than it had been nine months earlier, given the developments in the prosecution of Duwayne Brooks. Weeden none the less tried to persuade Youngerwood to attempt a prosecution in the Lawrence case on the grounds that there was a chance, albeit a small one, that a jury might convict. The prosecutor would have none of it. The CPS test was unequivocal: a prosecution could be pursued only if it had a better than 50–50 chance of success. There was no room for long shots. On 15 April, therefore, just one week short of the first anniversary of the murder, Gordon Etherington, the Chief Crown Prosecutor, wrote to Imran Khan.

After an 'extensive and diligent investigation', Etherington wrote, the police had completed their inquiries into the murder of Stephen Lawrence and the CPS had subsequently examined in the greatest detail all the evidence and information that had been gathered. 'Our unavoidable conclusion is that there is no prospect of a jury convicting on the evidence available,' he declared. He realized that this would be upsetting to Stephen's family and he asked Khan to pass on his continuing sympathy. If further evidence came to light – a possibility which 'should not be totally dismissed' – it would be closely examined, and if it proved sufficient the CPS would not hesitate to mount a prosecution. For the moment, however, no one would be prosecuted for murdering Stephen. Again, a door had slammed.

Chapter Twelve **The Fall of the Coin**

The end of 1993 was a bleak period in the case of Stephen Lawrence: the police investigation was running out of steam, the prosecution of Duwayne Brooks was under way and the Barker review had given the Fishpool operation a clean bill of health. But there was more to this affair than one murder; other assaults and other offences were involved and these cases too were playing themselves out in this period. Chief among them was the matter of Stacey Benefield, the white youth stabbed in the chest in the Brook estate six weeks before the Lawrence murder. What happened to Stacey, while apparently a sub-plot, was to prove of central importance to the Lawrence case, shedding an unexpected light on all that had gone before.

Although at the time he was attacked Stacey refused to identify his assailants, he later told the Fishpool team that David Norris wielded the knife and that Neil Acourt was with him. Stacey's friend Mattie Farman confirmed much of this story, and on 13 May Stacey and Mattie attended identification parades and successfully picked out Norris and Neil Acourt, who were promptly charged with attempted murder. Thus far it was a straightforward and promising case, but matters soon became more complicated. Dave and Neil had had no idea this attack was the subject of an investigation, still less that they were suspects, but once they were charged they were in no doubt about the identity of their accusers. Stacey and Mattie later gave statements to the police describing what happened next, and this is what they alleged.

A few days after the parades, Stacey and Mattie were approached in the street outside Mattie's house by Ray Dewar, a local man a few years older than they were, who had criminal connections.

'Someone wants to meet you,' Dewar said to Stacey. 'You'll be all right.'

Stacey knew what this meant and he was by no means sure he would be all right, in fact he had been dreading this encounter ever since he first gave his statement to DS Davidson. Dave Norris and Neil Acourt were in custody awaiting trial, so they personally could do nothing, but there were others who would be more than willing to threaten or injure on their behalf. And, of course, Stacey and

Mattie knew that Dave came from what they called 'a tasty family'. Cliff Norris, Dave's father, was known on the estates as a man who would not hesitate to hurt anyone who got in his way – and sending his eldest son to jail for attempted murder would surely count as that. Stacey told Dewar that he was not interested in a meeting.

Dewar did not take no for an answer and the following day he tracked Stacey down to the house of another friend called Stephen, where he was staying in the hope of avoiding trouble.

'He still wants to meet you,' Dewar said. 'He wants to give you some money to drop the case. You'll be all right.'

Stacey was still frightened but Dewar persisted. The man did not mean to harm him; he wanted to pay him £5,000 to change his statement, some of it immediately and the rest later.

'Who is it?' asked Stacey.

'I don't know, but you'll be all right.'

'How do you know I'll be all right if you don't know who it is?'

'He's a mate of my mate,' said Dewar, and according to Mattie, who was also present, at this point he let slip that it was Dave's father.

Stacey felt he did not have much choice; unless he ran away and went into hiding Dewar would always find him. So he agreed to a meeting. 'If I'm going to get shot,' he observed aloud, 'I'll get shot.'

'I'll go and arrange it. Be around tomorrow,' said Dewar.

The following day, 20 May, a white Sierra pulled up outside the house of Stacey's friend. Dewar was in the front passenger seat, with another man behind the wheel. Mattie said to Stacey as he left the house: 'If you're not back in an hour I'll phone the police.' Stacey got into the car and was driven about a mile along Rochester Way to Eltham Park, part of a band of green space that borders Eltham to the east. The Sierra turned right into the car park beside the tennis courts and there a smallish man with a tanned complexion – Stacey thought he was aged between twenty-five and thirty-five – was waiting beside a small white car. This man got in beside Stacey in the back seat, while Dewar sat on the other side, squeezing the young man in the middle. Then they had a conversation.

The tanned man, who was clearly in charge, said he was sorry that Stacey had been stabbed and it should never have happened. The Acourts were basically good lads, he said, and they would stand by Stacey and see him right. Stacey felt, however, that the man was less concerned about the Acourts than he was about Dave. 'I got the impression that he was Dave's father,' he said later. After a short chat clearly intended to reassure the young man and show him that the incident had just been a misunderstanding, the man reached into his pocket and produced a wad of £50 notes.

'This is the way I apologize,' he said, explaining that the bundle contained £2,000. 'Give £500 to Mattie and you keep the £1,500 and have a nice weekend.' Stacey took the money.

The tanned man made it clear that in return for this money he wanted Stacey to withdraw his evidence against Dave and Neil. 'This is the way I like to do business,' he said. 'I could have just pulled out a gun and shot you, but I shouldn't need to go around shooting people, should I?'

The driver of the car, still behind the wheel, offered the suggestion that Stacey should simply tell the police he did not see Neil or Dave on the night in question. 'That'll do,' he said, and the tanned man repeated, 'Yeah, that'll do.' Stacey said he would do as he was asked.

The man then opened the door of the car. 'We'll have another meet again soon,' he said, stepping out. 'I'm sure we can straighten this out. Don't worry about the police.' Dewar then accompanied Stacey back to his friend's house.

It would be difficult to exaggerate how frightened Stacey was at this time. Barely two months earlier he had been stabbed in the chest by, he said, David Norris, and medical opinion suggested he had been lucky to survive. Ever since, even before he spoke to Davidson, he had lived in fear, and so had Mattie. Mattie's mother would later say that she could not understand, during these weeks, why her son suddenly wanted to spend so much time with her. The explanation was that he felt safer. Now Stacey had been face to face, or so he believed, with Cliff Norris himself, and he had been bribed and told in so many words that he could just as easily be shot. From his remarks it was clear that the tanned man also knew about Mattie and that his message counted for him too. In this context, what happened next bordered on farce.

The first thing Stacey did was to present Mattie, as instructed, with £500, and he also gave their friend Stephen £50. Then he told them what had happened and they discussed it. The following day they went, with another friend called Chris, to nearby Bexleyheath. Stacey spent £360 on a Sega CD system, complete with games, while

Mattie chose a cheaper model for £190. Then Stacey bought a television for £200, a pair of jeans for £60 and boots for £30, and his friend spent £150 on clothes. Stacey gave Chris £100 and Mattie a further £100 or £200. He still had plenty left, so he and Mattie treated Stephen and Chris to a sunny weekend in Margate, by the sea. Stephen recalled the trip later: 'I left home with £50 and only managed to spend about half of it.' It seemed that Stacey and Mattie could not get rid of the big red banknotes quickly enough.

Another week or so passed before Dewar reappeared, once again inviting Stacey to join him for a short car journey. The same driver took them to the Black Prince Hotel in, appropriately, Bexleyheath, where he bought a round of drinks – lagers for Dewar and Stacey and orange juice for himself. Then the tanned man joined them again.

'How was my weekend?' he asked cheerfully, sitting down. They made a little small talk and then he became serious. 'It's time now to go to your solicitor and go to the police and tell them,' he said. He explained that when Stacey had done this, and when Dave was released, there would be 'a nice parcel' for him. Stacey took this as a reference to the outstanding £3,000. Stacey should not worry, said the tanned man, and at this point he mentioned that he himself was wanted by the police. Then he shook Stacey by the hand and left, saying as he went: 'The next time we meet, it'll be sweet.'

Another week passed and Dewar was in touch again, asking Stacey if he had 'any good news'. Stacey replied that he would be seeing his solicitor the following day.

'Make sure you do. The geezer's getting anxious,' Dewar replied. It was 11 June.

The two friends were in deep trouble and they had little idea of how to get out of it. By their account they had never really intended to change their story as the tanned man asked, but they were equally incapable of turning down the money. Polite refusal had not been an option. They knew that they were in grave danger – Stacey's family included some hard men, but nobody in Cliff Norris's league. Time, moreover, had run out, as they knew Dewar would be back the following evening looking for results. Stacey spoke to a relative, who took him to see a local councillor, who advised them to go to the police but to insist that they must have protection. So the following day Stacey called at Eltham station, where he provided a three-page statement to DS Davidson describing his encounters with the tanned man. Shortly afterwards Mattie also gave a statement and like Stacey he insisted on protection for himself and his family. Davidson found them a place of safety. The following day Mattie paid a fleeting return visit to his home, where he heard that three men had earlier been seen outside in a white Sierra.

The shadow of Cliff Norris had hung over the Lawrence case from its earliest days. The police had confirmed that he was the father of one of their prime suspects on the Monday after the killing and they were, or became, aware of his reputation for violence. Many times there had been hints that that reputation was inhibiting potential witnesses, although everybody was reluctant to discuss this with police. Even Gary Dobson and Luke Knight had been very reluctant to admit that they even knew young Dave. The police made no secret of their suspicions: after Neil and Dave were first arrested they opposed bail for Dave partly on the grounds that he was 'a member of a sophisticated and active criminal family who might attempt to pervert the course of justice'. But that was only suspicion; now Stacey and Mattie had produced evidence that pointed to Cliff. Stacey's description of the man who bribed him matched the elder Norris fairly well – Cliff was thirty-four and smallish, with a south London accent. He had said he was on the run, which Cliff had been since Customs and Excise intercepted his cannabis delivery in 1988. And he had a tan – rumour suggested that Cliff had spent time abroad in Spain or Australia. According to Mattie, Dewar had actually admitted to him that the man with the money was Cliff.

Brian Weeden was convinced, and he saw an opportunity: if he could capture Cliff Norris he would not only bring a high-level professional criminal to justice but he might also be better able to persuade people on the Eltham estates to talk about Dave Norris's role in the Lawrence affair. Weeden ordered a surveillance operation on Ray Dewar in the hope that this messenger might lead police to his master. For more than a week Dewar was watched and tailed, and the comings and goings at his house recorded. He went to Sainsbury's; he walked a Dobermann with a friend; he made an appearance in court on an unrelated matter. On 16 June he was followed all the way to Cambridge, where officers noted that he took an unusual interest in the HMV record shop. And then, on the evening of the 18th, he was again followed, this time to Canterbury, where detectives watched as he tried to break into a number of premises. This they felt they could not let pass, so Dewar was stopped, arrested and charged by Kent police with five attempted burglaries. He was brought back to London to be charged also with attempting to pervert the course of justice through his role in the bribing of Stacey Benefield. With this, the trail to Cliff Norris went cold; he would have known of Dewar's fate very quickly and almost certainly took steps to protect himself from discovery. A year was to pass before the police picked up the trail again.

The matter of the stabbing of Stacey Benefield, meanwhile, had reached the Crown Prosecution Service, where the usual cautious eye was cast over the file. The initial opinion was that attempted murder was an ambitious charge and that convictions were more likely on lesser charges of wounding with intent. These concerns were largely answered by a statement from the surgeon who treated Stacey at Brook Hospital. He confirmed emphatically that the wound resulted from a vicious thrust at the upper chest and that it was likely Stacey had survived only because the knife-point struck and glanced off his breastbone – instead of penetrating the chest wall with force, the blade slipped sideways, inflicting only a flesh wound, albeit one that required sixteen stitches. This was thought to support attempted murder charges. The other area of CPS doubt was the involvement of Neil Acourt. Since he was not accused of striking Stacey or of encouraging Norris to strike him, the charge in his case depended on the principle of joint enterprise: the notion that he shared responsibility because he was present and active at the scene on the side of the stabber. Some CPS lawyers doubted whether a jury would convict him on that basis, but they were overruled.

On 27 July Neil Acourt and Dave Norris appeared for committal at Thames Youth Court, where in brief proceedings the case against Neil was ruled insufficient and he was discharged. This was a lucky spell for him, for it was on the following day that he learned that the charge against him of murdering Stephen Lawrence had also been dropped. He was free. Dave Norris, however, was sent for trial at the Central Criminal Court on the charge that he had attempted to murder Stacey Benefield. This trial began four months later, on 16 November 1993, before His Honour Judge Richardson, and it lasted three days. Norris gave evidence in his own defence, suggesting that he was somewhere else at the time of the stabbing and had no knowledge of it. He called no witnesses and the rest of the defence case consisted largely of attacks on the credibility of Benefield and Farman, who both struggled in the face of hostile cross-examination. They were both skinheads, which may not have impressed the jury, while Norris was smartly turned out in suit and tie, with his mother, the blonde Tracey, sitting close by and occasionally weeping. At lunchtime on the second day, after all the evidence had been heard but before the judge delivered his summing up, both counsel were informed that something unusual and possibly important had taken place outside the courtroom. Norris was being driven to court each day from a secure unit by a driver from a private company and this driver had reported that he was approached during a recess by a member of the jury. The juryman, clearly believing the driver to be an associate or relative of Norris, touched him on the arm and asked for a quiet word. 'I'll tell you what the verdict is,' he said. 'It will be "not guilty", and that is what we all feel.'

Was this an innocent lapse of legal etiquette by a foolish juror or was it evidence that something improper was happening, that the jury had been nobbled? It was hard to tell. The two barristers spoke privately to the judge, who said that he was inclined to believe the former but that, if asked, he would consider an application to discharge the juror. Prosecuting counsel spoke to the police officer representing the Fishpool team at court, D C Martin Hughes, who wanted him to make the application, but the barrister had doubts about the legalities and instead secured an adjournment to the following day. Overnight both D I Ben Bullock at Eltham station and Philip Medwynter at the C P S formed the view that, given Norris's background, jury nobbling was more than likely. They wanted the whole jury discharged. For reasons that remain obscure, however, no application was made either for one or for all of the jury members to be discharged, and the trial proceeded to its conclusion. Amidst further tearful scenes, David Alan Norris was acquitted of attempted murder.

The matter did not end there. Immediately after the verdict the same juryman once again approached the driver, asking for Norris's address and saying that he wanted to offer the young man a job. As before the driver reported this to the court authorities and a meeting was held two days later in Judge Richardson's rooms to discuss what should be done. Present were counsel for the prosecution, a court officer and an officer from the City of London Police. 'On what I was told during the trial,' said the judge, 'I have reason to believe the jury may have, or some member of it may well have been nobbled.' He ordered a police inquiry. This inquiry found no direct evidence of nobbling but revealed that the juryman in question was at the time of the trial under investigation for dishonestly handling a cheque to the value of £23,000, part of what turned out to be a much larger theft of £100,000. A file on the juryman and his conduct at the Norris trial was subsequently passed to the CPS, but he was never charged or reprimanded and there was no retrial. If it really was David Norris who stabbed Stacey Benefield, he had got away with it. As for the juryman, years later he gave an interview to the *Daily Mail* in which he protested that he had not been nobbled. During the trial, he said, he felt sympathy for Norris, who seemed to him 'like a little lamb', or a 'mummy's boy'. He believed Norris's evidence and was convinced of his innocence, and for that reason had wanted to help him. As for the verdict, he said it was now 'the biggest regret of my life'. Since learning that Norris was also a suspect in the Lawrence stabbing – information that was naturally not revealed at the trial – he had become convinced of his guilt. 'I want to apologize to Stephen Lawrence's parents,' he said.

Three weeks after the Benefield verdict, Ray Dewar was found not guilty at Woolwich Crown Court of attempting to pervert the course of justice, although he was separately convicted of the attempted burglaries.

Meanwhile, the other loose threads in the Fishpool investigation, the other attacks and incidents that the detectives had pursued, were being drawn together in a manner no less disappointing for both the police and the Lawrences. One was the incident in Sainsbury's car park in Woolwich, when Doreen Lawrence and some companions said they were racially abused and threatened. This occurred on 30 April, eight days after Stephen's death, and was promptly reported to the police. Some time in September Chief Superintendent Philpott informed Doreen that the CPS had reviewed the evidence and that no action would be taken against the two white women involved. It fact the police had recommended to the CPS that the younger of the two women should face charges even though she denied the racial slurs. A CPS lawyer, however, concluded that it would be 'difficult to rebut' the woman's contention that she had taken a brick from the boot of her car as an act of self-defence. 'A woman who made the racist remark found herself confronted by three angry women who appeared not to show any sign of leaving. She has said that she feared for her safety. This would not at this stage have been an unreasonable fear.' The woman in question, it transpired, had also recently suffered a bereavement, and this too would have to be borne in mind. The chances of a conviction, therefore, were too small to justify prosecution.

Yet another case concerned the Witham brothers. Darren and Terrence Witham had alleged in May 1992 that they were assaulted by Dave Norris and Jamie Acourt in Chislehurst High Street, but although charges were laid they were eventually dropped on CPS orders. After the Lawrence attack the Fishpool team, in particular Ben Bullock, made a vigorous attempt to revive the case and additional evidence was gathered. But in July 1993 Graham Grant-Whyte of the CPS declared that there was still not enough to give a reasonable prospect of conviction. The grounds appear to have been broadly the same as they had been six months earlier: the cause and course of the fight were too indistinct to allow blame to be pinned firmly on one side, while Norris had no convictions at the time and was just fifteen years old. (The Witham file was effectively closed, although years later one more entry was added. In 1998 the boys' father made a formal statement claiming that, after Darren had first made his complaint against Norris, a man came to the door of the family home and offered to pay a large sum of money if the evidence was withdrawn.)

Lawrence, Benefield, Witham, Dewar, Sainsbury's: it is a depressing catalogue. In each case practical explanations were offered for the outcome, but in the eyes of the Lawrence family and their supporters – as, over time, they became aware of these developments – it amounted to a pattern. If they tossed a coin in the air and called heads, it seemed, they could be sure it would land tails up. The coin – the system – appeared to be weighted against them.

Chapter Thirteen **A New Investigation**

In the spring of 1994 change was creeping through the Metropolitan Police as Paul Condon, the man put in by the Conservative government to turn what had always been a force into what Whitehall regarded as a service, began to make his mark. 3 Area saw much of this reform: it was merged into a new, larger district covering more of south London and it acquired a new boss in Assistant Commissioner Ian Johnston. Classless and management-school in style, Johnston was very different from his predecessor, David Osland, an officer-and-gentleman type who retired to Surrey and became a Tory local councillor. These changes were to have profound implications for the Lawrences because Johnston and Condon decided that, as one of the first steps in the reform of 3 Area, they were going to do something about this notorious and highly damaging case. They invited Doreen, Neville and Imran Khan to a meeting at Scotland Yard. At last, it seemed, a door was opening instead of closing, and this was a very important door. The date of the meeting is significant: it was 20 April, five days after the CPS decision not to revive the prosecution, two days before the first anniversary of the murder, which was to be marked by protests, and four weeks before the inquest was due to reconvene.

Condon had written to the Lawrences once in the previous year, a tetchy letter influenced by the ill-humoured perceptions passed up the line from Osland, but they had not met before. Once they were all gathered in his office at Scotland Yard the Commissioner took care to get things off on the right footing. He was sorry, he said, that the relationship between the police and the family had not been successful in the past, but this was not a moment to apportion blame. As for the murder investigation, it was true that certain things might have been done differently but he assured the Lawrences that the officers had acted in good faith. And despite the latest CPS decision, he stressed that the Met remained determined to solve the case and catch the killers. In response, the family raised a number of matters that concerned them. What happened at the start of the investigation? What were the results of the internal review conducted by John Barker? Why had a planned *Crimewatch* television item on the case recently been dropped? Condon and Johnston did their best: the Commissioner promised that Johnston would give the family a briefing on the Barker review and would show them some documents in the case, although he stressed that there were legal limits to how open the police could be. As for *Crimewatch*, he said there was a risk of such a programme influencing witnesses in the case and perhaps tainting their evidence. Khan said he did not accept this, since a case could hardly be *sub judice* in this fashion if there was no prospect of a prosecution.

Throughout the exchanges there was no doubting the scepticism of the Lawrences; the past year had taught them not to trust. Khan explained that the family was considering a private prosecution and was looking at various ways of acquiring the information and documentation they needed. If the authorities agreed, they would like Michael Mansfield to be allowed to view the investigation papers in confidence, but if they did not, the family might attempt to force the release of the papers by legal action – by suing the Met or by dragging it out at the inquest. Condon warned that if the inquest went over the evidence too closely the chances of mounting a prosecution in the future might be compromised. It was all very frank. Then, winding up, Condon said he hoped that this would be the beginning of a process and that the family's confidence in the police might be restored when Johnston had briefed them. If they wished, he would be happy to see the Lawrences again.

It was a tense encounter but it was a start, and further progress was made at the next meeting, a fortnight later, presided over by Johnston. This took place at Plumstead station and on the police side Johnston was supported by his new number two in the area, Commander Perry Nove, and by Brian Weeden. 'At last we meet,' said Doreen to Weeden with some sarcasm when they were introduced. She had criticized him by name at press conferences and in newspaper interviews, but they had never been in the same room before. Johnston and Nove were surprised by this but Weeden pointed out that there were reasons: he had asked to meet the family in the early days but they had declined the invitations, and after that Bill Ilsley had taken over the liaison role from him. Johnston had other matters on his mind; he began as promised by providing some information about the police response on the night of the murder, suggesting that nothing out of the ordinary had taken place. Then, producing a copy of the Barker review, he crossed the room and sat between Neville and Doreen on a sofa. He didn't reveal the whole report but he showed them the findings on the first page: the investigation was satisfactory; family liaison had broken down because of misunderstandings on both sides and politically motivated groups hampered police relations with the media. The Lawrences were not impressed. The Assistant Commissioner then came to the crux of the meeting. Slowly and cautiously, he unveiled his proposal for tackling the case, a plan that was to dominate events for the coming year. The conventional methods of investigating the crime had been exhausted, Johnston explained, and the Met was looking at a new approach, involving radical new measures, in the attempt to solve it. By way of example, he said that it might be possible to persuade the CPS to offer immunity from prosecution to one of the suspects in exchange for direct evidence about the crime. This would be a difficult and delicate business, and he asked the family to think about the implications. Johnston also said the police were looking into ways of substantially increasing the £5,000 reward currently on offer. And, although he could give no further details, he hinted that there might be other steps that could be taken to give the investigation new life.

In the weeks that followed Perry Nove gave practical meaning to this promise of a new initiative and a second investigation took shape that was wholly different in character from the first. Weeden, who had extended his police service to stay with the case, retired. To replace him Nove brought in Detective Superintendent William Mellish, regarded as one of the finest detectives in the Met. A nephew of Bob Mellish, the long-serving south London Labour MP, Bill Mellish had worked under Nove on the extremely sensitive re-investigation of the murder of PC Keith Blakelock during the Broadwater Farm riot in north London in 1985. A tall, dapper cockney with a vocabulary borrowed from television's *The Sweeney*, he took the Lawrence case by the scruff of the neck. He was helped in this by levels of support which Weeden could only have dreamed of: the team, which had dwindled to just a handful of officers, suddenly swelled to fifteen, most of them members of Mellish's team from the Blakelock case. Resources in money and specialist support were suddenly available on a scale more often seen in anti-terrorist investigations than a civil murder, and above all there was enthusiastic new leadership from above. Chief Superintendent Bill Ilsley, who had overseen the case from the first day, found himself sidelined while Nove and Johnston drove matters directly.

There were clear professional and political motives for all this new activity. Johnston had recognized that the Lawrence case would not go away; the circumstances were too shocking, the family was too tenacious and the local black community too committed. He knew that if nothing was done his officers would find the case being cast up at them for years to come as proof of their unwillingness to tackle racist crime, and it would also remain a stain on the reputation of the whole Met, resurfacing every time there was a racist attack and every time there was an anniversary. Moreover, the prospect of another public battering by the family's lawyers when the inquest resumed was hardly one that a new assistant commissioner would relish. In short, Johnston saw that he had to do something. On the basis of the Barker review, it seems, he believed there was nothing to be gained by going back over the past, so he looked to the future. He wanted to reach out to the family and establish a worthwhile dialogue; he wanted to address the problem of Duwayne Brooks, and above all he wanted to solve the crime. If the killers were caught the file could be closed, the critics silenced and perhaps a measure of confidence restored among the black community. There was also the matter of pride. The Metropolitan Police still believed that its detectives were the finest in the country and many officers felt that the failure to crack this prominent case reflected on their collective professional ability. Johnston, as a new man in charge in the area, was keen to put this right.

Doreen and Neville, for their part, faced a difficult choice. Everything in them revolted at the idea of trusting the police, but their options were limited. They had been talking for nine months about a private prosecution but in reality this was a very long shot. Private prosecutions were rare, and for good reasons: the legal authorities frowned on them and even obstructed them, while the costs to the plaintiff could be ruinous. Private prosecutions for murder were virtually unknown; there had been just three in 130 years. Besides, the Lawrences did not have the beginnings of a case against the prime suspects, indeed they were not quite sure who all the prime suspects were, and they had very little understanding of what had happened on the night of the murder. They were ready to fight for the information they needed, to extract it from the police and the CPS by political pressure or legal action, but they knew that would probably be a legal battle in its own right and they might lose. Not for nothing did Michael Mansfield advise that a private prosecution could only be a last resort. And the alternatives were few and dwindling in number. To sue the police for negligence they would require much of the same information they needed for a private prosecution, and did not have, while their other idea, a public inquiry, now seemed beyond hope; the Conservative government had made its opposition plain. Reluctantly, and not unconditionally, the Lawrences decided that they must begin to engage with Johnston and Nove. They would support a new investigation, they said, but they made it clear that if this did not lead to a public prosecution they still intended to take legal action on their own, and they would be raising money in the coming months for that eventuality. They also continued to press for more information and to look for police help in other matters. In the words of Imran Khan, the family view was that this new-look Met was 'on probation'.

When Mellish took up his position in charge of the Lawrence case in mid-June 1994 his initial strategy was simple: to find out as much as possible about the prime suspects and their associates. To do this he deployed or was prepared to deploy the full range of surveillance and observation techniques permitted under the law, from covert video filming and undercover officers to following individuals and intercepting mail. The idea was to build an understanding of the group, to identify weak points, to catch them if they planned or committed any criminal acts or to acquire any leverage that might help in persuading one or more of them to accept immunity and give evidence against the others. Up to a dozen observation posts were established and the doings of the Acourts, Dobson and Knight were soon routinely monitored. David Norris was seen less often, principally because his home in Bickley was so difficult to watch without the watchers themselves being spotted, but he continued to visit the Acourts every now and then. While they built up their picture of the suspects in this way the Mellish team also kept their eye open for leads in a number of other areas, and one of these, specified almost from the first day, was Clifford Norris. Brian Weeden, who had briefed Mellish before retiring, left him in no

Stephen Lawrence. This photograph came to be the standard image (*Photo News Service*).

he funeral service in June 1993. eville and Doreen are in the reground. To the rear are oreen's sister, Cheryl Sloley, Paul ateng, MP, and Ros Howells *anDempsey/PressAssociation/Topha*).

Left Detective Superintendent Ian Crampton. Called out on the night of the murder, he led the investigation for the first three days (*Peter Jordan/PA*).

Right Detective Superintendent Brian Weeden, who took over from Crampton and led the investigation for a further year (*Chris Wood/ Star Images*).

Below Assistant Commissioner Ian Johnston, who oversaw the second investigation of the case in 1994 (*Universal Pictorial Press*).

Above Detective Chief Superintendent William Ilsley, who supervised both Crampton and Weeden (*National Pictures*).

102 Bournbrook Road. This shabby house on the Brook estate was the Acourt home at the time of the murder (*Garry Weaser/The Guardian*).

Duwayne Brooks, Stephen's friend, who was the principal witness (*Mark St George/Enterprise News*).

The barrister Michael Mansfield with Neville Lawrence. From December 1993 to the end of the public inquiry in late 1998, Mansfield provided the public legal voice for the family's quest for justice (*Samantha Pearce*/PA).

Imran Khan with Doreen Lawrence. He was the family's solicitor and trusted adviser (*Chris Wood*/Star Images).

Daily Mail

Jonathan Cainer: How you can find your Valentine

SEE PAGES 50-52

MURDERERS

The Mail accuses these men of killing. If we are wrong, let them sue us

Gary Dobson   Neil Acourt   Jamie Acourt   Luke Knight   David Norris

THE Daily Mail today takes the unprecedented step of naming five young men as murderers.

They may not have been convicted in a court of law, but police are sure that David Norris, Neil Acourt, Jamie Acourt, Gary Dobson and Luke Knight are the white youths who killed black teenager Stephen Lawrence.

We are naming them because, despite

COMMENT: Page 8

a criminal case, a private prosecution and an inquest, there has still been no justice for Stephen, who was stabbed to death in a racist attack almost four years ago.

One or more of the five may have a valid defence to the charge which has been repeatedly levelled against them. So far they have steadfastly refused every opportunity to offer such a defence.

Four have refused to give any alibi for

that night in April 1993. One initially offered an alibi, but it did not stand up when police checked it out.

This week the five refused to answer any questions at the inquest on Stephen, citing their legal right of privilege not to say anything which might incriminate them.

The Lawrence case threatens to damage race relations and the reputation of British justice.

If these men are innocent they now have every opportunity to clear their names in a legal action against the Daily Mail. They would have to give evidence

and a jury in possession of all the facts would finally be able to decide.

Yesterday the jury at Southwark Coroner's Court had little doubt of one thing. It took only 30 minutes to decide unanimously that the 18-year-old A-level student was unlawfully killed, the victim of 'a completely unprovoked racist attack by five white youths'.

The criminal cases against Norris, 20, Neil Acourt, 21, Jamie Acourt, 19, Dobson, 21, and Knight, 20, failed because of a lack of evidence. But if they thought they had got away with the killing they

Turn to Page 6, Col. 2

INSIDE: Andrew Alexander 12, Femail 19, Diary 39, Friday First 42-48, Letters 53, TV 54-56, Coffee Break 67-69, City 70-72, Sport 73-80

he *Daily Mail*'s front page of 14 February 1997, prompted by the conduct of the five spects at the inquest (*Enterprise News*).

Top Leaving the inquiry after the first day of the suspects' evidence, Neil Acourt responds to the chants of the crowd (*Justin Williams/PA*).

Bottom The following day, their evidence complete, the suspects and their supporters walked into a hail of eggs, fruit and bottles . . . (*Paul Hackett/Popperfoto/Reuters*).

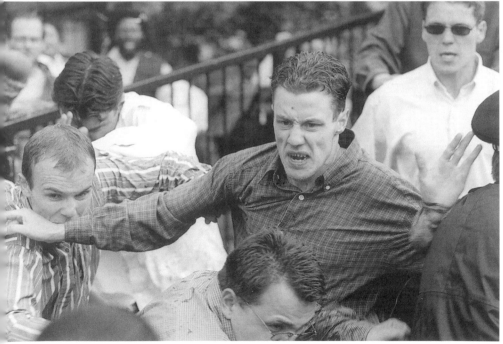

op ... and then fighting broke out. Left to right: Luke Knight, Bradley Lamb (half-
brother to the Acourts), Neil Acourt (partly obscured), Dave Norris, Jamie Acourt with
is fist raised, and, in the background, Bradley's brother Scott (*Paul Hackett/Popperfoto/Reuters*).

ottom The core of the group: Neil, Dave and Jamie at bay (*Paul Hackett/Popperfoto/Reuters*).

Neville and Doreen Lawrence at the inquiry in 1998 (*Kevin Lamarque/Popperfoto/Reuters*).

doubt that he saw Cliff as a vitally important figure in the case.

If they could not watch the Norris home in Berryfield Close, detectives could at least monitor events there in another way: they could search the dustbins. This was where they found their lead. Cliff had not been spotted since the Benefield incident and there had been rumours that he was in Australia but the police were hoping that he was still in contact with Tracey and the children. Sure enough, he sent his wife a birthday card and the card found its way into the domestic rubbish. It was the first evidence that Cliff was in the country. Mellish promptly switched the bulk of his surveillance effort to the Norris home, despite the difficulties, and soon they had another lead. On 9 August Tracey Norris and a woman friend left the house by car and were followed. Instead of a routine local trip this proved a longer journey as the two women headed out of London to the south and east, crossing the M25 motorway near Sevenoaks and continuing on past Tunbridge Wells in the direction of the Sussex coast. A few miles short of the town of Battle, near a village called Robertsbridge, they left the main road and took a succession of progressively smaller by-roads until eventually they turned up a lane marked as a dead end. The followers noted the spot, retired to a safe distance and waited. A few hours later Tracey and her friend drove out of the lane and went back to London. Checks showed, meanwhile, that at the end of the lane was a cluster of oast-houses that were available for rent as holiday homes. The following morning Tracey made the journey again, this time with Dave as her companion, and they stayed at the oast-houses for most of the day.

After Tracey and Dave had driven off, Mellish and three or four of his men remained behind to keep watch on the lane. Before long another car emerged and headed for a local pub, where two men got out and entered the bar. An officer followed them in and returned to confirm that one of the men was Clifford Norris. Mellish now summoned help, asking the local police to provide a team of armed officers and the Met's regional crime squad in south London to supply some detectives to carry out the arrests – he did not want his own involvement, or the link with the Lawrence case, to become known. While Norris and his companion, still under observation, drove back to the oast-house and turned in for the night, Mellish adjourned to a local police station to await his reinforcements. Before dawn the following morning he briefed his team and at 6 a.m.

they were in position, waiting. It was somewhat later that the occupants of the oast-house started their day and most of the morning had passed before they made it to a local café for breakfast. There they enjoyed their last meal at liberty for some time, paid their bill and walked through the door into the arms of the police. There was no fuss or trouble, although Cliff's companion proved to be carrying a loaded handgun and when the car was searched two more handguns were found, one of them hidden in a golf bag. A search of the oast-houses turned up a sawn-off shotgun and, packed neatly in its special padded briefcase, an Uzi machine gun. There was also what was described as 'a vast amount' of ammunition. Norris was charged with the firearms offences and with importing large quantities of cannabis back in the 1980s. While in jail on remand he slashed his wrists in an apparent suicide attempt (police maintained an open mind on whether it might have been the first step in an escape plan). Tried at Lewes Crown Court the following year, he was sentenced to a total of eight years in prison.

If it is true, as the police firmly believed, that Cliff was the principal intimidator in the Lawrence case, then there is a certain irony to his capture. Although he did not know it, it was his success in keeping Dave out of jail that was the cause of his own arrest and imprisonment. He had eluded the police and the customs service for six years and if he had not been targeted by the detectives investigating the Lawrence murder he would doubtless have remained at liberty for a long time. By protecting his son, however, he exposed himself. Mellish saw to it that the witnesses and potential witnesses in the Lawrence case – K, B, Emma Cook and the others – were quickly informed of the development. He also discreetly spread the word that the reward had been increased (thanks in part to a donation by an anonymous businessman) to £40,000. Perhaps something might change; it was a matter of waiting. The main focus of his efforts, however, remained the suspects, and within a week of the events in Robertsbridge there was another very important development.

On the night of 19 August Jamie Acourt went with some friends to the Stars nightclub in Greenwich, a favourite haunt of his, and in the course of the evening he became embroiled in an argument with another group of young men. According to witnesses, Jamie eventually pushed one of the men in the chest, prompting another man, Rico Mario White, to confront him. At this Jamie produced a knife and lunged at White, who dodged. A friend of White's, Darren Giles, then leapt on Jamie's back in an attempt to restrain him, but he was not strong enough. Jamie managed to inflict a cut on the stomach of yet another man, Richard Foord, before bringing the knife up sharply behind him and stabbing Darren Giles. Giles fell and Jamie backed away, still threatening with the knife, until he was seized and ejected from the club by bouncers. Moments later Giles too was thrown out and some of his friends went with him. Just another brawl, it seemed, except that Jamie's knife had penetrated Giles's heart. Before long he collapsed. The injury was so serious that he was thought to have been clinically dead by the time his friends carried him into the hospital near by, but he was saved by emergency surgery.

At the time of the fight some of Mellish's officers, including two pretending to be a couple, were in the nightclub maintaining surveillance on Jamie. While they were not close enough to have seen exactly what happened, they had no difficulty in pointing local detectives towards the perpetrator. Jamie was arrested a few days later, picked out of the line-up by several witnesses and charged with wounding Darren Giles and Richard Foord and attempting to wound Rico White. He was remanded in custody at Feltham Young Offenders' Institution in west London – where his brother Neil had been held on remand for the Lawrence killing and Dave Norris for the Benefield attack – and in October was committed for trial the following year.

One of the five, therefore, was in serious trouble, something that Mellish had been hoping for from the outset. His strategy had foreseen some bartering at this stage – a promise of leniency in relation to the new offence, or an offer of immunity in the Lawrence case – whatever was needed to tip someone into telling the truth about the night of 22 April 1993. Unfortunately, Jamie was not the boy Mellish would have chosen for this role. Bound so closely to Neil and to Dave Norris, he was thought far less likely to change his stance than Dobson or Knight. In the event, no approach was ever made to Jamie and the police had to content themselves with the hope that his arrest would destabilize the group in some way.

The difficulty of getting close to the boys had never been under-estimated. They were so young and close-knit and their circle of acquaintance was so well defined that there was no hope of inserting an undercover officer who might gain their confidence. They were kept under observation as far as possible, at home, on the street, in pubs, in pool clubs, nightclubs and even a health club. Jamie and Neil were watched at their uncles' bottling factory; but several factors were working against the police. Although these young men still associated, they were not active criminals who needed to plan their next robbery or burglary. On the contrary, more than a year had passed since the Lawrence murder and there was no prosecution in sight, so there was no particular reason for them to talk about the case at all, even if they were responsible. It was also becoming clear that they were on their guard in a way that was most unusual for teenagers. Neil Acourt, for example, always preferred public telephone boxes to private phones and was prepared to walk some distance to find one. Mellish was surprised by this and came to the view that they must at some stage have been sat down as a group and told by a professional criminal, possibly Cliff Norris, how to avoid incriminating themselves. Finally, these young men did not seem to have much privacy. There was no quiet place where they could meet regularly just to chat among themselves – the sort of exchange most likely to provide evidence. At one stage it seemed that they occasionally gathered in the bedroom of Gary Dobson's parents, possibly because Gary's own room was too small, but after some consideration senior officers decided that the police could not bug the bedroom of a law-abiding couple. These difficulties were frustrating, but Mellish was prepared to be patient.

Eventually there was progress. Somebody close to the suspects bought a car and they took to travelling around in it, particularly when it came to visiting Jamie at Feltham on the other side of London. The police bugged the car and although the results were technically very poor – the voices were largely drowned by engine noise and music – they did pick up an interesting line when one of the suspects was heard to remark: 'Gary can't hack the pressure.' This was hardly a revelation, since Gary had been identified as a potential weak link in the earliest days of the first investigation, but the mention of pressure suggested that things were changing in the group and that perhaps Cliff Norris's disappearance from the scene had made a difference. Mellish was keen to keep up this pressure: for example, at his suggestion Jamie's cell at Feltham was searched soon after he had received a visit and some cannabis was found. A prosecution followed, and Jamie was convicted. Time was pressing on, however, and still there was no breakthrough. In October the inquest was postponed again, at the family's request, and then at last came promising news: Gary Dobson and Charlie Martin (another member of the Acourt circle, on bail awaiting trial for the Kent caravan site stabbing were planning to take a flat together. The suspects and their friends would finally have a base where they could talk freely and which could be bugged without too many legal complications. Once this prospect was in view, Mellish decided to take steps to make sure that they did talk freely, and that they talked about the Lawrence case.

Through all these months the prosecution of Duwayne Brooks for public order offences at the Welling riot of 8 May 1993 was grinding on. Duwayne had been charged in October and his solicitor, Jane Deighton, was seeking evidence of his state of mind at the time of the offence. Before Christmas 1993 she wrote to the CPS asking for all statements by or about her client taken by the Fishpool team in April and May. Despite a number of reminders this met with a stony silence and by the 28 January she was writing: 'Could we please have replies to our letters dated 20 December, 24 December, 7 January and 14 January?' A week later she received a telephone call informing her that no CPS lawyer had yet been given responsibility for the case but that she would receive answers as soon as possible. Behind the scenes her letters were causing concern.

The police were aware of her requests and were very suspicious of them; Detective Inspector Ben Bullock of the Fishpool team (still, at this time, under Weeden's command) discussed the matter with the Metropolitan Police solicitors' department and they were of one mind, that the CPS should disclose only what a judge ordered them to disclose. The material Deighton was seeking was part of an incomplete investigation, they agreed, and was in any case irrelevant to the Brooks case. Deighton, meanwhile, was raising the stakes, for having sought counsel's opinion she decided that she would need more documentation and not less. 'In addition to the disclosure sought,' she wrote in her next letter to the CPS, 'we require copies of all material in the hands of the prosecution that relates to the murder of Stephen Lawrence.' In March she received a reply, very much in line with the police view: the CPS did not think such papers

215

relevant and if she really wanted them she would have to apply to the judge. While this sparring continued, a psychiatrist was examining Duwayne. His preliminary findings, available early in April, prompted Deighton to take a different line with the CPS.

'Dear Sirs,' she wrote, 'We make below anxious representations that the case against Duwayne Brooks be brought to an end. The two bases of these representations are, firstly, Duwayne's mentally disordered state, now and at the time of the offences charged, and secondly, the wider public interest.' The psychiatrist, she explained, had not only found that Duwayne was suffering from post traumatic stress disorder brought on by witnessing Stephen's murder, but also that the current legal proceedings were making matters worse. Besides this, she pointed out, the proceedings could hardly fail to have grave repercussions for the Lawrence case. Her client would be the key prosecution witness in any murder trial that might take place and the prospects of a conviction would probably hang on his credibility and reliability. 'To continue with the prosecution of Duwayne may be tantamount to handing the defence in any murder trial an acquittal.' And for what, she asked. He was charged with violent disorder at the Welling riot, yet the actions he was alleged to have committed were on the lower end of the scale of seriousness. In the videos of the demonstration, the figure alleged to be Duwayne took no leading or organizing part in the trouble. This trouble involved hundreds of people, yet he was one of only six to have been charged with violent disorder, and those charges had not been laid until six months after the event. The public, Deighton wrote, would regard it as a scandal if the CPS jeopardized the chances of a successful prosecution in a racist murder to pursue this belated and relatively minor case against Duwayne.

The CPS did not agree. The Duwayne Brooks file, which until mid-February had not been assigned to anyone at the service, by late April lay on the desk of the Branch Crown Prosecutor for the area, Howard Youngerwood. This was the same senior lawyer who had dealt with the Lawrence case, and it was because of Deighton's desire for documents from that case that he had become involved. Although technically he was not directly responsible for the Brooks file, given his seniority his opinions were decisive. After reading Deighton's letter he wrote in an internal memo:

There can be no question of the prosecution not proceeding on the basis of the evidence available, and the suggestion of Brooks's solicitors that it would be somehow in the public interest to stop these proceedings in order to preserve the credibility of Brooks for any future proceedings arising out of the murder is total nonsense and, frankly, improper.

So far as disclosure of documents was concerned he was inclined to be grudging, although he suggested that edited versions of some of Duwayne's statements might be released. In the event this was not enough to satisfy either Deighton or Judge Tilling, who was to try the case at Croydon Crown Court. Tilling delivered an interim ruling at the end of April requiring the CPS to notify the defence 'by using statements, police reports or in summary form, of any descriptions of Mr Brooks behaving "out of the ordinary" or of any "abnormal behaviour"'.

After Tilling's ruling, Youngerwood contacted the Fishpool incident room at Eltham and asked the office manager to look out any relevant documents and also to ask his colleagues and former colleagues on the investigation whether they remembered Duwayne acting oddly. If they did, he should write a summary of their recollections and send it on as soon as possible. In subsequent discussion with the police this suggestion was refined: a questionnaire would be sent out to every police officer who had had dealings with Duwayne Brooks during the relevant part of 1993, asking them to record any instances of abnormal behaviour on his part that they recollected. Through the month of May the forms were distributed, completed and returned, while Deighton, eager to get hold of useful evidence, urged the police to hurry up. In all seventeen officers responded, ranging from senior figures such as Ian Crampton and Ben Bullock to Inspector John McIlgrew, who met Duwayne at the Southwark identification suite, and the various junior officers who encountered him immediately after Stephen's death. The first part of the form was a statement: 'During my dealings with Duwayne Brooks I noticed / I did not notice that he displayed "abnormal" or "out of the ordinary" behaviour.' After that officers were required to state when and where they met Duwayne, and then there was a space for comments. Of the seventeen, nine said they did not notice any abnormal behaviour, four said they did and the remaining four did not cross out either option. But it was the comments beneath that told the story.

Only four of the officers who said they had noticed nothing abnormal, including Crampton and D C Cooper, the man who took Duwayne's long statement on the first night, left the comment section blank. In all, thirteen had something to say about Duwayne – generally just two or three sentences – and whatever their opinion about the normality or otherwise of his behaviour they showed a striking consistency of view. Five said Duwayne had been 'aggressive', four said he was 'uncooperative', four said he was 'anti-police', three thought him 'arrogant' and three said he was 'excitable'. Other words used included 'surly', 'unhelpful', 'flippant' and 'belligerent'. Two officers said that he showed no signs of emotional grief, one said he helped himself to drinks from a police station fridge without permission and one said that he 'apparently' broke a window in Plumstead police station. Of the seventeen officers, in fact, at least eleven offered views supporting a general picture of Duwayne as arrogant, uncooperative and aggressive. As evidence for the trial of Duwayne Brooks, all this was as likely to help the prosecution as the defence since it seemed to suggest that his behaviour after Stephen's death was characterized less by symptoms of trauma than by an irresponsible and high-handed hostility towards the police. As evidence in any future trial for the murder of Stephen Lawrence, moreover, these new documents would be extremely damaging to Duwayne's standing in the eyes of a jury.

While the questionnaires were being gathered, matters were moving on. With the trial still due in June (the judge later postponed it to December), pressure was mounting, and acrimonious correspondence flowed between Deighton and Youngerwood. Deighton suggested that her client was being persecuted and that the CPS was failing to comply with the judge's rulings on disclosure, while Youngerwood protested at her tone and rejected her accusations. 'I am sorry,' he wrote at the end of May, 'that you continue to impugn my integrity.' At the same time the CPS was coming under discreet pressure from another, unexpected quarter. Ian Johnston and Perry Nove were now running the Lawrence case on the police side and they were uneasy about the proceedings against Duwayne. This was a view in which they were encouraged by the Lawrences and Imran Khan, with whom they were having their first, tentative dealings.

At the end of May Johnston raised the matter directly with the CPS, and he wrote a note of this for Nove:

> This morning I telephoned Gordon Etherington of the CPS and indicated to him that we saw value in terms of community tension and social justice for him to give consideration as to whether or not the proceedings against Duwayne Anthony Brooks should go ahead. He was of the view that there were considerable difficulties with such a course of action, associated not only with the appropriateness of the withdrawal of proceedings in such a clear-cut case, but more significantly in that this would discredit Brooks as a witness who was giving evidence in return for a favour. I agreed with him about the difficulties, indicated that we would not stand in his way if on balance he saw such action as appropriate, and I agreed that the decision was very much one for him.

The CPS's justification for pursuing the case was this: they believed there was strong evidence that Duwayne had committed the two offences during the riot and those offences were sufficiently serious to call for prosecution. To drop the case in order to protect Duwayne's integrity as a witness in the Lawrence case would be improper and would give the impression that important witnesses to serious crimes had a licence to break the law. As Etherington said to Johnston, a discontinuance at this stage would not protect Duwayne's credibility as a witness in the Lawrence case; it would do the reverse. Defence counsel would be able to argue that Duwayne was only giving evidence in exchange for being 'let off' a prosecution of his own.

Deighton, however, could not understand the CPS's persistence. She had expert evidence to show that her client was probably not responsible for his actions at the time of the riot and that a trial was likely to worsen his condition. She was also increasingly concerned that he seemed to have been singled out for prosecution. The police videos she had seen showed protesters throwing missiles at buildings and police officers, but none of those was prosecuted. Yet Duwayne, who was alleged to have waved a stick and helped to push over a car, was being taken to court more than a year after the event. In desperation Deighton wrote to the CPS again. She described her client's state of mind: 'Duwayne Brooks is terrified by the public nature of the trial. He is terrified of being found by the [Lawrence] murder suspects or their agents. He knows they are violent . . . and he believes that the suspects have every incentive to attack him as he is the key to their prosecution and conviction.' She went on to paint a picture of a young man in the grip of despair, who sat in her office or waiting room with his face in his hands. It was, she said, 'a despair of an entirely different order than the fear exhibited by the many criminal defendants that pass through this office'. In response Tony Connell, a prosecutor working on the case with Youngerwood, suggested to her that the CPS would seek a second psychiatric opinion, and after some hesitation she and Duwayne agreed. A second opinion confirming the first would surely change the CPS's mind. But the finding this time was different: the second psychiatrist thought Duwayne might indeed have been suffering from mental disorder but said it was 'highly unlikely' that this rendered him incapable of controlling his actions at the time of the riot. On this basis any lingering doubts at the CPS (and there seem to have been very few) were dismissed; the case went ahead.

The trial of Duwayne Brooks began and ended on 13 December 1994; like many other legal processes associated with the case of Stephen Lawrence it followed a most unexpected course. Judge Tilling began by asking to see the video evidence at the core of the prosecution case and then he invited counsel for both sides to his room for consultations. There he told them that so far as he could see from the video and the documentation there was a case against Brooks but he was not sure that it was in the public interest to pursue it. He explained that given the mitigating circumstances – Duwayne had seen his best friend murdered only two weeks previously – it was unlikely in the event of a conviction that he would impose anything more than an absolute discharge. In other words, if Duwayne were found guilty there would be no punishment. That being the case, the judge asked the prosecution to consider whether it was really worth proceeding with a trial that was likely to last a considerable number of days while complex psychiatric issues were explored. This message was relayed to Youngerwood and Connell by CPS counsel, who offered his opinion that it was scarcely worth carrying on. This view was rejected. Nothing had changed, came the answer, and the case must proceed. After lunch, therefore, the trial proper began, and at least one person present formed the view that the judge was irritated by the turn of events.

The defence opened with a legal argument: the prosecution

amounted to an 'abuse of process' because, given the delay in bringing charges, Duwayne Brooks could not have a fair trial. The first psychiatrist to examine Brooks saw him only in early 1994 and was of the opinion that by then it was already impossible to say beyond reasonable doubt what his mental state was at the time of the alleged offence. The prosecution answered that the delay in laying charges was not unusual, especially for so complex a police investigation, and that satisfactory psychiatric evidence had been produced after similar delays in other cases. It now fell to the judge to decide. Judge Tilling began his ruling by observing that the power of judges to 'stay' or halt cases had always to be exercised with great care, and he noted that in his five years on the bench he had never once used this power. He went on:

> It is clear to me, reading the psychiatric reports, of which there are a number, that there is a real danger that a rehearsal of the incident concerning Stephen Lawrence could well have a serious effect on Mr Brooks's mental state. It is clear also that delay has taken place and, in my view, that delay does affect the quality of the psychiatric evidence available to the defence. I have also, in seeking to exercise my discretion, looked at the nature of the alleged offence as disclosed in the video film of this demonstration. I have also borne in mind the likely outcome, so far as sentence is concerned, even if Mr Brooks were to be convicted by a jury. All these factors drive me to the conclusion that this is one of those exceptional cases where I should exercise my discretion to stay these proceedings.

In plain language, Judge Tilling had aborted the trial on the grounds that the prosecution should never have been taken this far, and Duwayne Brooks was allowed to leave the court without a stain on his character.

It was a remarkable outcome, greeted with some irritation at the CPS. Howard Youngerwood wrote that the case illustrated 'the problems that arise when judges decide to enter the arena as to whether a prosecution is in the public interest', and Gordon Etherington thought that 'judges really should be discouraged from taking action in this way'. Tony Connell observed, however, that 'the decision of the judge cannot be viewed as so contrary to the evidence that it ought to be appealed'. The matter was thus closed.

The case left a legacy: abuse of process or not, the prosecution had brought into being important documents casting doubt on Duwayne's mental stability and reliability at the time he picked Neil Acourt and Luke Knight out of identification parades. These remained on file, ready to be disclosed to the defence in any future Stephen Lawrence murder trial. The Lawrences were well aware of this and they were equally aware that the psychiatric reports and police questionnaires would never have come into existence if the police had not charged Duwayne and the CPS had not prosecuted him. Doreen and Neville could not help contrasting the official determination brought to bear on this case involving a black defendant with what they believed had happened in the case of their son, a black victim. And while these events unfolded something else had happened to arouse their suspicions of officialdom. It concerned Detective Sergeant Christopher Crowley, whose account of a conversation with Duwayne did so much damage to the Lawrence case. In the spring of 1994 *Private Eye* magazine published very serious allegations about Crowley which were later the subject of a libel writ. They cannot be repeated here, but they concerned not only his conduct in relation to Duwayne Brooks but also his involvement in the case of Rolan Adams, the black teenager murdered in Thamesmead in 1991. The allegations, repeated in a television bulletin, shocked the Lawrences, and Imran Khan promptly raised the matter with Commander Perry Nove. Nove ordered a rapid internal investigation of the charges and promised Khan that any evidence of impropriety would be vigorously pursued. In the event, after two weeks this internal investigation was unable to substantiate the *Private Eye* claims and reported that there was no evidence Crowley had acted improperly.

In December Gary Dobson and Charlie Martin moved into their flat in Footscray Road on the south side of Eltham and, as had been hoped, the others in the group – notably Neil Acourt, Dave Norris and Luke Knight – began to hang around there. Very soon Mellish's team installed a bug, although not without difficulty. To overhear conversations the bug had to be placed in the living room and since the tenants had few belongings and the landlord provided the minimum of furniture this was somewhat spartan in character: a few basic armchairs, a television, a stereo and a small dining table with chairs. Mellish wanted not only audio surveillance but video as well, and though the device was small there were very few places where it could be hidden. In the end, it was concealed in a special socket fitted to a power point near the television. For a few weeks, starting on 2 December, the police listened to, watched and recorded the suspects and their friends as they came and went, watched television, listened to music, cooked, chatted and larked about. Mellish was not content merely to wait for the conversation to drift towards the events of April 1993, so he took steps to ensure that it was on the suspects' minds. Friends of theirs were stopped and questioned, for example, and the word was spread in Eltham that the Lawrence case was being reopened. Everything possible, short of a direct approach, was done to make the boys jumpy. The results were revealing in many ways, as the Lawrences discovered later, but in the eyes of Bill Mellish they did not produce one iota of evidence that could be of use in a prosecution. Not once did the suspects give themselves away, not once did they admit the murder; instead, at one moment Neil Acourt actually denied involvement. Around Christmas, Mellish called off the surveillance. His investigation, he knew, was running out of steam.

One evening at about that time, Christmas 1994, Doreen Lawrence went for a walk. She wanted to clear her mind and to have some time alone to think about what had happened to her and her family and about what should happen next. Since the murder they had moved out of the house they owned in Llanover Road because they feared an attack by Stephen's killers. While the suspects' identities had never been made public, Doreen and Neville were conscious that they themselves had appeared many times on television and at demonstrations – several of them in Well Hall Road. Their faces were known and their address might be too. There had been the incident when white youths were seen hanging around near by, and some weeks later the tyres of the family car had been slashed. The Lawrences had been genuinely afraid.

Doreen knew that her relationship with Neville had suffered, as even the strongest marriage would; they tended to cope with the strain in different ways, often on their own rather than together. She could see, too, that Stuart and Georgina had been deeply affected by what had happened. More than eighteen months after the murder the Lawrence family had moved very little closer to what the

223

therapists call 'closure', the moment when they would feel at peace with the past, when they could look back on what had happened without being overcome by emotion. Given the events that had intervened this was hardly surprising. On the one hand, the young men who had killed Stephen were free. Just a mile away in Eltham they could meet and laugh, drink, play Nintendo, catch buses, date girls, find jobs, grow into adults, father children of their own – in short, they could do anything they liked, while their victim was dead and lay buried thousands of miles away, all his hopes gone and his ambitions unfulfilled. On the other hand, the Lawrences were in no doubt that the police and the criminal justice system had failed, that for some reason, possibly incompetence and possibly racism, public servants who were paid and trusted to deliver justice had not done their duty. And those people too, it seemed, could not be brought to book. With Neville, Doreen had been prepared to give the police a second chance in 1994, but as the year drew to its close she found herself as bitter and angry as she had ever been.

Commander Nove had reported at the end of November that the time might have come to attempt the remedy of last resort: an offer of immunity to one of the suspects in exchange for his evidence against the others. This was something that Doreen had always dreaded, even though she had been promised that the offer would never be made to anyone suspected of actually wielding the knife. The idea that one of the attackers, however peripheral his role, might simply be absolved of responsibility for his actions revolted her. Worse, at the November briefing she learned something she had not anticipated: Nove explained that it was also possible that this person might receive the reward of £40,000. This was, as he put it, 'the real world', and that might be the price that had to be paid to secure convictions. Doreen was appalled. She told Nove she was very dissatisfied that things should have come to such a pass; the police were only in this position, she said bitterly, because they had failed to pursue the case properly in 1993. In the weeks that followed she found herself slipping back into her feelings of that time; it was as if she had been on ice since the second investigation began, and was now thawing. Her mind was filled by memories of incidents and experiences that she regarded as patronizing, racist, insulting, unfair or merely shabby. She was shocked that the original case should have been so damaged by the evidence of DS Crowley, a police officer. She was appalled that Duwayne should have been prosecuted when her son's killers were not. She resented the failure not to prosecute the white women in the Sainsbury's car park incident. She resented the way in which Imran Khan had been portrayed by some as a left-wing Svengali (not least because that left her and her husband appearing as dupes). Although she had more time for Perry Nove than any other police officer she had met, she disliked the way he spoke to her only in generalities, never giving names, for example. She knew that a defendant awaiting trial would be told more.

All this Neville felt too, but in a different way. Police officers and others were to say later that the difference between the two was that Neville was open to argument while Doreen was not, but that formula does no justice to either. Neville, for example, was capable of great stubbornness and tenacity: it was he who identified in the earliest days the problem of forensic evidence and who would never let the police off that hook. He asked D S Bevan two days after the murder whether forensic evidence was found at the scene and he saw very quickly that the delay in making arrests had made the discovery of forensic links to the suspects less likely. Well over a year later he was still questioning Nove on the issue. Doreen, for her part, was capable of compromise, as her cooperation with Johnston and Nove showed. But it is true that they saw and reacted to developments in different ways: Neville's anger, it seems, burned somewhere deep inside him and formed part of an internal dialogue; Doreen's was so near the surface that at times she could not contain it.

Her mind was in turmoil as she walked that December evening, and she paid little attention to where she was going. Nor did she really notice the passage of time. At home, Neville grew concerned; it was unlike her to disappear. He rang a few close friends and relatives but there was no word of her. After a while he tried again, this time casting the net more widely. Still nothing. Doreen, meanwhile, was walking and thinking. She thought about the suspects, the police, the documents; she thought about Stephen and Duwayne; she thought about her family; she thought about herself. She realized that she had had enough of trusting others, relying on others, waiting for others; none of them had done what she and Neville wanted. If the Mellish investigation had reached the end of the road, then she was not going to go begging the government or some branch of officialdom for help, for the result would surely be the same. What she needed, what the family needed, was to be in charge, to take control of events, and the only way of achieving that was to mount a private prosecution. The price would be high, both financially and personally; it would mean fundraising on a much larger scale than before and it would mean a long struggle through the courts. But Doreen was convinced that enough evidence either existed or could be found, and that if a jury heard it there would be convictions. High levels of commitment would be demanded, but that was something her family had – had always had – in abundance. Somewhere as she walked that night, while Neville worried for her safety and waited for her call, Doreen reached the decision that the private prosecution must go ahead, and when her mind was made up she immediately stopped at a public telephone and rang Imran Khan to tell him. Half an hour later she was home.

Over the next three months a delicate and unprecedented transition took place as a high-level police investigation slowly became a private prosecution. As Doreen Lawrence had envisaged, she and her husband, with Imran Khan and Michael Mansfield, took charge of events while Ian Johnston and Perry Nove slipped into the background. Nove had hinted as early as August that in the event of a private prosecution the Metropolitan Police would help (it would, he had said, 'consider cooperating with any strategy that was capable of putting Stephen Lawrence's killers before a court') and he was as good as his word. Various devices were proposed and employed to ensure that Khan would have sufficient documentation to prepare for legal action and many precedents were created in the field of police openness. The Crown Prosecution Service, characteristically, was more cautious. Howard Youngerwood remained convinced that a private prosecution would fail and in letters and telephone calls to Khan he repeatedly and passionately warned him of the consequence: any of the suspects who were acquitted could never be tried for the murder again, no matter what new evidence turned up. But the CPS position was that they would not stand in the way of the private prosecution or of police cooperation with it.

For a short period the interests of all three parties converged neatly, while the police offered Gary Dobson immunity. This was the last throw of the dice. Mellish's team took the initiative, the CPS provided the legal clearance for the offer and the family announced the private prosecution at a time calculated to increase the pressure on Dobson. Gary was chosen because he had been the most talkative and cooperative at the time of his arrest in 1993, because he had always been reputed to be the weak link and because the surveillance on his flat had confirmed the impression that, of the five, he was the least comfortable, the one who was having to struggle to keep up. There were other reasons: he was represented by his own solicitor, who did not act for any of the other prime suspects; he had a reasonable alibi for the night of the murder and he was the only one of the five not identified in some way as having been at the scene either by Duwayne Brooks or by Witness B. The police believed, moreover, that if he was a member of the attacking group he was the least likely of the five to have used a knife. On that basis, he was the best qualified to receive immunity on the CPS's terms.

The approach began in mid-January with a knock on the door of Gary's flat in Footscray Road. Detective Sergeant Tim White from Mellish's team introduced himself and asked if he could come in; he already knew that Gary, who had just woken up, was alone. Politely and without any suggestion of confrontation, he explained that he was investigating the Lawrence murder but that he had not been involved in the case at the time when Gary was arrested back in 1993. Gary was equally polite, even friendly, and he appeared to answer questions and give his views frankly. They talked for more than half an hour. Very gently, White carried out his mission, suggesting that if Gary would like to talk about the night of the murder they could meet in the company of an independent solicitor, from outside the area. The police, he hinted, might be inclined to take a rather different view of someone who cooperated with them and who was not actually a stabber. Gary should think about this but he should not mention it to his friends; it might be the smart thing to do. Gary, for his part, seemed to get the message, although he promised nothing, but as the conversation went on it appeared that his position had not changed much since he was first questioned by 'OJ' Davidson. 'None of us was involved,' he said, 'it was a bad case of misjustice.' He complained of a plot by the Tylers, by EE and his family and by K – all of whom had been named to him by Davidson – and said they 'lied and tried to put me and my friends in prison for something that we never done'. The police and the media had 'tunnel vision' on the case and had formed 'completely the wrong impression of us'. He stated: 'I just want a public apology in the newspaper when it becomes clear that it was not us.' Although this all appeared strongly felt – Gary had a particular animus for Davidson, whom he called a 'fucking nutter' – it was delivered confidently and calmly, and he seemed untroubled to be in conversation with a detective. After White left, however, Gary phoned the other suspects to tell them about the approach and they apparently instructed him to say nothing. But for some reason he also changed his solicitor, instructing Michael Holmes, who was based some distance away in Penge. Hopes were briefly raised when Holmes made contact with the police, seeking an appointment with Bill Mellish. They met, and Mellish explained to him the terms of the immunity offer; he seemed interested and he agreed to relay it to his client, but that was the end of the matter. Gary Dobson was not prepared, in Bill Mellish's terms, to 'come our way'. After just under a year, the bold strategy conceived by Johnston and overseen by Nove had come to nothing.

In March Imran Khan picked up the baton. 'It would be inappropriate to delay the private prosecution any longer,' he wrote to the CPS, asking for all the key documents within a week. It took a little longer, but by the end of that month an agreement had been reached under which Khan and his colleagues gave an undertaking that any materials they were given would be used for the private prosecution and no other purpose. By now the police had already contacted most of the hundreds of people who had given statements to the Fishpool investigation, asking them whether they would consent to the use of the documents by the Lawrences' legal team. Most gave their permission freely but a few dozen objected – their statements were 'redacted', the names being replaced by numbers or letters and the addresses removed. On 7 April the first tranche of documents, in several large boxes, finally reached Khan and Mansfield and just five days later they reported to police that they felt there was sufficient evidence to proceed. A further ten days passed before, in the legal phrase, 'informations were laid' at Greenwich Magistrates Court against Neil Acourt, Jamie Acourt, David Norris and Luke Knight for the murder of Stephen Lawrence on Well Hall Road on the night of 22 April 1993 – two years before, to the day. The police were ready, and the four were immediately arrested. Gary Dobson was left alone, for the moment.

Chapter Fourteen The Video

After the arrests, the next formal stage in the prosecution was the committal proceedings, at which a magistrate would decide whether the case was sufficiently strong to be put before a full court with a jury. In effect this would be a rehearsal for the trial, with defence barristers present to challenge arguments and cross-examine witnesses. It was set for 23 August. The hub of the preparations was Michael Mansfield's chambers, or offices, in an alleyway called Tooks Court close to the High Court on the Strand. The Lawrences and their legal team found this a period of revelations. So long in the dark about the case, they now had in their hands a mountain of paperwork generated by the Fishpool detectives, including Holmes computer records and witness statements, and as they read they began to form an impression of what had gone wrong. Two discoveries in particular astonished and outraged them: first, the volume and timeliness of information given to the police identifying the prime suspects, and second, the possible role of Clifford Norris. The Lawrences had long been aware that the identity of the killers was the subject of lively rumour in Eltham very soon after the murder, but they had had no idea of the contribution made by the man known as James Grant, nor had they heard about the two anonymous letters or the calls by the Female Anon. All of these, it could now be seen from the Holmes records, had pointed police towards the prime suspects within forty-eight hours – and yet no arrests were made for two weeks. In this light, the failure of the first investigation seemed more scandalous than ever. As for Cliff Norris, the vague explanations given by Perry Nove suddenly became vivid fact: the father of one of the suspects was a violent gangster. The Lawrences were appalled that they had never been told this, if only for their own safety. Such feelings, however, had to remain private, since Khan and his legal colleagues had undertaken to use the documents for prosecution purposes only. In any case the urgent priority was to assemble from the documents the strongest possible legal case against the four accused.

At Scotland Yard, senior officers and officials were making a discovery of their own. The video recordings made in Gary Dobson's flat before Christmas had never been given a wide circulation; once Mellish had decided that they provided him with no useful evidence it was normal that such covert materials should be discreetly handled. In the light of the private prosecution, however, the tapes were re-examined to see if they should be disclosed to the Lawrence lawyers and the result was dramatic. While it could be seen that in plain terms Mellish was right and that there were no admissions of guilt on the tapes, they contained revelations about the attitudes and behaviour of the suspects that might well be very damaging to them in the eyes of a jury. Moreover there was one scene in which they explicitly denied involvement in the murder, which on close examination might be construed as meaning the opposite, as being an ironic confession. Senior officers such as Commander John Grieve, who was the head of the anti-terrorist squad and the man with overall responsibility for covert activities, and officials such as Peter Essex of the Met solicitors' department came to the view that the tapes might be important evidence. The police even approached the CPS suggesting that the Lawrence case might be reinstated as a public prosecution, but they were rebuffed. They then resolved to put the tapes in the hands of the Lawrence team, although this presented some legal difficulties. A transcript containing edited highlights of the tapes was delivered to Tooks Court, where it provoked intense excitement, but the Met then explained that it did not feel free simply to hand over the tapes themselves. The problem was that, as with most covertly gathered evidence, the content revealed the method of surveillance. In this particular case the police were relaxed about such exposure, but if a precedent were created it could mean that many of their most sophisticated covert surveillance methods might ultimately be revealed to the criminal community. This obstacle could be overcome, however, since the Met was ready to hand the tapes over if instructed to do so by a judge. A hearing was arranged and in July a judge duly ruled that these tapes were not subject to public interest immunity since the public interest would be best served by their disclosure to the private prosecution team. The cassettes were handed over and, with just a few weeks to go before the committal hearing, Mansfield, Khan and their colleagues set about incorporating them into the case.

The tapes comprised dozens of scenes from inside the Footscray Road flat featuring Neil Acourt, Gary Dobson, David Norris and

Luke Knight as well as their friends Charlie Martin and Danny Caetano and one or two others. Jamie Acourt was in custody at the time, awaiting trial for the Stars nightclub stabbings. The black-and-white images on the video were a little blurred but the identities of those pictured were not in doubt. The frame, embracing about half the room, was always the same: to the right were a wall and window; in centre screen were some armchairs, with two doors beyond, one leading to the kitchen and the other to a small lobby and the front door; to the left, near the kitchen door, was the edge of the dining table. The scenes were recorded over about three weeks from 2 December 1994 onwards, some of them lasting just a few seconds and some several minutes, and the soundtrack was of mixed quality, with the subjects' voices often difficult to hear over the stereo or the television. At moments, the clearest voices on the tape were those of Desmond Lynam, Alan Hansen or Bob Wilson, dissecting the latest events in English or European football.

From the outset it is clear that the group knew or strongly suspected that they were being bugged, although it does not seem to have occurred to them that they might also be on camera. Shortly after the bug was installed, Neil and Gary returned to the flat and spotted that some of the electrical sockets had been changed. Neil demanded to know what had happened.

GARY: Landlord's been round and done the fucking things today . . . I didn't even know he was coming round, mate. I came in and I seen all the plugs and that, fitted on.

NEIL: Was Charlie here?

GARY: No, not that I know of. I come in and . . .

NEIL: What, he come in your house . . . ?

GARY: He comes in. He comes in to fix things. He come in to fix the cupboards, but we knew about the cupboards . . .

NEIL: You're joking.

GARY: No, I didn't even know, Neil, I didn't even know myself. He said to Charlie, 'I'll be coming round Monday to do the door in your bedroom . . .'

NEIL: Who put all them cassette things in there?

GARY: He must have. I didn't even fucking realize.

NEIL: I don't believe you're letting the geezer in your house. So what if he's the landlord . . . phone him up.

GARY: I can't say . . . He's gonna turn round and say, 'Well get out of my flat then.'

NEIL: You say, 'Bring the deposit down and poke it up your arse. It's my fucking house.' What's he doing coming in?

GARY: I know that, Neil.

NEIL: Gal, it don't matter who he is he can't just walk in here like that.

Neil appears to have been concerned not only because he believed Gary's rights had been infringed but also because he suspected that the landlord had seen an electric stun gun that was in the flat, an illegal object that was a favourite toy of his. Gary remained defensive and apologetic and eventually observed that it was the first time he had noticed that the landlord had done such a thing. This prompted Neil to say: 'It ain't the first time he's been here. This gaff could be bugged up to the eyes, mate . . . I bet this gaff's bugged up to the eyebrows, mate.' For days afterwards the landlord's visit and the sockets remained a topic of conversation, aired before every visitor to the flat. Neil's suspicions appeared to turn into firm convictions. 'Let's speak so we can only understand each other, just to be safe, 'cos the geezer come in the other day with someone and done all that plug,' he told Luke and Charlie. Then, fortissimo: 'Anyone's listening, they already know that they suck horses' cocks, so we ain't got to really say nothing, have we?'

While those in the flat heard Neil's warnings, they were not overly inhibited. Here, for example, Luke and Neil are watching a football match on television and Luke complains about the commentary.

LUKE: I think it was Cameroon, a fucking nigger country.

NEIL: Who was saying that?

LUKE: Fucking our presenter. English presenters saying, 'Oh, yeah, we want Cameroon to win this.' Why the fuck should he want niggers to win it when they're playing, like, Italy or something, like a European fucking football team?

NEIL: It makes you sick, dunnit?

LUKE: Gets on ya nerves.

NEIL: (*to television*) You rubber-lipped cunt. (*Laughs*) I reckon that every nigger should be chopped up, mate, and they should be left with nothing but fucking stumps.

233

LUKE: D'you remember that Enoch Powell? That geezer, he knew straight away. He went over to Africa and all that, right?

NEIL: Is that what happened?

LUKE: Yeah, he knew it was a slum. He knew it was a shithole and he came back here saying they're uncivilized and all that and then they started coming over here and he knew, he knew straight away. He was saying, 'No, I don't want them here. No fucking niggers; they'll ruin the gaff.' And he was right, they fucking have ruined it.

NEIL: Is he still alive?

LUKE: I seen him on a programme the other day.

NEIL: What was he saying?

LUKE: He wasn't saying nothing about niggers and all that, he was just saying about . . . something else.

NEIL: I wanna write him a letter: 'Enoch Powell, mate, you are the greatest. You are the don of dons. Get back into Parliament mate and show these cock suckers what it's all about – about all these flash, arrogant, big-mouthed, shouting-their-mouths-off, flash, dirty rapists, grass cunts.'

LUKE: Yeah, fucking rapists and everything.

Neil, Dave Norris and Luke discussed the national lottery.

DAVE: Why on earth do old grannies want to play? They'll all die before . . .

NEIL: At least they are white.

DAVE: (a little later) See if I was there, if I was one of the crowd, I tell you I would mug them.

NEIL: What, rob them?

DAVE: If I was in the crowd, I'm telling you I'd fucking mug 'em, I'm telling you. For 500 grand . . .

NEIL: So would I, mate.

DAVE: I would mug 'em. I'd kill the cunts. I'm telling you.

NEIL: You've got to wait till they've cashed it, gone to the bank.

The lottery was a novelty at the time and it cropped up several times in conversation. Neil was impressed by the millions of pounds to be won, while Gary had an observation of his own.

GARY: The Spanish one's good. The Spanish one's good and all, the Spanish lottery.

NEIL: Well, Gal, tell me one thing. What's the matter with ours? Seventeen and a half million . . .

GARY: I know. There's nothing the matter with ours. I'm saying the Spanish lottery's good as well.

The following day they learned who had won the first jackpot.

GARY: It's a Paki!

NEIL: Fuck off.

GARY: It's a Paki, mate.

NEIL: Fuck off.

GARY: A Paki who won. Look: 'The lottery jackpot is a married Asian factory worker with three sons . . .'

NEIL: You're joking.

The boys watched a good deal of television, often supplying commentary of their own. Neil and Luke watched the BBC's *Sports Personality of the Year* programme together.

LUKE: I guarantee I know who wins it: Linford fucking Christie.

NEIL: Fuck off. Damon Hill.

LUKE: He's good.

NEIL: (*to television*) Bollocks, you nigger. I want Montgomerie to win it. Or Sally Gunnell.

LUKE: Ah, she might win as it goes.

NEIL: A macaroon better not win it, mate.

LUKE: I guarantee it's a macaroon. Either Colin Jackson or Linford Christie.

For the record, it was Damon Hill who won. On another evening Neil Acourt watched a Royal Command Performance on his own, and a singer could be heard performing 'Luck be a lady tonight'. 'Black cunt,' he observed. 'Get off our fucking royal performances, you.'

Once, Gary took exception to an advertisement.

GARY: This is racist, this advert.

NEIL: Is it?

GARY: Niggers having a good time in the sun. All the white people
waiting at a bus stop. All the niggers are having a good time at the
bar drinking. The white fat bouncer looks a cunt. Good-looking
black geezers in the club all having a good time and the fucking
white geezers are all boring.

NEIL: That's racist that advert . . . How d'you complain?

GARY: You have to write to fucking television complaints division or
something, give your address or something.

While he spoke, and sometimes in silent mime, Neil Acourt could
often be seen playing with a knife. When he was not holding it, it
usually lay at the end of the window-sill, ready to be picked up and
slipped into his waistband as he went out. But it seemed that he
could not leave it there for long. As he talked or listened, he would
casually swing it over his shoulder in a bowling motion, or he would
slash the air, back and forth at neck height, or hack at a chair, or
silently practise stabbing on one of the others, stopping just short
of injury in a sort of dare. Once, on his own, he stabbed the door,
muttering to himself, 'I am hard. I can punch doors.' On another
occasion he sat watching television with the five-inch blade resting
on his thigh, running his fingers up and down it in an unconscious
simulation of masturbation, his eyes and thoughts on the screen.
His other games with the knife and the stun gun seemed to be played
more against his friends than with them. 'Start talking little man,'
he says as he points the knife at Luke, who is sitting. Then, 'What
do you reckon on these shoes? Do you like them or not?' Luke replies
that they seem fair enough and Neil again launches into a mock
attack, saying casually, 'I reckon they're all right. Fuck all the matter
with them.' To Charlie he says when he finds a nick in the blade,
'That's the bit that fucks you on this . . . Look, I was showing Luke
the other day, you know these things, look if you want you just
push it in.' He pushed the knife into the chair. 'Look, it goes straight
in.' Charlie complains: 'Neil, ah, ah, it really hurt yesterday.' But
Neil completes the lesson: 'It goes right in like, if you want to cut
somebody you just put that bit on their face and go . . . Feel it on
your hand.'

There are samples, too, of almost absurd violence, perhaps rage.
A large parcel flies across the room and lands on the floor near the
door. Neil jumps on it and kicks it with all his strength. 'Do him!'

he says. The parcel contains leaflets that Charlie has undertaken to distribute door-to-door. 'That'd hurt 'em, mate!' says Neil, still kicking. Luke remarks: 'It would hurt them. It would kill 'em.' Once, too, Neil hurls a chair across the room, shouting, 'Smash it up! Let's beat the cunt off the gaff, mate.' Charlie, who as one of the tenants is responsible for the contents of the flat, feebly tries to calm his friend: 'The thing is, right, if we didn't have this flat nowadays, where would we go?'

If Neil dominates the flat, bullying, butting into conversations, arguing, waving the knife and showing off, Dave Norris is not one of the underdogs. He has his position; he is quieter, but violence is not far from his thoughts. Here he is, reflecting on his life.

DAVE: Do you know, the last two years of my life, all it is, it's been really tensed up so much you know. When I was inside: non-stop fighting 'cos I was so tense. Come out, I rowed with me mum every fucking night. I ain't got no money; I'm still tense now two years later. Like, fucking, I must have felt happy, what, one week? So, like, do you know what I mean by one week? Seven days out of two fucking years. I ain't depressed but the rest of the time I'd just got the hump. I mean I don't want to be like that. I want to be happy. I want to be like, loads of money, go on holiday to America . . . [Refers to his girlfriend] I want to get her a tidy car. Then I can sit, I can sit, I can sit here every night and think to meself, me bird's got a brand-new Golf GTI convertible or whatever she gets, or a Carlton or whatever, and I'm sitting there, I've got meself, like, two or three businesses. Jamie's out, d'ya know what I mean? It ain't been too bad since I've been out, but then again if we never got fucking nicked for something we never done, mate, then we might have been earning a lot more, d'ya know what I mean? We'd be a lot further than we are now. Then again that's past, mate. Fuck 'em [the police]. Do you know the best way to get at them cunts is to earn millions and millions of pounds, straight as a fucking die, and then we'll park, we'll pull up outside fucking, I don't know, pull up outside Bromley nick or fucking Greenwich nick, just sit there for two minutes and let them see your car and then wind them up, mate, just sit there and wind them up. That's all I'd do. Fucking cunts. Let them know you're there, mate, like play your music so they'd look out the window or something and then say, 'Look what I've got, mate. Do you want to come and nick me, like, for having all this money?'

This leads on to a discussion of suicide.

DAVE: If I was going to kill myself do you know what I'd do? I'd go and kill every black cunt, every Paki, every copper. Every mug that I know, I'm telling ya. I'm not talking about the people I love and care for, I'm talking about the people I don't like. I'm telling ya, I'm telling ya, then I'd just go home and go boom, straight in me head. That's if I was going to do it, but that's madness . . .

NEIL: I reckon the only thing you could do is to jump off the highest building.

DAVE: No, that's like the worst way to go, mate, know what I mean? Your head's like . . . poooof.

NEIL: Can you imagine jumping off a building and watching it come, come at ya. You just think, yeah, just watching it come, just spinning, yeah . . . I ain't talking a thirty-foot jump. I'm talking Canary Wharf like, to make sure you're fucking dead . . .

DAVE: I'd go down Catford and places like that, I'm telling you now, with two sub-machine guns and I'm telling ya, I'd take one of them, skin the black cunt alive, mate, torture him, set him alight . . . I'd blow their two legs and arms off and say, 'Go on, you can swim home now.'

NEIL: Just let them squirm.

DAVE: They'd be bobbing about like that.

And Dave brags. Here, he gives a confusing account of a violent encounter in the park.

DAVE: I had a fight with an old man, didn't I, about fucking four months ago. I was walking over the park, anyway an old geezer comes up and he was with his wife and kids and that, anyway he was moaning about the dogs being over the field and he came up to me and he was a big cunt and he started going, started going like that, and he was going 'I'll fucking take you on.' I said, 'Leave it out, I ain't gonna hit you.' All of a sudden he went bop on me jaw. So I just stood there and I went to him, smack, upper-cut, and he went crack, and all of a sudden I just flipped. I went and got me screwdriver and all that old lark and come running out and like so I deal with him, and all of a sudden the geezer (*another man*) come and I went to get a club and he grabbed the club and he's like, his daughter's husband or something – so it was his son-in-law . . . Went down the glove compartment, got me brother's club, so I picked it up and started smacking him around the mouth and all of, this nigger come along and I just kneed the cunt right in the bollocks.

CHARLIE: And what, then the nigger joined in?

DAVE: He was a fucking grown man. He was about forty years odd, and his grandad. Smacko. And I was knocking the grandad.

CHARLIE: And then what, the nigger come along?

DAVE: Yeah, a big nigger come along and said, 'Leave the fucking kid alone, you silly cunt.' (*He is stepping in to protect Norris*)

CHARLIE: What? Saying to you . . .

DAVE: And I was going, 'What you talking about?' I start going and called him a black cunt and all that saying he was a fucking coon. He was going, 'Leave it out, mate,' and all of a sudden I just flipped and he was holding the geezer and so I went smack, punched the nigger like that and he was going fucking like, 'What's going on?' He was a massive bloke, definite fucking bodybuilder, definitely, Neil, he was massive mate . . . Fucking nigger's going, 'I'm sorry I helped now.' I said, 'Well, don't butt your nose in then anyway.' We started having an argument. I went, 'Fair enough.' Just walked off.

Gary Dobson cuts a feeble figure beside Dave and Neil. This is his attempt to impress.

GARY: There's a nigger there like me brother used to know years ago. He ain't a nigger but he's black.

NEIL: He's a black cunt.

GARY: He's a black cunt but he ain't, like. Yeah, he ain't a rude boy. He like talks like a normal white geezer, does normal white things, not mug old grannies and things like that, but like he's just one of them type of people who, not on purpose, but like drive you mad, get on your nerves. The other day I nicked his hat. He was getting on me nerves the other day like, he's forever got his hat on. He's like one of the niggers who don't never takes his hat off, so I nicked his baseball cap and he didn't catch me, I got away. He seen me later on and like he got me arm and twisted it behind me back and started mucking about, tapping me on the back of me legs. It weren't hurting but I didn't like it. I just didn't like him doing that and I had the Stanley knife in me pocket, pulled it out and I bit the thing off and I said, 'That'll do there Mick, before I end up fucking cutting ya . . .' All fucking day he was getting on me nerves, Luke . . . I said, 'You tap me once more, you silly cunt, I'm going to just fucking slice this down you.' And he let go me arm and said, 'Ah seriously, Gary, where's me baseball cap?' He's put like the broom handle down, 'cos he's picked a broom handle up. He's gone, 'Seriously, Gary, where's me baseball cap?' I went, 'All right, since you've asked nicely I give it to ya.' So I go downstairs and say, like, 'Here it is.' He went, 'Ah cheers.'

Of all the conversations on the videotape, one struck Michael Mansfield as vitally important, as a key to the case of Stephen Lawrence. It was a discussion about the police, probably for the benefit of police listeners.

NEIL: They all suck cocks. We ain't done nothing. They probably use it on themselves. They probably shag it up the arse.
DAVE: (*Laughs*)
NEIL: Bunch of social worker black cunts . . . The only way they can get in the police force is if the fucking commissioner sucks it for them. Gaylords are back on the scene, trying to fit people up again, mate. They're presuming we're guilty, saying and saying . . .
DAVE: For some reason, Neil, they keep driving us all mad . . . Because I tell you what, for some reason they think there's definitely a gap in their promotion, that's what, mate.
NEIL: Oi Dave.
DAVE: Don't they? For some reason they think we know something. Fucking dense mate.
NEIL: And they ain't got nothing still. The thing that's making me laugh, we ain't done nothing, that's what I mean. There's none of us done fuck all. But the thing that makes me laugh, Dave, they're

gonna be doing it for the rest of their lives, mate, and I'm just
gonna be laughing all the way to the Leeds.

DAVE: Do you know what? Listen, next time they turn up at my door
I am gonna, I am gonna moon at them. Yee, oh!

NEIL: Fuck off you cunts! I'll say, 'Yeah, I know you fancy me boys
but there's no need to keep coming back, I ain't queer. Go away. I
don't take it up the arse and I don't give it so fuck off.' . . . Let
them go wherever they fucking want. For all we know it was that
mob over the East End done it. They're all the fascist people, mate
. . . that's where all that racist attacks happen.

DAVE: Load of bollocks, all it is . . .

NEIL: I fancy they've had a crack deal meself, I fancy. [This refers to
Stephen Lawrence and Duwayne Brooks.]

DAVE: Yeah, they probably did. They probably had.

NEIL: Crack.

DAVE: Yeah, came down to get a bit of toot or something, or had a
bit of crack. It's all gone wrong, the coon's got knackered up and
all of a sudden . . . four innocent people are getting done for it.

NEIL: Yeah, that's what I fancy has happened.

DAVE: That's definitely what's happened, Neil. Every time it comes
on the news the real people are sitting laughing their nuts off.

NEIL: What, the real people . . . ?

DAVE: Yeah, the real people are sitting laughing their nuts off.

LUKE: Thinking they've got away with it, mate. Fucking scot free.

NEIL: Yeah, they're definitely doing that.

LUKE: Here Neil?

NEIL: What?

LUKE: You reckon Man U will go through?

Chapter Fifteen Committal

The committal hearings began on the morning of Wednesday 23 August 1995, at Belmarsh Magistrates Court in Woolwich. The courtroom was modern, bright and open, but the Lawrences were dismayed to discover how small it was, for this was the first time they had seen the men accused of killing Stephen and they were uncomfortably close. Neil and Jamie Acourt, Dave Norris and Luke Knight were neatly turned out, mostly in dark suits, and their mothers sat close by. Neil was now twenty years old – he had been seventeen at the time of the murder – and this was the first time he had ever been prosecuted for a crime. Jamie was nineteen and could not make the same claim: besides his driving and drugs convictions he had recently been tried for the Stars nightclub stabbings – and acquitted on the grounds that he had acted in self-defence. Dave, now a father, had celebrated his nineteenth birthday on the previous day; he too had experience in court, having been cleared of the attempted murder of Stacey Benefield. Luke, still eighteen, had no criminal record.

Presiding was a single stipendiary magistrate, David Cooper. The prosecution, in the form of Michael Mansfield QC, believed it was fortunate to have this particular magistrate on the bench and that he was likely to be sympathetic to their case. Perhaps for that same reason the defence believed they were unfortunate, and they opened the proceedings by trying to persuade Cooper to disqualify himself. One by one the defence barristers – the accused were represented separately – rose to explain that they thought it inappropriate that the same magistrate who had presided over bail hearings involving their clients should also preside over the committal proceedings. At the bail hearings Cooper had heard information about their backgrounds, including police views on how dangerous they were, and defence counsel said this might be thought capable of influencing him against them. The argument was put with oleaginous courtesy. 'One is talking here,' declared Charles Conway, representing Neil Acourt, 'not of bias, but the *appearance* of bias.' Michael Bromley-Martin, acting for Norris, agreed. Appearance, he said, was everything, 'whatever we may think of your own (if I may say so) *clear* abilities'. Trevor Burke, Jamie's counsel, said he spoke for the defendants' families: '*I* will of course accept an assurance that this will not influence you at all. My concern is *they* will not.' Cooper would have none of it. The legal test in such circumstances was whether there was a real danger of bias, he explained. 'Not only is there no real danger in this case; there is no danger of bias whatsoever. I do not want to sound or be pompous, but like all my colleagues I have sworn an oath to be impartial in short terms and that is what I am going to be. So I decline the invitation, as it was put to me, to disqualify myself.'

The real business then began, with a summary presentation by Mansfield of the case against the defendants. He relied, in effect, on just three witnesses: Duwayne Brooks, Witness B and Maureen George, who between them implicated all four of the accused. Brooks had picked Neil Acourt and Knight out of line-ups, Mansfield said, and he had also later recognized a man who could only be Jamie Acourt outside the Starburger restaurant and in the Plough pub. Witness B had seen Norris and Neil Acourt fleeing the scene moments after the stabbing, and heading in the general direction of the Acourt home, and B also thought he had seen Jamie Acourt at the same time. Maureen George, for her part, heard a group of boys running past her house, one of whom called out either 'Hurry up J' or 'Hurry up Jamie'. 'If you put those three elements together,' said Mansfield, 'we say that the group that is running away down Dickson Road comprises David Norris, Neil Acourt and Jamie Acourt . . . and of course Luke Knight.' And there could be no doubt, he went on, that all who were in that group shared responsibility for the murder of Stephen Lawrence. 'It must have been plain to all of them that the object of the exercise was to inflict serious harm to the extent of death.'

Mansfield then turned to knives. First he pointed out that a knife consistent in size and shape with Stephen's wounds had been found in the front garden of the house in Wendover Road. While it could not be proved that this was the murder weapon, it remained a fact that this house was very close to the Acourt home. More directly relevant, perhaps, was the armoury of weapons discovered at 102 Bournbrook Road when Neil and Jamie Acourt were arrested: ten knives, including a Gurkha knife, a tiger-lock knife and a small sword with a scabbard. 'We say that upon arrest plainly there were materials there indicative of certainly possession – I cannot go further than that – possession of the kind of weapons that plainly must have been used to inflict the two vicious injuries on Stephen Lawrence.'

Next came the videotape, for Mansfield an essential pillar of the prosecution. The tapes showed three of the defendants, Neil Acourt, David Norris and Luke Knight (Jamie was in custody at the time), expressing a deep hatred for black people, he explained. Not only did they use 'abusive and almost unrepeatable' language whenever a black person was mentioned or appeared on television, but they also spoke of a desire to cut up black people, torture them and set fire to them. And they could be seen to admire and play with knives and to carry them out into the street. Taken together, Mansfield said, this was evidence of motive; the subjects of the video showed both a propensity to violence with knives and a violent hatred of black people. And he went further, arguing that the tapes also proved that it was no mere accident of mistaken identity that linked the defendants to the racist murder of Stephen Lawrence. Brooks and Witness B, independently, had identified members of the group as being responsible, and now the tape showed these same people to have extreme, violent racist views. This was surely more than a coincidence. Finally, he turned to one particular conversation on the tape, in which the Lawrence murder was discussed. The defendants knew they were being bugged, he pointed out, and were so conscious of it that they often laced their conversation with remarks clearly intended as insults to the police listeners. They were capable, in other words, of acting up for the bug. Mansfield then described the exchange in which Norris suggested that Stephen was killed because of a drug deal:

NORRIS: Yeah, [he's] came down to get a bit of toot or something, or had a bit of crack. It's all gone wrong, the coon's got knackered up and all of a sudden . . . four innocent people are getting done for it.

NEIL ACOURT: Yeah, that's what I fancy has happened.

NORRIS: That's definitely what's happened, Neil. Every time it comes on the news the real people are sitting laughing their nuts off.

NEIL ACOURT: What, the real people . . . ?

NORRIS: Yeah, the real people are sitting laughing their nuts off.

KNIGHT: Thinking they've got away with it, mate. Fucking scot free.

NEIL ACOURT: Yeah, they're definitely doing that.

What these three did not know was that they were also being filmed, said Mansfield, and this meant that their physical reaction to these words was extremely revealing. As the exchange ended, he said, they were smiling or laughing. When they spoke of 'the real people' – the killers – 'sitting laughing their nuts off', Mansfield was suggesting that these young men were doing just that: sitting laughing their nuts off, in the belief that they could not be seen. He explained: 'It is as if someone is saying, "Ha ha, we did not do it, nudge-nudge, wink-wink." In other words it is capable of the opposite inference, given their demeanour when they said those words.' It was an admission of guilt. The tapes, Mansfield concluded, thus provided evidence of motive, confirmed the identity of the attackers and showed them implicitly admitting their guilt. It was 'the final cement for this case', since in all these ways it corroborated the key evidence supplied by Brooks and B.

This, then, was the sum of all the detective work carried out since the murder by the likes of Crampton, Budgen, Weeden, Davidson, Tomlin, Chase, Wilkinson, White and Mellish. And this, too, was the case that the Crown Prosecution Service had rejected. They had rejected it in the summer of 1993, when it depended only on the word of Duwayne Brooks; they had rejected it when B had changed his evidence at the end of 1993 and they had rejected it when they were alerted to the video in May of 1995. Now the various strands had been drawn together, the vital elements identified and the supporting arguments mustered by a leading QC, albeit one more accustomed to defence than prosecution. Although journalists were present, none of this evidence and none of Mansfield's oratory could be published in the media because the proceedings were subject to reporting restrictions. Committal proceedings were public only in the sense that members of the public could sit in the gallery; unless the defence asked for the restrictions to be lifted (which in this case they did not) the press could say nothing about what went on unless and until the case came to trial. It remained now for Mansfield to run through the evidence in detail, with witnesses where appropriate, and for the defence barristers to mount their separate and various challenges, which they did with vigour and some success. The process took ten more days.

Duwayne Brooks was the first important witness and he had a rough ride. He was clearly nervous and uncomfortable as Mansfield led him slowly through the evening of the murder and, in considerable detail, through the attack itself. Asked to describe the attackers, Duwayne spoke of a tall youth with short, black hair who stabbed Stephen, a shorter one with black hair and another shorter youth with long blond hair. His answers were short, often just yes or no, and given so quietly that occasionally Mansfield had to ask him to speak up. Once, when Duwayne was struggling to describe events after the murder, the magistrate broke in to say: 'Mr Brooks, I know this is an ordeal for you. Can you do your best?' For the most part, his evidence closely followed his many statements to the police, which he had been allowed to re-read before testifying, but when it came to the Starburger and Plough pub encounters, he added something new.

MANSFIELD: What is the description of the one you had definitely seen before, that you can now recollect?
BROOKS: He was tall, medium build, short, black hair.
MANSFIELD: Where had you seen that person before?
BROOKS: At Eltham.
MANSFIELD: Where do you mean in Eltham?
BROOKS: At the time of the incident.
MANSFIELD: Can you recall what that person had been doing at the time of the incident?
BROOKS: He stabbed him.

Mansfield's case was that the young man whom Duwayne had seen in these two encounters could only have been Jamie Acourt, because Duwayne commented that he looked like the brother or twin of the first man he picked out of an identification parade – Neil. In effect, therefore, Duwayne was now saying that Jamie had stabbed Stephen.

Charles Conway, for Neil Acourt, asked not what Duwayne had seen, but how clearly he had seen it. How soon after seeing the white boys did he call out to Stephen to run? How soon after that did he himself start to run? When he was running, he looked back, but from where? And for how long? The questioning was sharp, even aggressive, and the object was clear: Conway was implying that no one could have seen or remembered much in such circumstances. In the witness box Duwayne, who had not been put under pressure in this way before, showed the strain. At one point he said he saw the stabbing itself, but then Conway produced Duwayne's original statement, made hours after the attack, and read a passage that included the sentence: 'I didn't see the knife go into Stephen.' It was at the moment when Conway was pressing home this point, implying that Duwayne was contradicting himself, that something else happened in court. The passage read from Duwayne's statement did not stop with the reference to the knife going in, but continued: 'Stephen immediately screamed in pain, high-pitched and loud.' Doreen and Neville Lawrence, sitting together in the increasingly tense courtroom, heard this with shock. They had never read the statement and they had never been told that Stephen had screamed, indeed a great deal of what Duwayne was recounting was new to them. For Neville the reference to the scream was more than he could bear. 'I felt the pain myself and I could not stand it,' he said later. He rose from his seat, left the chamber and was heard to cry out and collapse in the hall outside. Proceedings were halted as an ambulance was summoned and moments later Neville, with Doreen, left for hospital, where he recovered within a couple of hours.

When proceedings restarted in the courtroom Conway moved on to the descriptions that Duwayne gave police after the murder, and again he read from the statement given in the early hours of 23 April 1993. This was how Duwayne described the man who struck Stephen: 'I would describe his hair as being long, over his ears. It was frizzy and stuck out at the sides. Most of his hair was down at the sides and I could clearly see his forehead. He had an oval face. I can't really describe his facial features but I think I would recognize him again from his hair and general look.' Conway asked: 'That is the stabber, right?' And Duwayne said: 'No.' Conway did not press the point – he scarcely needed to – but moved on to the identity parades, the Welling demonstration and the involvement of Detective Sergeant Christopher Crowley. The thrust of the questioning was now an implication that Duwayne had been angry after the murder, had wished to take revenge, had been 'fed' the name and descriptions of the Acourts by friends and had picked out Neil on that basis. Duwayne proved more comfortable on these subjects, and particularly on matters relating to Crowley, and he yielded little ground.

Jamie Acourt's counsel, Trevor Burke, rose next and returned to the problem of the stabber's description. 'What is the more accurate description?' he asked. 'Is it short black hair or long frizzy hair?' Duwayne replied: 'Short black hair.' His original description had been wrong, he said. Then Burke went over once again the occasions when Duwayne saw the man with short black hair at the Starburger restaurant and the Plough pub. He referred to the statement Duwayne gave police after these sightings and said: 'The statement is to hand if you want to have it, but will you accept from me that you never indicated that the man you had seen in the pub or at the Starburger was the stabber?'

DUWAYNE: I never indicated that?
BURKE: No. Why not?
DUWAYNE: I don't know why not.
BURKE: Weren't you sure?
DUWAYNE: I can't remember how I was thinking at the time.

Duwayne's ordeal ended soon after this exchange, but the defence, and Jamie's counsel in particular, had scored some palpable hits. The case against Jamie was from the outset the weakest of the four: Duwayne had not picked him out of a line-up, Witness B was vague about whether he saw him running from the scene and he did not appear in the video. The sightings in the pub and at the burger restaurant were crucial, but it had never been confirmed that Jamie was at either location at the appropriate time. Now Jamie's counsel was clearly implying that Duwayne had changed his story about those sightings and about the role of the man he saw. Such doubts benefited not only Jamie but Neil and Luke, since anything that brought Duwayne's reliability into question would erode the standing of his identifications. At the same time, Conway and Timothy Kendal (acting for Luke) were mustering evidence to suggest that those identifications were a classic 'fleeting glance' case under the Turnbull rules and therefore unsafe.

Witness B, the young man who said he had seen something from the top of a bus, had only agreed to give evidence on the promise of anonymity, saying he feared for his own and his family's safety.

He was thus referred to in court only as Witness B and arrangements had been made for him to testify from behind a screen. Before he could enter the witness box, however, the defence challenged this arrangement as unfair; they wanted to know who he was. The attack was led by Michael Bromley-Martin, representing Dave Norris, who pointed out that this witness's evidence was the central pillar of the prosecution's case against his client – Witness B said he was sure he saw Norris running from the scene. As far as Bromley-Martin was concerned, this was a witness 'whose creditworthiness is only marginally above zero' and whom police had previously dismissed as a Walter Mitty character (DS Davidson's verdict). B had told the police one story in May 1993 and sworn it was true for six months. Then he suddenly changed his story completely and swore that the new account was true. Why should he be believed? As for anonymity, Bromley-Martin said that, since Witness B claimed to have recognized Norris from the top of a bus at night, it was vital to establish how well he knew him, and for that he would have to ask B how and when he had met Norris and how often he had seen him. Such questions would be impossible with an anonymous witness, he said. Legal arguments followed, taking up the best part of a day, and it was the following week, Tuesday 29, before Cooper gave his ruling: Witness B *could* give his evidence anonymously. Bromley-Martin then appealed to the High Court against this decision, but was rebuffed. On the Wednesday, Witness B took his place in a screened witness box, before a special microphone that lent his voice what listeners agreed was a Dalek quality.

Mansfield took him through the story of how he was travelling home on the bus when he saw four youths running out of Cobbett Road and into Rochester Way. The one in front he did not recognize but the second was David Norris and the third Neil Acourt. For the defence, Bromley-Martin questioned briefly but effectively. He established that the sighting had been made at some distance and lasted only a 'short time'. Then he turned to the issue of recognition.

BROMLEY-MARTIN: When was the last time that you had seen David Norris?

WITNESS B: I couldn't honestly tell you. He was always around the area.

BROMLEY-MARTIN: Have you ever spoken to David Norris?

WITNESS B: Yes.

BROMLEY-MARTIN: How long prior to this incident had you spoken to him?

WITNESS B: I can't remember. Not an actual date.

BROMLEY-MARTIN: Are you a friend of his?

WITNESS B: No.

BROMLEY-MARTIN: Who told you what his name was?

WITNESS B: The friends I used to go around with. They knew him and that's how I got to meet him.

BROMLEY-MARTIN: Was it they who told you his name?

WITNESS B: I just picked up his name.

BROMLEY-MARTIN: That is the only way you know his name?

WITNESS B: Yes.

Conway followed this with a string of questions stressing that B had only ever had a side view of two of the people he saw. Indeed, at first he had a back view, until the bus drew closer. 'You saw the group for a total of five to seven seconds?' he asked. 'Yes,' said B. 'It must follow that whatever view you had of the side of their faces must have been less than five to seven seconds. You have to agree.' 'Yes,' came the reply. Once again, a 'fleeting glance' case was being built. Like Bromley-Martin Conway wanted to know how well Witness B knew his client, and here B was surprisingly forthcoming for a man wishing to protect his anonymity. He revealed that he had known Neil at the Sammy Montague club, where he played football with Jamie. And finally, Conway pressed him: was he sure it was Neil he had seen, or Jamie? This was B's most vulnerable spot, for since making his statement to police in November 1993 he had been interviewed again, and a doubt had crept into his evidence. Conway probed at it.

CONWAY: So the position today is that you cannot be sure which it is; is that right?

WITNESS B: That is correct.

CONWAY: You felt it was Neil because he was bigger than Jamie?

WITNESS B: Yes, he is bigger built.

CONWAY: And taller?

WITNESS B: Not really that much taller.

This was all damaging to the prosecution, not least because Neil was *smaller* than Jamie and, in 1995 at least, not noticeably better built. Mansfield re-examined, hoping to carry out some repairs. Witness B, he established, was 'not 100 per cent sure' he had seen Neil rather than Jamie, but he was 'quite sure'. As for Norris, Mansfield tried to undo the impression that B knew him only slightly. B had been aware of Norris around the Brook estate for a matter of years, seeing him on average once a fortnight, usually in the company of the Acourt boys. How had B learned the name? He had heard other boys call him Dave. And the surname? He had picked that up in the same way. At this Bromley-Martin rose again and asked whether B had ever heard both names used together, and B replied that he had not.

As far as the prosecution was concerned, things were going badly. Bromley-Martin had laid the groundwork for an argument that would run something like this: B had a fleeting glance, from the top of a moving bus at night, of the side of a man's face; he recognized this as a man who might be called Dave, and might be called Norris, and might be called both. Given that there was no other identification evidence against Norris, this could only be described as a very weak case. During a lunchtime recess Mansfield consulted with his junior, Stephen Kamlish, and they opted for a bold measure. They asked Bromley-Martin if Norris would stand in an identification parade for Witness B. After consulting with Norris and his solicitor, Henry Milner, Bromley-Martin agreed and an appointment was made at Southwark police station for the morning of Saturday 2 September. This was a gamble for both sides: Mansfield was confident that Witness B had known Norris well enough to recognize him back in 1993, but he was also aware that B had not seen Norris since then. Young people change in their late teens; would B know his man? As for Milner and Bromley-Martin, they were already in a strong position which would be badly damaged if B picked out Norris. But on the basis of his answers in court they had come to the conclusion that B hardly knew Norris, so they felt it a chance worth taking. On the Saturday morning Norris sat in the line-up in Southwark station while B walked up and down behind the one-way windows. He took his time, and then he picked out the wrong man.

This development was reported to the court when the case resumed on 6 September, and then battle was joined over the video. The defence argued passionately that the tapes were inadmissible as evidence for a great range of reasons. Something that was filmed twenty months after the offence, they said, could not be used to prove a motive – a motive had to exist, and be shown to exist, *before* the crime. And while it was true that the tapes showed Knight, Norris and Neil Acourt to be racists, they had no monopoly on such views. 'These views are, from my personal point of view, disgusting and unpalatable,' said Conway, 'but all over England there are young men with extreme racial views of this nature. They go to football matches. They are in pubs. They are even on television sometimes.' As for Mansfield's argument that their denial of the crime on tape amounted to an admission, counsel for Knight and Norris insisted that their clients were *not* smiling or laughing when the key words were spoken, while Conway pointed out that Neil Acourt was clearly smoking a joint at the time, and that may have explained his demeanour. In any case, said Conway, it would be perverse for a court to take people's words and read into them the direct opposite of their meaning. Above all, however, Conway pressed the argument of prejudice. 'I submit that this tape screams out with prejudice,' he said. And he went on:

> A jury in their jury room will look at these tapes and say to themselves: 'Mr Neil Acourt is so unpalatable and has such wicked views that he must be guilty because he is just the sort of person who would have done it.' They will therefore be swamped by the sea of prejudice into not considering what I submit are the real issues in this case, namely, can we rely on the identification of Brooks and B? If this evidence is admitted, the tapes will become the main aspect of the case . . . and they will dwarf the real evidence.

Mansfield, in a long and very detailed response peppered with the foul language of the tapes, answered these arguments. He elaborated on what he said were the probative elements of the recordings, such as the similarity between the bowling action used by Neil Acourt when he was playing at stabbing in the flat and the action that must have been required to inflict the wound on Stephen Lawrence's chest. Painstakingly he went through the conversation which he claimed was an admission of guilt, drawing on the many other moments when the boys appeared to be performing for the microphone. And equally carefully, he showed the instances of violent racial hatred. The magistrate sided with Mansfield. In a long ruling he rejected one by one the defence arguments, dealt one by one with the legal precedents and came to the conclusion that the tapes could be admitted as evidence. 'I bear in mind the method and weapon used to kill Mr Lawrence, the number and likely type of youth to be involved, the joint enterprise alleged, the words used by one of the youths prior to the murder. Light is thrown on each of these important aspects by the videos.' He did not himself accept Mansfield's argument about the supposed admission in the tapes, he said, but that would be a matter for a jury if there was to be a trial. Over the vociferous protests of defence counsel, Cooper also ruled that the tapes should be screened in court, and this was promptly done. The defendants watched without notable reaction, as did their mothers.

Would there be a trial? Not for Jamie Acourt. After Duwayne Brooks's evidence about the Starburger and Plough pub sightings, after B's equivocal evidence about which Acourt he had seen, and given that Jamie did not appear in the video, the prosecution team decided that it was hopeless to continue against him. Once the arguments about the video were concluded, Mansfield informed the court that he would no longer be seeking to have Jamie committed for trial. After a few satisfied words from the defence, Cooper turned to the dock and said: 'Mr Jamie Acourt, would you stand up please? You are discharged. You are free to go.' And not for David Norris either. After Witness B failed to pick him out at Southwark, he too was discharged. Both these young men had been charged in the Witham case, but never tried. Norris had been tried in the Benefield case, and acquitted. Jamie Acourt had been tried in the Stars nightclub case, and acquitted. Now they were both walking away from the case of Stephen Lawrence.

For Neil Acourt and Luke Knight it was not over. A further day was devoted to the evidence of Christopher Crowley and in a very hostile interrogation Mansfield undoubtedly shook the detective sergeant. But there was no knockout and that shadow still hung over Duwayne's evidence. After Crowley left the box the various counsel made their closing submissions and on the morning of 11 September David Cooper gave his final ruling. With reference to legal authorities he explained that his role was clear: he was not to try the case but to decide whether there was sufficient evidence to justify a trial. This meant that when it came to arguments about the credibility of a witness – by implication Duwayne Brooks – it was not for him to make a judgment but for a jury. He praised the defence counsel for their efforts but said that he had found the prosecution arguments compelling: 'I am therefore of the opinion that there is sufficient evidence to put Neil Acourt and Luke Knight on trial for the murder of Mr Stephen Lawrence.'

'Yes!' said Doreen Lawrence, in relief and delight. She had been optimistic at the outset, but anxiety grew in her by the day, and the events surrounding Jamie Acourt and David Norris had left her fearful that all four might escape. Now, however, there would be a trial at the Central Criminal Court – the Old Bailey – and most importantly the evidence would be heard by a jury. Doreen, Neville, Mansfield and Khan were of one mind on this: a jury was their best hope. British people may be generally conservative by nature and often prejudiced in one way or another, but defence lawyers know that in cases which challenge the system and cases which involve an apparent underdog those same British people can be sympathetic, defiant towards tradition and the authorities, and even radical. This was such a case. And besides such thoughts for the future, there was the sense of vindication. In the family's view, David Cooper's decision proved that the CPS had been wrong. Outside the court, Doreen read a statement:

> It has been two years now since the Crown Prosecution Service dropped charges against two men for the murder of our son, without even caring to consult or advise us of their decision. It was an act as hurtful and as painful in its effect as the news that Stephen had been killed. Since that time we have fought against tremendous obstacles to reach this stage. These obstacles have been overcome by our own private efforts, with the help of our family and many supporters who have joined us along the way, and at great financial risk . . . No family should ever experience the last two years of our lives. This is the worst kind of fame. We have been brought into the public spotlight not by our own acts, but by the failure of others who were under a public duty to act. The decision of the court today stands as the first clear indictment of that failure.

She added:

We have come this far without the Crown Prosecution Service and it is our wish now to continue to the end without their involvement. Through this prosecution we have had a role and a voice. We are not about to lose that freedom to a body that was stone deaf to our experience, our needs and our concerns.

While Doreen was reading this, Assistant Commissioner Ian Johnston approached the family group in view of the press, shook hands with Stephen Kamlish and spoke briefly to him. 'I just wanted to wish the family well and to promise them continued support,' he told reporters.

Gary Dobson was not forgotten. At the start of the private prosecution it was agreed that he could not be prosecuted, since neither Duwayne Brooks nor Witness B, nor any other witness, had identified him as a member of the attacking group. Alone among the five suspects originally arrested, therefore, he appeared to have consigned the Stephen Lawrence case to the past. Before long, however, the police were once again knocking on his door.

One of the earliest decisions taken by the private prosecution team was to seek a complete review and reassessment of all the forensic evidence in the case. As Neville Lawrence had been pointing out since 1993, this was a dog that did not bark. Why, in a case the Metropolitan Police now described as one of London's biggest-ever murder hunts, had no traces been found by scientific means to link the prime suspects to the victim? It was well known that almost any human interaction involved exchanges of fibres and other tiny particles, and the Lawrence murder had been a sudden and violent contact involving the shedding of blood. Even allowing for the destruction or loss of evidence in the time between the murder and the arrests – when clothes were washed or discarded, or when stray fibres simply fell off clothing – Neville could not believe that no such traces survived. Nor could Khan and Mansfield. When they received the Fishpool documents in the spring they looked urgently for the explanation. They found that in 1993 and 1994 a large number of tests had been carried out by the Met's forensic science laboratory on the various knives associated with the case, on a variety of clothes and shoes taken from the suspects, and on Stephen's clothes and his bag. The findings, summarized by Dr Adrian Wain of the laboratory

255

in a letter of 8 June 1994, were broadly but not totally negative. On Stephen's jacket and trousers he had found a grey cotton fibre matching the component fibres of a jacket that was taken from the home of David Norris at the time of his arrest. Another grey cotton fibre matched the component fibres of a jacket taken from Gary Dobson's home. In both cases, however, the fibres were common and could easily have come from elsewhere. Wain's view of these discoveries was pessimistic: 'On their own, I can attach no significance to these fibres whatsoever.'

Since the beginning of the year the family and their supporters had been raising money to fund the prosecution. A Lawrence Family Campaign was set up, staffed mainly through Imran Khan's connections in the Southall Monitoring Group in west London, and it sought funds in every way it could. A letter entitled 'The Price for Justice' was sent out to thousands of people soliciting donations, while raffles, auctions and collections were held at a large variety of events, political and otherwise. Public sympathy was high, and the trades union movement in particular gave support. The initial target of £10,000 was soon passed but the family knew that if they failed to secure convictions at the Old Bailey and were ordered to pay both their own and the defence's costs they would need at least ten times that sum, so the fundraising effort was sustained. In the meantime, however, they made the difficult decision to dip into this kitty to finance a new forensic effort, commissioning an independent scientist, Dr Angela Gallup, to see if more evidence could be found.

Through the spring and early summer, Gallup worked with Wain to take the forensic tests as far as they could reasonably be taken, pursuing even the more remote scientific possibilities. 'Only in terrorist cases would you go any farther,' one forensic expert said later. They soon confirmed that none of the spots on the suspects' clothing that might have been blood could possibly have come from Stephen; either they were not blood at all or they were the wrong group. They examined the many knives now in the collection of Fishpool exhibits and again found no relevant traces. This left fibres. Hundreds of thousands of fibres had been removed from the surface of the relevant garments on strips of Sellotape by Wain and his colleagues in 1993 and 1994. Of these, 646 had been judged worthy of further examination and it was from that work that the grey cotton fibres emerged. Now, with Gallup, the process was restarted and once again all the strips of Sellotape were laboriously scanned under the microscope, along with additional fibres retrieved from the polythene bags that had been placed over Stephen's hands after he died (the contents of these bags had not been examined before). This time 1,071 individual fibres were identified as promising and were studied separately. They were compared by eye under magnifications of up to 400 times actual size; if appropriate their fluorescence was tested under ultraviolet light, dye colours were analysed by a process known as microspectrophotometry and dye chemistry was also scrutinized.

At the end of all this, they found three additional fibres of interest, all from the bags on Stephen's hands and all possibly relating to Gary Dobson. Two purple-brown wools, the scientists concluded, could have come from a cardigan taken from Gary's bedroom in May 1993, and a colourless polyester might have come from the same jacket as the grey cotton found previously. Neither Gallup nor Wain, however, saw these matches as proof of Dobson's involvement in the murder, principally because all the fibres and dyes in question were very common – the cardigan, for example, was sold by Marks & Spencer. 'Even in combination,' wrote Gallup, 'these fibres provide only very weak evidence of any association between Lawrence's and Dobson's clothing.' But the story did not end there, for the jacket in question had long been of particular interest to police. It matched more closely than any other confiscated garment a description given by Duwayne Brooks in his original statement. Duwayne had spoken of the lead attacker 'wearing a grey-coloured bomber jacket with a zip-up front, the lining of it was white and I recall that the front may have had a white strip at either side of the zip'. Dobson's jacket was grey with two vertical white stripes.

The prosecution team – Khan, Mansfield, Kamlish and other lawyers from the Tooks Court chambers – took these two elements together and began to build a case against Dobson. Although he had an alibi, provided by his parents and their friends, no one could say with certainty that Gary had not gone out at the time of the murder. He himself had lied to police officers making door-to-door inquiries about his movements on the night. Gary was also associated with a knife: the one found at the home of his girlfriend, Gaynor Cullen. This too was thought by the pathologist to be consistent with Stephen's wounds, and no one could say for sure that it was in the Cullen house on the night of the murder. Furthermore, Gary appeared on the videotape, not only as a racist with violent tendencies, but also as someone who occasionally played with knives. Reviewing all this, the lawyers decided they had enough to begin proceedings and on 28 August, with the committal hearing involving his friends already under way, Gary Dobson was arrested and charged with murdering Stephen Lawrence.

Once again Gary talked. Unlike the other four, who exercised their right to silence, he agreed to be questioned by police. The interview, conducted by Detective Superintendent Mellish, took the form of a final appeal to Gary to tell the truth about the night of the murder. Patiently and persistently, Mellish spelled out the evidence against Gary, casting it in the blackest terms. The position, he suggested, was very grave indeed and time was running out. 'I would seriously ask you to consider your position,' he said. He told Gary he should not be afraid of his friends, and as for Clifford Norris – 'a wicked bugger', Mellish called him – he was 'out of harm's way'. Halfway through the interview, Gary and his solicitor were left together to watch the video and discuss it. Then Mellish returned and put on further pressure: 'Your friends on that video don't treat you particularly well. I ask you this: why do you continue to protect them, because they and their activities and their influence have ruined your life?' He pleaded: 'I want you to help yourself.'

It was impressive but it was a waste of time. Gary insisted that he was 'absolutely not' present at the murder and that he had 'no idea' about how the fibres came to be on Stephen Lawrence's hands. As for his friends, he insisted Mellish misunderstood them. 'We ain't animals,' he said. 'We've been best of friends for years and we will be best of friends for years. They won't never threaten me.' Whatever the tape suggested, he was not a racist and neither were they: 'I've got nothing against black skin itself . . . The only time that I've ever felt angry toward black people on the whole is when they've got a chip on their shoulder against white people.' He had told the truth all along about the night of the murder, he said. 'I wish I could tell you something . . . There ain't nothing I can tell you.' Even the prospect of a prison term, it seemed, could not separate Gary from his mates. The one point at which he got into difficulties in the interview was in his explanation for the red-handled knife found at the Cullen home. According to Gaynor and her mother it had been in the house since well before the murder, but Gary said he bought it some time *after* the murder. He could not remember who sold it to him but it was a friend 'who was getting kitchen cutlery' at the time. Mellish did not press the matter; these were contradictions that could be explored in court.

Gary's committal hearing, also before David Cooper at Belmarsh, proved a brief affair with only one moment of drama. Beryl Cullen, called as the only prosecution witness to confirm her version of the story of the red-handled knife, refused to testify. Cooper sent her to the cells with a warning that she would face contempt charges unless she changed her mind, and after considering her position there during the lunch break she agreed to cooperate. Otherwise the proceedings were straightforward and on 7 December Cooper ruled that there was a case to answer and that Gary Dobson should be tried alongside Neil Acourt and Luke Knight for the Lawrence murder.

Chapter Sixteen The Trial

The trial at the Old Bailey began on Wednesday 17 April 1996 and ended on Thursday 25 April, straddling the third anniversary of the murder. The case was now a *cause célèbre* in British race relations as well as a rare and historic private prosecution and on the opening day it received fuller coverage in the national press and on television than at any previous stage in the story. Even after three years the most basic facts of the case had remained vague to many – Stephen was simply 'the black boy murdered at the bus stop' – but now it could not be avoided, and almost all the coverage had the same message: Neville and Doreen were taking on, not only the three accused, but also the criminal justice system.

Not much had changed since the committals in the character of the prosecution case, which looked like this.

Neil Acourt had been identified by Duwayne Brooks and was seen running from the scene by Witness B. The videotapes showed him to be a knife-obsessed racist who repeatedly demonstrated exactly the kind of downward stabbing movement used to kill Stephen. He was also captured on tape denying the murder while smiling or laughing, in a way that could be construed as an admission.

Luke Knight had also been picked out of a line-up by Brooks and also had a fervent hatred of black people. A party to the taped 'admission', he had lied to police about his association with the others.

Gary Dobson was another racist, associated with the others, who was seen on tape playing with knives. Fibres linked him to Stephen, particularly fibres matching a jacket of his resembling one described by Duwayne Brooks as worn by one of the attackers. In circumstances that remained obscure, Gary had given his girlfriend a knife which might have been used in the attack. He had also lied to police about his movements on the night of the murder.

If these charges were to be proved, a terrible burden rested on Duwayne Brooks. Now aged twenty-one, Duwayne remained an unsettled and unhappy young man and psychiatric assessments suggested that his depression was aggravated by talking about the attack. He was also subject to bouts of terror brought on by the belief that he might be murdered as Stephen had been, and for the duration of the trial he was given full police protection and was continuously escorted when not in court. If Duwayne's importance was clear to Michael Mansfield it was equally clear to the defence, and before the jury had even been empanelled defence counsel informed the judge in open court that they intended to challenge his evidence as inadmissible. Since the defence was funded from Legal Aid, junior barristers had done the work at committal; now, for the trial, the defendants retained QCs: for Acourt, Stephen Batten; for Knight, Ronald Thwaites; for Dobson, James Stewart. Duwayne had had a rough time at Belmarsh court but he had reason to fear worse from these men. And that was how matters unfolded. What was listed as the trial of Acourt, Knight and Dobson soon became, in effect, the trial of Duwayne Brooks.

On the bench was the Honourable Mr Justice Curtis, a former Recorder of Birmingham who had become a circuit judge a year earlier. The first test of his attitude to the case was the defence challenge to Duwayne's evidence, and matters did not fall favourably for the prosecution. To Mansfield's dismay, Curtis ruled that if the admissibility of Duwayne's evidence was to be disputed in the course of the trial, then the prosecution could not mention it in its opening statement to the court. When Mansfield declared that this would leave him with very little to say to the jury, Curtis replied that he was sure he could think of something: 'You are a much better advocate than I ever was. Can we get on?' Soon, however, the defence also suffered a setback, albeit a lesser one. They proposed that prospective jurors should be asked whether they had formed any views on the case as a result of media reporting; if they had, then they should not be allowed to sit. Mansfield opposed this and so did the judge, who said he did not want jury-vetting in the American style; he was accustomed to instructing juries to put press coverage out of their minds and that was what he would do in this case. He did accept, however, that the jury should not include anyone living in southeast London. Seven men and five women were duly sworn, all of them white.

The first witnesses were the French au pair, Alexandra Marie, who spoke through an interpreter, and Royston Westbrook. They set the scene, describing the events they had seen as they waited at the bus stop. Then came Duwayne Brooks. He was examined first by Michael Mansfield, who carefully and slowly took him through the story: the arrival at the bus stop, the waiting, the attack, Stephen's collapse. As he had been at the committal, so now Duwayne was nervous, softly spoken and generally monosyllabic, but with Mansfield's help he managed to present the evidence fairly clearly and fully. By prior arrangement Mansfield carefully left any questions relating to descriptions and identifications until last, and when he reached these there was a pause. This was the evidence whose admissibility the defence had challenged, and their arguments had to be heard before it was given. The judge thus asked the jury to withdraw, explaining merely that he had to rule on a point of law. The argument that followed took the form of a trial-within-a-trial, with both sides questioning not only Duwayne himself but other witnesses in order to establish how far Duwayne could be relied upon.

Again, Mansfield began. Given its long and tangled history, this evidence was now a minefield and it was impossible even for Mansfield to traverse it without the odd detonation. One such occurred when he was taking Duwayne through his first statement and came to the frizzy-haired man in the forefront of the attack:

MANSFIELD: What did he do?
BROOKS: He ran into Stephen and stabbed him.
MANSFIELD: He stabbed him?
BROOKS: Yes.

There was another when they were dealing with the identification parade of 3 June.

MANSFIELD: You picked someone out. How does that person relate to the scene in Dickson Road and the group of white youths?
BROOKS: I think he was the person that stabbed him.
MANSFIELD: You think he was the person that stabbed him?
BROOKS: Yes.

These two assertions would be extremely difficult to reconcile, for Luke Knight, who was picked out on that occasion, was not frizzy-haired but had short, dark hair.

It was Stephen Batten QC, for Neil Acourt, who rose when Mansfield sat down, and his cross-examination of Duwayne was as merciless as it was cool. He devoted particular attention to the identity of the stabber. It was odd, he observed, that Duwayne now said the man he picked out on 3 June was the stabber, for he did not mention this to the police at the time of the line-up.

BATTEN: Do you want to withdraw your answer given earlier that it was the one on the third parade who was the stabber?

BROOKS: No.

BATTEN: You say you thought then it was the stabber but you decided not to tell the police?

BROOKS: I don't know what I thought then.

BATTEN: You do not know what you thought then?

BROOKS: No.

BATTEN: You have, and indeed did at committal, suggested somebody else entirely different for the stabber, have you not, Mr Brooks?

BROOKS: I don't know.

BATTEN: Mr Brooks. A very close friend of yours was killed.

BROOKS: Yes.

BATTEN: You were there. Do you take these identifications seriously?

BROOKS: Yes.

BATTEN: Most of all, no doubt you would like to see the man who stabbed your friend convicted, would you not?

BROOKS: Yes.

BATTEN: Who stabbed him is very important to you; that must be so, Mr Brooks, must it not?

BROOKS: Yes.

BATTEN: Let me try again, please. You have identified somebody totally different from the man on the third parade as being the stabber, have you not?

BROOKS: I identified someone different?

BATTEN: Yes.

BROOKS: From my description?

BATTEN: Let me see if I can help you in order to keep things short. Do you remember that in December you gave a statement to the police about having seen people you recognised out and about, in

263

one case in a public house and in the other on a street outside a burger house?

BROOKS: Yes.

BATTEN: Do you remember what you told the police about the roles of people you recognised, one of them in particular, the one you had seen in the pub and on the street? Do you remember what you told the police?

BROOKS: I don't remember.

BATTEN: Do you remember what you told the magistrate, what you had seen that person do?

BROOKS: No.

BATTEN: Mr Brooks, do you not remember that at the committal proceedings you suggested that the man you recognised in the public house, outside the burger bar, was the man who did the stabbing?

BROOKS: Do I remember saying that?

BATTEN: Yes.

BROOKS: No, but I probably did say that.

BATTEN: Would it have been true by any chance?

BROOKS: If I said that, yes.

BATTEN: Well, did you also tell the magistrate that the person you had seen in the public house and the person you had seen in the burger bar was not a person who had been on the parade?

BROOKS: Yes.

BATTEN: Then it cannot be the man on the third parade, can it?

BROOKS: From what you are saying, then, it can't.

This went on for hours. Duwayne's many statements to the police, his evidence at committal and his examination by Mansfield were clinically dissected and every apparent inconsistency or contradiction was run past him again and again. Such interrogations are everyday fare at the Old Bailey – they are exactly what is expected of a good defence barrister – but for Duwayne Brooks the experience was plainly torture. He was not fit or equipped to cope, and when he tried to explain or justify himself he often stumbled, creating new contradictions, new confusions. The more mistakes he made the more dispirited he became, and the more his head went down the more easily he was led. Systematically, Batten challenged every little detail surrounding the identifications.

BATTEN: When did it first occur to you that two of the people in the crowd [of attackers] looked so like each other that they must be brothers, or possibly twins?

BROOKS: I don't remember.

BATTEN: It did not occur to you that night [the night of the murder], did it?

BROOKS: No.

This was the basis of Batten's third main argument. The first was that Duwayne saw very little of the attackers on the night of the murder; the second was that he was hopelessly confused about which attacker was the stabber and the third was that, by the time of the identification parades, Duwayne had been coached in who to look for. Not only did he fail to mention brothers in his original statement, but he also made no reference to a man with distinctive short, black hair. These details, Batten insisted, had been supplied to Duwayne by someone else in the weeks after the murder and he used them to pick out Neil Acourt and Luke Knight. To support this argument he drew on Duwayne's own words and on the statement and testimony of Detective Sergeant Christopher Crowley, but there was also another source. In an unusual departure, Imran Khan, the instructing solicitor on the prosecution side, entered the witness box to be questioned about his contacts with Duwayne Brooks in the weeks after the murder, and in particular about the meeting on 2 May recorded in a note by Khan's colleague Ahmed Ratip. The note had been disclosed to the defence with some reluctance by Khan, who had argued, in vain, that it was subject to client–solicitor privilege. It was Ronald Thwaites, acting for Luke Knight, who examined Khan.

The focus of his questions was a single passage:

There were other people at the bus stop. Police said one of them said he saw the fight with Stephen and the other six boys. I have seen his statement.

The implication was clear: that these were Duwayne's words and that Duwayne had seen a statement about the attack made by another of the bus stop witnesses. Thwaites asked Khan if the note was accurate and he said it was not. He had no memory of what was said, but he was sure that in this respect the note was wrong: 'He could not have said it to me because had he said so alarm bells would have rung.' Thwaites agreed that bells should have rung and explained why: 'If that passage is true it is capable of destroying the eligibility of witness Brooks as a witness of identification.' Khan accepted the hypothesis but stressed that the passage was *not* true. Why, he was asked, would he bring a colleague to a meeting to take notes and then not accept what the notes said? Khan replied that he had not brought Ratip for that reason; he was there because it was unusual for a victim's solicitor to meet a prosecution witness and he wanted someone present in case there was any suggestion of impropriety. Ratip did take the note? Yes, said Khan, but on his own initiative. And he added: 'He wasn't the best note-taker . . . It was a Sunday and he was the only person I could get.' When Ratip himself appeared in the witness box to give his account of these events, he certainly did not cut an impressive figure. Asked about the notes, he declared: 'I cannot vouch for their accuracy at all.' He had merely taken them because Khan and Duwayne were talking and he wanted something to do. When Thwaites pointed out that a clumsy attempt had been made to change the date on the document from 2 May to 8 May – which was *after* the first identification parades – Ratip was unable to account for it.

Crowley was called, and taken through his account of the conversation with Duwayne Brooks by Batten and Thwaites. He stood by his key claim: that Duwayne said friends had told him how to recognize the Acourt brothers. Michael Mansfield, cross-examining, attacked Crowley's credibility as ruthlessly as Batten had attacked Brooks's. Was it not true that the statement in which he recorded the conversation with Duwayne was written hours afterwards, and was thus not a verbatim account? Yes, said Crowley. Did he regard himself as reliable in such matters? Yes, again. Then why, asked Mansfield, had Crowley dated the statement 4 June when it was written on 3 June? It was a mistake, conceded the detective. From there, Mansfield turned to the defence claim that Duwayne had failed to say at the time of the parade that he thought the man he picked out was the stabber. Did Crowley ever ask him whether he had anything to say about the man's role? Yes. What did he say? That he had nothing to add. Then why was that not in the statement? And why did Crowley also fail to record another exchange he now insisted had taken place:

that after their conversation he had asked Duwayne to put what he had said in writing, and that Duwayne had refused?

Mansfield was implying that Crowley's statement, apparently so damaging to Duwayne, was in fact flawed, partial and imprecise – in short, unreliable – and that there were better grounds for believing Duwayne's account. And the interrogation was not over. Inspector McIlgrew, who oversaw the identification parades, had testified that Crowley came to him after the conversation and asked what he should do. McIlgrew said he told the detective to report it to the Fishpool incident room and make a statement. Crowley, however, denied that this exchange had ever happened and insisted that he had made his report to the Fishpool team on his own initiative. Was one of them lying? Was it Crowley? Mansfield left the implication in the air. As for some of the things that Crowley claimed Duwayne had said, they were made to appear absurd. The story that he had picked someone out because they looked as though they had spent the night in the cells: would any solicitor or supervising police officer allow such a thing at a parade? Of course not. The story that Duwayne had been told he would recognize the Acourts because he had been to school with them: why would he say such a thing when it was a certain fact that he had *not* been to school with them? It was a somewhat battered Detective Sergeant Crowley who left the witness box when the cross-examinations were over.

The defence summed up first in this trial-within-a-trial and there were few surprises. This was, said Batten and Thwaites, a 'fleeting glance' case, which in itself should render the identifications invalid, but it was more than that. Deliberately or by accident, Duwayne had acquired information about the Acourts and he had used this information at the line-ups because he himself remembered almost nothing about the appearance of the attackers. The source may have been a police officer or it may have been a friend, but the effect was the same: Duwayne was looking for two brothers with short, dark hair. It was on this basis that he picked Neil Acourt out of a parade on 13 May – perhaps he recalled seeing, but not identifying, Jamie Acourt at a previous parade and noticed the similarity. And it was on this basis that he picked out Luke Knight on 3 June; Knight had a similar haircut and was 'the closest person he saw' to the man he had previously identified. In the months and years that followed, it was said, Duwayne had changed his story so many times that even he could not make sense of it. The defence also drew on the fruits of Duwayne's own prosecution to cast doubt on his mental state in May and June 1993. Psychiatric reports from that case, it was pointed out, showed that he was suffering from post traumatic stress disorder and that his symptoms included 'patchy amnesia'. And one of the police questionnaires was produced to suggest that Duwayne was unstable and awkward. If ever there was a case where a judge should exclude a witness's evidence, said Thwaites and Batten, this was it.

Mansfield rose. He stated, very simply, that Duwayne denied receiving descriptions of the suspects from third parties and that the defence had failed to prove that he had. Where their case was not based on artful speculation it was based on the testimony of Crowley, which, Mansfield said, had no credibility whatever. Most, if not all, of the supposed problems with Duwayne's descriptions could be ascribed to a single factor which was a commonplace with witnesses. They see faces and events and they store these in their memory; because of trauma, because the memories are stored too deeply or simply because of an inability to put things into words, they can have difficulty initially in describing what they have seen. Only later do the recollections return, and in some cases witnesses only remember a face when they see it again. This was what had happened to Duwayne Brooks. No one had suggested that there was impropriety of any sort in the conduct of the identification parades and defence solicitors had been present at each to make sure of it; Duwayne had picked out his men fair and square. As for the long arguments about who was the stabber, Mansfield conceded that there were inconsistencies in Duwayne's account but asserted that they did not matter. The prosecution saw this as a case of joint enterprise and would not seek to prove that any one of the three defendants had used the knife, so it would be happy for the jury to be instructed to set aside that question.

The judge gave his ruling immediately, and his view of the matter was apparent from the outset. He said bluntly: 'This is a fleeting glimpse case.' On that point alone he could have excluded Duwayne's evidence, but he went on to catalogue the contradictions and confusions identified by the defence. When he reached the conflict of evidence between Duwayne and Crowley he paused to say that he did not need to decide which of the two was telling the truth and which was lying. If he relied only on those parts of the conversation which were not in dispute he felt there was sufficient evidence of contamination. He concluded:

> I have heard Brooks's evidence and seen him. I am entirely satisfied that where recognition or identification is concerned he simply does not know, in ordinary parlance, whether he is on his head or his heels. (This, I hasten to add, is understandable: he was undoubtedly shocked at the terrible events I shortly described at the beginning.) Second, he only had a snap look at one and no more than one of his friend's attackers. Third, since then by many people and at many times he has been asked about identification matters. Next, nearly three years further on in effect he has identified three if not four people as the stabber: the man we have called Curtains [this is the frizzy-headed man, whose hair was said to hang like curtains on either side of his face]; Jamie Acourt effectively; Luke Knight, and the Starburger man, making four . . .

> What is the duty of the judge? However horrific the crime, and however objectionable the motive for it may be, that does not enable any judge to remove or alter the legal safeguards already in place to prevent, so far as humanly possible, the conviction of anybody on a misidentification. The perils of misidentification are well known, and an Act of Parliament and the established cases require the trial judge to act as a screen to see that the material to go before the jury is material on which they can properly convict according to law.

> It will be obvious to any intelligent listener that Mr Brooks's evidence of identification is impeachable not just on one but two grounds, that is to say no true identification recognition at the time and identification thereafter not by recognition, but which is also tainted . . . I shall direct that Brooks's identification of each of these defendants [Acourt and Knight] does not go before the jury; to do so would amount to an injustice. Adding one injustice to another does not cure the first injustice done to the Lawrence family.

> I so rule for the reasons that I have given.

Hearing these words, Doreen Lawrence collapsed – she later left the Old Bailey in a wheelchair. Overnight, the legal team reviewed the position and acknowledged that it was hopeless. Without Duwayne's evidence they had nothing at all to link Luke Knight to the murder and only the equivocal word of Witness B to suggest that Neil Acourt might have been there. Duwayne had also provided a vital link in the

Dobson case, since it was he who remembered seeing the distinctive jacket during the attack. The following morning Neville was present in court, but Doreen was not, to hear Mansfield announce that in relation to all three defendants 'we do not intend to proceed with this prosecution'. The judge, after expressing sympathy for the Lawrences, 'who have been put in the most terrible situation', summoned the jury. It was now Wednesday afternoon and they had not been in court since the previous Thursday (in fact the judge had allowed them to remain at home for much of this time). All they had heard in the case was the evidence of Marie, of Westbrook and of Duwayne Brooks up to the issue of identification, and they had no idea what had been going on since then. With evident surprise and bewilderment, they listened as Mansfield and Curtis explained that the trial was over. The judge told them that their duty was now clear. They would be asked if they had reached a verdict and the jury foreman must reply, 'yes'. Then they would be asked whether on the direction of the judge they found each defendant not guilty and again the answer must be 'yes'. Had they chosen a foreman? They had not. 'Would you mind doing so?' asked Curtis. 'If you wish to retire to do it, please tell me.' At this there was some whispering and one of the jurymen declared: 'We would like to retire.' It was not clear whether this was merely for the purpose of choosing a foreman or whether the jury, in their surprise, wished to discuss what had happened and what they had been asked to do, but Curtis allowed them to leave. They returned after a few minutes and did as they were bid: Neil Acourt, Luke Knight and Gary Dobson were declared not guilty of the murder of Stephen Lawrence and discharged. In the final act of the trial the judge declared that, since the case had been properly referred for trial by a magistrate, it was right that the Lawrences' costs should be met out of public funds.

After three years, this was the ultimate calamity for the family. All the effort, all the sacrifice, all the struggle had come to nothing. Doreen and Neville had long believed that if they could only get the evidence before a jury there would be convictions; they had come within sight of that – the jury was sworn and ready – but were denied at the very last moment. To them the judge's regrets and expressions of sympathy meant nothing and they were offended that, without even retiring to consider the matter, he should have taken it upon himself to exclude evidence and sink the case. They had no doubt that any jury, even this all-white jury, would have believed and trusted Duwayne, for all his confusion, and would have rejected the clever browbeating of the defence. They had no doubt, moreover, that once the jury saw the videotapes they would convict. Yet now this prospect had been dashed away and they had nothing. Less than nothing, for not only did these boys walk free, but having been found 'not guilty' they could never again be tried for the murder. Perversely, the two remaining suspects who were not beyond justice – Jamie Acourt and David Norris – were the two against whom there was least evidence. Neville told reporters in measured terms: 'I believe in fairness and I don't think what happened today is fair at all.' Asked about Doreen, he explained that she was too distressed to attend: 'You can just judge how she feels.'

Michael Mansfield and Imran Khan were bitter too. They also had wanted to put the evidence before the jury and they felt that the judge had been unfair to intervene so early. At the very least, they thought, he should have let the proceedings run to 'half-time', the moment in a trial when the prosecution has finished presenting its case and the defence first shows its hand. Then the defence could have put forward the argument that there was no case to answer, including its views on Duwayne's credibility, and a fuller and more balanced debate would have been possible. Perhaps then the outcome would have been different. Khan told reporters: 'We are extremely disappointed with the judge's ruling and would have hoped the identification evidence could be put before the jury – something that happens in nearly every case . . . The criminal justice system has let this family down.' He added a note of recrimination: 'It must be remembered that we would never have been put into this position if the first police inquiry into the murder had gathered sufficient evidence.' From Scotland Yard, Assistant Commissioner Ian Johnston issued a statement: 'We will never give up on this inquiry. We will never close this case and we will go on looking for ever. We will meet with the family in a few weeks when the dust has settled.'

At the Crown Prosecution Service, where the view had always been that any prosecution would fail, discretion was the order of the day. The formal line with press inquiries was to make no comment on the verdict and to express sympathy for the family. Internally, however, there was relief and even quiet satisfaction at the outcome; had there been convictions the service, already so unpopular, would have been lambasted for failing to pursue the case. On the day after the verdict Barbara Mills, the Director of Public Prosecutions, wrote a memorandum to Howard Youngerwood:

I know that you have been heavily involved in this case which has caused all of us much anxiety. I am particularly grateful for all the help which you gave over the many months during which we deliberated about it. I am sure that you are as pleased as I am that your judgement about the sufficiency of the evidence has been vindicated. We all, of course, feel much sympathy for the Lawrence family over the tragic and quite unnecessary death of their son, but we have to maintain an independence of approach to cases despite their emotive and emotional background. I know that this case has had particular difficulties because of the allegations of racism, and I am grateful for the way in which you and those who worked with you on the case have dealt with such a difficult problem.

Chapter Seventeen **The Inquest**

In July 1996, three months after the collapse of the trial, the Lawrence family left to take a holiday in Jamaica. They were accompanied by a film crew who were making a documentary for Channel Four. These film-makers had been following the case since the start of the private prosecution and had recorded a series of interviews with the couple which illustrated, among other things, the widening differences between them. On the eve of the trial, for example, they sat together for the cameras as Neville said: 'It doesn't matter what happens at the end of the day. We've made a statement that there was a case to be answered and if we haven't got it right, well, we're not prosecutors.' Doreen disagreed: 'I look at it completely differently. The end verdict does matter because after all this time somebody's got to answer for Stephen's death.' It seemed that Neville was exhausted while Doreen's anger still drove her on. After the trial they were both bitter, telling the camera that they were the victims of an establishment conspiracy. The judge, said Neville, 'had been brought down from Birmingham to do a special job and he did it'. Doreen said they had never had a chance because the justice system would never tolerate a successful private prosecution. It would 'open the floodgates'.

What should they do next? And what would they do with the rest of their lives? The holiday was part of the process of deciding. The marriage was in trouble and a rest among friends in the homely atmosphere of Jamaica might help. But Neville's mind was turning once again, as it had in the summer of 1993, to thoughts of a permanent return to the island. He was fed up with Britain and believed his family would be safer and happier in Jamaica, removed from the racism and the memories. There was also the question of what to do about the murder case: should they press on with the campaign for justice and if so what could they do? What the television camera saw in Jamaica was two people moving in opposite directions. They were filmed visiting Stephen's grave in the countryside near Kingston. As they approached, Doreen was speaking in voice-over of how they had been 'grieving separately'. 'We don't seem to know how to get close,' she said. 'This thing has ruined our lives so much that no one could ever, ever understand.' At the grave she and Neville stood together a moment and then, in that fussy way that mothers have, she began to tidy things and change the flowers, weeping as she did so. When she had walked out of camera-shot Neville leant down and put his hand on the stone. 'It's been a long time, boy,' he said to his son, and his voice went. He sagged and sat and wept, his tall frame heaving with great sobs.

When they talked about the future the gulf between them was even clearer. Neville spoke with warmth of Jamaica, of his relatives and friends there, of the comfort of the church, of racial harmony. He had had enough of the struggle: 'I've been through three hard years of pain and suffering and I don't think I can take any more. I'm at the end of my road. Be it right or wrong, that's how I feel.' He plainly wanted to stay. Doreen, by contrast, would not contemplate moving for good; that was just what the racists wanted black people to do, to pack up and go, she said, and she would not give them that satisfaction. In her mind she was still fighting: 'It's anger that keeps me going. Without it I think people would just walk all over me. They tried it in the early days.' When the summer was over Neville remained in Jamaica while Doreen returned to London with the children.

The inquest came next. Convened and abruptly adjourned in December 1993, it had been postponed several times in 1994 and then, when the private prosecution began, deferred until that was concluded. Sir Monty Levine, though now very close to retirement, had followed developments closely and intended to preside when the inquest was held. It took place in February 1997 and it proved to be his last and one of his most remarkable cases.

Throughout the final phase of the private prosecution the relationship between the Lawrences and their legal team on one side, and the Metropolitan Police on the other, was exceptionally close. Although Perry Nove was no longer involved, Ian Johnston kept a watching brief, while Bill Mellish was in direct contact with the prosecutors – he personally arrested and questioned Gary Dobson. Another officer, Detective Chief Inspector John Carnt, worked full-time on liaison between police and prosecutors. The ultimate symbol of this close relationship was the scene at the Lawrences' eve-of-trial conference at Tooks Court, which was filmed by the Channel Four crew. Around a large table in Mansfield's office sat the QC himself, his junior Stephen Kamlish, Imran Khan, Doreen and Neville Lawrence and various other lawyers. With them, participating in the exchanges, were two police officers: Mellish and Carnt. It was a situation without precedent. It carried some legal risk for the police – would they be obliged to assist another private prosecution in the same way? – but there were considerable benefits. Senior officers could say, with hands on hearts, that they had done everything within their power to help the Lawrences since the private prosecution began and that since the investigation was relaunched in the spring of 1994 they had gone 'to the limits of legality' in the effort to have Stephen's killers brought to book. Their desire to do so was sincere and the Lawrences were genuinely grateful to officers such as Nove and Mellish. But the effort was also important to the Met for reasons of public relations: it put them on the side of the angels.

This relationship was doomed from the moment the trial collapsed. In their outrage the family and their lawyers, particularly Doreen and Imran Khan, immediately asked themselves: 'What is the root cause of this disaster?' The answer, which Khan expressed to journalists on the steps of the Old Bailey, was that none of this would have happened, neither the failure of the private prosecution nor the CPS refusal to take on the case that preceded it, nor for that matter the long disintegration of Duwayne Brooks as a witness, if the first police investigation had been properly conducted and the evidence gathered when it was fresh. Once again all the feelings of July 1993 came flooding back. The Lawrences did not give up, and never would give up, the hope of seeing the suspects punished in some way, but their thoughts were now turning towards calling the police to account for what went wrong. And whereas in 1993 they had next to nothing to support their suspicions, now they had seen much of the Fishpool documentation. They had evidence.

Before the inquest reopened on Monday 10 February, the Met had an idea of which way the wind was blowing. Doreen had given press interviews in which she criticized the police, and the list of witnesses sought by the family included an unusual number of police officers. To protect the police interest Jeremy Gompertz QC was instructed to represent the Commissioner in the coroner's court. Once the proceedings were under way it was soon clear that this was a wise precaution: in the very first moments, for example, Sir Monty took the unusual step of checking that no member of the jury was related to a police officer. While the coroner said that no one was on trial, there could be little doubt that the police were about to be judged. And within an hour Doreen Lawrence was in the witness box, delivering the case for the prosecution. Questioned by Sir Monty, Mansfield and, briefly, Gompertz, she gave her account of the night of the murder, with frequent reference to the absence or inactivity of the police. 'We drove down to Well Hall Road,' she said. 'We didn't know how far to go. We went past the pub and there is a bus stop near the pub, and we looked down the road. We didn't see anything.' Sir Monty asked: 'What? No police or anything?' 'No, we didn't see anything.' And later: how soon after Stephen was pronounced dead at 11.17 p.m. did the police speak to the family? 'A police officer didn't come to our house until about eight o'clock in the morning.'

Doreen had also written a statement, or a speech, in advance, and Mansfield invited her to read it. She gathered her thoughts for a moment and then began.

My son was murdered nearly four years ago. His killers are still walking the streets. When my son was murdered the police said my son was a criminal belonging to a gang. My son was stereotyped by the police – he was black then he must be a criminal – and they set about investigating him and us. The investigation lasted two weeks. That allowed vital evidence to be lost.

My son's crime is that he was walking down the road, looking for a bus that would take him home. Our crime is living in a country where the justice system supports racist murderers against innocent people.

The value that this white racist country puts on black lives is evident, as seen since the killing of my son. In my opinion what happened in the Crown Court last year was staged. It was decided long before we entered the courtroom what would happen – that the judge would not allow the evidence to be presented to the jury. In my opinion what happened was the way of the judicial system making a clear statement, saying to the black community that their lives are worth nothing and the justice system will support anyone, any white person who wishes to commit a crime or even murder, against a black person. You will be protected. You will be supported by the British system. To the black community: your lives are nothing. You do not have feelings. You do not have any rights to the law in this country. That is only here to protect the white man and his family, not you.

Since my son's murder we as a family have not been able to grieve for the loss of Stephen. Even though the system was against us we tried to redress the injustice against us. We felt we had to and with the dedication of our legal team and supporters we mounted our own private prosecution to seek justice for our murdered son. I hope our family will be the last – even though there is no sign of it to date – the last to be put through this nightmare, which it has been for us. There need to be changes for the future. The Establishment needs to have in place a system that will allow all crimes to be treated in the same way and to be investigated in the same way regardless of who is the victim, of who the perpetrators might be, not to have one rule for the white and another for the black people. We as a family felt that in the early stages, which would have given the evidence that would have ensured that those who killed my son would have paid for their crime, they [the police] wasted that time. As far as they were concerned, for them to come across a young black man who has no criminal record, who is studying, that is something they seem to be unaware of.

They were very patronising to me in the early stages, and instead of them being a support to us they came to be an injury. Because they were not supporting us as a family, every time we spoke to them it was like a banter that we had to go through. We had to fight. On one occasion – it was the first time that I ever went to a police station, with my husband and a group of us – I felt that maybe they didn't get all the information, the names that were coming to us. I personally wrote the names down and I took it to the station. As I walked in I presented it to one of the officers and while we were there talking I sat and watched him. He folded the paper and rolled it into a ball in his hand and at the end of our meeting I said to him, 'You are going to put that in the bin now.' He said to me, 'No, no. We treat all the information we have seriously.' But at the time they were not taking my son's case as seriously as they should have done.

Passionate and moving, this speech proved a pivotal moment in the case of Stephen Lawrence. To the police it announced that with the failure of the private prosecution all their efforts since 1994 were null, and they must now face the reckoning for what went before.

To the public – the speech was widely reported – it announced that the Lawrence case was not over and that the family held the police, the justice system and white Britain responsible for the injustice they had suffered. This was no longer a legal matter but a political one. Doreen, who had once before spoken of having to endure 'the worst kind of fame', was now embracing fame. As a wronged and grieving mother she had moral authority and she was ready to use it in a new way.

The inquest continued for four days and heard from a great many witnesses. Duwayne Brooks, Royston Westbrook and Joey Shepherd all testified, as did Geoffrey Mann, the ambulance service paramedic, and the pathologist, Dr Richard Shepherd. The court also heard from police officers, including James Geddis, the off-duty constable who stopped at the scene, Linda Bethel and Tony Gleason, the first uniformed officers to arrive; and Ian Little, who attended the scene and the hospital. Mansfield set about these police witnesses like the criminal defence barrister he is, challenging their memories, picking holes in their notes when they had notes and portraying them as unreliable when they did not, and at times implying that they were making things up. The picture he painted through these cross-examinations was a sorry one: no one, it seemed, gave Stephen first aid as he lay bleeding on the ground; no one, Mansfield insisted over the denials of police officers, spoke to the family in the hospital; no one showed any urgency about looking for the attackers. Did anyone run a quick check of local police files that night for information about young racists who used knives? No. Were such files kept? Yes, but they were locked up at night. Mansfield criticized the quality of the search of Dickson Road and expressed outrage that house-to-house inquiries did not begin until fourteen hours after the murder. The police, he said, were 'remiss in the extreme'; they would not have wasted so many opportunities to gather evidence and catch the killers if the victim had been a police officer.

In an attempt to counter some of these charges Gompertz called Detective Chief Inspector Carnt, who had not been on the original Fishpool team but who gave a general account of the first investigation, stressing its scope and scale. The records showed, he said, that there *were* some house-to-house inquiries on the night, but it was true that the full effort did not begin until 10 a.m. the following morning. This became a very large operation and by the time it was concluded 1,600 people had been seen. As for the remainder of the investigation, by November 1993 the team had pursued 943 lines of inquiry and taken 443 statements from 326 witnesses. Carnt also gave some account of how events unfolded, telling the story of the anonymous letter found at the Welcome Inn pub, the surveillance operation, the finding of the Wendover Road knife and the arrests. Fear, he said, had been a factor in the failure to find more eyewitness evidence. Carnt's was a competent performance but it was over-shadowed by a little piece of theatre. He had brought with him to court the original sheet of paper handed to Chief Superintendent Ilsley by Doreen Lawrence on 6 May 1993, the sheet which she alleged he folded and rolled into a ball. Sir Monty asked to see it and it was passed to him. He held it up for all to see and counted aloud: 'One, two, three, four, five, six creases going one way and about eight or nine going the other.' It looked, he said, as though it could be folded 'into something the size of a postage stamp'. And this he proceeded to do, folding and refolding along the creases while the court watched, rapt. 'Look at this,' he said eventually, holding aloft a wad of paper that was, indeed, not much bigger than a stamp, and from the public gallery came a burst of laughter and applause. Gompertz tried to suggest that folding was one thing and rolling into a ball was another, but it was in vain. Doreen had been vindicated.

The inquest was notable for two other events: the appearance of the five suspects and the verdict of the jury. It was unusual that people acquitted of a murder should testify at a subsequent inquest and these five did not do so willingly. They were summonsed to appear and when they did four of them brought their barrister, Charles Conway, to argue that they should not have to give evidence. (The exception was Gary Dobson, who was represented by his solicitor, Michael Holmes.) Sir Monty said no: they must give evidence, albeit he would not allow them to be tried again. So it was that, for the first time, Neil Acourt entered a witness box to be examined about the murder. He swore by Almighty God that he would tell the truth, the whole truth and nothing but the truth. He sat. He listened while the coroner explained that this court did not apportion blame and that he had the right not to answer questions 'if by doing so it will incriminate you'. Asked if he understood, he said, 'Yes.' Then Sir Monty began. 'Were you present at the scene or close to the scene when an incident took place on 22 April 1993 around the period of time between 10 p.m. and 10.30?' At this Conway rose and said: 'I claim privilege on his behalf in relation to that question on the grounds that he has previously been asked these questions at his trial.' (This was not the case.) Sir Monty turned to Neil: 'Do you wish to answer that question?' 'No,' came the reply.

There followed a short legal argument and then Sir Monty tried again.

> CORONER: Can you assist the court in any way on how Stephen
> Lawrence came by his injuries on that night?
> ACOURT: I claim privilege on that question.
> CORONER: Do you know anyone who could assist with knowing
> how Stephen Lawrence came by his death?
> ACOURT: I claim privilege on that question.

Mansfield had a go. He asked Neil if he knew what he was doing, and whether he realized that he could change his mind at any time and help the court, to which Neil replied: 'I'm claiming privilege, yes, full stop.' Where was he living at the time? 'I claim privilege.' Was it close to Well Hall Road? 'I claim privilege.' Did he have close friends living there? 'I claim privilege.' The pattern was set. The privilege in question was the one Sir Monty had mentioned, the right not to say anything that might incriminate him, and though Mansfield protested vigorously that Neil could not incriminate himself in this matter since he had been tried and acquitted, it was useless. But Mansfield pressed on, for if he could not hope to elicit information he could at least ensure that this strategy was exposed to the full. While Conway protested 'Enough is enough', and Sir Monty tried to restrain him, Mansfield asked question after question, always receiving the same answer. Did he know what had happened in Well Hall Road? 'I claim privilege.' Had he ever spoken to anyone about those events? 'I claim privilege.' Did he know a young woman called Michelle Casserley? 'I claim privilege.'

Luke Knight came next, and was asked directly: 'Were you present at the scene?' He replied equally directly: 'No, I wasn't.' But any hopes this raised were short-lived. To the next question: 'Do you know anyone who was?' he answered: 'I claim privilege on that question.' With Norris it was the same. There was laughter in court when he was asked: 'Are you called Mr Norris?' and he replied: 'I claim privilege.' No amount of verbal gymnastics by Mansfield made the slightest difference, not the double-negative questions, not the nice-guy talk, not the outrage, not the sarcasm and not even attempts at provocation. A member of the jury had a go, asking Norris: 'Did you know Stephen Lawrence at school or college?' The answer was the same: 'I'm claiming privilege.' A mood of frustration and anger began to grip the court and Sir Monty contained it with difficulty. While Jamie was in the box the arguments between Mansfield, Conway and the coroner intensified, and Jamie eventually produced a small speech to explain his position:

> Every time you involve this so-called incident what you keep coming up with, I'm gonna come up with claiming privilege. You want to ask me how I got here, I'll tell you, but if you want to ask me anything else, or to do with anything involving things like what you're talking about, then I'm gonna claim privilege.

Gary Dobson, usually the most forthcoming of the five, was no different. In an effort to make him respond, Mansfield produced the jacket taken from Gary's home in May 1993 and asked if he recognized it, but the answer again was: 'I claim privilege.'

It was a mockery of justice but, as the coroner made clear, the young men were exercising their right, a right explained at the outset by him when Neil Acourt entered the witness box. Sir Monty was also conscious that these exchanges were taking place very close to the limit of the remit of a coroner's court – there was no question of forcing the five to be more open. But as Dobson left the witness box having claimed privilege for the last time he closed an episode which was much more eloquent than it seemed. Ever since the committal hearings the boys, and particularly Neil, had always been cocky in court, smiling and whispering together, looking around with a defiant air. But they had never spoken in court before and it made a difference. This time their stubborn refusal to help the court combined with their attitude and behaviour to create a powerful impression, not only of cynicism and dishonesty, but also of menace. The whole affair, from Neil's entry to Gary's departure, had lasted barely three hours and shed no light on Stephen's death, but it was to have important consequences.

The first of these was seen after Sir Monty asked the members of the jury for their verdict. There were ten: six men, one of them Asian, and four women, one of them black. The coroner told them that there was no doubt Stephen was unlawfully killed and he was sure that would be their finding. Beyond this, he explained, they had other responsibilities: they must identify the cause of death and they must state the time, date and circumstances. When they were describing circumstances, they should summarize very briefly what they believed had happened. For example, said Sir Monty, they might like to say how many people were involved in the attack. But they must not add any riders, make any recommendations or attach blame to any person. The jury retired and, to the surprise of some, remained out for more than thirty minutes. When they returned they confirmed that Stephen Lawrence had indeed been unlawfully killed in Well Hall Road on the evening of 22 April 1993. As to the circumstances, the jury declared that he had died 'in a completely unprovoked racist attack by five white youths'. This was surely a form of words calculated to suggest that, if they had been allowed to say who was responsible, this jury – the first and only jury ever to deliver a verdict of any kind in the Lawrence case – would have convicted *those* five white youths.

For the Lawrence team the inquest was an unqualified success. Once again public interest in the case had grown and the press coverage was if anything fuller than at the trial. The five suspects had finally been dragged into the witness box and their character exposed in the harshest of lights. Doreen had once spoken of her wish to 'wipe the smile off their faces'; while she did not succeed in doing that, she managed to make millions of people aware of their cruel smugness. And a strong case had been made against the police over their handling of the first investigation, which appeared to have been lackadaisical and unorganized, if not cynically negligent. At Scotland Yard, Assistant Commissioner Ian Johnston now made a fateful decision. As the inquest ended he released a personal press statement to the press responding to the criticisms that had emerged. In essence it was a point-by-point defence of police conduct, both at the scene on the night and in the subsequent weeks.

It was an off-duty police officer who was the first officer on the scene, and he immediately telephoned for an ambulance. Other officers were

282

quickly on the scene. It was considered whether to take Stephen to hospital by car but, on checking, it was found that the ambulance was only minutes away. The officers made sure that, according to their first aid training, Stephen was in the right position and tried to keep him warm with a blanket from the first officer's car. There was blood, but they did not know where it was coming from. From the time the off-duty police officer was on the scene until the ambulance arrived was only a matter of a few minutes. I honestly do not know what more they could have done.

As for the investigation, he stood by it. It was thorough – over three years there had been 2,600 interviews and 1,500 lines of inquiry – and if evidence was not found it was not for want of effort.

We started the investigation immediately, but all we had that evening was one witness who was very emotionally affected by what he had seen. Two days later we received anonymous information which alone was insufficient to warrant an arrest, but we took immediate action on it. It was thoroughly researched and we mounted a full surveillance operation. More than two weeks later Mrs Lawrence gave a piece of paper to a police officer with six names on it. It is a matter of record that the information was immediately fed into our system and acted upon, but four of the people named have never featured in either prosecution.

Johnston made the same points in radio and television interviews. His strategy, therefore, was rebuttal, always accompanied by expressions of sympathy for the family and regret that the killers were not in jail. But Johnston had only been in charge of policing southeast London since the spring of 1994; how did he know what had happened in 1993? In part, he relied on the evidence at the trial and inquest, where Geddis, Bethel and Gleason, among others, had given accounts of their actions. Johnston and his colleagues knew that there were direct conflicts of evidence about some events that night and they felt that the police case had not been given a fair hearing. For example there was the Lawrences' complaint that no police officer spoke to them at the hospital. Gleason's contemporaneous notes stated that he took Neville into the resuscitation room to identify Stephen's body, while another officer, Ian Little, recalled being present when this happened. This could hardly have occurred without an exchange of words. Gleason's notes also contained the Lawrences' address and telephone number, which he believed Neville had given him. While it was true that these notes were not signed by Neville, which might have put the question beyond doubt, the police view was that there was enough evidence to show they had *not* ignored the family.

As for the first investigation, Johnston was relying in part on Carnt's knowledge of the files, but most important of all in establishing his confidence in the work of Crampton, Weeden, Ilsley and the rest was the Barker review. This was the internal assessment written by Chief Superintendent John Barker in the autumn of 1993 which found no fundamental flaws in the first investigation. In a revealing phrase, Bill Mellish would later refer to the Barker report as a 'comfort cushion' – having read it, you could be sure that the first detectives on the case had done a broadly competent job. The Met now rested on that cushion. They would acknowledge that perhaps some mistakes had been made in the early days but they always stressed that these made no difference to the outcome. The essential problem had been the reluctance of key witnesses to cooperate and not a lack of police effort. Barker proved it.

The differences of view between the family and the police were about to be tested thoroughly for the first time, for when Imran Khan emerged from Southwark Coroners Court after the inquest verdict he announced that the family had decided to take the case to the Police Complaints Authority, the national body responsible for policing police forces. Khan also indicated that the family were considering taking a civil action for injury against the five – another rare legal procedure. And one further course was suggested that afternoon by Sir Herman Ouseley, the chairman of the Commission for Racial Equality. He issued a statement calling for an independent public inquiry into the case. The Home Secretary, Michael Howard, said he would consider the matter 'very carefully'.

While the inquest was still drawing to its close on that Thursday 13 February 1997, on the other side of central London Sir Paul Condon was having lunch as a guest of the editor of the *Daily Mail*, Paul Dacre. Several of Dacre's senior journalists were also present and the atmosphere was convivial – there is no national paper friendlier to the police than the *Mail*. The Lawrence inquest was raised. Dacre and his colleagues had been particularly struck by the refusal of the five suspects to cooperate, and their repetition of the words 'I claim privilege.' The *Mail* journalists discussed the background with the Commissioner.

That afternoon, back on the editorial floor, Dacre learned of the inquest verdict – 'a completely unprovoked racist attack by five white youths' – and an idea began to form in his head. Dacre is acknowledged as a brilliant editor, with particular gifts for identifying stories that will interest, shock or appeal to his readership and for presenting them in dramatic style. The idea he had was, he knew, perfect for the *Mail* and its readers but it was also legally dangerous, so he consulted the in-house lawyers. They reflected and then told him he was safe, so he immediately gave the appropriate orders.

The result, on the Friday morning, was one of the most famous newspaper front pages of the 1990s. The headline was a single word, underlined and in letters two inches tall: 'MURDERERS'. Under it, in bold type, came the challenge: 'The *Mail* accuses these men of killing. If we are wrong, let them sue us.' And beneath that, running right across the page, were photographs of each of the five. The article began:

> The *Daily Mail* today takes the unprecedented step of naming five
> young men as murderers. They may not have been convicted in a
> court of law, but police are sure that David Norris, Neil Acourt,
> Jamie Acourt, Gary Dobson and Luke Knight are the white youths
> who killed black teenager Stephen Lawrence. We are naming them
> because, despite a criminal case, a private prosecution and an inquest,
> there has still been no justice for Stephen, who was stabbed to death
> in a racist attack four years ago.
>
> One or more of the five may have a valid defence to the charge
> which has been repeatedly levelled against them. So far they have
> steadfastly refused every opportunity to offer such a defence. Four
> have refused to give any alibi for that night in April 1993. One
> initially offered an alibi, but it did not stand up when police checked
> it out. This week the five refused to answer any questions at the
> inquest on Stephen, citing their legal right of privilege not to say
> anything which might incriminate them . . .

285

> If these men are innocent they now have every opportunity to clear their names in legal action against the *Daily Mail*. They would have to give evidence and a jury in possession of all the facts would finally be able to decide.

This caused a sensation. The *Mail*'s action was not, in fact, unprecedented – the *Mail on Sunday* had earlier done something similar in the Rachel Nickell murder case, although in a lower key – but it was timely, flamboyant and perfectly judged. Dacre had correctly read the popular mood and nothing that the Lawrences had done in four years, in the private prosecution or at the inquest, had a fraction of the impact of that front page. The *Mail*'s action led the radio and television news, dominated the discussion programmes, was reported and analysed in depth by the paper's rivals and filled the comment and letters pages for days. In Eltham the London *Evening Standard* knocked on Gary Dobson's door in Phineas Pett Road and got the briefest of responses from him through the letter-box: 'Fuck off.'

Was this trial by newspaper, or even lynch law, or was it a fitting retribution for men who had escaped justice and now held the law in contempt? The debate was especially compelling because of the unusual way in which opinion was divided. Paul Foot, the left-wing journalist, declared the *Mail*'s initiative to be excellent. 'I don't normally think it's right for people to be witch-hunted in this way, but in this case the legal process had run its course and the case against these men was overwhelming.' Darcus Howe, the black writer and broadcaster, said that he was 'fully in support' of the *Mail* because of the special circumstances of the case. Peter Preston, the editor of the *Guardian*, said it was 'a valid way of expressing the extreme anger at the state this case has been left in'. None of these three would normally be expected to support the actions of the *Daily Mail*. Liberal doubts about the paper's action were expressed in muted terms, although there were some who pointed out that the five had merely exercised a right of silence which left-wing lawyers never tired of defending. Where there was criticism of the *Mail* it came from other quarters. Lord Donaldson, a former Master of the Rolls, argued that the paper had committed 'a gross contempt of court'. Its brash announcement of the guilt of the five, he said, compromised any possible future prosecution involving them.

Ronald Thwaites, the barrister who acted for Luke Knight at the Old Bailey trial, said that his client and the other defendants had been acquitted in entirely proper circumstances and that the *Mail* was guilty of 'a cynical exploitation of a truly tragic event'. Michael Beloff QC wrote in *The Times* of a new and worrying phenomenon which he called 're-judgement'. It seemed, he said, that when the media were not satisfied with verdicts given in court according to well-established legal practice, they would now simply supply their own. Another barrister called it 'guilt by smear'.

Underpinning this debate was the almost certain knowledge that the five would not sue the *Mail* for libel. For one thing they could not afford it; legal aid is not available for libel cases and such a suit would cost a small fortune. For another, as the *Mail* had pointed out, if they wanted to prove the paper wrong they would have to account for their movements on the night. Having refused to do so for four years they were hardly likely to break cover at this late hour. When Dacre had consulted his lawyers about the front page, libel had hardly entered his mind; he was concerned about contempt of court and they advised him he ran little or no risk. So it proved, for although the Attorney General's office agreed to consider Lord Donaldson's views it concluded that no contempt case could be mounted.

The blanket coverage of the *Mail*'s coup threw up two facts which had not previously been publicly known. The first was that Dacre had known Neville Lawrence personally before the murder, since Neville had done some painting and decorating in the editor's home. The second was that Dacre had met Sir Paul Condon on the day the front page was conceived. Both facts were presented as explanations for the paper's action, but the truth was somewhat different. Dacre's knowledge of, and liking for, Neville Lawrence gave him some personal interest in the case, but not a strong one. Through all the years since their telephone conversation in early May 1993, Dacre's *Mail* had taken no more and no less interest in the Lawrences than any of its rivals. As for the lunch with Condon, it had some influence on the front page – the Commissioner was clearly asked about the strength of the case against the suspects – but the Lawrence affair was not the only topic of conversation at the table and when the lunch ended none of those present had any idea of what was to come. Inside the *Mail* there was no confusion about what had happened. Dacre was personally appalled by the behaviour of the five and on consulting his newsdesk he found his suspicions about them confirmed. Staff reporters had been investigating the history of the suspects, he was told, and the conclusion was that they were guilty and they were, to use a *Mail* word, 'scum'. Dacre felt that these people should not be allowed to get away with murder and they should not be allowed to get away with holding two fingers up to British justice. From there it was merely a matter of how to achieve the effect he wanted, and whether it would be legal.

If it was primarily a 'white-on-white' matter – white youths versus white justice – that triggered the *Mail*'s involvement, the paper did not shrink from the consequences. For days afterwards the *Mail* ran pages of coverage of the family, the five youths and the case, with a special logo and slogan: 'Justice for Stephen'. Months and even years later they were supporting the Lawrences, even when it came to reporting their criticisms of the police. Doreen Lawrence, for her part, was delighted when she saw the front page and she showed her gratitude by granting the *Mail* a long, frank and exclusive interview.

It was now March 1997 and everything in the case of Stephen Lawrence was about to change. The years of desperation, of crying out for public attention and official action, were drawing to a close. It may not have seemed so at the time, but brick upon brick the family had been building their case over those years, from the early protests through the committal and the trial to the inquest. They had tried every course imaginable and never given up, never accepted no for an answer. Their very endurance had become part of the argument – surely something could be done for this long-suffering family? Now Doreen's speech, the behaviour of the suspects in the witness box, the verdict of the jury and the *Mail*'s front page – all these had settled the matter. Something would be done.

Part Three Reckoning

Chapter Eighteen The Kent Investigation

The Lawrences first asked for a public inquiry in the summer of 1993 and a Home Office minister, Peter Lloyd, turned them down. The idea had been raised occasionally since then, whenever the case made news, but always with the same result – Conservative Home Secretaries in the 1990s, preoccupied with rising crime, had little interest in holding the police up to public scrutiny. However, by February 1997, when after the inquest an obviously reluctant Michael Howard was obliged to consider the matter once again, things were changing, for it looked likely that the decision would soon be taken out of his hands and out of the hands of anyone in his party. A general election was due within weeks and all the opinion polls indicated that the Conservatives would be heavily defeated. Howard's replacement was expected to be Jack Straw, who was both personally and politically much more sympathetic to the Lawrence case. Discreet contacts with the Labour Party had raised the family's hopes that, once elected, the new government would approve an inquiry. This would mean a long, thorough, public examination of what had gone wrong before a senior legal figure, and it was what the family now wanted most of all.

Even before the election, however, another process had begun which would prove vitally important to the case of Stephen Lawrence. Those in charge at the Police Complaints Authority responded swiftly to the family's statement after the inquest that they would register a formal complaint against the Met. Although the Lawrences did not give this a high priority – their attention quickly turned towards the improving chances of a public inquiry – the PCA pressed ahead with the procedures to mount a full-blown investigation of the Met's handling of the case. In the absence of a complaint document the PCA drafted its own, drawing on statements made by Doreen at and after the inquest and on interviews she had given in the press. It proved a formidable list, and was condensed into the following terms of reference:

> To investigate the Metropolitan Police handling of the Stephen
> Lawrence murder on 22 April 1993 and any related matters, but with

specific regard to: 1) the initial response, 2) family liaison, 3) the conduct of the murder investigation up to and including the review carried out by the Metropolitan Police.

The PCA identified seventeen police officers who were or might be the subject of personal criticism by the family and the investigation's central task was to establish whether there was evidence to justify disciplinary action against these seventeen. They fell into four groups: Geddis, Bethel, Gleason, Groves, Little, Pye, Benn and Jeynes, who were involved only in the first few hours of the investigation; Crampton, Ilsley, Bullock and Weeden, who directed Operation Fishpool; Bevan and Holden, the family liaison officers; and Barker, Osland and Blenkin, more senior figures. PCA practice is to use officers from other forces to conduct investigations and so the Lawrence brief was allocated to a team from Kent Constabulary under the supervision of the Deputy Chief Constable, Robert Ayling. This raised some eyebrows, for not only was Kent a next-door neighbour to the Met in southeast London, but Sir Paul Condon and Ian Johnston had both held senior positions in the Kent force in the past – it was thought to be too cosy an arrangement to permit objectivity. The PCA management took a different view. On the one hand they had a high regard for the quality of work of Kent police and on the other they felt that to assign the job to a force farther afield would be unnecessarily cumbersome and costly; far better to locate the investigation just a short trip away from Eltham.

The Kent Constabulary headquarters is a large, red-brick building on the edge of Maidstone, and behind it lie some playing fields. On the far side of these fields, somewhat incongruously, stands a modest, detached house of classic 1960s suburban style that was once the residence of an assistant chief constable. From March 1997 this house was the discreet base for a formidable police investigation under the code name of Operation Bridge. In charge, reporting to Bob Ayling, was Detective Chief Superintendent David Clapperton, young, blond and relentlessly efficient and systematic. His team comprised two inspectors, a sergeant, six detective constables and a Holmes system specialist, while he could also draw on the services of an intelligence analyst. The first step in the investigation was to secure all the surviving Fishpool documentation from 1993, including thousands of Holmes records and hundreds of witness statements.

From there they set about dissecting the events of the night of 22–23 April and the subsequent investigation under Crampton and Weeden. Operation Bridge lasted nine months, or twice as long as the events it was examining, and involved hundreds of interviews, both with people on the periphery and with figures central to the story. In a few cases, these interviews were conducted over several days. The result of all this effort, completed around Christmas 1997, was a 400-page report which transformed the terms of the debate over the case of Stephen Lawrence.

Many of the family's specific complaints related to the first few hours after the murder – the police response to the attack, the treatment of Stephen as he lay on the ground, the start of the murder investigation at the scene and the treatment of the family at the hospital. The Kent team traced everyone who was present and could conceivably have any memories or observations to contribute, and then weighed the evidence. Their conclusions on these matters did not, for the most part, coincide with the views of the Lawrence family. The police, the Kent investigators concluded, responded well in the first instance: the off-duty officer, PC James Geddis, was one of the first to stop, while Gleason and Bethel arrived in the area car three minutes later. Before the ambulance arrived another two police vehicles had reached the spot: a panda car containing PC Joanne Smith and a vanload of officers from the mobile Territorial Support Group under Inspector Steven Groves. Their first actions at the scene, Kent said, were 'prompt and professional'.

Among the most vivid of all Doreen Lawrence's complaints, made in a statement after the inquest, was a suggestion that these officers failed to give her son the appropriate medical help because 'they did not want to get their hands dirty with a black man's blood'. Kent looked at the question of first aid, interviewing not only the officers but also the Taaffes, who prayed at Stephen's side, and other members of the public who stopped at the scene. The police officers gave a broadly consistent account: they had been advised that Stephen had suffered a head injury and they believed this to be the source of the blood on the pavement; they did not move him because they believed he was already in the 'recovery position'; two of them – Gleason and Bethel – said they took his pulse, while Geddis spread a blanket over him; they felt that the Taaffes and Angela Geddis were comforting him so far as was possible; they did not take him to hospital in a police car because they thought it safer to wait for the ambulance. As to Doreen's suggestion that they neglected Stephen because he was black, the officers were indignant. Race, said PC Bethel, 'had absolutely nothing to do with anything'. Geddis observed: 'I can totally understand her feelings but that is a totally scurrilous allegation to make.' The fact remained, however, that none of these officers, all of whom had received training in first aid, attended in any way to Stephen's wounds, indeed none of them established that he had been stabbed. The medical consensus was that nothing they could have done at that time would have saved Stephen's life, but Doreen's point was that they should have *tried*. On this, the Kent team consulted two experts and got two different answers. A senior Red Cross training official took the view that the police officers had acted in accordance with current Red Cross teaching. The other expert, Graham Cook, an accident and emergency consultant at Maidstone Hospital, thought there had been a failure of first aid. The proper course, he said, would have been to establish the true nature of the injuries and to ensure continuous monitoring of the patient's condition, and neither of these had been done. He blamed inadequate training. The Kent team weighed the evidence and once again they came to the view that it did not support Doreen's complaint. So far as first aid was concerned, the officers at the scene had done everything that could reasonably have been asked of them. The expectations of Graham Cook, the A&E specialist, were unrealistic.

So it was with the issue of 'scene management' – the police operation on Well Hall Road after Stephen had been taken to hospital. Cordons were in place within ten minutes and over the ensuing four and a half hours no fewer than fifty-five officers attended the scene, among them three of very senior rank: Chief Superintendent Philpott, the officer in overall charge of the uniformed branch in 3 Area; Chief Superintendent Christopher Benn, in charge of support services over much of south London, and Detective Superintendent Ian Crampton, the senior investigating officer on the case. For two chief superintendents to visit a crime scene in this fashion, Kent observed, was 'quite unique'. The Kent team also tested another of Doreen's striking allegations about the night. At the inquest she said that, when she and Neville were searching for Stephen near the

Welcome Inn, they looked down Well Hall Road and saw no sign of police activity. Could this be true, that the Lawrences had looked down the road to the crime scene from a distance just after 11 p.m., and there was no one there? The Kent officers conducted an experiment one evening in Eltham. They posted a police car with a flashing blue light by the spot where Stephen fell and then drove a van carrying a camera slowly down the road towards it from the Welcome Inn, recording what could be seen at every stage. They found that, because of the gradient and a gentle bend in the road, the van had to travel 140 yards beyond the pub before the camera picked up a flashing blue light at the spot where Stephen fell. In other words, it was possible that before they turned back for the hospital the Lawrences looked down the road and saw nothing, even though there was some police activity at the scene. Another matter that Doreen had raised was the testimony by Bethel, at both the trial and the inquest, that she had written her notes on the night while sitting on a park bench. There was no doubt that this comment left an impression of casualness but Kent found that Bethel had acted sensibly and under orders. By the time she started to write there were plenty of other officers at the scene to carry on more urgent work, and it was important that she should record what she had witnessed as quickly as possible. The public bench on the corner of Dickson Road was merely a convenient spot to do so.

As to the searching of the crime scene and the house-to-house inquiries on the night, the Kent investigators encountered some difficulty in establishing exactly what took place because of a shortage of written records. Inspector Groves said he had taken full notes at the time but they could not be traced. Chief Superintendent Benn told the same story. The Territorial Support Group documentation was sparse in the extreme and it emerged that, contrary to best practice, no one at all had kept a 'scene log' – the formal record of who attended the crime scene and at what times. However, from interviews with officers and with people living close to the scene the Kent team established that searches *were* carried out near the bus stop and in Dickson Road, using both dogs and powerful lamps. To find out how far house-to-house inquiries were conducted, they mounted their own house-to-house inquiry, revisiting the area in 1997 and knocking on doors close to the scene. They called at eighty-one homes and found that ten householders remembered either receiving a visit from a police officer or speaking to one on the night. This tallied broadly with the recollections of senior police officers, who said that door-knocking was concentrated on the houses which were still showing lights. In sum, Kent found that the police attended the scene in numbers and to senior levels and, with the exception of the failure to keep a scene log, carried out the normal operations required after a street murder. Doreen Lawrence's impressions, it appeared, were based on misconceptions. When the Kent investigators looked at the scene management as a whole, therefore, they came to the view that the Met's performance was 'of a high standard' and officers behaved 'correctly and professionally'.

On police conduct towards the family at Brook Hospital, the verdict was similar. This time there was a direct conflict of evidence: two officers, Gleason and Little, said they had spoken to Neville and that he identified his son's body; Neville and Doreen flatly denied this and insisted that the first officers they spoke to were the two who visited them at home the next morning. The Kent detectives delved deeper but only added to the uncertainty. No member of the hospital staff could remember seeing the police talking to the Lawrences and nor could they recall police officers taking Neville to see the body. On the other hand, Gleason's contemporaneous notes stated clearly: 'At 12.02 a.m. I was present when Mr Neville Lawrence identified the body of his son at the Brook Hospital in Resuscitation One.' The notes also gave the Lawrence address and telephone number. Balancing these, Kent decided that the Lawrences' ability to recall what happened had 'apparently' been affected by trauma. The conflicts could not be resolved, but 'from the facts so far as they can be determined' it seemed that Gleason and Little had not neglected their duty.

This general picture of police professionalism and proper conduct was very different from the one that had emerged from the inquest, and the Kent investigators offered an explanation for the contrast. In the coroner's court, they suggested, it was the junior officers who gave most of the evidence and they had no overall knowledge of what had happened and 'were not in a position to give the reassurances sought by the Lawrence family'. This, in fact, was an argument put forward at the time by the Met itself, but it was only half true. The coroner heard evidence from one chief inspector and two inspectors, who should have been well placed to describe what happened. Absent from the inquest, however, was Chief Superintendent Benn, who might have been able to give the most authoritative account. Kent pointed out that the Met could only blame themselves for failing to anticipate events at the inquest and put forward their best witness.

In many ways closest to Doreen Lawrence's heart was the matter of family liaison. Repeatedly, she had alleged that the conduct of Detective Sergeant Bevan and Detective Constable Holden towards her family was unsympathetic, patronizing and even insulting. Although they were supposed to be liaison officers they provided almost no information and they behaved as though Stephen had been a criminal, she said. As for Chief Superintendent Bill Ilsley, who had taken over responsibility for relations with the family after the first ten days or so, she believed he was no better. The Kent team approached these matters with their customary thoroughness, assembling all the information they could. Every officer who had contact with the family was questioned, while the three key figures, Bevan, Holden and Ilsley, were interviewed at length and in the presence of solicitors. Progress was hampered, however, by the family's reluctance to cooperate with the PCA inquiry. Despite a number of requests it was only in September, six months into the investigation, that the Lawrences finally agreed to visit the house in Maidstone, where they met Ayling, Clapperton and the other Kent officers. Neville, who had returned to Britain from Jamaica during the summer, subsequently provided a statement, and thereafter the Kent detectives were also able to fill out the picture by approaching other members of the family.

Still there were direct conflicts of evidence, or at least of interpretation, over family liaison. Bevan and Holden, for example, firmly denied Neville's claim that when they showed him a pair of gloves in the first few days they were implying that Stephen was a burglar. And they said the presence of a large number of people in the Llanover Road house was a barrier to their attempts at building a relationship with the Lawrences. As for Ilsley, he admitted folding up Doreen's list of names but insisted passionately that he would never have thrown it away, and he pointed out that he took it straight to the Fishpool incident room to be dealt with. Holmes records confirmed that this was the case. Kent went over the matters that affected relations between police and family – the mortuary visit; the involvement of Imran Khan; the arguments over Holden's mobile telephone – and in the end were unable to allocate responsibility. The liaison officers *had* encountered some difficulties, the investigators said, because of 'the intervention of others', but it was also clear that there was never much warmth between them and the family and that as time passed matters deteriorated. Gestures by the two, such as Holden hand-delivering a birthday card from Doreen to Georgina (who was in Kent on a school trip), failed to bridge the gap. Other attempts to redeem the situation also failed 'because of the conflict between the family's thirst for information and the need for the investigating officer [Weeden] to protect the integrity of his investigation'. So far as Bevan and Holden were concerned, Kent's verdict was that they personally could not be blamed. But when it came to the involvement of more senior officers there was criticism: the liaison officers had been poorly supervised and when things went wrong the officers in overall charge failed to take the initiative and find innovative ways to overcome the problem. For example, when he was offered by Philpott the services of uniformed officers who had 'experience and aptitude for dealing with ethnic minority people', Chief Superintendent Ilsley politely declined.

Thus far, the findings of Ayling and Clapperton were not likely to cause much anxiety at Scotland Yard. The same could not be said of their observations on the investigation itself. This was the first time since the Barker review that professional detectives had examined the conduct and progress of Operation Fishpool and judged the performance of Crampton, Weeden and the other officers; indeed this was a far more thorough examination than Barker's, not least because it was much better manned and had more time. In effect, the Kent team relived the first investigation, carrying out their own evaluations of the evidence in step with the original sequence of events and attempting to establish what best practice demanded. Although it was not part of their brief – for Fishpool remained a live investigation – they too inevitably found themselves trying to solve the murder, to see ways of patching up the gaps in the evidence, to reinterpret statements and to make sense of the mass of detail. Unlike their predecessors in this quest they did not have to endure pressure from the political world or the media – the Kent investigation was largely ignored by the press – although as the months passed they found the PCA increasingly impatient for results.

What they found horrified them. From the first day of the Fishpool investigation until the autumn, the Kent team came to believe, the hunt for Stephen's murderers was ill-judged, mismanaged and lacking any spark of inspiration. At the heart of the failure, they found, was one fundamental mistake and it was the same mistake that the Lawrences had identified as early as 4 May 1993: the delay in making arrests. Why this decision was wrong and how it came to be taken were questions the Kent investigators explored in the minutest detail.

Within twenty-four hours of Stephen Lawrence's death the incident room had received three tip-offs, all pointing to the same suspects, and yet each of these was in some way under-exploited or neglected. The first anonymous telephone call, at lunchtime on that Friday, was not reported to Crampton or Bullock. The two calls that evening from the Female Anon were similarly not reported to the SIO. None of these, nor any of the thirty-nine anonymous calls received by the Fishpool team by the end of 1993, was recorded on tape, nor were they ever subjected to detailed comparison and analysis and nor were any determined efforts made to identify and trace the callers. And then there was the man called James Grant, who walked in off the street to report what he knew and proved to be a mine of valuable information. Kent found the documentation relating to Grant fragmentary and elusive, not least because most references to him were cryptic, quoting neither his real name nor his cover name. But bit by bit they were able to complete the picture of what happened that night: how he was questioned by Detective Constable Budgen, who wrote only a short account of the interview; how Detective Inspector Bullock did not see him and how Detective Superintendent Crampton was not informed that night about the new information.

The Saturday, Kent found, was scarcely better. The same prime suspects were named in the two anonymous letters that came to hand that day, one left in a telephone kiosk and the other placed on a police car in the Welcome Inn car park. Yet very little priority was given to tracing the author of the letters and the girl who found the telephone kiosk letter was never even interviewed. The Kent team placed great emphasis on the need to identify these anonymous informants: very often such people know more than they say and are prepared to help when interviewed. Informants who make contact very soon after a crime can be especially important, too, since their information is fresh and unlikely to be contaminated by frequent repetition. Saturday was also the day when Mrs D D told P C Bennett that her son, E E, and his girlfriend, Emma Cook, were potentially vital witnesses, but that information was simply lost. The Kent investigators were unable to establish what had gone wrong and in interview both Bullock and Crampton were aghast at the lapse, but it was clear that, although the message was written promptly on the day, nobody knew of its contents until six days later.

The police need 'reasonable grounds for suspicion' before they can make arrests and Kent did not directly suggest that Crampton had such grounds by Saturday night. By the following night, however, they felt he did. Once Davidson had in hand the statement of Stacey Benefield implicating Dave Norris and Neil Acourt in an attempted murder, Kent concluded, he could have acted. And if they had arrested those two the police would have been able to search two homes for clothing and weapons which might have yielded a forensic link to the Lawrence murder. They would also have reduced the ability of the prime suspects to intimidate witnesses and prepare alibis for themselves. In addition, police could have arranged identification parades in relation to the Lawrence case while witnesses such as Duwayne Brooks, Joey Shepherd and Royston Westbrook still had the events fresh in their minds. This was, said Kent, 'a golden opportunity', but it was lost. Crampton did not learn of the Benefield statement until the next day, by which time he had handed over control of the investigation to Brian Weeden.

Crampton was interviewed by Ayling and Clapperton in October 1997. Although it was a formal affair, conducted in the presence of Crampton's solicitor, like almost all the Kent interviews it was calm and polite. First names were used. The procedure was slow and methodical, without any artifice: issues were tackled in chronological order, with much reference to documents, and Crampton was given every opportunity to put his point of view. He was asked whether he considered making arrests on the Saturday:

CRAMPTON: We considered it. We discussed it. Mr Ilsley, myself and DI Bullock, we obviously discussed it. We determined what our strategies would have to be, or would be.

CLAPPERTON: And your decision was not to arrest?

CRAMPTON: Not to arrest.

CLAPPERTON: Can you tell me where that decision is recorded?

CRAMPTON: No. It isn't. Again, you would expect perhaps to find it in the policy file. It wasn't as if we had evidence and decided not to arrest in spite of evidence. To a degree we had information but no evidence and we decided not to arrest on that information.

He went on to explain that he had been told by the pathologist that, because Stephen was wearing so many layers of clothing, it was unlikely that his attackers' clothes or shoes would be splashed with blood. As a result it seemed less urgent to make arrests and search for bloodstained clothing. In addition, if he had arrested the prime suspects on Saturday he would have had very little to put to them in interview, while he believed at the time that he would soon trace witnesses who would vastly strengthen the case. Thus he preferred to wait. Clapperton then asked him whether, if he had known of the Benefield statement on the Sunday night, he would then have ordered the arrest of Neil Acourt and Norris. Crampton said no. The courts, he argued, would probably take a dim view of arresting people for one crime when you were really looking for evidence of another. In this, Kent concluded, he was wrong: the law allowed it.

If Crampton did not know of the Benefield statement on the Sunday night the same could not be said of Weeden the following afternoon, but he too chose not to arrest. Interviewed by Ayling and Clapperton over three days in early November, he explained that to have done so would have made nonsense of the surveillance operation that Crampton had ordered, which was just getting under way. He was also concerned about the public perception of such arrests: the police would appear to be more concerned about the attempted murder of a white boy than the actual murder of a black one. The Kent team were not impressed. So far as the surveillance was concerned, they had already formed the view that it was never much more than a nonsense. They commissioned a study by a Home Office surveillance training specialist, Phil Pitham, who found that the planning and preparation of the operation were inadequate and the paperwork was incomplete. As for the rest: 'In my opinion the surveillance team would appear to have been deployed in an *ad hoc* fashion with no apparent direction towards the achievement of specific objectives or the collation of evidence to assist in the prosecution of an offence.' Twice, bags were seen leaving 102 Bournbrook Road, but nothing could be done because of a lack of communications. As for the photographs, once they were taken they appeared to have been ignored: pictures showing Norris and Dobson together could have been used at Dobson's interview to refute his claim not to know Norris, but they were not.

As far as the Lawrence case was concerned, Weeden said that in the Lawrence investigation he adopted Crampton's approach and attempted to find evidence before carrying out arrests. Partly, this was because he accepted Crampton's judgement and was happy to rely on it while he made himself familiar with the detail of the case. Partly, he told Kent, it was because four days had already passed since the murder and the culprits had had time to destroy any forensic evidence. And partly it was because he believed he still did not have 'reasonable grounds to suspect' in the Lawrence case. Kent had little patience with these suggestions. The advantages of early arrests were obvious – greater potential for forensic evidence, the prevention of intimidation and the chance to mount early identification parades – and they far outweighed any advantages of delay. Yet Weeden waited for eleven more days. For the first five, by his own account in interview, he was not quite on top of the case and the bank holiday weekend had arrived before he could 'start really trying to do some pro-active work'. He explained: 'I was in truth on the back foot for the first few days because of the sheer volume of incoming information and things I had to absorb and decisions I was making as well as press interviews.' One victim of this delay was the process of preparing E-fit images with the witnesses; the Kent team were appalled that Duwayne Brooks was not asked to prepare one until thirteen days after the murder, Joey Shepherd was not asked until twelve days after it and Royston Westbrook was never asked.

Weeden gave himself time, but when he and Ilsley finally decided to make their move the operation was poorly planned and went off at half-cock. On the eve of the arrests, Kent found, Detective

Constable Budgen reported to the team briefing on his latest conversation with the informant called James Grant. One of the things that Grant had told him was that the Acourt boys were known to hide knives under the floorboards. Yet when Jamie and Neil were arrested and the house at 102 Bournbrook Road was searched, it appeared that the floorboards were never lifted. What was more, no attempt was made to find blood traces on towels, shampoo bottles or furniture – places where deposits might have been made after the suspects returned home. Although no fewer than twenty-one officers were involved in the raid on that house alone, and although they included a number of search specialists, they lacked the information and guidance to do their job properly, Kent concluded. As for the attempt to arrest Norris at Berryfield Close (he was not at home), the Kent detectives saw it as a fundamental error not to have established where this suspect was.

Once the suspects were in custody the interviews were equally badly handled. Again an expert analysis was commissioned, this time from Christopher Mould, the head of Kent Constabulary's interview training department. He took the view that all four interviews showed a lack of planning and he was particularly critical of the handling of Jamie Acourt. Jamie was questioned for only seven minutes and he faced just twenty-nine questions of which twenty concerned practical and procedural matters. In other words, he was asked just nine questions relating to the murder of Stephen Lawrence. Mould acknowledged that Jamie, like Neil and Norris, made it clear at the outset he would only answer 'no comment', but he insisted that police officers should not surrender so easily to such tactics. Jamie should at the very least have been put under pressure. As for the questioning of Dobson and later Knight, who answered every question put to them, it was just as ineffective. Mould said these interviews were unplanned, rambling and lacking in clear objectives. And this same lack of planning infected the identification parades, Kent found: they were organized at the last moment; the paperwork was not ready and there was a scramble to find 'stooges' to stand alongside the suspects. In the end only two parades were held on the arrest day, which meant that more valuable time was lost in which the witnesses' memories could grow stale.

Completing this narrative, the Kent investigators noted something else. The arrests took place on a Friday, and the following Monday

Brian Weeden took emergency leave for six days because his mother-in-law had been killed in a road accident. Kent did not reproach him for this but they wanted to know who took charge in his absence. Was it Weeden's immediate superior, Detective Chief Superintendent Ilsley, or his deputy, Detective Inspector Bullock? In interview, Ilsley was asked and he said it was Bullock. When Bullock was asked, however, he said it was Ilsley. These were six important days for the investigation, in which Norris was arrested, Neil Acourt was identified and charged with the Lawrence murder and Neil and Norris were also charged for the Benefield stabbing.

While many failures were identified that involved junior officers, the thrust of Kent's criticism of the Fishpool investigation was directed at management, and the harshest words were reserved for Weeden. Most of the errors and omissions could be traced directly to a lack of supervision and rigour. Weeden had a 'trusting style' and a '*laissez-faire* approach', and once he had given an order he seemed to assume his officers would carry it out fully and effectively. He did not check or challenge their performance as he should have. And in the eyes of the Kent team Weeden also failed in the SIO's basic task, to 'see through the maze', to distinguish what was important from what was not and to pick out the leads and opportunities that promised to yield hard evidence. He also lacked drive, attention to detail and the determination to get the most out of witnesses, informants and suspects. 'Nothing less was good enough,' Kent concluded.

It did not end there, for the Kent detectives had many important criticisms of the remainder of the investigation. When they examined the handling of forensic evidence, for example, they found it to be just as erratic as Neville Lawrence had always feared. As was routine with murder victims, on the night of his death Stephen's hands were enclosed in plastic bags to ensure that any traces remaining from the attack were preserved. When these bags were later sent to the forensic laboratory, however, they were marked simply 'for retention' and the contents were not analysed. Thus it was only in 1995, when the Lawrence family set in motion their re-examination of the forensic evidence, that the bags were studied. And then, as we have seen, fibres were found in them that matched clothing taken from Gary Dobson's house. The Kent team simply could not understand why these bags were neglected in this way. Nor could they understand why two bloodstained tissues found on Rochester Way were not subjected to the most rigorous testing, and how one of them came to be lost.

And there were other serious failures, one of which stands out from the others. When Duwayne Brooks gave his first formal statement to police on the morning after the murder he said there were six boys in the attacking group. 'I made a mental note of how many of them there were,' he said, 'because I wondered what they were doing.' Most of the other witnesses were less sure, speaking of four, five or six boys, and Linda Williams, the nurse who saw the attacking group from behind as she drove by, was confident that she had counted just four. The Fishpool team had four prime suspects initially, and then added a fifth: Luke Knight. But they could not be sure that they had all the attackers, or even exactly the right ones. Gary Dobson had an alibi, as did Luke; what if one or both of them was genuine? There was a possibility, recognized by Weeden and his detectives, that there might have been one or two young men in the attacking group who were not among the prime suspects. This meant that inquiries could not stop with the five: there might well be other culprits to be caught. The Kent investigators examined how the Fishpool team dealt with this part of the case: in general terms, they found, the inquiries that were carried out lacked organization and consistency, and in particular Weeden failed to apply systematic criteria for eliminating possible suspects.

Looking at the evidence, moreover, the Kent team came to realize something which they felt was of the utmost importance. They analysed all the descriptions given by all the witnesses, both those at the bus stop and others such as Williams and the one or two local people who had seen something from their windows, and they found a surprising common thread. Several of them had said that one of the attackers had fair or blond hair. This was not something that the original investigators had missed altogether, but they did not consider it particularly significant – Bullock and Weeden suspected that one of the prime suspects might have had fair hair at the time, or that the witnesses had been misled by the effects of orange street lighting. Kent did not believe this, and Clapperton and Ayling took the view that this 'blond offender' was an important line of inquiry which had been neglected. They identified several figures on the general suspect list – known associates of the Acourts, youths named in tip-offs and so on – who might fit the description and in almost every case they found that the original investigation had failed to deal thoroughly with these men. Here is one example.

An eighteen-year-old associate of the Acourts, who was 5' 5" tall with short blond hair, was suggested as a suspect by an informant on 28 April. This man was seen by police on 14 June and he stated that on the night of the murder he was at a local social club with a friend, whom he named. The friend was seen on 6 July and he confirmed this, but when officers visited the social club in question they found that the register of visitors did not quite support the story. The date beside the suspect's name was 21 April, not 22. A club official said that this was probably just a slip of the pen, but since he was the father of the suspect's friend there were grounds for scepticism. Yet Weeden marked the relevant docket: 'No further action.' This was the more remarkable because the original tip-off about this suspect included the information that he wore a black jacket with 'NAFNAF' on the back. In the first week of May a local woman called Eileen Gooch had reported a suspicious conversation she overheard in the street in which a youth appeared to be talking about police and saying to a friend that he was not scared. The boy then threatened her. Mrs Gooch described the boy as aged nineteen or twenty, 5' 5" tall, with blond collar-length hair. He was wearing a jacket with the logo 'NAFNAF' on the back. Given this background, Kent could scarcely believe that Weeden had been prepared to dismiss this young man without attempting all possible avenues of inquiry. Why were members of the social club not questioned? Why were taxi firms not approached, since the man said he had taken a taxi home from the club that night?

A further mystery uncovered by the Kent investigators concerned the fate of James Grant. Both Budgen and Davidson insisted at interview that the man called Grant was officially registered as a police informant. This would mean that he could be paid for his information and that he could be contacted again for criminal intelligence purposes. Kent, however, were unable to find any of the documentation that would normally show someone had been registered. The only relevant paperwork they turned up was a file containing a memo written by Davidson during the summer of 1993 recommending that Grant should receive a reward for his efforts. Brian Weeden had endorsed it, suggesting a sum of just £50. When he was questioned about this, Weeden said that the decision about payment was Ilsley's and that he knew Ilsley did not believe in paying generously for information. So it proved, for he recalled that when he discussed the matter with Ilsley even the £50 proposal was rejected. Grant received no reward. Kent's verdict was that this was symptomatic of Fishpool's failures in connection with Grant: they did not recognize his importance when he walked into the station on the day after the murder and they still did not recognize it months later when it came to paying a reward. His information was worth hundreds of pounds, possibly even thousands. Worse, the Fishpool detectives never established clearly that Grant's source was K (the man who visited the Acourt house on the night of the murder). When he was questioned by Kent detectives Grant confirmed that he had heard the story first from K, but when Clapperton revealed the connection in interview, Weeden clapped his hand to his forehead in shock. Other questions about Grant remained unanswered even after Kent's scrutiny, and one in particular was later to acquire great importance in the eyes of the Lawrences and of Michael Mansfield: why were there no registration papers?

Kent's terms of reference did not limit them to the events up to the discontinuance in July 1993 but specifically included consideration of the Barker review, conducted in the autumn of that year. In fact the review was one of the first documents to be studied by the Kent team and they felt disquiet about it from the outset. Once they had studied the original investigation for themselves they returned to the review with an even more doubtful eye. Detective Chief Superintendent John Barker was interviewed by Ayling and Clapperton on 10 September 1997 and, alone among officers and ex-officers approached by Kent, he proved reluctant to cooperate. He answered questions about the background to his report and on what happened when he handed it over, but he would not comment on the content and on how he reached his conclusions. He later submitted written answers but the Kent team were not happy with them. On the content of the review, Kent had a number of detailed criticisms to raise with Barker: why, for example, did he appear to belittle the quantity and quality of information reaching the police in the earliest days of the investigation? There also appeared to be a number of errors of fact; but these were relatively minor. What really concerned the Kent team was that they had been able to identify and catalogue twenty-eight significant shortcomings in the first investigation, including missed opportunities, incomplete lines of inquiry and errors of judgement, but Barker had missed all of them. Where they had been shocked at the poor quality of management and detective work, he had been happy with what he found. 'The investigation,' he had written, 'has been progressed satisfactorily and all lines of inquiry correctly pursued.' Asked about this during his interview, Barker repeatedly insisted that he would 'reserve his position' on such matters. However, he eventually made a surprising claim. He said that he deliberately chose not to include criticisms of police officers in his report because the report was 'potentially disclosable to the defence' in any future Lawrence prosecution. Instead, he had made these criticisms known verbally to the senior 3 Area officer who commissioned the review, Deputy Assistant Commissioner Osland, during a 'frank exchange' after the final report was submitted on 1 November 1993. Osland, in his interview with Kent, had made no mention of hearing such criticisms from Barker.

It was not just the workmanship of the Barker review that was shocking, the Kent team noted, but its consequences. First, it failed to give any new impetus to Weeden's investigation at a time when that was urgently needed – in that sense it was a missed opportunity in its own right. Second, the review misled senior officers, who as a result presented a completely false picture of the investigation to the Lawrences and the public. Third, and probably most damaging of all, it effectively closed down whole avenues of inquiry for years, since officers who read it believed there was no point in revisiting areas which had been professionally dealt with in the first place.

Two matters remained and both related to the question of why this dreadful chain of events occurred. From the outset, the Kent investigators were under instruction to probe the issue of race: was police conduct on the night of the murder, or in the days and weeks that followed, influenced by racism? This was the perception of the Lawrence family and much of the black community in 1993, and by 1997 it was a suspicion shared by a large part of white Britain as well. Kent concluded, however, that they could find 'no evidence to support the allegation of racist conduct by any Metropolitan Police officer' in the case. This was to be a very controversial finding, although perhaps not a surprising one given the character of Police Complaints Authority investigations. Their job was to establish whether there was evidence of wrongdoing by individual, named officers. In the Lawrence case seventeen officers, serving and retired, had been identified as subject to complaint, and Kent could find no evidence of racism that could be used in disciplinary proceedings against any of these seventeen. By nature this would have to be specific and overt, and no such evidence was found. This was by no means the last word on the role of race in the case.

The other issue to be tackled was the possibility of corruption. The Kent team did not even consider this line of inquiry until after the visit by the Lawrences to Maidstone in September. During that visit Doreen and Neville (now back from Jamaica) suggested that the pursuit of the killers might have been deliberately sabotaged by one or more police officers who were acting in collusion with the five suspects or their families. The Kent investigators agreed to look into it, but by now time was short and they were unable to carry out more than a cursory hunt for evidence. They established that no Fishpool officer was directly related to the suspects (as had once been rumoured), and that there was no known link between any of the Fishpool officers and either Clifford Norris or the Acourts' uncles, the Stuarts. As with race, others would take up this issue where Kent left off.

Kent's brief had been to determine whether any of the seventeen named officers should face disciplinary action and here again their findings were to be the subject of dispute. Ayling and Clapperton concluded that four officers, Crampton, Weeden, Bullock and Barker, had neglected their duty while a fifth, Ilsley, had performed unsatisfactorily. Of these five, however, all but Bullock had retired by the end of 1997. There was nothing unusual or suspect about this, since they had each completed the normal thirty years' service after which it is unusual for police officers to remain, but the effect was to place these four beyond the reach of police discipline. Kent were left to conclude, a little limply, that Crampton, Weeden and Barker should have faced discipline *if they had still been serving*. Likewise Ilsley should have been 'admonished' if he had still been serving. Only in the case of Detective Inspector Ben Bullock (still just over a year from retirement) could they recommend action with the expectation that proceedings would actually occur. When all this became public some time later, it left the impression that police officers were escaping justice.

By December of 1997 the Kent investigators were under acute pressure to finish their task. A public inquiry – ordered by Jack Straw, the new Home Secretary – had been in preparation for nearly six months and the PCA report had to be in hand before it could begin. This report would not be made public – they never are – but on 15 December a 23-page summary of its conclusions was issued to the media. This spoke of 'weaknesses in the leadership, direction and quality of work of the first murder investigation', of poor handling of informants and witnesses, of delays and missed opportunities and of the 'highly damaging' Barker review. No evidence of racism or corruption had been found, it said, but 'serious shortcomings' were now evident and these would never have been uncovered without the determination and persistence of the Lawrences. This caused a sensation. 'Lawrence: the damning facts' was the front-page lead headline in the *Daily Mail* the following morning, and the other national papers adopted the same tone. Kent's peer review had shamed the Met and, in important ways, vindicated the Lawrences, and the public inquiry was still to come.

Chapter Nineteen **A Necessary Pillorying**

At 10 a.m. to the minute on Monday 16 March 1998, Sir William Macpherson brought down his gavel to declare open the public inquiry into the case of Stephen Lawrence. More than seven months had passed since Jack Straw had announced the inquiry and placed Sir William, a former High Court judge, in charge. Considering the burden of work Straw shouldered on becoming Home Secretary in May, he had acted extremely promptly. The decision that Labour, if elected, would order such an inquiry had been taken in opposition, but the announcement of this was overtaken by the calling of the general election. Once he was installed at the Home Office, Straw invited Neville and Doreen Lawrence to a formal meeting in June and a month later he was ready to act. He wrote to John Prescott, the Deputy Prime Minister (who was standing in for Tony Blair at the time), to inform him that he had decided to set up a judicial inquiry under the Police Act. 'I want to see the proper concerns of the Lawrence family and the wider community addressed,' he wrote, 'while at the same time not undermining the police service and devaluing the progress it has made in recent years in improving its relations with the communities it serves.' This balancing act would prove to be impossible. The inquiry was announced in the House of Commons on 31 July and given the following task:

> To inquire into the matters arising from the death of Stephen
> Lawrence on 22 April 1993 to date, in order particularly to identify
> the lessons to be learned for the investigation and prosecution of
> racially motivated crimes.

These terms of reference were 'narrowly focused', Straw told Prescott, but in truth they were not as narrow as they might have been. 'Matters arising' is a catch-all; the words 'and prosecution' were carefully inserted to ensure that the Crown Prosecution Service and indeed the private prosecutors could be called to account, and 'to date' meant that anything that happened up to the time the report was completed might be deemed relevant. Macpherson had a lot of ground to cover.

The Lawrences' legal team, mindful of previous experience, had offered suggestions to Straw as to who should chair the inquiry – a shortlist of liberal judges – but the Home Secretary had ideas of his own. Sir William Alan Macpherson of Cluny and Blairgowrie is the twenty-seventh hereditary chief of his clan and master of Newton Castle in Perthshire. He comes – it should be no surprise – of warlike stock: his great-great-great-grandfather was killed leading several hundred Macphersons in the service of Bonnie Prince Charlie, and more recently his father was a twice-decorated artillery officer in the First World War. Sir William, after an English education at Wellington College, would have followed this martial tradition had the Second World War lasted a little longer. Instead, after brief peacetime service in the Scots Guards, he went to Oxford and then to the Bar, becoming a Queen's Counsel in 1971 and, from 1983 to 1996, a High Court judge. The army, meanwhile, remained a hobby, albeit a rather serious one: in the 1960s he commanded a territorial regiment of the SAS (whose tie he often wore at the inquiry). On the day he opened the public proceedings of the Stephen Lawrence inquiry, Macpherson was two weeks short of his seventy-second birthday. He looked, perhaps, a little younger than that; his wiry figure seemed to owe more to his military side than to the sedentary life of a judge, and his manner certainly had a youthful briskness.

This quintessentially establishment personality – an elderly, white, Scottish aristocrat – was given three 'advisers' who would sit with him: John Sentamu, the Anglican Bishop for Stepney, who had once been a judge in Uganda; Tom Cook, a former Deputy Chief Constable of West Yorkshire, and Richard Stone, a doctor from Notting Hill who was chairman of the Jewish Council for Racial Equality and had a long record of race relations activism. As their title suggested, these three advisers could not make findings of their own but were there to assist the chairman.

Although Straw had moved quickly, the inquiry encountered many delays before it could get down to business. First, there was the housekeeping. A home was eventually found at Elephant and Castle in south London, in Hannibal House, a shabby office block rising above an even shabbier shopping centre painted, ingloriously, in a thick coat of puce-pink. Here the third floor was smartly refurbished as offices and the fourth as the inquiry chamber. After much negotiation, nine parties were allowed representation, and they could be divided broadly into prosecution and defence. On the prosecution side were the Lawrences, Duwayne Brooks and the Commission for Racial Equality, while the defence comprised the Metropolitan Police, the Crown Prosecution Service and, as two discrete groups, the three superintendents – Ilsley, Crampton and Weeden – and the lesser, or federated, ranks. Chief Superintendent John Barker, by now retired, was also separately represented, as was the borough of Greenwich. Besides these, the inquiry had its own counsel, making ten legal teams in all. No fewer than twenty-one barristers were accredited to the inquiry, of whom six were QCs. When proceedings got under way each of these ten teams would be entitled to question witnesses, although the chairman made it clear from the start that he was extremely anxious to avoid repetition and deviation.

The second cause of delay was the Kent report. Sir William quickly saw that he could not sensibly begin until Kent had completed their work (even though the findings were not in any way binding upon him) and on that basis he was obliged to defer the opening session until January 1998. Once the report was in hand, complete with its appendices and supporting documents, it took time to digest, and indeed the weight of paper became the third cause for delay. It was to be an electronic inquiry, with documents from the huge files of evidence displayed on screens at the lawyers' desks rather than presented in hard copy form, but the process of scanning and cataloguing was lengthy and laborious. Disclosure – the release of relevant papers by each party to the inquiry and the other parties – also took time, and once the tens of thousands of pages were in hand they had to be read and assessed. So January became February and, at the request of the Lawrence team, February became March. And when Sir William formally opened the inquiry he found, to his dismay and annoyance, that he had to adjourn it once again almost immediately.

On the previous day, under the headline 'Father may ask Lawrence judge to step down', the *Observer* newspaper had reported that the Lawrence family were concerned that Sir William's record as a judge suggested he was 'insensitive' on issues of race. The paper had unearthed from his career on the bench various items which it presented as evidence of this insensitivity. In 1991, notably, Sir William had found against the Commission for Racial Equality in a case brought against Cleveland Education Authority. The authority was within its rights, he had ruled, to allow a white Cleveland woman to transfer her child from a class after she wrote complaining that the girl came home from school singing 'in Pakistani'. He was quoted as saying in court that 'real racial discrimination' would be overcome by goodwill and common sense rather than statutory provision. The *Observer* also quoted a study of decisions in immigration cases which suggested that out of fifteen judges Sir William had been the most likely to refuse would-be immigrants the chance to have official decisions against them reviewed by the courts. And there was more, for the paper also repeated something that had appeared in the pages of *Private Eye*: the QC appointed as counsel for the inquiry, Edmund Lawson, had in the past defended police officers accused of wrongdoing. The implication of these facts, as presented by the *Observer*, was that the judge in the Lawrence inquiry was a man without sympathy for black people and the official inquisitor might be a man with a particular sympathy for the police. If all this was true it hardly augured well for the inquiry. There was a response from the judge in the *Observer* article in which he defended his record on the bench and asked: 'Might it not be a good idea for the critics to wait for the inquiry to start? I want it judged on its conduct and results.' But the Lawrences took the view that to wait for the results might be to leave things too late, and that if they remained silent they might find themselves left with nothing at the end, just as they were left with nothing after the private prosecution. They chose to speak up.

Sir William's first words on declaring the inquiry open the following morning were a condemnation of the *Observer* report and a vague threat of legal action against the paper. When he had finished speaking he turned to Michael Mansfield, who in somewhat anguished terms asked for an adjournment of two weeks. Mansfield was struggling to be tactful, for he was in a similar position to the defence lawyers at the committal who opened their case by asking the magistrate to disqualify himself. The Lawrences, Mansfield said in carefully unspecific terms, had requested an interview with the Home Secretary to express 'very legitimate concerns', particularly about 'the context in which the inquiry is held'. Macpherson, flushed and shocked, asked if the Lawrences were proposing to raise the *Observer* report with Straw and Mansfield replied that their concerns were 'in part triggered by the *Observer* newspaper'. At this the chairman retired to consider the position, emerging after five minutes to say that although a further delay was 'a great blow' he felt he had no choice but to grant an adjournment of one week. The family, with Mansfield and Khan, duly saw Jack Straw the following evening: although he said that he would not remove Sir William from the inquiry, the Lawrences later issued a statement saying they had received 'assurances'. The implication was that the chairman was under notice that his 'sensitivity', or lack of it, would be closely monitored.

These events were to prove characteristic of the inquiry, which lasted more than six months and remained tense and ill-tempered throughout. The 'prosecution' teams were in varying degrees sceptical about the whole inquiry process and one lawyer went so far as to remark that it had been 'set up to fail'. The 'defence' teams, representing the police and the CPS, accumulated their own grievances over time, both against the 'prosecution' teams and against the inquiry itself, while the inquiry staff – counsel, secretariat and panel – felt themselves to be caught in the middle and unfairly criticized. These undercurrents of suspicion and resentment infected many behind-the-scenes discussions of legal and procedural matters and frequently surfaced in the open hearings. It was to be a bruising process for all concerned.

The inquiry resumed, with Sir William in the chair, on Tuesday 24 March and the proceedings began with a series of endorsements of the chairman by his advisers. Bishop Sentamu said he had 'complete confidence in the chairman's ability to conduct this inquiry with fairness and sensitivity', while Richard Stone said that the whole panel shared a determination to get to the heart of the matter. After a short prayer for Stephen ('We will remember him') and a minute's silence, they got down to business, the chairman calling for opening submissions. The pattern of proceedings as they unfolded was to some degree influenced by the geography of the chamber, so it is worth pausing to describe it. The panel of chairman and advisers sat on a raised dais with their backs to a wall, overlooking the chamber. Immediately before them, to their left, was the witness box and to the right were the stenographers. Farther off and directly in front, stretching out over four rows of desks, sat the legal teams. In the front row were the inquiry counsel, led by Edmund Lawson, and the Lawrence team, led by Mansfield and with Imran Khan usually in attendance. The Lawrences themselves often sat with their lawyers to hear evidence. The second row held three police teams: Jeremy Gompertz QC for the Met; Sonia Woodley QC for the superintendents and Michael Egan for the lower ranks. In the third row were Ian Macdonald QC for Duwayne Brooks (Duwayne attended only one session), Jeffrey Yearwood for the CRE and the representative of Greenwich borough. And in the fourth and last row were Brian Barker QC, for the CPS, and Mukul Chawla, representing former Chief Superintendent John Barker. The scene was a crowded one, for besides the leading barristers there were juniors and often solicitors as well – Jane Deighton, for example, on behalf of Duwayne. The desktops were no less crowded: each team had a large screen on which documents under discussion were displayed; they also had laptops and disks, water jugs and glasses, lever-arch files, loose bundles of paper, Post-its and all the usual legal litter. Beyond the rows of desks, to the rear and to one side, lay the seating for the public and the press.

The opening submissions began, as all subsequent examinations of witnesses were to begin, in the front row. Lawson rose to speak first and quoted a description of Stephen given by a police officer who had known him through Cambridge Harriers athletics club:

> During the period I knew Stephen I found him to be polite and respectful. He was a dedicated athlete, by far the best athlete in my group, and although he was very aware of this fact he was never big-headed about it. On the contrary, he appeared embarrassed about his talent. I never saw him display any form of aggression and would describe his temperament as the same as his father: quiet and unassuming. He was of good character – exemplary character. He was a young man who had never come into contact with or to the notice of the police.

Lawson went on to say that his task was to probe, on behalf of the inquiry, what went wrong and why. He made no apology for stating at the outset that something had gone wrong because, he said, that was self-evident and demonstrated by a mass of documentation. As he elaborated on this, another pattern for the months to come became apparent. The full, 400-page Kent report, that damning assessment of the Met's performance, had not been made public, but the lawyers found themselves relying heavily upon it. Consequently, the sensational details uncovered by Kent emerged at the inquiry in dribs and drabs, more often from the lips of barristers than witnesses. Lawson thus spilled out the story of the many tip-offs given to the police in the days after the murder, and of the half-dozen other attacks that the prime suspects were alleged to have committed. He mentioned the various delays in following up leads, the 'particularly crass failure' of the surveillance operation, the omissions relating to the 'blond offender' and, above all, the delay in making arrests despite the evidence in the Benefield case. Much of this was new to the public and to the press, and it included some vivid images – the surveillance photographer who had no radio to alert police that washing was being taken out of 102 Bournbrook Road; the bags around Stephen's hands that were not submitted for forensic examination; the failure to use photographs to challenge Gary Dobson at interview.

Mansfield was the next to speak and he began by quoting from Vernon Johns, a black Baptist minister in Alabama who was a forerunner to Martin Luther King. 'It is safe to murder Negroes,' Johns had said in 1948. Mansfield spoke of the climate in which racism flourishes and declared that this climate was created, in part, 'by law enforcement agencies which fail to take speedy and effective and committed action to pursue illegality'. He then set out the family's basic position:

> The magnitude of the failure in this case, we say, cannot be explained by mere incompetence or a lack of direction by senior officers, or a lack of execution and application by junior officers, nor by woeful under-resourcing. So much was missed by so many that deeper causes and forces must be considered. We suggest that these forces relate to two main propositions. The first is, dealing with the facts themselves, that the victim was black and there was as a result a racism, both conscious and unconscious, that permeated the investigation. Secondly, there was the fact that the perpetrators were white and were expecting some form of protection . . . The inordinate and extensive delays and inactions give rise to one plain inference and one plain question which we suggest has to be boldly addressed: was the initial investigation ever intended to result in a successful prosecution?

317

Mansfield thus served notice that the Lawrence family was looking far beyond Kent for its explanations of what went wrong. The actual errors and failures of procedure identified by the Kent detectives were only the symptoms, he was suggesting, and the disease was far worse than 'mere incompetence'. The investigation was infected by conscious racism and by corruption – it was deliberately prevented from succeeding.

Gompertz followed, expressing the great regret of the Metropolitan Police that the killers had not been punished and the sympathy felt by all officers for the Lawrence family. The Met, he said, acknowledged that mistakes had been made and was 'determined to learn every possible lesson from any constructive criticism which emerges from the inquiry'. In general terms, he presented the defence case. The Lawrence murder was investigated from the outset by a large and committed team. Under pressure and swamped with material, they worked long and hard to find evidence but were defeated by the reluctance of witnesses to cooperate. Kent had found many faults in their conduct but it should be remembered that these officers did not have the benefits of time and hindsight available to the Kent team. 'Once the crossword is completed,' he said, 'the clues often appear easy.' As for racism, Gompertz made clear that the Met would contest the charge: 'It is quite possible to get things wrong, perhaps even very wrong, without being racist.'

Like any defendant in court, the Met was ready to concede what it knew the prosecution would prove, but no more. Even this, it is easy to forget, entailed an enormous shift in position from the attitude it had adopted before the publication of the Kent report summary by the PCA the previous December. Until then, with the 'comfort cushion' of the Barker review behind them, senior officers had maintained the line that the first investigation was basically sound, and if mistakes were made they did not affect the outcome. Now such arguments were simply untenable and important errors and failures were acknowledged; the argument would henceforth be about how serious they were, the context in which they took place and why they occurred.

Just how bruising an experience the inquiry would be became plain in the first few days of witness evidence, which were devoted to the events of the night of the murder, both in Well Hall Road and at the hospital. On these matters Kent had given the Met a clean bill of health and it may be that a relatively easy ride was expected. Mansfield and his team had no such intention and they tackled the likes of Bethel, Gleason and Little with extraordinary ferocity. Within a minute of first rising to cross-examine, Stephen Kamlish was challenging Linda Bethel's recollection of the scene as Stephen Lawrence lay on the ground: was she really saying there was blood near his head? Yes. That was odd, because she was the only person among all those who had given statements to say so. Was she aware that his wounds were on the chest and arm? Yes. So the blood could not have been around his head, could it? Well, it might have seeped out that way, said Bethel. But there is no slope at that point in Well Hall Road, is there? There is a slight incline, she said. Kamlish is built like a bull, with a large, stubbly head and suits straining at the buttons; in full cry he can be very intimidating and he seemed to have reached full cry almost immediately. The whole chamber was taken aback, including the chairman, who observed: 'All the witness can do is give her recollection.' But Kamlish's purpose was to shake that recollection. She had received first aid training and refresher courses; why she did not try to staunch the bleeding, as first aid procedures require?

BETHEL: If we hadn't been told it was a head injury, then
    perhaps I would have started searching through his clothing.
    But I believed, I mean, he had a lot of clothing on him; it was
    dark.
KAMLISH: Why is the fact that it was dark relevant?
BETHEL: Because I couldn't see where any blood was coming from; it
    wasn't obvious.
KAMLISH: You had a torch in your car?
BETHEL: Yes.
KAMLISH: That was parked a few feet away?
BETHEL: Yes.
KAMLISH: Did you go and get the torch?
BETHEL: No.
KAMLISH: Did you ask anyone else to get the torch?
BETHEL: No.
KAMLISH: Why not?
BETHEL: I don't know.

It was the same with Gleason. Had *he* seen blood on the ground beside Stephen's head?

GLEASON: Yeah (*gestures behind his head*). Back there some-where.

KAMLISH: That is simply not true, Mr Gleason.

GLEASON: I am sorry. I cannot remember.

KAMLISH: Well, please do not say something which you do not remember, which cannot be true. The blood was not behind his head, was it?

GLEASON: I don't remember. Well, I believe it was there, but . . .

KAMLISH: Did you bend down and do anything at all to this young man?

GLEASON: Yes, I did.

KAMLISH: You did. Tell us, then, what you did to look for the source of the bleeding after you had discovered it was not the head.

GLEASON: I checked his outer clothing.

KAMLISH: What do you mean, you checked it?

GLEASON: I looked down the body to see if there was any obvious, visible wound.

KAMLISH: You did not touch it, did you?

GLEASON: I cannot remember.

KAMLISH: You cannot remember touching his body at all, can you?

GLEASON: No, sir.

And Geddis, who stopped in his car to help, was given no special treatment. Kamlish all but accused him of lying about the blood, and later asked why he had taken no notes of what he had seen.

GEDDIS: Sir, I was off duty and I wasn't, I didn't make any notes. I wasn't asked to . . .

KAMLISH: You were not asked by anyone?

GEDDIS: Not to make notes, no.

KAMLISH: You accept that being off duty is irrelevant? If a police officer gets involved in an incident, you are a police officer as if you were on duty?

GEDDIS: That's correct, yes.

320

KAMLISH: You should have made notes?
GEDDIS: With hindsight, sir, yes, I should have.

With Sergeant Nigel Clement, one of the officers with the Territorial Support Group, Kamlish went up a gear. Clement maintained that he had arrived in the first TSG van to reach the scene, shortly before the ambulance. Inspector Steven Groves was in charge, said Clement, and he sent the van off to tour the streets on the west side of the Progress estate in search of the attacking group. Kamlish's first words to him established that he too had no notes of what had happened on the night and that the van's log, known as its 'tag sheets', had gone missing. He asked about the nature of the tag sheets: 'If, for example, you are not telling the truth about getting there when you said you did, the tag sheet might help . . . ?' To which Clement replied: 'The first thing I would say is that I am telling the truth . . .' But Kamlish had his doubts. Clement had stated that, although he got out of the van while Stephen still lay on the pavement he saw no blood on the ground, and he suggested that this might have been because the body was shadowed by a tree. Kamlish produced photographs of the scene taken later that night which showed no shadow; in fact the body had been close to a lamp-post. When Clement, now struggling, said the street was simply dark, Kamlish retorted: 'It was not that dark. It is ordinary city orange street lighting. Nobody could have missed the blood, I suggest, if they were standing close to him as he lay on the pavement. It is just impossible to miss it.' When Clement went on to say that he did not see Duwayne at the scene either, Kamlish dropped all pretence: 'You were not there, were you, at this time?' As for the search of the streets in the van, Kamlish did not believe in that either. And Clement had said he paid a visit to the Welcome Inn to question staff and drinkers; Kamlish was sceptical.

At this point, after four days of evidence, the onslaught was brought to a halt. Kamlish had been questioning almost everything that police officers said and drawing repeated attention to the absence of written records. At first it had seemed that his purpose was to show that the police case was flawed by poor recollection and contradiction, but as time passed it had become clear that he was implying something altogether worse. Without using the term, he was saying that there had been a cover-up. The Lawrences had been right about the events at the scene and the police wrong, he was suggesting, but the Met officers had convinced Kent that they had performed professionally by telling lies, perhaps even coordinated lies. The absence of contemporaneous notes to support the police case, Kamlish kept saying, was deeply suspicious. Jeremy Gompertz, representing the Met, rose to his feet and protested:

> We are becoming extremely concerned, sir, about what is happening. This witness was asked to come here without the service of any form of Salmon letter upon him. All kinds of allegations have been put to him, of which he had no notice whatever, and it seems to us to be directly contrary to the principles with regard to the warning of witnesses and their entitlement to personal legal representation if this course of conduct is going to be followed, either with this witness or indeed with any subsequent witnesses.

This was an appeal to the chairman to order Mansfield and Kamlish to give notice to witnesses of any allegations that would be made against them, in accordance with rules for inquiries laid down in the 1960s by Lord Justice Salmon. Sir William said his thoughts had been running in that direction:

> I certainly had not expected a barrage of questions suggesting that this officer has lied in respect of practically every piece of his evidence . . . If this is going to happen again I must have notice of it, because fairness works both ways, and if officers are going to be asked questions in the way they are being asked . . . they must be given notice.

Mansfield grumbled a good deal but found the chairman increasingly prickly on the subject; he had no choice but to comply. The result was a hiatus of three days in which evidence was heard from non-police witnesses while Mansfield, Kamlish and their colleagues drafted the so-called 'Salmon letters' serving notice of what they would allege.

If counsel for the police hoped that this would tame the Lawrence camp they were mistaken, for one of the first officers to be questioned after the proceedings resumed their course was Inspector Steven Groves and his ordeal at the hands of Michael Mansfield was at least as punishing as anything Kamlish had dished out. A neat, dark man with a moustache and a fussy air, Groves had arrived at the scene of the murder in the same TSG van as Clement and believed that he remained in effective charge of operations there for two hours or more. When Mansfield came to cross-examine his first step was to read aloud from Groves's Salmon letter, making clear that the Lawrences did not believe he had done his job properly that night. He then asked the inspector which TSG van he travelled in that night. Groves said he was in van U325, with Clement. A long flow of gentle questions tended to strengthen his conviction about this fact until Mansfield revealed with aplomb that Clement was in van U326 and not U325. 'Mr Groves,' he went on, 'I am going to suggest that this inquiry cannot rely on a single word you are saying. Do you think you are totally unreliable?' 'No, sir,' came the sullen reply.

Groves, who said he always carried a clipboard on duty, had told Edmund Lawson of the 'fairly comprehensive' notes he had taken at the scene, of his 'complete log' of the street search he ordered and of his elaborate sketches showing the positions of cars, bins and the like. He had later handed these notes over to local police, he said, but they were now missing, as were his own photocopies. Mansfield went over all of this again in the manner of a world-weary school-teacher dealing with a particularly stupid child and then asked: 'Is there any possibility, officer, that you just never took any notes that night because you were not that bothered about this incident? Is that a possibility?' Groves, by now flustered and a little angry, denied it. Mansfield asked him why he had used the word 'fight' in relation to the incident and Groves said he believed that when he was first called to the scene by radio a fight was mentioned. 'Mr Groves, I suggest to you very clearly, this is one of your assumptions because it is a *black* victim, is it not?' 'No, sir. You are accusing me of being a racist now and that is not true. I would like it noted that I do not think it is fair either.' Mansfield was not convinced: he asked about a passage in Groves's Kent interview in which he used the word 'coloured'. Groves attempted to explain the context and then realized what Mansfield was getting at. 'I am in a sort of quandary here,' he said. '*He* [pointing at Edmund Lawson] is a white man; *that* [Margot Boye-Anawoma, on the Lawrences' team] is a coloured woman. What else can I say? I have to make some description. I do not think that is being racist. *He* [Lawson again] is a white man; *that* [this time Neville Lawrence] is a coloured man.'

Half of the public gallery at the inquiry, the half with the better view, faced across the room towards the witness box. In these early days the green seating was rarely full; in fact there were usually no more than twenty or thirty people watching and listening, about half of them black. During police evidence, and particularly when Kamlish or Mansfield were tying officers in knots, the audience was plainly absorbed by the spectacle and laughter or groans would greet some of the more unexpected answers. This would not normally be allowed in a court of law. When Groves's interrogation reached its most uncomfortable moment, however, Gompertz rose to complain about 'constant interruption and background noise' from the gallery. The chairman's response was revealing:

> Mr Gompertz, you must realise that persistent interruptions from me are not going to help anybody [by which he meant that he had no intention of helping Groves]. I make it crystal clear that if there is laughter in the public gallery at answers given by officers who are under heavy cross-examination then the public gallery will be cleared. Mr Mansfield, I ask you: if you will, remember that you are eliciting facts. There is no jury. There are four of us and we are aware of the position of this officer. He does not need to be pilloried . . . (*slight pause*) unnecessarily.

This was a warning to the public but also to Mansfield, who by implication was accused of treating the gallery as he would a trial jury. The final words, moreover, told their own story. Perhaps without intending to, Sir William had implied that a certain level of pillorying would be accepted as necessary. This was little more than a statement of the obvious, for if public opinion, and indeed black opinion, was to be satisfied that the inquiry was doing its job then the police would have to be placed under pressure. An inquiry that took officers at their word and granted them the benefit of the doubt would convince or help no one. It was presumably for this reason that, although he plainly disliked the tactics of Mansfield and Kamlish, the chairman allowed them more time than anyone else for their questions, and usually as much time as they wanted.

Did this process shed any light? Did it help the Lawrence case? Taking as the starting point Kent's conclusions that the police had done nothing wrong on the night of the murder except fail to keep a scene log, these early exchanges at the inquiry certainly moved things along. On first aid, for example, testimony by the Maidstone Hospital A&E consultant, Graham Cook, left a firm impression that police officers properly trained in first aid would have known that they should examine a bleeding body for wounds and if possible attempt to staunch the flow of blood. As far as scene management was concerned, it emerged that Inspector Groves was not the only officer who thought he was in charge: acting Inspector Ian Little, Chief Superintendent Christopher Benn and Detective Inspector Philip Jeynes all claimed to have been in command at some period of the night. These periods, however, overlapped – in other words there were times when two or even three officers thought they were running things at one time. Kamlish quoted a remark by Bethel in her Kent interview to striking effect. She had been asked who was in charge and she offered various names, adding: 'I know there were quite a lot of senior officers standing around with their hands on their hips.'

Close scrutiny of events at the hospital produced little that was new. Gleason gave his account of events there and maintained it in the teeth of a bruising assault by Kamlish, while Ian Little, who joined Gleason at the hospital for a time, could not add much. The mysteries remained. Did Neville Lawrence identify the body in Gleason's presence? Did he provide Gleason with the family telephone number? In both cases the conflict of evidence remained. A further mystery surrounded the source of the suggestion, passed on to Ian Crampton in the early hours, that the Lawrences had said they did not want to be disturbed until the morning. On this the family and Gleason were agreed: they knew nothing about it. But if new facts were in short supply that did not prevent the chairman from forming an opinion that appeared to be quite different from Kent's, for he remarked that he thought early liaison with the family was 'hopeless'. 'It doesn't look as though there was a plan to deal with the family at all,' he said.

Chapter Twenty Up Through the Ranks

Between March and mid-July the inquiry sat for fifty-six days, usually four days a week from 10 a.m. to 4.30 p.m. Then in September it reconvened for a week for closing submissions before embarking on a shorter second phase devoted to hearing recommendations not specific to the Lawrence case. For the first phase the various parties had agreed in advance a running order of issues to be addressed but in practice this timetable could not be strictly followed. One witness might have knowledge relating to three separate issues – say, race matters, surveillance and the treatment of informants – and the only practical course was to deal with all three in a single session. Thus the inquiry proceeded witness by witness, and in broad terms the movement was upwards through the police ranks, starting with Bethel and Gleason, who were lowly uniformed constables, moving on to detectives such as Budgen, Tomlin and Davidson and then their superiors, Bullock, Crampton and Weeden, before reaching the lofty heights of the police managers, Ilsley, Osland and Barker. Scattered among these was the odd civilian, some of them expert witnesses.

The pattern of activity established at the outset remained constant to the end. A witness would be sworn and would first face questions from counsel for the inquiry, usually Edmund Lawson. Brisk, organized and matter-of-fact, but with a tendency to dry wit, Lawson displayed none of the abrasiveness of the Lawrence team but often extracted just as much useful information. 'There is no guile to my question,' he told Groves at one stage. 'I only ask simple questions; it's part of my personality.' Somehow this was not reassuring. From Lawson the witness would pass to Mansfield or Kamlish, who would display their very different styles. Though a radical, left-wing man, Mansfield could be a very old-fashioned barrister, conducting a cross-examination like a three-act play. There would be quiet passages of highly detailed questioning, punctuated with phrases such as 'Think very carefully now, officer,' which were designed to unsettle. Slowly he would build up to a moment of challenge, when a killer fact – or failing that a killer accusation – was thrown out and the witness would have to frame a single, all-important answer.

And then Mansfield, angry, sarcastic, incredulous and bitter by turns, would pound the witness box with questions, rolling his eyes, shrugging, provoking and teasing. 'Are you really telling me that . . .' he would ask. 'You surely don't have to be a Maigret to understand that . . .' he would declare. Then, suddenly, the indignation would evaporate and, turning to his next topic, he would revert to analytical mode. Groves, Davidson and Ilsley fared especially badly under this treatment; all made the mistake of arguing. Kamlish the bulldog may have lacked this range, but he made up for it in ferocity.

After the Lawrence team came the barristers acting for Duwayne Brooks. Ian Macdonald, a veteran of race cases over thirty years, was polite, hesitant and slow, but rarely failed to elicit the essential facts from witnesses or to put key information from the documents before the public. This camp was often at odds with the chairman, who would cut them off when he felt they were going over ground already covered or pushing the questions into areas he thought irrelevant. At times both sides struggled to contain their anger in public. From the Brooks team the witness might be passed to the Commission for Racial Equality if race questions were appropriate, or to the various police counsel. Here the running order varied but broadly speaking the approach was consistent. The police had a poor case. After Kent it was obvious that no matter what they did the chairman's report would be damning on the issue of competence, so in many ways the less they said about that the better. On other issues – the allegations concerning race and corruption – it was up to the Lawrence team to prove their case and the police were confident, initially at least, that they would not do so. Thus for the most part the police counsel's questioning was brief, unemotional and highly factual. Once they were finished there were often a few questions from the chairman and his panel, and then the witness was free to go. The ordeal might have lasted anything from one hour to three days.

Rarely in those fifty-six days did the inquiry sink into routine or tedium; the highly charged atmosphere and the brisk pace dictated by the chairman ensured that even the examinations of the most minor witnesses were lively, and they almost always contributed facts and insights which illuminated the important issues. Some passages and moments, however, stood out, and among these were the appearances of John Bevan and Linda Holden, the family liaison officers. Bevan made a poor start in the witness box when, questioned by Edmund Lawson about the failed attempt to arrest Dave Norris at Berryfield Close, he admitted that the subsequent search of the house had been 'cursory'. Why only cursory, asked Lawson.

> BEVAN: It is hard to actually describe why, but the property was a mansion, in short, a very, very expensive property, very expensively decorated, and carpets, for example, were top quality fitted. I felt and I obviously made a decision at the time that the extent of my search was an adequate one, whether it be for the fact that David used that address on a temporary basis, which might have been indicated due to the fact he wasn't there.
> LAWSON: Mr Bevan, forgive me. That might be taken to suggest that if you have a posh house you are not going to be the victim of a proper search whereas if you live in a grubby council flat you will have it torn apart.

By now disbelief and laughter had gripped the public gallery, and it was in vain that Bevan tried to explain that he would have known if, for example, the top-quality fitted carpets had recently been lifted to hide something.

He had recovered a little by the time Lawson asked him to explain what went wrong with family liaison.

> That is something, as you can imagine, sir, that I have mulled over for five years and I would love to have an answer to that. I tried everything I could to communicate with the Lawrences. I wanted to be there for them. I have said in all documentation to Kent and on statements that I still want to be there for them today, and I wish I could be. There was a tremendous barrier to communication. It is very, very hard to put my finger on exactly what it was. I do not think I will ever be able to. I think they were taken over – that is possibly a bad way of putting it – by lots of outside bodies who wanted to make their own statement through the Lawrences and I think it is perhaps that that had the biggest effect on the lack of communication, because very, very soon after our initial meetings we were viewed with suspicion and mistrust.

He went on to deny that he had been unsympathetic to the family and that he had treated them in an offhand fashion because they were black. Asked what information he gave them about the course of the investigation, he said: 'It was an extremely difficult task trying to balance what information I could give to the family without prejudicing any subsequent police action, particularly in relation to arrests. I was not in a position to furnish, certainly not names. I found it a hard task to balance that, to keep everyone happy.' 'Is the answer to my question none?' asked Lawson, and Bevan said he had told the family that some suspects had been identified, but probably not much more than that.

Bevan returned to the box the next morning to face Kamlish, but there was a delay before the questioning could start. At the chairman's suggestion proceedings were adjourned for ten minutes to allow the Lawrences, who were delayed by heavy traffic, to take their seats. They had expressed a particular wish to be present for this cross-examination, and once it was under way it was easy to see why.

KAMLISH: Family liaison: firstly, to confirm a few matters, you had never done it before?
BEVAN: That's correct.
KAMLISH: You had not had any training?
BEVAN: There is no training for family liaison, sir.
KAMLISH: You had not seen the guidelines?
EVAN: I don't believe I had, no.
KAMLISH: You had not done it before and you did not even look at the guidelines . . . Do you not think that was something, with hindsight, you should have done?
BEVAN: Using that lovely word 'hindsight' again, sir, quite possibly . . .

This was just a build-up, for soon Kamlish turned to the nub of his challenge to Bevan. He and the Lawrences had read closely all of Bevan's evidence to the Kent investigation and they had formed a distinct view of this officer's approach to the liaison task. 'I want to put to you what is perceived by the Lawrences as your true motivation for doing this job – do you understand? – and why it broke down, and it is all to do with self-gratification, is it not?' He then produced a list of quotations from Bevan's statement and interview with Kent:

he had said he 'relished the opportunity' of a 'very demanding job' and believed his 'caring, supportive' character would be 'an asset to that role'. One of his 'greatest attributes', he had told Kent, was that he could 'speak to different levels of people'. And he believed he could 'offer something to this role' which would be 'mutually beneficial to them [the Lawrences], to me and to the inquiry in general'. Later he said 'it would be a big feather in our cap' if he and Holden could resolve the problems over the mortuary visit. Kamlish was suggesting that Bevan was less interested in helping the Lawrences than in gratifying his own vanity. It was a devastating assault, almost impossible for Bevan to answer, and Kamlish followed it by pressing him about his inability to understand the position that the Lawrences found themselves in. 'You did not appreciate how they were seeing you; you only looked at it in terms of how they reacted to you. Do you understand?'

To Kent, Bevan had spoken of the differences between Doreen and Neville Lawrence, how Neville would occasionally smile at him but Doreen would not. He had also described Doreen as aggressive. Kamlish, with Doreen sitting close by, was merciless.

> KAMLISH: You described her in your interview as aggressive, this grieving mother, from day one, did you not?
>
> BEVAN: Mrs Lawrence did adopt an aggressive stance.
>
> KAMLISH: Was it aggressive for somebody whose son had just been killed a day or two earlier in a racist attack, for her not to smile at you and not to talk much to you? Is that aggression?
>
> BEVAN: We can analyse, I am sure, all the words used throughout those interviews and we can pull them apart now, sir. What I have felt is – I felt at the time and I feel now to some degree – that Mrs Lawrence's stance was aggressive. It is not a criticism; I was trying to explain how she was dealing with me.
>
> KAMLISH: Do you want to take that word back now, with hindsight – that she was aggressive, a day or two after her son had died?
>
> BEVAN: We can analyse all the interviews and all the statements and we could pick out words, as we have done, like 'elated' and now 'aggressive' . . .

Pressed again on the information he had supplied to the family he accepted that he provided 'very, very few specifics'. On the role of Imran Khan, Bevan said he was 'just one more barrier to communication'. On the atmosphere in the Lawrence house, Kamlish stressed that the people Bevan met there were family, friends and a couple of members of the ARA; there could be nothing sinister about that. Finally, Bevan was confronted with a remark he had made in his Kent interview about Linda Holden, the other liaison officer. He described her as 'quite hard'. In the witness box he was plainly embarrassed, and insisted the words were 'a little harsh'. 'She is a lady who can hold on to her emotions, where I class myself as far more emotional than her.'

Two days later Holden gave evidence. She had had previous experience of family liaison, although not in a murder case. Kamlish began on a curious note, saying that Holden had passed Neville Lawrence in the inquiry building the previous week without acknowledging him. She insisted that she had encountered both Neville and Doreen Lawrence and had greeted both of them – 'I have never been rude to Mr Lawrence.' Then Kamlish turned to 1993 and Holden's dealings with the family then.

KAMLISH: You were patronising. Maybe you didn't intend to be, but you were.

HOLDEN: I am sorry if they took the view that we were patronising, but there was no other way of sometimes speaking to them. We were absolutely straight down the line with the family. Whatever they needed to know we told them. If there were things that we couldn't tell them, then obviously we would take guidance from the senior officer.

KAMLISH: You agree that sometimes you may have been patronising?

HOLDEN: I was never patronising.

KAMLISH: You did not treat them as equals, as people of equal intelligence?

HOLDEN: I did treat them as equal. I treated them as a family that had had a tragic circumstance. They had just lost a child and it was somebody that could never be brought back. I just treated them the same way as I would have treated every other family who had a loss.

331

KAMLISH: For example, you took the view that Mr Lawrence did not understand what you were telling him.

HOLDEN: Absolutely not. As I said just now, Mr Lawrence was very, very shocked. His son had just died. How could you expect him to fully understand everything that was being said to him?

There were several such passages, in which Kamlish put forward the Lawrences' view of what had taken place and Holden responded with her own, without the gap closing an inch. They covered the late-night telephone conversations, the other people in the house, the inquiries about Stephen's background and the questioning of Stephen's friends. In spite of Kamlish's approach, Holden yielded almost no ground. The chairman, however, seemed unimpressed by Bevan and Holden as witnesses; he remarked in passing that the closing submissions by the various parties on the issue of family liaison would probably be pungent – 'and probably quite rightly so'.

By the time Holden gave her evidence the temperature at the inquiry had risen perceptibly. Four weeks in, the Metropolitan Police had reviewed the proceedings to date: dozens of officers had been mauled in the witness box, the Met appeared to be losing every argument and the headlines in the press were uniformly hostile and embarrassing. Sir Paul Condon issued a statement.

The Commissioner appreciates the need for a thorough and fearless investigation, which may well include criticism of police officers, but he is concerned that the confrontational nature of cross-examination of some of the police officers and the selective use of evidence has not assisted the search for truth, which is, of course, the prime objective of the inquiry. Such cross-examination . . . may lead to witnesses failing to do themselves justice by adopting an unduly defensive attitude.

More seriously, the Commissioner is extremely concerned about the damage which is being done to the relationship between the police and the black community. If police witnesses are constantly pilloried by a barrage of confrontational cross-examination, the attempts by the Metropolitan Police service to rebuild that relationship, which was seriously harmed in the aftermath of Stephen's murder, could be set back significantly. That would be a negation of the second objective of the Inquiry, namely to achieve a reconciliation and a more positive future.

This was a challenge to the chairman to restrain Mansfield and Kamlish, and it was a challenge he declined to take up. Soon he was under quite contrary pressure, in the form of a petition 'from the people of the public gallery' complaining that counsel for the police were attempting to discredit the Lawrences and Duwayne Brooks and to disrupt the inquiry by raising legal technicalities. 'We are not happy to see you are always obliging their wishes, yet seeming to cut short the cross-examination by Jeffrey Yearwood, Ian Macdonald QC, Rajiv Menon, Michael Mansfield QC and Stephen Kamlish,' it said. This, too, had no apparent effect on the chairman. Yet the character of the public gallery had changed; thanks mainly to the recruitment efforts of the family's supporters, larger numbers of people were attending and the majority were clearly committed to the Lawrence cause. The murmurs and sniggers which greeted lurid testimony in the early days were replaced by more open expressions of feeling. These in turn provoked complaints from police counsel and appeals for calm from the chair. Emotion was running high.

It ran higher when Duwayne Brooks made his appearance at the inquiry. That was day 27, in mid-May, and by then Jane Deighton and her barristers, Macdonald and Menon, had succeeded in stamping on everyone's mind the fact that Duwayne was not merely a witness to the murder but the surviving victim of the attack. They also missed no opportunity to challenge the observations made about Duwayne's behaviour by police officers in the questionnaires circulated at the time of his prosecution. In particular, one former officer was brought to the witness box to explain that the story that Duwayne had broken a window in the front office of Plumstead police station on the night of the murder – a story which found its way into one of the questionnaires – was entirely false. It was established that Duwayne was never in the front office and that he had been linked to the breakage by mistake; somebody else was responsible.

A theme of the Brooks case was the attempt to link the Lawrence murder with the murder of another black youth, Rolan Adams. Two connections were made, and the first involved the red Astra. This was the car seen twice by police officers on Well Hall Road in the minutes after Stephen was taken to hospital. It was carrying five youths, and they were laughing. Officers took a partial registration

333

and by a stroke of luck stopped the same car two days later. The driver turned out to be Daniel Copley, a young white man from Thamesmead who had been convicted of threatening behaviour in connection with the Adams murder. That much of the story, made public for the first time during evidence at the inquiry, was enough to prompt headlines in the press, but more emerged when former DC Mick Tomlin entered the witness box. Tomlin had retired to Spain and appeared at the inquiry as if still dressed for the beach – chinos, sweatshirt and sandals. His approach to giving evidence was just as casual. Holmes records showed that although Copley was stopped in April, it was early June before an action was raised requiring Tomlin to interview him. Tomlin had difficulty remembering this, but he was reminded from the papers that he took a statement from Copley identifying two other passengers in the car. These were Jason Goatley, another young man convicted of threatening behaviour in the Adams case, and his friend Kieran Hyland, who also had a conviction for a race-related attack. When they were questioned, contradictions emerged in their accounts of that night, notably that Hyland alone accepted that there were five people in the car. He also refused to name the other two. Tomlin simply had no memory of all this, and was quite unable to explain why the matter was never investigated further. 'Does it ring a bell?' Menon asked him. 'There are a lot of bells to ring, because it's now, what, five or six years ago. No,' came the reply. Menon carried on regardless: 'What did you do about it?'

> TOMLIN: What do you expect me to do?
> MENON: You have a statement from a witness telling you that five people were in this car. He has agreed to name two of the others that were present.
> TOMLIN: Yes.
> MENON: He has refused to name the fourth and fifth occupants of the car. Both the other people who have been interviewed . . . say, 'No, there weren't five people in the car on the night in question, there were only three.' Surely that is an important lead that should be properly investigated by the police?
> TOMLIN: I don't really know what to say. I mean what would you like me to say to him? 'You must tell me who the other people are'?

334

MENON: The difficulty here is that we know that these people have criminal antecedents involving racist attacks and racist murders.

TOMLIN: Yes.

MENON: Surely this is a matter that should be further investigated by yourself or other officers?

TOMLIN: Certainly not by me, no.

The Brooks team thought it possible that the occupants of the car knew the prime suspects in the Lawrence case and might even have had contact with them on the night of the murder, although no evidence was ever found to support this.

The other link with the Rolan Adams case was Detective Sergeant Christopher Crowley, who once again gave evidence. Thickset, with a ruddy complexion and a mop of black hair, he proved a nervous witness. After a brief examination by Edmund Lawson, Ian Macdonald rose (this was a witness he had asked for) and read out the allegations he intended to put to Crowley. The first of these was 'that you were either lying about or misunderstanding what Duwayne Brooks said to you following the identification parade on 3 June, thereby undermining the credibility of Duwayne Brooks's identification evidence'. And another was 'that you acted in a manner which had the effect of undermining the credibility of Nathan Adams, the principal prosecution witness, surviving victim and brother of Rolan Adams'. Macdonald questioned Crowley at length about the Lawrence case, but to the chairman's evident irritation he devoted almost as much time to the Adams case. He first demonstrated that in the course of the 1991 investigation Crowley had taken two statements from the same witness in the space of six weeks. In the first Crowley recorded that the witness was a schoolboy aged fifteen and in the second he identified him as a factory worker aged 'over twenty-one'. 'So in six weeks,' Macdonald observed with feigned bafflement, 'Colin Cattini has gained at least five years in age and has changed from being a schoolboy to a factory worker?' As the officer squirmed, the public gallery laughed. However obliquely, this was another attack on the reliability of Crowley's evidence about Duwayne Brooks.

The nub of the argument about the Adams case was the treatment of Rolan's younger brother Nathan, who was with him when he died and was also injured in that attack. The details were familiar to the Brooks camp because Jane Deighton had acted for the Adams family in 1991. Weeks after that murder, Nathan, who was fourteen at the time, was arrested and charged with an attack on a white youth. Crowley conducted the interview, in which Adams gave only 'no comment' answers. The case was dropped months later, but on the following day Nathan Adams was arrested again, for another offence (this charge was also later dropped). The second arrest was carried out by officers 'working to D S Crowley', the records showed. Both these arrests took place before the trial of Rolan Adams's attackers and Macdonald insisted that the charges could have been raised during Nathan's testimony at that trial in an attempt to discredit his evidence. This, then, was the evidence for the charge that Crowley had acted in a manner that had the effect of undermining Nathan Adams's credibility. Crowley countered it in some detail: he said he had acted entirely properly and according to routine procedures over the first arrest, and he had had nothing whatever to do with the second arrest, which happened to be carried out by one of twenty-five officers under his command. 'I did not do anything wrong,' Crowley said. 'I acted professionally and correctly and I did not undermine any of the investigations. I carried out my job to the best of my ability.' In short he denied the charge outright. These matters had been investigated by a senior Met officer who found nothing untoward, but the Brooks team argued that his report was flawed and the Met eventually conceded that the investigation was hurried and perhaps incomplete. This, however, was still some way short of proof that Crowley had done what was alleged.

Duwayne Brooks, when he appeared at the inquiry, did not testify. Police counsel in particular had wanted to question him, but after long delays while psychiatric advice was sought, the chairman agreed that he would not have to enter the witness box. Nor did Duwayne personally read out the statement he had prepared; he sat with his lawyers while Rajiv Menon read it on his behalf. It told once again the story of the night of 22 April 1993, but this time the emphasis was not on issues of identification but on his relationship with the police. He described his state of mind as Stephen lay bleeding on the pavement:

> I was pacing up and down, up and down. I was crying. I was
> desperate for the ambulance. It was taking too long. I was frightened

by the amount of blood Steve was losing. I saw his life fading away. I didn't know what to do to help him. I was frightened I would do something wrong.

He conceded that he had used strong language at this stage, although he denied using the words 'pig' and 'cunt', as one officer had suggested. When PC Bethel questioned him, for example, he told her where the attackers had run but she made no use of the information. When she asked again, he said: 'I fucking told you where they went. Are you deaf?' He insisted that he was not out of control or hysterical. 'I was perfectly capable of answering sensible questions.' He spoke of seeing several police officers, only one of whom asked him if he was all right. Later, when he was taken to the police station to make his statement, he said he felt he was being treated more like a criminal than a victim. When it came to his account of the attack, he claimed that officers had reacted with suspicion.

> They kept saying, 'Are you sure they said "What, what nigger"?' I remember someone, maybe the same senior officer, saying, 'You know what this means if you are telling the truth? Are you sure they said "What, what nigger"?' I said, 'I am telling the truth.' He said, 'You mean you have done nothing to provoke this in any way?' I said, 'No, we were just waiting for a bus.' I thought either they thought I was lying or they wanted to do a Jedi mind trick on me so I would lie and say it didn't happen.

None of the officers at Plumstead station ever asked him whether he had been touched or hurt in the attack, he said.

Duwayne had a good word for DS Bevan, who was his liaison officer. While he complained that he was not seen as a victim or offered counselling (something the police disputed), he felt Bevan treated him more seriously and so he trusted him more. As for other officers, he was bitter:

> I made nine statements, went on three identification parades, went to the magistrates' court, Crown Court and the inquest. I kept meeting the police when they asked me to. It was hard when they kept treating me like they didn't believe me and when they treated me with attitude and they didn't seem to care for my safety.

On this last point, safety, he spoke of his terror both after the murder and in the years that followed – a constant fear that 'the fascists', as he called them, would come to get him. During the Old Bailey trial, he recalled, he was given constant protection but this was not thoughtfully handled. On one occasion he was guarded by the officer who had arrested him in 1993 for his part in the Welling riot, and on another he was surprised to be taken to a hotel in Eltham. 'It was the worst area in London they could have chosen. It felt like they took me to Eltham to break my spirit. I didn't sleep that night, because I was frightened to be in my room.'

When he came to the identification parades, he described the second day, 13 May, when a series of line-ups was held. He was brought there in a minibus and was surprised and alarmed to find himself in company with a skinhead. This turned out, however, to be Stacey Benefield and the two young men chatted. 'Stacey Benefield said that the boys who stabbed him were known to stab people and not to get done for it. He said they knew people in the police.' After the parades – at which Duwayne picked out Neil Acourt and Stacey picked out Neil and Norris – the two travelled home together in the minibus. 'Stacey Benefield said something like he knew the people who had attacked him. The one he just picked out was obvious anyhow, because he looked like he had spent the night in a cell and he was wearing something like tracksuit bottoms. I don't recall seeing anyone myself in tracksuit bottoms.' While this story was told by way of explanation for what later happened with Crowley, it was hardly calculated to rebuild Duwayne's credibility as an identification witness. If the defence at the Lawrence trial had known of this conversation with Benefield they would have presented it as further proof that Duwayne was 'tainted'.

He described his feelings at the private prosecution in vivid terms.

I remember I felt that I had not prepared and I felt unsupported. I was frightened of the atmosphere. I was frightened for me. Another witness [Witness B] was allowed to be anonymous and I wasn't. I wanted to know why . . . I remember going out of the court so I could read my statements . . . I felt everything was depending on me and I was going in blindfold. I was alone on a big ship full of pirates. The pirates had me trapped. Mr Kamlish told me the case was going to be dropped. I said, 'Why?' He said because the judge wouldn't allow my evidence to go to the jury. I felt upset. I felt guilty that I wasn't able to give my evidence properly.

With that the statement to the inquiry ended, but Menon said that he wished to read out Duwayne's original statements to the Fishpool investigation as well. The chairman resisted, stating that they were on record and he and his advisers could consult them if they wished. Menon persisted, with the public gallery on his side, and Sir William gave way. The whole episode was one which left the police side with a sense of grievance. Duwayne's main statement to the inquiry contained many accusations against the police in general and against named officers, but it came relatively late in the proceedings and after most of the relevant officers had given their evidence. There was thus no chance to put the allegations to them and hear their reaction, and no chance, given the chairman's ruling, of questioning Duwayne. Worse still, from the Met's point of view, the statement inevitably received wide and sympathetic coverage in the media.

These same issues of fairness were in the air when Doreen Lawrence entered the witness box. She and Neville had both provided statements to the inquiry, read on their behalf by members of their legal team, but it had always been envisaged that they would also be questioned in person. This moment came in June. The task of leading for the police fell to Jeremy Gompertz, a small, neat, grey-haired man notable for his brevity and courtesy. For the occasion of his encounter with Doreen, the public gallery was packed. She was questioned first, briefly, by counsel for the inquiry, and then Gompertz rose.

> Mrs Lawrence, I want to ask you some questions on behalf of the
> Commissioner. In doing so can I please make it absolutely clear that
> my purpose is not to criticise you and your husband? Secondly, can I
> make it clear that I am mindful of the chairman's ruling that counsel
> who wish to ask you and your husband questions should confine
> themselves to matters of fact and not opinion?

He tackled two matters. The first was whether there had been a delay in passing to the police certain information received at the Lawrence home soon after the murder. Much detail about this was put to Doreen but to cheers from the gallery she swatted it all aside, suggesting that any delay was more likely to be on the police side. 'From what I can see, what is happening is that the police are looking to cover their backs.' Her manner was a mixture of disdain and suppressed anger; it seemed she might erupt at any moment. Gompertz pressed on, asking about names of suspects that the family had heard in the early days after the murder, but again he was brushed aside. Then he turned to the journey to the hospital. Doreen could see where this was leading: at the inquest she had spoken of looking down Well Hall Road and seeing no police activity, but Kent's experiment had suggested that this proved nothing, for unless she and Neville had travelled a good way down the road they could not have seen the spot where Stephen had fallen. Gompertz was planning to explore this.

> GOMPERTZ: You went, did you not, to the Welcome Inn?
> MRS LAWRENCE: No.
> GOMPERTZ: Where did you go then?
> MRS LAWRENCE: We passed the pub and we went down to the next junction and that is where we turned around. We went past the bus stop to the road on the left, and that is how far we went. We passed the Welcome Inn pub.
> GOMPERTZ: Yes. Well, we have maps. I wonder if you could be given one, please? I am sorry that I did not make that request earlier.
> MRS LAWRENCE: Can I ask a question here? Am I on trial or something here? I mean, from the time of my son's murder I have been treated not as a victim. I have not been treated as a victim since my son's murder. Now, I can only tell you or put in my statements what I know of what went on that night, and for me to be questioned in this way, I do not appreciate it.

By now there was uproar, cheering and applause in the public gallery, which had been restive from the outset. Gompertz was being howled down, and he addressed the chairman.

> GOMPERTZ: Well sir, I must be in your hands.
> CHAIRMAN: I think you should use your discretion. Is there any vital matter of fact that you feel you ought to ask?
> GOMPERTZ: I have to confess that there are a number of other

matters I was going to ask about, but I respect your judgement in these matters more than anyone else's, and having . . .

CHAIRMAN: I should indicate, and I am sure the public would accept, that I understand Mr Gompertz's position, but I think your discretion should be exercised in favour of not asking further questions.

GOMPERTZ: Sir, I will, of course, accept your guidance.

That was that. When, a little later, Neville Lawrence entered the witness box, there were no police questions at all. In the media Doreen was presented as the David who slew the police Goliath, but the truth was subtly different, for she had long since ceased to be the underdog. There could have been no more graphic illustration than those scenes at the inquiry of the extent to which, by the summer of 1998, power had shifted from the Met to the Lawrences.

And there were even worse humiliations for the police. The testimony of John Barker was one. Barker had been a reluctant witness for the Kent investigation, but he had no choice about appearing at the inquiry, which he did on day 38. He followed Bill Ilsley, the other former detective chief superintendent, who had put up a wretched performance under examination by Lawson and Mansfield and was left looking chippy and narrow-minded. Barker fared even worse. Lawson led him first through his own account of events, presented as a statement to the inquiry, in which he described an early meeting with Commander Blenkin in 3 Area to discuss the remit of his review.

> Blenkin warned that the review would have to be carried out with a great deal of sensitivity to avoid undermining the position of Weeden, who was still SIO at the time. . . The clear implication was that I should ensure that the conduct of the review was not heavy-handed . . . The review should be constructive and not a form of complaints investigation.

On the report itself, he insisted as before that it was framed as it was because of fears that it might have to be disclosed in a future prosecution – 'It seemed to me inappropriate to record in that document criticism of any specific officer if it was relevant, which could then be used by the defence by way of discrediting prosecution witnesses.' Be gentle, be constructive, be discreet; Lawson wondered if these alleged hints and fears had influenced the review and Barker said they had. Where he had criticisms, he communicated them only verbally to the likes of Blenkin, Weeden and Deputy Assistant Commissioner Osland. Then Lawson led Barker through a humiliating comparison between his own findings and those of the Kent PCA team, and Barker agreed that he no longer took such a rosy view of the Fishpool investigation as he had in his review in late 1993.

Kamlish, as ever, went for the jugular, accusing Barker almost in his opening breath of being the author of a cover-up. 'You were worried that if the review got to anyone outside the Metropolitan Police Service, such as lawyers in a future case, and thereby possibly the general public, you were concerned that you did not want to be seen to be criticizing Metropolitan Police officers.' 'That is not the case at all,' came the reply. Kamlish asked where the records of the review investigation were and Barker answered that they had been packed up when the review was complete and sent to the incident room at Eltham. 'I understand,' he added, 'that they are no longer available.' Kamlish made hay with this and then, pressing his case for a cover-up, he quoted again from one of Barker's statements: 'At one point I did consider producing a second, more critical report for the Metropolitan Police's internal purposes only.' Did this not clearly imply that the real report concealed or covered up failings? Barker disagreed. Kamlish then ploughed through some of the inaccuracies in the report – mostly minor matters of fact – asking Barker to account for them, until the chairman interrupted.

CHAIRMAN: Mr Barker, can I have a look at the situation? I want to ask you one or two questions myself. Did you think that the public interest immunity would apply to this document, your review?

BARKER: No.

CHAIRMAN: Did you think it was disclosable to the public or to the parties in any litigation that might follow?

BARKER: I thought it would be disclosable, sir, yes.

CHAIRMAN: It is right, is it, that your position is that you therefore toned down what you said for that reason?

BARKER: Yes.

CHAIRMAN: Can you defend this report?

BARKER: I would . . .
CHAIRMAN: In general and in particular?
BARKER: I would like to, sir.
CHAIRMAN: Well, there you are, Mr Kamlish.

The final remark was ambiguous but the chairman's expression and tone were not. He plainly thought Barker was being a fool and it was scarcely worth Kamlish's effort to continue. Barker himself asked for a drink of water and then, line by line, Kamlish pursued his demolition. After forty more humiliating minutes, he changed tack. 'You were a trusted, high-flying officer, were you not?' 'Yes.' 'Your career background reads like the perfect police officer's CV, does it not?' 'Thank you.' 'You are the *crème de la crème*, are you not?' 'I can only take your view on that.' Then how, Kamlish wondered, could he have made so many mistakes and missed so much? With the witness floundering, Kamlish in full cry and the chairman visibly irritated, it was time for lunch.

When the hearing resumed the chairman announced that he had a short statement to make. To a silent, expectant chamber, he read:

> My advisers and I have given careful consideration to the present state of this witness's evidence. We feel it necessary and right that we should say that, in our view, his value as a witness and his credibility in vital matters has already been much undermined for reasons which will be perfectly obvious for anyone here today. Our present view, although we await the conclusion of all the witness's evidence and submissions, is that we feel we ought to indicate that this review is likely to be regarded by us as indefensible for what must be obvious reasons in these circumstances. We wonder whether further questioning – other than by Mr Chawla, should he see fit to examine his client – is required.

It was an extraordinary moment. Here was a former senior officer at Scotland Yard, a former head of the Flying Squad, being dismissed by the inquiry chairman as an unreliable witness. Sir William's earlier intervention had identified the fault in Barker's position: once he accepted that he had toned down his report, it could not be defended. He had admitted producing a review that did not accurately reflect the facts as he knew them and as far as Sir William was concerned nothing more that he had to say after that could be of any value.

Two matters remained to be clarified from the Barker episode: first, his claim that he had been told by Blenkin when he began work on the review that he should be tactful in dealing with Weeden and his team, and second, his claim that after it was completed he told Blenkin and Osland of the criticisms he had omitted from the review. Osland was the next officer to testify. A tall, patrician figure, apparently posher than most of his former colleagues, Osland had by now retired from the Met and become a local councillor for the Conservative Party in the Croydon area. Questioned by Lawson about Barker, Osland repeatedly stated that when he commissioned the review he was hoping for reassurance that the investigation had been conducted properly, an approach that Lawson found odd on the grounds that it was not an attitude likely to encourage due scepticism. When it came to the delivery of the completed review, Osland described how Barker called on him to present the document. 'What did he tell you about further criticisms that he had to make that were not contained in the report?' asked Lawson. 'Nothing. I mean, if he had mentioned to me any criticisms I would have insisted they were in the report.' As for Blenkin, his account of briefing Barker ran as follows: 'I told him that it was a particularly sensitive investigation. I told him that both Mr Weeden and Mr Ilsley were somewhat unhappy – because they had told me this – that DAC Osland had decided on a review. I handed him the terms of reference. I read them through with him and I didn't speak to Mr Barker again.' He specifically denied suggesting to Barker in any way that he should treat Weeden gently. Afterwards, did Barker privately express criticisms of the investigation to him? They did not speak again, insisted Blenkin. No one, therefore, would corroborate Barker's story.

Osland had suffered badly in the witness box, pilloried in particular for two things. The first was his 1993 memo to Scotland Yard that began: 'Our patience is wearing thin on 3 Area, not only with the Lawrence family and their representatives . . .' and the second was an interview given to the *Croydon Advertiser* in December 1997 in which he suggested that any officers accused of racism by the Lawrences should sue. Doreen and Neville Lawrence were both present in the chamber when Kamlish asked Osland about these, and he struggled to defend himself. But Osland, like Ilsley, represented the

old order of Metropolitan Police managers, the generation super-
seded in the years after the appointment of Paul Condon as Commissioner. Assistant Commissioner Ian Johnston, the man who in
1994 ordered the Mellish investigation and who subsequently oversaw police cooperation with the private prosecution, represented
the new order. His appearance at the inquiry was clearly intended
by the Met to mark a turning of the page, and it began in dramatic
style. Tall, slim, dark and nervous, he took the oath, sat down and
asked to make a statement. The Lawrences had been forewarned
but were not in the chamber and there was a delay before Neville
appeared and sat beside Mansfield. Johnston, wearing uniform,
asked if he could stand but the chairman told him to remain seated
– 'I am sure that will be regarded as no discourtesy.' Having started
with the constables, the inquiry had now reached almost to the
pinnacle of the Met, and what followed was a landmark event in
the case of Stephen Lawrence.

Clearing his throat and addressing himself to Neville, Johnston
read:

> Mr Lawrence, I wanted to say to you that I am truly sorry that we
> have let you down. It has been a tragedy for you. You have lost a son
> and not seen his killers brought to justice. It has been a tragedy for
> the Metropolitan Police, who have lost the confidence of a significant
> section of the community for the way in which we have handled the
> case. I can understand and explain some of what went wrong. I
> cannot and do not seek to justify it. We are determined to learn
> lessons from this. A great deal has changed and will yet change. We
> have tried, over the last four years since the first investigation, to
> show imagination and determination to prosecute Stephen's killers. I
> am very, very sad that we have let you down. Looking back now, I
> can see clearly that we could have and we should have done better. I
> deeply regret that we have not put his killers away. On behalf of
> myself, the Commissioner – who specifically asked me to associate
> him with these words – and the whole Metropolitan Police, I again
> offer my sincere and deep apologies to you. I do hope that one day
> you will be able to forgive us.
>
> Finally, I would like to add my own personal apologies for
> supporting the earlier investigation in ways in which it has now been
> shown that I was wrong. I hope the reasons for my support will be

understood and I hope that, eventually, you will forgive me for that as well, Mr Lawrence.

If words alone could have done it then those would surely have been good enough, but as many newspapers observed the next day, it was too late for that. The Lawrences had issued a statement of their own:

> It has taken five years of trauma, heartache and suffering for our family to reach this stage of our struggle. The Commissioner now accepts that the first investigation was flawed and incompetent. What will happen to those officers? Will they be disciplined? Will those now retired lose their pensions? Maybe we need another public inquiry into police corruption for the Commissioner to then accept that these boys were protected in some way. If it hadn't been for this inquiry the Commissioner would still be saying that officers did everything they could to bring our son's killers to justice. Whilst we accept the Commissioner's apology, we do not forget that Stephen's killers are still free.

The Met had approached the inquiry hoping to fight its corner, defend the defensible and then face the consequences of the report. Scotland Yard was well aware that Kent's was a dreadful indictment and the force was ready, as one official put it, to 'take a beating', but it had not expected things to get so much worse. As the police witnesses paraded by, the chairman, his advisers and the public got a glimpse of the hidden wiring of the Metropolitan Police, the inner functioning of the machine, and it was most unflattering. This went beyond Kent and addressed deeper questions. Why was the investigation so poor? How was so much shoddy workmanship permitted? What was the calibre of the people in charge? Was there something fundamentally wrong with the management of the Met? And the Lawrences were pushing beyond Kent in other directions, too. They and others were probing in the hidden wiring for evidence of racism and as their statement made plain they suspected that corruption, too, had played a part. These questions were still unanswered when Johnston delivered his apology. It was not yet time to turn the page.

Chapter Twenty-one Race

If the Lawrence case was not about race and racism – and the Metropolitan Police contended that it was not – then its importance was drastically diminished. Without race this was merely a dispute about the effectiveness and probity of a single police force, albeit the biggest in the country, but with race it might challenge the whole of British society. The black community had no doubt that what Neville and Doreen experienced at the hands of the police and the justice system would not have happened to the parents of a murdered white boy, and a large proportion of the wider public sympathy for the family was surely prompted by the uneasy feeling that this might be true. This was reflected in the inquiry's terms of reference, which assumed that there would be 'lessons to be learned for the investigation and prosecution of racially motivated crimes'. And yet when the hearings began and Michael Mansfield spoke of race as a 'deeper force' in the case there was concern, even gloom, among the 'prosecution' teams – Lawrences, Brooks, CRE – that it might be impossible to prove. The example of the Kent investigation stood before them: employing the same standards of evidence and proof that they used with such effect to identify neglect of duty and incompetence, the Kent team had been unable to construct a single charge of racism against a single officer. The 'prosecution' view was that Kent's approach had been crude ('Are you a racist?' – 'No', was Kamlish's caricature), but they were aware that alternative strategies offered no guarantee of a different outcome. In the police service, racists would hardly broadcast their views or commit them to paper, nor was it likely that officers would begin to denounce one another as racists from the witness box. If racism had been at work, how could it be exposed?

One method used with some success by the CRE in other cases was to conduct comparative studies – if a black man complained of discrimination by his employer the CRE might look at the treatment of similar employees who were white to see if a clear contrast could be demonstrated. At the Lawrence inquiry such an approach was ruled out from the earliest days: Sir William was scrutinizing one murder and he would not contemplate spending time and energy examining others for the purposes of comparison. What he promised instead was that he would not necessarily demand the same standards of proof with racism that he expected with other matters – he was prepared in principle to 'infer' that something might have happened as a result of racism. How far he might be prepared to go in drawing such inferences, however, was a matter of some concern, and the suspicion that it might not be far at all undoubtedly underlay the Lawrences' early criticisms of Sir William. It was true that in Dr Richard Stone and Bishop Sentamu he had advisers who were very familiar with issues of race, but no one knew how much weight he would give to their views. As a former High Court judge, after all, the chairman was used to making the most important decisions on his own.

In the early days of the inquiry it seemed likely that the experience of Kent would be repeated, for while the barristers succeeded in shaking the Met's position on the issues of first aid and hospital liaison they had difficulty pinning down any evidence of racism. The Lawrence team adopted an indirect approach.

KAMLISH: Do you have any experience of equal opportunities or race awareness training?

BETHEL: I believe we had training at Hendon [police college].

KAMLISH: How many years ago was that?

BETHEL: That would be 1989.

KAMLISH: What did that consist of?

BETHEL: I can't remember specifically. I think we sat down, had discussions, certain scenarios were possibly put to us, how we would deal with it, what we would think . . .

KAMLISH: What ways do you consider in this country racism manifests itself?

CHAIRMAN: I do not think that as broad a question as that is probably appropriate, Mr Kamlish. That will be discussed later.

KAMLISH: Perhaps I will ask a more focused question, dealing with your personal experience. Have you ever been present when someone has suffered racism, in whatever form?

BETHEL: No.

KAMLISH: Never?

BETHEL: Not that I can think of right at this minute.

KAMLISH: Ever been present when a colleague of yours has said
something or behaved in a racist way?

BETHEL: No.

KAMLISH: Never?

BETHEL: Not that I can think of, no.

KAMLISH: Never heard a racist comment in the Metropolitan Police
by any officer?

BETHEL: I'm aware that comments were made and, yes, they are
heard, but I can't specifically recall any. I am not saying it doesn't
exist.

There were similar exchanges with other junior officers, but while
they clearly made the witnesses uncomfortable they led nowhere.
And when Gompertz rose on behalf of the Met he would put the
straight question: are you a racist? The answers came in varying
forms but they were all in essence the same: no. Geddis, for example,
was shocked: 'That is an insult. I mean, I'm a Christian. We have
black people in our church – many – that we mix with, and they are
brothers, if you like, of mine.' Chief Inspector Jonathan McIvor,
one of the officers who visited Well Hall Road on the night, said he
regarded racism as 'unacceptable' and spoke of how ethnic diversity
could 'enrich and benefit society'. Joanne Smith, the fourth officer
to reach the scene, said she loathed racism and observed bitterly: 'It
is very easy to brand somebody a racist.'

There was one revealing exchange, but it did not involve a police
officer. Conor Taaffe, the passer-by who went to Stephen's help and
who prayed at his side, was asked about the moment when he and
his wife first became aware of a problem. They saw Stephen fall, he
said, but they did not immediately go to him. Duwayne saw this
hesitation and it increased his desperation at that moment, so Ian
Macdonald asked about it. Taaffe explained that he and his wife
had 'sensed danger', and it passed through his mind that this might
be a ploy to lure them across the road to be robbed. 'Was that
because it was two young black men?' asked Macdonald. 'I would
say that was part of my assessment, yes.' It was an important
moment, for Taaffe was a sympathetic witness who acted towards
Stephen with exemplary kindness and he was admitting that, for
that one moment, he had applied a racial stereotype to Stephen and
Duwayne. The lesson was plain – ordinary people, even good people,

can have such thoughts; what matters is what they do. Recognize a racist thought for what it is and you can set it to one side; fail to recognize it and it can more easily influence your actions. Such ideas are hardly revolutionary, yet in the whole course of the inquiry no one else would ever admit as much as Conor Taaffe did.

The police position on racism was a simple one: it played no part in the Lawrence case. As a general principle, the Met was prepared to concede that there might be racists in its ranks, but no more than there were in society at large. Any suggestion that there was a general problem of police racism, or that the institution of the Met was in some way collectively racist, was rejected outright. This view harked back to the findings of Lord Scarman in his report on the 1981 Brixton riots. He concluded that the direction and the policies of the police were not racist and that the force was not 'the oppressive arm of a racist state'. In so far as there was racism, Scarman said, it was to be found in 'the ill-considered, immature and racially prejudiced actions of some officers'. This became known as the 'bad apple theory'. But the Met insisted, as Kent had found, that there was no evidence that even a bad apple had been at work in the Fishpool investigation, and in the absence of such evidence it held that the charge of racism was nothing more than a slur. Indeed, the Met's counsel argued that the original team had made a considerable positive effort on race: a senior officer (Ilslcy) publicly acknowledged on day one that this was a racial crime; a specialist officer from the Racial Incidents Unit (Fisher) was attached to the investigation in its early stages, and Crampton and Weeden had both addressed their team on the need for sensitivity.

The race issue remained elusive and intangible in the early days of the inquiry, and a certain frustration showed among the 'prosecution' lawyers. They could hint or they could accuse, they could mock officers for their inability to remember hearing racist jokes, or for their claims that they had many close friends who were black, but this was hardly enough. Unless something changed, it seemed, the inquiry might end up reaching a conclusion similar to Kent's. It was during Mansfield's questioning of 'OJ' Davidson, the detective sergeant at the heart of the first investigation, that things began to change. This was one of the most explosive cross-examinations of the inquiry, with Mansfield at his most aggressive and Davidson barely able to contain his anger. 'I don't want to sit and take this, sir,' said the detective at one point, addressing the chairman. 'Do I have to sit here?' Mansfield threw the book at him, accusing him of being suspiciously slow in tracking down key witnesses and then suspiciously quick to dismiss them as useless (it was Davidson, for example, who classed Witness B as a 'Walter Mitty character'). He suggested that Davidson deliberately sabotaged the efforts of James Grant to point police towards the killers, and he implied that Davidson had lied in various statements he had made relating to the case. All of this the detective denied in vigorous and often emotional terms. The key exchange about race, when it came, was a relatively calm one. Mansfield asked Davidson whether anything in particular had struck him when he first read the papers on the case. Davidson said he did not see the point of the question; it was a heinous murder. 'And?' asked Mansfield imperiously. 'Is there an "and", sir?' asked Davidson. 'Yes. There is an "and",' came the reply, 'I am not going to take all day about it. I just wondered if it occurred to you that it was a race attack?' This was Davidson's response:

At the stage of reading the statements I was aware there was alleged four or five white lads attacked two black lads. In my mind I would think that may have been a race attack. There was a call out, I believe, of a racial nature [this was 'What? What? Nigger!'] which again would put it in my mind that it may be a race attack. From other information I gleaned during the inquiry I would say that the persons that were believed to be allegedly responsible were persons that would have killed anyone had they been there at the time. I do not think in my own mind this was a race attack. I believe this was thugs attacking anyone, as they had done on previous occasions with other white lads.

He emphasized his point:

I believe this was thugs . . . they were thugs who were out to kill, not particularly a black person but anybody, and I believe to this day that that was thugs – not racism, just pure, bloody-minded thuggery.

This appeared to put Davidson at odds with his superiors, Crampton, Weeden and Ilsley, and indeed with the national police policy laid down by ACPO, the Association of Chief Police Officers. ACPO defined a racial incident as 'any incident in which it appears to the reporting officer or the investigating officer that the complaint involves an element of racial motivation, or any incident which includes an allegation of racial motivation made by any person'. In other words an incident was 'racial' if anybody at all said it was, and by these terms there could be no doubt that the Lawrence murder was a racial murder.

Davidson had opened a can of worms. The question of racial motivation and racial classification became a recurring theme of the weeks that followed as five officers told the inquiry they shared Davidson's doubts – one of them said that 'up to 50 per cent' of the Fishpool team took a similar view. This was DC Martin Hughes:

MANSFIELD: Nobody could possibly say that this incident had nothing to do with colour, could they?

HUGHES: I believe that the motive for Stephen Lawrence's death had nothing to do with colour. I agree that it is a racist attack. Stephen Lawrence in my opinion was killed because he was there, not because he was black.

MANSFIELD: Many of us would like to know what the distinction is. If this is a racist attack, how is it that it had nothing to do with colour?

HUGHES: I'm not saying it isn't a racist attack, sir. What I am saying is that the reason for the attack had nothing to do with Stephen's colour. The fact that he was black and was there was the reason in my opinion that he was killed. It is a racist attack because it is perceived as being a racist attack.

Linda Holden insisted that the motivation of the attackers could not be established until it was known what was in their minds. This drew a trenchant series of questions from Tom Cook, the former policeman among the advisers.

COOK: If you are given a crime to investigate which involves three men who go into a post office and discharge a firearm, demand the money and run out with the money, what would you say the motive was?

HOLDEN: A robbery, sir.

COOK: You are not inside the minds of the people committing it.

HOLDEN: No, but obviously the fact they have got a shotgun and

352

gone and held up a post office, it would give me some idea.

COOK: There is no other alternative evidence that points to another motivation, is there?

HOLDEN: No, sir.

COOK: And there is not in this either.

HOLDEN: I can only stick by what answers I have given.

The effect of such exchanges was to suggest that, while a clear definition of a racial crime existed, it had little relevance for officers carrying out investigations. This impression was confirmed by Inspector Ben Bullock, who was asked about the process of registering a racial incident. Documents were sent to Scotland Yard, he explained, for inclusion in race crime statistics. 'Just for statistics?' Lawson asked him. 'Yes, I believe so,' said Bullock. 'How does it being a racist attack affect, if at all, the conduct of an investigation?' 'It does not affect the conduct of an investigation. It obviously hypes up the media outside.' The Lawrences were outraged to find that, as they put it, the racial motive was being denied. White officers, they said, were stubbornly refusing to acknowledge the obvious. Stephen and Duwayne had been attacked by white boys who used the word 'nigger'; there had been no prior provocation or contact of any kind and the white people at the bus stop near by had been left untouched: if that was not a racist attack, what was?

The officers responded that their feelings and opinions on this matter were of no importance. A murder was always a very serious crime, whoever the victim, and they gave their all to solve it. Barristers for the 'prosecution' teams did not accept this, and they set about showing that the race motive should have had practical significance for the detectives and thus that the denial of it actually hindered the investigation. Mansfield pointed Davidson to the interview with Gary Dobson conducted by himself and DC Hughes after Dobson's arrest in May 1993. Dobson made clear at one point that he was upset by the suggestion that he was accused of a racist attack, but instead of exploiting this feeling to put pressure on the suspect, as Mansfield suggested they should have done, the two detectives reassured him. 'Personally, I don't think it was particularly a racist attack,' Davidson told Dobson. Pressed on this at the inquiry, both men brushed it off as an attempt to put the suspect at his ease and gain his confidence. They were, they said, more concerned with gathering evidence on the murder than making a point about race.

Further evidence that doubts about the race motive had a practical impact on the investigation emerged during the closing spell of Brian Weeden's evidence. Weeden was always certain to receive rough treatment in the witness box and his testimony was notable for his palpable effort of control. He breathed so deeply, especially in the tenser moments, that each breath was picked up by the microphones and could be heard throughout the chamber – this was a man straining every muscle in the effort to avoid mistakes. It proved an effective approach, for despite a characteristically abrasive assault from Mansfield, Weeden managed – unlike Groves, Davidson and Ilsley – at least not to make things much worse for himself. His one significant error in the witness box, which was paid for in outraged headlines the following morning, was to betray confusion about the legal powers of arrest. It was the day after that, in the closing phase of his evidence, that he was questioned by Jeffrey Yearwood, for the Commission for Racial Equality, about the matter of racial motivation. Weeden accepted that, although he had made it clear to his team that the Lawrence case was to be treated as a racial attack, some doubts persisted among the junior officers, particularly after evidence emerged to suggest that the prime suspects had stabbed white people. Yearwood then mounted his challenge.

What had Weeden done, he asked, to establish the racist motives of the suspects? What had been done to find evidence that might show that they would carry out such an attack? The detective was at sea; he could not see where this was leading. Yearwood pressed on, asking what efforts had been made to find out about the suspects' relations with black people, and Weeden was unable to rebut the implication that these efforts were occasional, half-hearted and unorganized. For example, Yearwood could find no trace in the case documents to suggest that any of those who gave statements to the police and who were familiar with the five suspects were ever asked about the boys' racial attitudes.

> YEARWOOD: Does that surprise you now, when you think about
> it – particularly bearing in mind that Detective Sergeant Davidson
> had been given the task of dealing with some of these more
> difficult witnesses, [and] knowing that he held the view this was

not racially motivated – that this evidence was not forthcoming?

WEEDEN: If I can stop you there. I do not accept that I knew this was Sergeant Davidson's view.

YEARWOOD: You know now. Does it really surprise you, looking back on it now?

WEEDEN: That those questions were not asked?

YEARWOOD: Indeed.

WEEDEN: Well, I think ideally it would have been better to have asked that, and possibly other questions.

The racist background of the suspects – Jamie's exploits at Kidbrooke School, Neil and Dave painting 'NF' on a wall, Neil allegedly threatening a black footballer with a knife – all of these, and anything else that might have been discovered, had a very low priority indeed in the Fishpool operation. It was, it seemed, as if detectives investigating the murder of a woman by her husband failed to ask family friends whether they had been aware of any difficulties in the marriage.

Over time the wider questioning brought out many signs of unreconstructed attitudes to race among police officers. Steven Groves's flounderings on the word 'coloured' were not the only example; a dozen officers were in the habit of using the term, while one could see no problem with calling someone a Negro. There were instances, too, of officers who seemed to have given little or no thought to issues of race, and among these none was more striking than Detective Chief Superintendent Ilsley.

MANSFIELD: What do you understand to be the meaning of the word 'racist' or 'racism'?

ILSLEY (*pause*) . . . People making derogatory remarks about people of a different colour.

MANSFIELD: Is that all? Is that all you want to say about that?

ILSLEY: I am sure there are other things, but I can't think of them at the moment. I am sure if I sat down and worked it out, I'm sure I would think of other things.

MANSFIELD: It is a difficult scenario, sitting in a witness box being asked questions in this way, and it may not be easy to get the mind working in this way, but I want to give you the fullest opportunity to deal with this. If there is anything else you want to add . . .

ILSLEY: There are a lot of things. Equal opportunities as well, sir.

MANSFIELD: Do you agree that racism does not necessarily show itself in the most obvious ways, like, you know, using the word 'nigger'?

ILSLEY: I understand that, sir, yes. People have a bias or prejudice, something like that.

MANSFIELD: Have you been aware of the more difficult kind of racism that sometimes appears within the police force?

ILSLEY: No, I haven't.

MANSFIELD: Never?

ILSLEY: Never, sir.

These child-like perceptions can hardly have been what the inquiry panel expected to hear from a man who had been in charge of all detective work in 3 Area, and who had thirty years of experience in the Met. Despite southeast London's long record of racial tension, very few of the officers who passed through the witness box could recall receiving any race training in their careers, and where they had it seemed to have left little mark. When Assistant Commissioner Ian Johnston gave evidence he explained that for some time the Met had had a 'golden thread' policy, in which race matters were not treated separately but woven through all training given to officers, and he accepted that this did not seem to have worked. Johnston's testimony was poor, particularly as he followed two of his former subordinates who had been impressive: Perry Nove and Bill Mellish. (Mellish's account of the arrest of Cliff Norris drew a round of applause from the public gallery, a unique achievement for a policeman.) The Assistant Commissioner began with his apology but soon spoiled the effect by giving long and muddled answers to subsequent questions, which gave an impression of evasiveness and soon brought a testy put-down from the chairman. When Johnston was asked about the word 'coloured' he roundly condemned its use by his officers as outdated and insensitive, but a few moments later he used the word himself.

Another area where racism was explored to some effect was in the alleged stereotyping of Duwayne Brooks. Here a collection of fragments was shaped into a case. Duwayne said that the first officers at the scene treated him as a suspect; if true, was this because he was black? He said that officers at Plumstead station cast doubt on his claim that the attackers used the word 'nigger'; if true, was this because of Duwayne's colour? And so on. The most telling evidence in the stereotyping argument, however, was the questionnaires about Duwayne's behaviour filled out by officers at the time of his prosecution. However they were looked at, the words used on these forms seemed to sum up the clichéd white vision of young black males – aggressive, surly, uncooperative, arrogant, anti-police. That Duwayne was accused in one of breaking a window that he did not break merely completed the picture. And above all else in this argument about race stood the treatment of Doreen and Neville. In the hospital, in their home, at the mortuary, at the first meeting with Ilsley and long afterward in their dealings with the police they felt that they had been rebuffed, patronized and marginalized because they were black. Doreen was especially eloquent on the subject. She wrote in her statement to the inquiry:

> We were seen as gullible simpletons. This is best shown by Detective Chief Superintendent Ilsley's comment that I had obviously been primed to ask questions. Presumably there is no possibility of me being an intelligent black woman with thoughts of her own who is able to ask questions for herself. We were patronised and we were fobbed off.

None of this would have happened to a white mother or a white family, she insisted.

As the inquiry moved towards its close it was still the case that no evidence had been produced of a single act of deliberate, malicious racism by a single officer. Nor had it been shown that racism in any form had been the primary cause, or even one of several primary causes of the failure of the Stephen Lawrence investigation. But this did not mean that the Met won the argument, for the chairman still had the power to 'infer' racism and his occasional remarks in these later sessions left the impression that he might do just that. His views and those of his advisers came into the open when Sir Paul Condon finally made his appearance at Hannibal House.

It was not until October 1998, and phase two of the inquiry, that Sir Paul gave evidence. This phase was in principle devoted to general matters and recommendations, but Sir Paul was also questioned directly about the Lawrence affair. He began his testimony with an apology to the Lawrences for the failures of his organization, as Ian Johnston had done before him, and he added a further, spontaneous apology to Duwayne Brooks, which was something new. He then made a series of confessions: his officers sometimes stereotyped black people; the response to racist crime had been inadequate; the internal struggle to root out racist officers had been ineffective; the 'golden thread' training approach had not worked. Some of this, he said, had become evident in the course of the inquiry and some of it had been recognized much earlier; he and his staff had prepared a programme of reforms to put things right. As he began to explain these reforms there was noise from the public gallery, which was packed, and Sir William appealed for calm. The feeling was that these reforms were coming very late in the day.

Soon the Commissioner reached what was to prove the nub of the matter. The words 'institutional racism' had been in the air at the inquiry for some weeks, and the chairman had spoken of it as a complex concept with which he and his advisers were grappling. Sir Paul tried to warn them off.

> I have serious reservations for the future of these important issues if the expression 'institutional racism' is used in a particular way. I am not in denial. I am not seeking weasel words . . . If this inquiry labels my service as institutionally racist then the average officer, the average member of the public, will assume the normal meaning of those words. They will assume a finding of conscious, wilful or deliberate action. They will assume that the majority of good men and women who come into policing to serve their fellow men . . . go about their daily lives with racism in their minds and their endeavour.

Here was the Met's bottom line. Sir Paul said he was prepared to acknowledge many failings – insensitivities, clumsiness, lack of awareness, lack of consideration, stereotyping and more – but he could not accept the notion that these were anything more than a number of individual failures, he could not allow that they might add up to a single, thematic failure by his service. 'My anxiety is with this notion of some collective will, that people – intelligent, well-meaning people – don't actually know what they are doing,' he said.

In phase two of the inquiry there were no barristers and it was the chairman and his advisers who asked the questions. Sir William put to the Commissioner the proposition that the patronizing treatment of the Lawrences and the reluctance to accept the racial motive were both collective failures. Did he accept that they might amount to institutional racism? No, said Sir Paul, because most people would interpret that as a declaration that all the Met's officers were racist. Sir William replied: 'I do not think that would be my approach, but it would be my approach that it [institutional racism] exists.' Tom Cook, the former policeman among the advisers, took up the argument, asking: 'Would you accept the premise that unconscious racism by individual officers is widespread and leads to discrimination in the service?' No, came the reply, not if you say 'widespread'. Condon was standing firm, but the tension in the chamber was growing. Next, Bishop Sentamu asked about more general evidence of inappropriate language and behaviour by officers which often went unchecked by their superiors; did the Commissioner not see that this was what many people understood as institutional racism? The bishop was free to use the term, said Sir Paul, but he could not because he had to think practically and constructively about the future. 'You have heard me say . . .' he continued, but the third adviser, Dr Richard Stone, interrupted: 'You have told us ten times and please don't tell us again that you are not in denial.' Then Stone made an emotional appeal:

> It seems to me, Sir Paul, that the door is open. It is like when Winnie Mandela was challenged in the Truth Commission in South Africa by Desmond Tutu to acknowledge that she had done wrong and she just did it and suddenly a whole burden of weight, of sort of challenge and friction, melted away . . . If we are to go forward, I say to you now, just say, 'Yes, I acknowledge institutional racism in the police,' and then in a way the whole thing is over and we can go forward together. That is my question. Could you do that today?

It was an approach that pleased the public gallery, and the pressure on the Commissioner was intense. Sir William chipped in: 'You have been given the challenge, or the question, Sir Paul. What is the answer?' But the Commissioner would not shift: 'The answer is that it would be very easy to please the panel, to please this audience, to walk out of this room so that very superficial media coverage says,

"Yes, they have said certain things." I actually think that would be
. . . dishonest, for me to say that just to please you all.' Over the
uproar from the gallery, Sir William called for quiet and moved the
discussion into other areas.

Although Sir Paul's stand made headlines and gave additional
strength to the 'Sack Condon' campaign that had been gathering force
with the open encouragement of the Lawrences over the previous few
months, these exchanges were more significant at the time for what
they revealed about the thinking of the panel than what they said
about the leader of the Met. There was clear unanimity between the
ex-judge, the ex-policeman, the bishop and the doctor on the subject
of racism: they agreed that the evidence they had heard over the
previous eight months pointed to the existence of a serious problem
within the Metropolitan Police, a problem that was widespread and
caused practical disadvantage to black people. The chairman himself
had linked this problem directly to the Lawrence case, both in the
treatment of the Lawrence family and the denial of racial motive.
While Sir Paul repeatedly suggested that the gap between the two
sides was narrower than it seemed, and that the argument was about
terminology, this was not the case. He had explicitly rejected the
notion that usually well-meaning officers might harbour unconscious
racist attitudes and he had denied that this could be widespread.
The panel members were of one mind on this, and the Met had been
warned.

Chapter Twenty-two **Corruption**

Of the 'deeper forces' that Michael Mansfield detected at work in the Lawrence case, racism was one and corruption or collusion was the other. At an inquiry notable for the anger often expressed both in public and behind the scenes, nothing caused more bitterness than Mansfield's dogged pursuit of corruption and the Met's total denial of it. The police themselves had unintentionally painted the backcloth to this argument early in 1998 when Sir Paul Condon announced that he believed there were about 200 corrupt officers in his force and declared that he was waging a crusade to identify them and root them out. Although in Sir Paul's mind this was a quite separate matter from the Lawrence case, Mansfield insisted at the inquiry that one or more of these corrupt officers must have been involved in Operation Fishpool and that he or they acted to subvert and frustrate the investigation, almost certainly in collusion with criminal relatives and associates of the five suspects. As with race, this argument went beyond Kent, which found no evidence of corruption and which pinned the blame for the failure of the first investigation squarely on incompetence. But in contrast with his experience in the race debate, to sustain his case on corruption Mansfield found himself relying heavily on Kent's researches. For before they reached their conclusions the Maidstone team had made some curious discoveries.

With customary thoroughness, they examined the family backgrounds of each of the five suspects. The Dobsons had no known criminal connections and neither did the Knights – no evidence could be found to support a rumour, widely circulated and accepted, that Luke was related to the East End gangster Ronnie Knight. The Acourts and Norrises, of course, were different. Besides Cliff Norris there was also Alex Norris, his older brother who, Kent found, had 'a vast amount' of convictions to his name. During the 1970s Cliff and Alex had associated and been arrested with Terry Stuart, an uncle to Neil and Jamie Acourt. Like Cliff, Terry Stuart went on to become a drug-importer and distributor on an industrial scale, and this had led to his arrest and imprisonment in France in 1990. Two of Terry's brothers, Melvin and William, had criminal records, but for lesser offences. These were formidable connections for the young suspects. Kent then investigated whether any of the Fishpool officers or their superiors had links with these people. What they found was not enough to persuade them that anything improper had occurred in relation to the Lawrence case, but it was enough to arouse the suspicions of Michael Mansfield and his team.

One trail led to Ian Crampton, although not, Kent found, in any way that cast doubt on his honesty. Alex Norris's wife belonged to another south London criminal family, the Frenches, and in 1989 one of her brothers, Gary French, was under observation by the police. He was followed to a meeting with another man, but at the last moment he realized he was being watched, sped away and escaped. Police managed, however, to stop the other man, whose name was David Norris. This was not young Dave, the suspect in the Lawrence murder, who was then only thirteen years old, but a 44-year-old man. Questioned, this older David Norris denied any knowledge of Gary French but he told police that he was a cousin of Clifford Norris. In fact this David Norris was well known to police because he was a paid informant, and it was because of this that he was murdered two years later, almost certainly by a contract killer. This was the case that Ian Crampton spent most of 1992 investigating, a very tangled affair that linked south London criminals, drug-running and loyalist paramilitaries in Northern Ireland. It was to attend the trial of the five men accused of conspiracy to murder David Norris that Crampton left the Lawrence investigation on 26 April 1993.

The Lawrence team wanted to know more about this. Was Crampton, during his three days as SIO in the Lawrence murder, aware of the connection between the two cases, and how much did he know about Clifford Norris? Kent, moreover, had found a connection between Clifford and the other SIO, Brian Weeden. Metropolitan Police files showed that in 1976, when he was still a teenager, Cliff Norris was arrested in south London and that an administrative document relating to him had been signed by Weeden, who was then an Acting Detective Inspector. Again Kent could find nothing to criticize in this: it was a 'very tenuous link'. But again Mansfield and his colleagues were not satisfied. Cliff Norris, after all, was a powerful criminal who was known to intimidate and who was very strongly suspected of bribing Stacey Benefield to protect his son. Now it seemed that both SIOs on the Lawrence case had some previous connection with him, and however remote these connections were they would require very close scrutiny.

Suspicious as it was in the eyes of the Lawrence team, all this was dwarfed by the next of Kent's revelations, which involved an officer who became known as Sergeant XX. During the years 1987 and 1988 the Customs and Excise service, which is a police force in its own right, mounted an operation designed to trap Cliff Norris and his associates and to shut down their drugs racket, which involved bringing the goods in by lorry from France, through Dover, to depots south and east of London. This customs operation involved sustained surveillance and in the course of it the customs officers discovered that Norris had 'a friendship of sorts' with Detective Sergeant XX, who was serving on the Flying Squad. XX was subsequently reported to the Met's internal discipline body. Kent found that he had no connection with the Lawrence case, but Mansfield and his colleagues smelled a rat. Here was a Metropolitan police detective in a dubious relationship with Norris. How far did it go? And did XX have any connection with officers in the Fishpool team?

This picture of Cliff Norris and his connections was made all the more tantalizing by the knowledge that Cliff had escaped arrest for so long – from 1989, when the customs service pounced and he got away, to 1995. In that period, it seemed, he was abroad for some of the time, but there were also signs that he continued to be active in southeast London. Fishpool detectives had found an entry in the records of a Greenwich wine bar showing that he had held a birthday party there in 1992, while Eltham gossip suggested that he had been seen there more than once in the same year. And then there was the Benefield affair, which prompted the strongest suspicions that Clifford was active in the area, protecting his son, in the aftermath of the Lawrence murder. How could a wanted man come and go like this in 1990s Britain? The Lawrence team firmly believed that he must have enjoyed some form of illicit protection and that as a result no serious effort was made to catch him. This belief was underpinned by the knowledge of what eventually happened in 1995: when Detective Superintendent Bill Mellish arrived in the area that summer and decided to remove the influence of Cliff Norris from the Lawrence case he was able to do so in just a few weeks.

Like so much else about the Kent investigation, all this information – contained in an appendix – was not made public before the inquiry began. Hinted at on a number of occasions, it emerged properly with dramatic suddenness about six weeks into the proceedings, during Mansfield's cross-examination of Detective Sergeant Crowley. The two men had already been sparring for some hours when the barrister asked Crowley whether he had known the name Norris before the spring of 1993. Yes, came the reply, he was an active criminal.

> MANSFIELD: Is there a link, officer, between the Norris family and certain police officers?
> CROWLEY: I have no knowledge of that, sir.
> MANSFIELD: You have no knowledge?
> CROWLEY: No, sir.
> MANSFIELD: Do you know a Detective Sergeant [XX] on the Flying Squad?
> CROWLEY: No, sir, I do not.
> MANSFIELD: Never heard of him?
> CROWLEY: No, sir. No.

Like many cross-examinations in the inquiry, by all parties, this was one in which the witness had very little part. Barristers rehearsed information or put forward theories and witnesses were often merely a foil. So it was in this case: it was not Crowley's answers but Mansfield's questions which supplied the revelations, and their effect was electrifying. While the press and the public gallery leapt to attention at this first suggestion of an improper link between a named police officer (and Mansfield had used XX's real name) and Norris, the Met's barrister, Jeremy Gompertz, leapt to his feet to interrupt. He argued that Mansfield had never, in any letter of notice to witnesses, made such an allegation and until he did so it was unfair and wrong of him to put questions on the subject. Mansfield, he said, had simply floated a name and then left it in the air without demonstrating that it had any relevance to the witness. Asked by the chairman to explain himself Mansfield said:

> May I make the position entirely clear. I cannot and do not suggest that this officer had any corrupt connection with the Norris family. What we do infer from the circumstances of this case, given the way in which intelligence was not used in the early days, is that an officer

somewhere *must* have known the Norrises. The Norris family are capable of corruption and that is beyond dispute, and that because of a connection between a police officer – it is not known which, since very few files, including this officer's, have been made available . . .

He did not complete the sentence but the point was made. The Lawrence team did not intend to be discreet about this matter, but instead would probe every possibility in the search for evidence of corruption. From that day onwards they kept the Met, the inquiry staff and the chairman under unrelenting pressure to produce documentation on the careers and disciplinary backgrounds of officers, on the case of Sergeant XX and on the criminal backgrounds of Cliff Norris and his associates. On several occasions, in public sessions, they dropped hints or made accusations to the effect that this information was being withheld, and this prompted resentment on all sides. Both Edmund Lawson, counsel to the inquiry, and the chairman himself firmly and angrily denied obstruction and foot-dragging, while the Met insisted it was doing all it could to trace and supply documents. At the same time it was made clear to Mansfield that some of these files were too sensitive to be laid open before a public inquiry. They contained, it was said, information from vulnerable informants, or information about secret ongoing investigations, or information about confidential matters not relevant to the inquiry. Although they were not disclosed to legal teams, most of these files were read privately by Sir William and his advisers to establish whether they were relevant. Mansfield never publicly acknowledged that he was happy with this arrangement and until the very end (when he grudgingly accepted that all important papers had been produced) remained openly frustrated about the documents in the corruption argument.

When Crampton and Weeden appeared in the witness box, however, he ensured that he was able to question them at length. With Crampton he began by examining the case of the other David Norris, or David Norris (deceased), as he became known at the inquiry. This was Norris the murdered informant, who had told police in 1989 that Cliff Norris was his cousin. Crampton was able to show that while he was investigating this murder he had taken steps to establish whether this claim was genuine. Two brothers of David Norris (deceased) were interviewed and asked whether they were related to a Clifford Norris and both stated that they were not. Why had Crampton been so interested in this matter? Because Clifford's family, the Deptford Norrises, were 'notorious at the time', he replied. And why would the dead man have claimed a relationship that did not exist? Here there was no clear answer, except perhaps that he had been trying to build up his own importance. In fact Mansfield did not accept that Norris (deceased) had no relationship with Cliff, and the Met attempted to resolve the matter by consulting the official records of births, marriages and deaths. Gompertz told the inquiry that no family connection could be found, but still Mansfield denied that this was conclusive.

Cousin or not, the Norris (deceased) matter proved one thing beyond doubt: Crampton knew of Cliff Norris at the time he took charge of the Stephen Lawrence murder and became aware that a boy called David Norris was a suspect.

> MANSFIELD: When the name Norris crops up you are the one officer in southeast London who would have bells ringing all over the place, would you not?
>
> CRAMPTON: It didn't ring bells all over the place . . . It did not ring bells that this 16- or 17-year-old boy had to be a member of that family at all.

Mansfield did not hide his scepticism at this. He pointed out that in his Kent interview Crampton had said that the Norrises of Deptford were 'amongst police officers a fairly well-known family going back over a number of years, particularly the father of young David Norris'. But Crampton insisted that he was speaking there of his knowledge *after* his involvement in the Lawrence case and not before it; it never occurred to him during the three days he was in charge of the Lawrence case that Dave Norris the suspect might be related either to Norris (deceased) or to the 'notorious' Clifford Norris. It was a fairly common name, he said, and this was Eltham and not Deptford; there was no reason to make the connection. Through a long and detailed cross-examination he never shifted from this position.

Despite the pressure there was nothing in Crampton's demeanour that suggested defensiveness or evasiveness – something that could not be said of every police witness. He appeared both thoughtful and helpful if not exactly comfortable under fire, and he resisted the temptation to argue or complain. This did not spare him the most critical treatment – even Edmund Lawson, usually brisk and matter-of-fact with his witnesses, could not hide a certain contempt as he rehearsed with Crampton the many mistakes and omissions of the first three days. Mansfield, who followed, was at his most bitter and robust, and he made no secret of his view of the reason for Crampton's mistakes. When he came to discuss the handover briefing Crampton gave Weeden on the Monday morning, Mansfield pointed to its gloomy conclusions on the prospects for the case. 'I am going to suggest, Mr Crampton, very clearly, that what you were doing over that weekend was fudging it all, quite deliberately, and then you do exactly the same on the Monday morning so that you ensure no arrests and no identifications. That is what you have been doing, is it not?' To which Crampton replied: 'That is totally and utterly untrue, sir.'

Meanwhile, behind the scenes, the case of Sergeant XX had been further investigated at Mansfield's urging, and during a break in Crampton's evidence Edmund Lawson reported what had been learned.

> The position, put briefly, is that the officer in question was investigated concerning his contact with Norris but not disciplined. There were no disciplinary proceedings brought against him for that matter, but during those investigations it became revealed that the police officer had falsely claimed to have been at the Old Bailey one day when in fact he was off on personal business of his own, and he was disciplined in relation to matters such as falsehood and prevarication, which led in due course to a disciplinary hearing taking place in May 1989. From our perusal of the file it was revealed that, in fact, Mr Crampton had been his Detective Chief Inspector while he and the officer concerned had been at Bexleyheath between 1985 and 1987 and had provided what I describe as a character reference in writing for the officer for the purposes of the discipline hearing.

This was new: Crampton personally knew XX, the officer who had dubious connections with Cliff Norris, and had written a reference for him. And there was now the peculiar fact that XX had not been disciplined for having contact with Norris – why was that? There followed further rancorous exchanges between Mansfield, Lawson and the chairman about the availability of documents, and an adjournment while the full XX file was fetched from Scotland Yard (it arrived in a three-deck filing cabinet heavy with bolt-on locks) and assessed by Sir William and Tom Cook. After this there was further delay when a barrister appeared, representing XX, and declared that the inquiry had no business investigating his client and dragging his reputation through the mud. Arguments were heard in camera and eventually the chairman ruled in public that Mansfield could ask Crampton about his links with XX, but that the details of XX's disciplinary record were indeed irrelevant to an inquiry into the Stephen Lawrence murder. Even Mansfield had accepted, he said, that there was no evidence to show XX had a connection with that case.

Questioned at last about this, Crampton pointed out that his link to XX dated from the mid-1980s, which was before XX was known to have associated with Norris. As for the reference he later wrote (which remarked on XX's honesty and integrity), Crampton said that he had supplied it in good faith and without knowing the nature of the disciplinary charges against the officer. 'I think you are building this into something that didn't exist,' he told Mansfield. When Gompertz rose to question Crampton he established that the detective believed his involvement in two cases involving different men called David Norris was nothing more than chance. And the Met counsel could not resist drawing attention to another link between the case of David Norris (deceased) and the case of Stephen Lawrence.

> GOMPERTZ: It just so happened, when the [Norris] matter came to
> trial, that appearing as defence counsel on behalf of one of the
> alleged killers of David Norris was Mr Michael Mansfield?
> CRAMPTON: Yes.
> GOMPERTZ: Again, no doubt, just chance . . .

Brian Weeden, whose turn in the witness box came next, testified that he had never heard of Clifford Norris before the evening of his first day in charge of the Lawrence case, 26 April 1993. Mansfield challenged this, and Weeden conceded that he had recently learned that twenty-two years earlier he had signed a piece of paper with Norris's name on it. This was, he said, a 'purely administrative function' and he could hardly be expected to have remembered the name. But surely, merely in his capacity as a long-serving London detective, he knew of the 'notorious' Cliff Norris? No, said Weeden. Why not? There were hundreds of prominent criminal 'names' in south London. Could you name a couple, asked Mansfield. Weeden could only think of one: Francis. Out of hundreds you can only remember one? Weeden pleaded that he had been retired five years and would have known more if he was still in the service. This was barren terrain, and Mansfield soon switched to other, more fertile fields. Later, prompted by Gompertz, Weeden summed up his views.

There was no conspiracy at any stage and I think that the attempts to portray such a conspiracy are frankly ludicrous. When one looks at the matters that have been advanced I think they can be seen as being very, very thin if not transparent. My officers did everything they possibly could to see this case through to a successful conclusion.

When Bill Ilsley testified it was a different story in every way. Much of Ilsley's career had been spent in criminal intelligence, and he was a specialist in handling informants. In this capacity he had come across the name of Clifford Norris in 1989, for it was one of his informants who passed on the information that Cliff was responsible for shooting a woman in the throat. Ilsley insisted, however, that when the name of Norris came up in the first days of the Lawrence case he did not immediately think of Cliff, and nothing Mansfield could say would shake him from his certainty of this. 'Norris is quite a common name,' said Ilsley. 'He [Dave] is a sixteen- or seventeen-year-old kid. He could be anyone's son.' With that Mansfield moved on to XX, and by now he had more information. In June 1988, he revealed, the customs service had swooped on a drugs consignment and made a number of arrests, but Cliff and Alex Norris had managed to escape in a fast car. This occurred on the day after the last of Cliff's known meetings with Detective Sergeant XX of the Flying Squad, in a pub called the Tiger's Head in Chislehurst. Ilsley knew nothing of all this; it was not Met business. But the implication about XX was left in the air.

It was plucked out of the air by Rajiv Menon, junior counsel for Duwayne Brooks, who had a point to make. Menon asked Ilsley: 'Should an officer who has previously associated with a dangerous

369

criminal who was the father of one of the suspects in the case be engaged in witness protection?' Ilsley, and everyone else, was baffled, until Menon spelt out what he meant. But first he added a few details to the XX story: when XX was seen with Norris 'he was observed making notes; he used a calculator; on one occasion he was carrying a carrier bag which contained a number of oblong slabs or packages; and on one occasion Clifford Norris handed a carrier bag to him'. After this customs officers were naturally suspicious of XX, but when confronted he said that the reason he was seeing Norris was that he was trying to cultivate him as an informant. XX, however, had no authorization for this, said Menon, but when it came to disciplinary action he was only given 'words of advice'. It was true that he was eventually sacked, but that was only for faking his work schedules, and when he appealed he was reinstated at the lower rank of constable.

All of this astonishing information Menon presented by way of background to his main point, which was no less astonishing: 'Bringing it closer to home, XX, we have recently discovered, guarded Duwayne Brooks on at least one occasion during the period of the private prosecution.' Ilsley, once again, had nothing to say about this – he did not know XX and he had retired from the Met by the time of the Lawrence trial in 1996 – but the chairman did not let it pass. He was, he said with visible irritation, aware that XX had been involved in protecting Duwayne Brooks, but he believed that it was only after Duwayne had concluded his evidence at the Old Bailey. Menon angrily asked to see the relevant papers and, during a coffee break, was shown them. Once the session resumed he pointed out that, yes, the occasion on which XX had guarded Duwayne was the night after he concluded his evidence in the trial-within-a-trial at the Old Bailey, but that at that time the judge had not yet given the ruling that brought the case to an end. In other words, it was still possible that Duwayne would testify again and so he was still vulnerable to pressure. Menon did not suggest, however, that XX actually tried to exert any pressure, and neither had Duwayne himself made such a claim in his statement to the inquiry.

All this information stirred a fever of public speculation which was only increased by the sideways manner in which it emerged. Had Cliff Norris pulled strings to ensure that the Fishpool investigation failed? Was XX the link? Had Norris, even though he was behind bars at the time, been poised to 'fix' the Lawrence trial if necessary in 1996, by intimidating Duwayne? What was the significance of the link to David Norris (deceased)? And was somebody *still* trying to prevent the public from finding out about this? The police response, as expressed by Weeden, was that this was nothing more than a conspiracy theory, and one that was constructed, as so many such theories are, on the absence rather than the presence of evidence. In the end, nothing more of substance was learned about XX or the other Norris and the matter remained one of questions rather than answers. Although the whole affair generated much more heat than light, there was nothing false or opportunistic about Mansfield's line of attack. His conviction was evident, and even after proceedings closed on those tempestuous days in May and June he could be seen banging his desk and passionately revisiting the arguments with his colleagues. Yet the essential proof was not there and he seems to have known it; he had the smoke but not the gun. The XX story in particular was extraordinary, but as Sir William pointed out there was nothing to show that it was relevant to the Lawrence case. Mansfield's answer was to press for more documents, and more documents after that, but still the proof did not come. And he also suggested that in the search for corruption, as in the search for racism, the inquiry should be prepared to settle for inference. 'No officer is going to say yes to the question, "Am I corrupt?" any more than any officer is going to say, "Yes, I am a racist." One has to ask questions about the circumstances under which certain things were not done.' The questions were asked, but there was no sign that the chairman shared Mansfield's view of the answers.

The same pattern of surprise, anger, recrimination and a desperate search for documents was seen in the other principal matter put forward by the Lawrence team as evidence of corruption at work. Again this was something that the Kent investigators had turned up, and again it was something on which Mansfield and his clients placed their own interpretation. It concerned the fate of the man called James Grant and the information he supplied.

When the Lawrence lawyers reviewed the sequence of events relating to Grant that was set out in the Kent report, they came to the conclusion that this prime informant had been deliberately sidelined. Here was a man who presented himself at a police station, gave his true name and volunteered extremely valuable information. Over the following two or three weeks he had a number of further contacts with police, during which he gave them other useful leads. Then, mysteriously, he vanished from the record. His role was not mentioned in the Barker review and any remaining awareness of him in the Fishpool incident room simply faded away. It took the arrival on the scene of the Kent team in 1997 to resurrect him. Mansfield's view of all this was that one of two things must have happened. Either the police deliberately 'lost' almost all of the evidence of Grant's role after the event because they felt the manner in which his assistance had been squandered was so embarrassing it must never become known, or else one or more detectives in the original Fishpool team conspired to marginalize Grant even as the investigation was going on. Detective Sergeant Davidson, Grant's principal handler (who chose the man's pseudonym in honour of the whisky brand), proved to be the focus of inquiries on this matter.

One key weapon in Mansfield's hands was a note written by a Kent officer of a conversation with Grant in 1997, in which Grant complained of his handling by Davidson and Budgen and asserted that he had made clear to both officers from the outset that the source of his information was Witness K. This second point was a remarkable one, for the Holmes records suggested that it was not until Sunday 2 May that the Fishpool team learned of the identity and importance of K (the young man who visited the Acourt house an hour after the murder). If what Grant said in 1997 was correct, then Davidson and Budgen had known about K for at least a week by then, and done nothing to find him. One difficulty with this was that the Kent report itself did not rely on Grant's 1997 claim, which was not a statement and was not made under oath, and another was that both Davidson and Budgen denied it outright from the witness box at the inquiry. Grant had insisted, they said, that he would not name his source to them. When Mansfield pointed out that there was no contemporary record of this refusal they merely shrugged and indicated that they would not have written down a negative. It was, it seemed, a dead end.

When Davidson gave evidence, Mansfield hammered at him for hours about his role in the case, the sequence of his actions, his relationship with the witnesses K and B and his handling of the informant Grant. Davidson, he said, had 'put witnesses off' and 'queered the pitch' for the investigation. He had missed or neglected important leads in the information he received and dragged his feet in contacting people with knowledge of the crime. When it came to Grant, Mansfield said, 'you really did not want this informant's material to be followed up'. Taken together, Mansfield would later say, the failures and mistakes that could be laid at Davidson's door were 'sufficiently fundamental that they provide a basis for inferring either gross negligence or, worse, an attempt to thwart the effectiveness of the investigation'. Davidson, flushed and emotional, denied it all: 'I would give everything in every murder to solve it and I don't like the fact you are inferring I would do anything different in this. [To chairman] Once again, sir, he is accusing me of racism, and bad racism.'

Mansfield was particularly concerned with what happened to Grant. Davidson and Budgen said they had formally registered him as an informant at Greenwich police station on 28 April 1993; if this was true, why were there no registration papers? Both detectives insisted that they *had* filed the proper papers, and their work schedules from the time confirmed that they both visited Greenwich station on that day. But the officer to whom they said they had given those papers, Detective Chief Inspector Les Owens, testified at the inquiry that he had no memory of their visit and no Eltham informant on his files called James Grant. To further complicate matters there was the file of papers found at Eltham police station which showed that in the summer of 1993 Davidson had recommended that Grant be paid a reward. In that document, Grant was described as 'this recently registered informant'. The picture was confused, but Mansfield was as convinced of the importance of these matters as he was of the importance of Sergeant XX, and he would not let go. Davidson and Budgen were eventually recalled to go through in detail their accounts of their visit to Greenwich station to see if they could be reconciled with that of Owens. In fact they could hardly be reconciled with one another, for Davidson insisted that the papers had been handed personally to Owens while Budgen said they had merely left an envelope on Owens's desk. There matters rested.

The strength of the corruption case lay in the eye of the beholder. The lawyers, the journalists and the public gallery at the inquiry were more divided about it than they were about any other issue, including race. To some it was conspiratorial nonsense – one police witness spoke of 'a Merlin's broth of magic and mirrors and innuen-does and nudges' – while to others it was ludicrous and naïve to imagine that all this smoke might exist without a fire. Yet smoke it was, and in his closing submission to the inquiry Mansfield was still pressing the need to accept inference of corruption in lieu of proof. The evident reluctance of the chairman and his advisers to do so was undoubtedly one explanation for the passion that Mansfield brought to this argument.

Chapter Twenty-three **Mitigation**

The most devastating criticisms in the Kent report related to incompetence and there was never much chance that the inquiry would make this picture any blacker than it already appeared. So it transpired. The four central figures – the SIOs, Crampton and Weeden, their immediate superior, Ilsley, and their immediate subordinate, Bullock – were each questioned in detail about the mistakes, omissions and delays identified by Kent. Since the full Kent report had never been published, much of this was new to the public, and item by item the shocking catalogue was reported in the press, from the missed telephone message of the Friday to the mishandled interviewing of the suspects after arrest. But this was not new to the inquiry panel (who had read Kent), and little of substance was added by the long cross-examinations of the four. For the police barristers this was naturally a bleak period. While they could try to fend off the charges of racism and corruption, there was little or no defence to the charge of incompetence. The best they could hope to do was pick up on details, highlight whatever it was that the officers had got right and enter pleas of mitigation. Among these last was the matter of hindsight.

The key mistake identified by Kent was the delay in making arrests, and when Ian Crampton entered the witness box to account for his three days in charge of the Lawrence investigation he had a point to make about this. Edmund Lawson, the first to question him, was obviously aware of it and for the occasion he borrowed an opening question that was usually Mansfield's.

> LAWSON: With hindsight, is there anything now that you wish you
>   had done differently?
> CRAMPTON: Yes, sir.
> LAWSON: And what is that?
> CRAMPTON: Well, one of the things I would have to say with
>   hindsight is that knowing what I know now I would have arrested
>   earlier.
> LAWSON: What, in particular, is it that you know now that causes

you to be of the view that you would have arrested earlier or should have done?

CRAMPTON: The strategy that I adopted was unsuccessful.

LAWSON: Because it did not work?

CRAMPTON: Because it did not work and I had gone for an option, then clearly the other option may well have worked. Obviously, I cannot say it would have done, but the answer to the question is, with hindsight, yes, I would have done something differently.

The fundamental mistake, therefore, was admitted from the outset, but Crampton was careful to repeat the phrase 'with hindsight' and to make the point that early arrests would not necessarily have led to convictions. All four key figures ultimately testified that they chose or supported the strategy of deferring arrests in good faith because it felt like the right thing to do at the time. All four were forced to concede, as Crampton did, that the strategy failed, and that when the arrests were eventually made on day fourteen of the investigation they had no more substantive evidence than they had had on day three. In that time, too, they acknowledged, the suspects would have been able to dispose of evidence, prepare themselves for questioning and possibly threaten witnesses. But the senior detectives insisted that this was easier to see from a distance of five years than it was at the time. Hindsight, one police barrister observed caustically, is the only exact science.

Just as it was generally accepted that 'with hindsight' fourteen days was too long to wait for arrests, it was accepted that the surveillance operation was poorly planned and executed, but here the police managed to redeem one small thing from the wreckage. One error listed by Kent was the failure to use surveillance photographs to disprove Gary Dobson's contention during his interview that he did not know Norris – one picture showed the two of them together outside 102 Bournbrook Road. This point was raised several times at the inquiry and Davidson expressed shock that this evidence was not given to him before he questioned Dobson. However Bullock stated that despite considerable effort the Fishpool team did not have a photograph of Dave Norris in advance of the arrests, so they did not realize that he was the youth pictured with Dobson. The first photograph of Norris (a holiday snap) was collected from the

Norris home in Berryfield Close on the day of the arrests – too late, apparently, to help Davidson.

Besides hindsight, there was also resources. The senior detectives pointed out that Kent had taken no account of the meagre supplies of men and money available to the Metropolitan Police at the time, particularly in southeast London. Crampton and Weeden 'did the best they could with the resources they had and in very difficult circumstances', said Ilsley. '3 Area at that time was the busiest area in the Met . . . so we were under tremendous pressure and these people were working very, very hard.' The Amip (Area Major Investigations Pool) was undermanned and underfunded, and it was simply accepted as the norm that no investigating team would meet the staffing levels recommended in national police guidelines. 'You worked within the resources you had,' Ilsley insisted. Against this background, by common consent, Operation Fishpool was relatively generously staffed, having the full quota of 'outside' officers. However, the 'inside' team, in the incident room, was under strength. This was why Sergeant Flook found himself doing four jobs – office manager, Holmes receiver, statement reader and action allocator – and why there was also a shortage of Holmes indexers. Crampton told Lawson that this, too, was a general problem:

LAWSON: Did you have enough people to run the Holmes system effectively?
CRAMPTON: Well, I never had enough . . . You would never have enough to run the Holmes system.
LAWSON: Would you ask for any more, then?
CRAMPTON: There wasn't any more to have.
LAWSON: Is this just a resource problem?
CRAMPTON: It is. It is just the number that were trained in the area, the number of murders we were dealing with and the situation. It is no different to the situation that we face in every murder. We were always complaining about it but nevertheless that was the situation that prevailed.

A picture was thus painted of a chronically weakened force, struggling with a heavy load of serious crime. And the senior detectives received some support in this from an expert witness, Detective Chief Superintendent Michael Burdis of South Yorkshire Police, who testified that he would have assigned about forty-five officers to a murder investigation of this kind, and that West Midlands Police would have assigned forty. Operation Fishpool, however, was given about twenty-five.

There was also the argument – put forward with steadily increasing vigour – that the inquiry itself was unfair. It had begun with the dispute over Salmon letters, when the cross-examination of Sergeant Clement had to be interrupted because he had not been duly warned that he would be accused of lying. And it continued with the complaint by Sir Paul Condon that his officers were being pilloried, to the detriment of race relations in London. More and more the police barristers – notably Sonia Woodley QC, for the superintendents – found themselves rising to complain about noise from the public gallery, which they said distracted or even intimidated their clients. Above all, perhaps, they resented their inability to cross-examine those who made accusations against the police. Doreen Lawrence's cross-examination had been brought to an abrupt end at the judge's request, while Neville's was over in minutes. Duwayne Brooks, on psychiatric advice, was excused from having to enter the witness box. Yet all three had been allowed by the chairman to present statements which contained not only specific allegations against the police but sweeping denunciations. These complaints were made outside the chamber, too, when Mike Bennett, London chairman of the rank-and-file trade union, the Police Federation, wrote to the *Police Review* in June. 'I seriously question whether the Met deserves to be painted as the disgrace we read about day in, day out since the inquiry started,' he declared.

> With the majority of people in the public gallery prepared to voice their prejudice against the police, is it any wonder that police officers have not wanted to get into a verbal slanging match with the lawyers and have appeared to be incompetent? The day before the inquiry started, the judge was the victim of outrageous accusations which ensured that he has to be careful of his actions and comments for fear of being branded racist. That hardly makes for an independent inquiry. I fail to understand how the Home Secretary can accept the final report of the inquiry, given that it has been the most controversial long-term cross-examination in living memory and not conducive to the truth . . . It is stage-managed to such an extent that

questions cannot even be put to the parents for fear of upsetting them, or upsetting the crowd in the gallery.

At the time, such views received short shrift in the press, where any sympathy for the police was comprehensively outweighed by outrage at the unfolding evidence of incompetence and worse, but they were to surface again when the inquiry report was due.

If police counsel had been denied the chance to question the Lawrences and Duwayne, they were determined to tackle Imran Khan, whatever the reaction from the public gallery. Over the years the slim, bearded, neatly-groomed solicitor had become the focus of a good deal of ill-will, particularly among officers on the original Fishpool team. In the incident room his letters to Weeden in the early days, demanding information about the investigation, had been notorious, and the two family liaison officers both regarded him as a 'barrier' to their efforts at communication with the Lawrences. As for Bill Ilsley, in his Kent interview he said:

Mr Khan was never, ever supportive of anything we did. He had his own agenda . . . We knew that, whatever we were going to say to them [the Lawrences], it would be spread around and could hamper our inquiry. He had a totally different agenda all the way through and was totally critical of the police for every single thing we did.

Khan was clearly perceived as one of the 'outside agencies' so many officers complained of, which were said to have hindered the investigation and by implication to have stirred up the feelings both of the family and the black community against the police. For some time, perhaps for years, officers believed he was linked to the Anti-Racist Alliance, the group whose members worked at the Llanover Road house in the weeks after the murder, but this was a misconception. He first appeared in response to an ARA appeal for a lawyer to help the family, but he was not an ARA member. Khan had worked for several years in an east London 'monitoring group', supporting victims of racism who were in many cases in dispute with the police. In 1991 he qualified as a solicitor and began to practise in Ealing, in the west of the city. There he was associated with another 'monitoring group', based in Southall, which, through him, came to play a leading role in the Lawrence family's formal campaigning and fund-raising activities. Like Michael Mansfield Khan is left-wing, indeed the two men share an attachment to the politics of Arthur Scargill, the miners' leader, and in the 1997 general election Khan stood in an east London constituency as a candidate for Scargill's Socialist Labour Party – polling well by the party's modest standards. In the eyes of police officers these credentials established his 'agenda': he was regarded as anti-police and, to borrow the *Daily Mail*'s term, a 'race militant'. That he had been involved since 1993 in a number of other high-profile legal cases that involved black defendants who were critical of the police served only to strengthen their suspicions.

It is also likely that resentment felt by police officers towards the Lawrences themselves over the years was transferred to Khan. Doreen and Neville had criticized the police in the harshest terms but as grieving parents they could hardly be challenged; not so their solicitor. And it clearly suited some officers to believe that Khan was manipulating the couple, something that the Lawrences and those closest to them always rejected as insulting nonsense. 'When you know Doreen Lawrence,' said Ros Howells, her friend and confidante, 'you know that she is not led by anyone.' It is obvious that Khan gave legal advice and that this was influential, among other things, in focusing the family's efforts on the remedies available in law. It is also obvious that he was trusted by them and remained so for the whole six years from the murder to the inquiry report. But equally, it is obvious that his manner of doing business, as demonstrated by the letters, faxes and telephone calls to the incident room at the end of April 1993, left some officers frustrated and angry.

There were a number of preliminaries to his appearance in the witness box, and chief among these was the brief testimony of Ahmed Ratip, the assistant who had accompanied Khan to the meeting with Duwayne Brooks in May 1993 that gave rise to the disputed notes. These notes, disclosed with some reluctance at the trial by Khan, had prompted suspicions that Duwayne had read a statement by another identification witness in the Lawrence case, something that would have tainted his own evidence. When Ratip had testified at the trial in 1996 his memory of this meeting was already fuzzy and his view of his own notes was dismissive – 'I cannot vouch for their accuracy at all.' By 1998 he remembered even less. To Edmund Lawson's evident surprise, he declared that he had no recollection of the meeting at all, not just of what took place, but of the very fact that there had been a meeting. He could not explain why the date on the notes had been changed and he could not shed any light on its ambiguities. He managed to interpret a little of his own writing, but that was all. Questioned by Stephen Kamlish he revealed that he had not worked with Imran Khan since that occasion and that they were no longer acquainted, although a little later he told Jeremy Gompertz they had previously been friends. There had obviously been a falling-out. This was the nearest Ratip came to supplying new information and his answers steadily grew quieter and more opaque. Gompertz lost patience with him: 'Apply your mind, please,' he snapped, 'rather than saying "I don't know" like an automaton.' After a few more muttered responses it was the chairman's turn to lose patience. 'Can I ask what may seem a strange question,' he said, addressing the whole chamber. 'Who seeks to rely upon the evidence of this witness?' No one responded, so after the briefest pause he turned frostily to the witness and said: 'Thank you, Mr Ratip.' And that was that.

The other important preliminary to Khan's appearance was the discussion of rules of engagement. On the eve of his testimony, Michael Mansfield rose to request a precise list of all the documents that would be quoted or referred to by all the parties intending to question Khan. 'His files are extensive,' explained the barrister, and this would help him to 'isolate' the relevant papers. Mansfield did not say, although it was the case, that it would also enable Khan to anticipate and prepare himself for the lines of questioning he would face. The chairman was sympathetic and suggested that this would be appropriate but then, sensing dissent in the room, he asked: 'Surely that is acceptable to everybody?' Gompertz replied: 'I observe in passing that this will place Mr Khan in a position in which no other witness to the inquiry has been placed, but we make no objection to that.' Woodley, for the superintendents, complained of double standards, while Michael Egan, for the other ranks, protested that Khan ought to be satisfied with the same general Salmon letter which had been supplied to other witnesses. The chairman, however, stood firm:

If I had ever been asked during the inquiry for prior notice to be given
of documents to be used I might well have given an instruction or
made a recommendation that that should be done. But I was not so
asked. I have now and it will be done.

It was a revealing moment. Mansfield and Khan were obviously
worried about a vengeful and damaging police onslaught the following day, and Sir William plainly thought his concession was a price
worth paying to avoid legal or procedural arguments over Khan's
testimony. The police lawyers, however, could scarcely hide their
fury.

It was Gompertz who led for the police the next day. He was as
polite as ever, and Khan in turn was at his most courteous and
helpful. Gompertz began by addressing the Lawrences' view – he
called it their perception – that the police had investigated them
rather than the suspects. If Khan had taken a more active role in
explaining to them why it was necessary and normal for the police
to question relatives of a murder victim, would that not have helped
to prevent the subsequent breakdown of relations? No, said Khan,
'I do lay the blame squarely at the Metropolitan Police's feet.'
Gompertz put it to him that when Kent police looked into this they
found that in the first two weeks after the murder the Met officers
spent only nine and a half hours investigating Stephen's background,
out of a total in the thousands – 'That is not an inordinate
amount of time, is it?' Khan suggested that it might not be the full
picture.

From there they moved to the letters Khan had written to the
incident room, which were described by police as a bombardment.
Gompertz went through them one by one, carefully noting the
timings, the follow-up phone calls and the threat to raise the matter
with the Commissioner. Was this not, he asked, at least a mini-
bombardment? 'It's sniper fire,' came the reply.

GOMPERTZ: What I am suggesting is that this course of
correspondence and telephone-calling, suggesting that the matter
would be brought to the attention of the Commissioner's office, got
relations between yourself, and therefore the family, and the police
off on the wrong foot. Do you agree?
KHAN: No, sir. That may be the perception, but I think it's a matter

of routine that police officers are able to deal with such
correspondence.

GOMPERTZ: Did you ever stop to consider the effect upon liaison?

KHAN: The effect it was having was that the family were not getting
information. That was my prime objective.

GOMPERTZ: So, is the answer to my question, 'no'? You did not
think about the effect that all this might have on liaison?

KHAN: Not in terms. No, I don't think I did.

Gompertz asked about the meeting with Duwayne Brooks on 2 May.
Why did it take place? When Khan said he couldn't remember,
Gompertz pressed him. Surely he had thought a good deal about the
events of this time in the succeeding years?

KHAN: Yes, I imagine. Yes.

GOMPERTZ: It is a case of great importance, is it not?

KHAN: Yes.

GOMPERTZ: By far the biggest case that you have ever been involved
in?

KHAN: You could put it that way, yes.

GOMPERTZ: Yes. So you are saying that you really can recollect
nothing about the reasons why Mr Brooks wanted to see you on 2
May?

By now Gompertz had adopted a tone of disbelief, but it was not
entirely genuine, for he had his own hidden agenda. This was a
script that Mansfield and Kamlish had used time and time again
throughout the inquiry to challenge and ridicule any forgetfulness
by police officers. It was not only policemen, Gompertz wanted to
show, who could forget things.

By the same token he demonstrated that it was not only policemen
who failed to keep full records and who mislaid documents, for
Khan was forced to admit that his files were incomplete because
they had been 'reshuffled'. In relation to Duwayne Brooks, moreover,
Gompertz extracted an admission from Khan that as Brooks's solicitor he should have done more to protect his client's interests. But
the traffic was not one-way. When Sonia Woodley suggested that his
confrontational approach had intimidated her client, Brian Weeden,
Khan replied: 'He was an officer with thirty years' experience dealing

with solicitors. I was a solicitor with eighteen months' experience. You would have expected me to be the one affected.' Had he been operating to a hidden agenda? The idea was an insult to the Lawrences. Was he sorry about anything he had done? Only that he had not been firmer with the police. It was something of an anticlimax; the police barristers threw up a few sandbags with the attack on Khan, but it was far too late to turn back the tide.

Chapter Twenty-four **The Suspects**

The appearance of the five suspects at the inquiry had been fore-shadowed from the very earliest days. It was, after all, their behaviour at the inquest, and the protection given to them there by the right to silence, that had done most to bring public opinion behind the case for an inquiry. There was a powerful public desire for them to be examined again. But the question remained open: could they be forced to answer? The terms of reference allowed no room to conduct a fresh murder trial, as Sir William pointed out on the eve of the first session. 'This inquiry,' he said, 'is not about finding the killers of Stephen Lawrence; it is about how the subsequent investigation and prosecution was conducted.' He left no doubt, however, that he was determined to see the boys brought forward to give some account of themselves and that in law he believed they had no choice in the matter.

Summonses were issued in May and were immediately challenged, the suspects' solicitors announcing that they would seek a judicial review of the matter. On 18 June, therefore, in Court Three at the Royal Courts of Justice in the Strand, Charles Conway put forward the argument that any questioning relating to the supposed involvement of the five suspects in the murder would amount to a retrial and would thus be improper. The judges, Lord Justice Simon Brown and Mr Justice Hooper, were clearly inclined to agree, and they wondered aloud whether there should simply be a test: any question that went to the guilt or innocence of the applicants, rather than the true issues – what or who caused the police failures? – should not be allowed. Lawson, responding, said that the chairman had no intention of allowing unfettered questioning but that it had to be possible to broach the question of involvement since, at the very least, if these five were not responsible that would mean the police had pursued the wrong suspects. In plain words, he claimed, the question 'Were they in fact the murderers?' was entirely appropriate to an inquiry into police conduct. Mansfield rose to say that 'we do not shrink from questions whose incidental effect may be to lead to innocence or guilt', and that the direct question might indeed arise in cross-examination.

The judges consulted and then Simon Brown briskly dismissed the arguments of all three barristers. What mattered in terms of the police role, he said, was not whether the five were guilty but whether there were good grounds to suspect them.

> Whilst the inquiry involves in a real sense the trial of the police who investigated this crime, it is in no sense a trial of these applicants [the five] and must not be allowed to become one. The temptation to use the opportunity of these applicants' appearance as witnesses to explore in depth their involvement in this appalling killing – acute though it is, given one's profound lack of sympathy for them – must be firmly resisted. One might have thought that if the applicants were, in truth, innocent, they would be clamouring for this chance to proclaim that innocence and clear their names. But that is not their position and their rights must be respected.

In short, they could not be asked questions 'going essentially to their guilt or innocence', but beyond that the chairman had discretion. 'I add only this,' said Simon Brown. 'I would be surprised if the chairman thought these applicants' evidence of sufficient assistance to justify more than a very few hours of the inquiry's time.' This was an outcome that disappointed many who wanted the five called to account, and notably the Lawrences, but which surprised few.

At least they were to come. On the morning the five appeared the approaches to Hannibal House were lined long in advance with police and crowd barriers, and those going to the hearing had to pass through a metal detector. Seating in the chamber was limited by fire regulations to a little more than 250, and with all the barristers and legal teams to be included that left places in the public gallery at a premium. Among the first to install themselves were about thirty members of the Nation of Islam. They had been coming to the inquiry once or twice a week for six weeks or so and had always been very quiet. They were, however, distinctive, the men in their dark, double-breasted suits, white shirts and red crescent-moon-and-star bow ties, the women in full powder-blue dresses with matching headgear that made them look like nuns. When one very senior officer saw them at the back of the room after his testimony he was overheard to say: 'They're smart, aren't they? Are they a choir?'

Security in the chamber had been a delicate issue. There was a fear that the suspects might be so provocative that they would be attacked, or that the session would at least be disrupted, but at the same time the inquiry team were conscious that a large police presence might be no less provocative. The decision was taken to invite the Lawrence Family Campaign to take some responsibility for order. As a result, on that morning there were just three police officers in the chamber, while the campaign provided several dozen members and supporters as stewards, most wearing T-shirts bearing a picture of Stephen and the slogan: 'Murdered by racists; killers on the loose'. Seats had been arranged, moreover, in such a way as to box in the ordinary members of the public. Much of the front row was reserved either for stewards or members of the wider Lawrence family.

Although no real crowd had formed outside, there was tension inside, and a feeling of impending drama. The five – Neil Acourt, Jamie Acourt, David Norris, Gary Dobson and Luke Knight – entered the building via the ramp at 8.50 a.m., two of them wearing sunglasses, to desultory shouts of 'murderers' and 'scum, scum'. Jamie blew a kiss to one of the shouters. Word that they had 'strutted in' soon reached the fourth floor. At 9.15 a.m. there was a brief session to discuss the questions and the admissibility of matters relating to the Benefield case, and then they adjourned. At 10 a.m. the chairman once again led his panel to their seats. The Lawrences were not present and he asked for them to be called. Then, after a minute's silence and a few words from the bishop, Jamie Acourt was brought in. As he entered about a third of the people in the gallery, including members of the Nation of Islam and the stewards, stood, turned their backs to the chamber and gave a clenched-fist salute.

Jamie, now twenty-two, is solidly built with short black hair, a broad forehead and high cheekbones. Wearing a black suit and a dark shirt without a tie, he looked smart but hard. Lawson opened the questioning in an otherwise silent chamber. He read him his rights, eliciting a string of yes answers which were so quietly delivered the chairman had to tell Jamie to speak up. Lawson then established that Jamie had known Luke Knight since school and there had never been a time (as Luke had once asserted) when they had not been friendly. He asked about the knives and the sword and the revolver, all of which Jamie shrugged off, and then he asked whether Jamie or his group carried knives in public. When he said no, Lawson confronted him with a number of incidents, but this did not ruffle him. Were they racists? No. Jamie said he had never heard any of the group use the word 'nigger' and he had never come across racists in his home area. He and his brother had never called themselves the Krays; he had not known before his arrest that he was even under suspicion for Stephen's murder, or under surveillance; he did not know the Astra car group, but he did know Cliff Norris, although 'I ain't seen him in years'.

By this point Jamie had made at least a dozen statements which, if they were not downright untrue, were so improbable as to be incredible. Lawson asked him if he was really willing to help, and the chairman interrupted – for once, to applause from the gallery – to warn the witness that if he committed perjury he might be prosecuted. Jamie, however, had settled into his pattern. He was calm though earnest, resting his head at moments on his hand or occasionally rubbing his chin.

Mansfield got up (Lawson had taken just fifteen minutes) and reminded Jamie of the circumstances in which he saw the video at committal. He asked if he really could not remember the contents. 'Yeah, I can't remember.' Then Mansfield put to him a series of extracts from the video, drawing the comment: 'I ain't shocked. It's nothing to do with me.' Are these your views? No. Asked about Clifford, he said he met him when he was 'a kid', but could not be more specific. Dave, he said, had never mentioned that his father was on the run and Cliff never spoke to the boys after the murder. On knife-carrying, Mansfield pressed but got the same responses as Lawson had. 'You're not treating this as a joke, are you?' Almost an hour had passed by now and the chamber remained tense and quiet, but there were signs that something was up. The bishop had left his seat and Doreen Lawrence had an urgent, whispered conversation with an inquiry official. A police inspector wearing an earpiece had emerged from the back room. While Mansfield asked Jamie about the revolver the inspector moved with another officer down through the room towards the public entrance.

Very suddenly, a group of men from Nation of Islam burst into the room, led by one who was wearing a small earpiece and microphone. 'This is a sham!' he shouted as he marched with his followers through the chamber until he was standing behind Doreen Lawrence's seat. He pointed at the chairman: 'You are stopping the public coming into the inquiry and you are disrespecting black people. Police, you are out of order. We are going to do you. This is disrespectful. You are a bunch of racists. Why are you spraying CS gas at our people?' Dramatic and impressive though this was, there did not seem to be a direct intention of harming Jamie Acourt, but the police took no risks. By the time the leader of the group had reached Doreen's seat, Jamie had been grabbed by several officers and bundled unceremoniously out through the back door. Some of the intruders got close enough to touch him as he departed, but no blow was struck. In the back room the other suspects and their companions were preparing to defend themselves.

The chairman promptly declared the session suspended and in the hubbub Doreen took a microphone: 'Hello everybody, this is Doreen Lawrence speaking. I am going to ask you this on behalf of me and my family. At no time within my life or my son's life have we ever interrupted anything whatsoever. The whole idea of having these boys here is for them to answer questions into what happened on the night of my son's death. With people behaving in this manner . . .' She was interrupted by a cry of: 'They're using CS gas on our side, sister.' She went on: 'Well, I'm sorry to hear that. Since the time of our son's murder the police attitude to us and our family and people in the black community has been disgraceful. Now, all I wish to say is, for the safety of everybody, please could you keep calm . . .'

The background to the interruption soon became clear. Upwards of 100 people had failed to gain admission to the chamber for the hearing and, feeling aggrieved, they had remained below chanting: 'Let us in! Let us in!' Among those putting the complaints to police and others were members of Nation of Islam. At one point the crowd, with members of Nation of Islam to the fore, surged forward. Officers and private security guards fell back towards the lift and one or two officers used their CS sprays. Some people, principally Nation of Islam members, got through and made their way up to the fourth floor to join others outside the chamber before bursting in. A police spokeswoman later said that the CS spray had been used because a chief inspector had been knocked to the floor and kicked by a group of seven or eight people. The police were accused

389

of over-reacting and of failing to listen to complaints and warnings that had been given.

Before long the situation calmed. At 12.40 p.m. Neville Lawrence and the bishop, who had both been downstairs to address the crowd, went to the microphone in the inquiry chamber and Neville appealed to people not to disrupt the proceedings further. 'If anybody feels that they cannot comply with this inquiry then I would ask them to leave and make their protests elsewhere.' When the chairman reopened the session Charles Conway, for the five, rose to ask whether his clients could give their evidence by video link and was told they could not. The chairman complimented the people in the chamber on their conduct and said that proceedings would resume properly when a video link of a different sort had been set up to provide a feed of the evidence to the overspill audience downstairs. In the interval that followed, a rally took place in the shopping centre at which Doreen again pleaded for calm: 'The police are out there in numbers; they have this thing that if there's a group of black people there has to be a problem. I'm begging you, don't show that's true.'

At 2.55 p.m. Jamie was back in the witness box, with Mansfield questioning. From now on, matters proceeded in an orderly and largely quiet fashion, inside the chamber at least. Jamie's strategy was already clear: he would divulge as little information as possible and he would accept as little of what was put to him as he could get away with. He just didn't know or couldn't remember. Mansfield reminded him about various knives that had been found in his possession at various times, and he stonewalled. Then he asked whether Jamie was banned from Kidbrooke School on 2 October 1991.

JAMIE: I don't know, you tell me.

MANSFIELD: No, no. I would like you to remember. Have you forgotten that?

JAMIE: Yes, I have, yes.

MANSFIELD: Were you banned from the school – I will ask you if you even remember the teacher's name. Sue Davidson, do you remember her?

JAMIE: No.

MANSFIELD: For, in fact, possessing at school an offensive weapon. Can you help about that?

JAMIE: Is this what you're saying I got expelled for?

MANSFIELD: Why are you smiling? Do you think it is fun?

JAMIE: No, I am trying to remember.

MANSFIELD: Please help us, what was the offensive weapon in October '91 which caused you to be banned from Kidbrooke School?

JAMIE: Are you talking about being expelled?

MANSFIELD: That is right.

JAMIE: Yeah, it was a monkey wrench.

It was tedious, frustrating, slow. Mansfield went on to say that Jamie was cautioned on 23 October 1991 for carrying an offensive weapon. Also in that year he was cautioned for threatening a woman with an offensive weapon. Then on 30 May 1992 came the Witham brothers attack, when Jamie was carrying a truncheon. On request Jamie listed his uncles, denied he was related to the Norrises and denied knowing any of the Astra group. When Mansfield sat down the chairman remarked: 'I think we have had enough from this witness.' And Jamie left, smiling.

Neil entered a silent chamber dressed in black trousers and a light blue shirt with no tie. He is smaller than his brother and slighter of build, though he looks wiry and tough enough. His hairline has receded a good deal and he wears his mouse-brown hair short. His face and brow have that peculiar sharp-cut, bony look. At the witness box he took a gulp from the glass of water before affirming with his hands in his pockets. When it came to testifying he showed a few signs of nerves, blinking a lot and touching his face, but he was clearly more relaxed and confident than his brother, and less cagey. He denied taking knives out in public, except at the time of the video, when, he said, he had feared for his safety: 'After I was accused of murder I received loads and loads of life-threatening calls and letters, so I thought to make sure I was safe I would do that.' He also denied being a racist, although he said he had used the word 'nigger'. 'Listen, black people call each other niggers, so why does it matter if white people refer to them as that? That is hypocritical.' He had said what he said on the tapes out of 'stupidness, anger'. Anger at what? 'At what I had been going through for the last year or so for the time we have been talking about. It is just anger. It was not like I was going to go and do it, is it? I have been through a lot, so when you have been through a lot like that you get angry and you just say stupid things.' He described the story of being banned from the Samuel Montague as a 'definite fairy story'. On the video he waved a knife around from 'boredom, it was just boredom'. The stun gun in the flat was a replica which only made a noise. The Krays story was just nonsense and he had never heard of the Astra group. When he claimed privilege at the inquest it was on the advice of his legal team.

All this was for Lawson. By the time Mansfield stood up Neil was thoroughly comfortable in the box, with his head tipped back and his eyebrows raised. He gave every sign of thinking that a lot of what was being put to him was nonsense or trivial and he openly described one early suggestion from Mansfield as a silly question. The chairman soon rebuked him for laughing. Neil firmly denied any blood relationship between his family and the Norrises: 'I would know if they were family or not, and they ain't.' When Mansfield began to ask him about a fishing trip he was known to have made to Frant Lakes in August 1994 he was bemused. Mansfield suggested that this was very close to the oast-house holiday home that Cliff Norris was living in at the time, but Neil treated the idea of a link as ridiculous. He revealed, however, that he had twice visited Cliff since he had been sent to prison. And when Mansfield strayed towards the matter of guilt or innocence in relation to the Benefield case, Conway was quick to protest and the chairman closed things down.

Mansfield took Neil through much of the videotape transcript, with Neil portraying all the remarks as childish or light-hearted. Pressed, he said: 'It's not funny, but when you're young at that age you are angry and you're laughing and you're joking, you say things, you don't mean them.' Asked why he seemed to be aware that they were being bugged he denied it, but said instead that they had a 'light suspicion' that they might be observed. At this Mansfield sat down frustrated. He had extracted next to nothing of value.

David Norris proved a ghostly figure, small, slight, pale, spotty and apparently very nervous. His face was long, with a light stubble, and topped with short dark hair, and he wore a baggy black suit and a blue shirt with no tie. When he spoke, his voice was thin, fragile and whiney, with a tendency to rise towards the end of the sentence. Under questioning, he gave every appearance of being

392

slower-witted than his friends, using even fewer words and requiring more that was put to him to be repeated or explained. Whether this was genuine or a form of dumb insolence was hard to tell. He said that his friends never carried knives; he had never heard them use racist language, and he had only visited Dobson's flat once or twice. Lawson put it to him that he had carried a butterfly knife and he denied it.

LAWSON: Were you charged with wounding the Witham brothers in
   November 1992?
NORRIS: I think I was, yes.
LAWSON: And with possession of a butterfly knife?
NORRIS: No.
LAWSON: Not possessing a butterfly knife?
NORRIS: No. Allegedly, but . . .
LAWSON: Was there any truth in the allegedly?
NORRIS: Certainly not.

Like Neil, he insisted that the language on the video tape was the result of anger. He was 'very angry, yes. Using my anger in the wrong way.' He said the murder of Stephen Lawrence was 'appalling'. Asked whether he was expelled from school in 1989 for uncontrollable and violent behaviour he said he couldn't remember. Then proceedings were adjourned for the night.

There was a crowd below and as the boys emerged there were shouts. Neil Acourt, wearing sunglasses and presumably high after surviving his turn in the box, smiled broadly at the hecklers behind the crowd barriers and, holding out his hands palms upwards, waved his fingers inwards. 'Come on then, try it,' the gesture said. Moments later as they reached the open air, Jamie bent his body back from the waist and then threw himself forward to propel a gob of spit into the crowd. Then the five, with their companions, marched jauntily down the ramp to a waiting van. A traffic cone was thrown, but it missed them by some distance. All of this was captured on television and by the press, and the exploits of Nation of Islam vied with the offensive behaviour of the suspects for the lead position in the media reports. In the event, by the following morning most papers were agreed that the top of the story was the Lawrences pleading for calm. 'Don't wreck our crusade' was the headline in the *Daily Mail*, beside a picture of Neil Acourt, described as a 'swaggering suspect'.

The first day set the scene for the second. There were no incidents before Norris resumed his place in the witness box and Mansfield produced the clawhammer-head with a strap strung through it which had been found in Norris's bedroom in Berryfield Close. It was a shocking object but it produced no reaction at all from the witness. Then, over objections by Conway, Mansfield asked whether Norris was at the Acourt house at 11.40 or 11.45 p.m. on 22 April 1993. 'I don't remember. If I could I would tell you but I cannot remember.' This was close to the wind, and eventually Conway had his way. Mansfield altered course, asking whether Norris had been to the Bournbrook Road house at any time in the two weeks that followed. 'I don't think so.' The surveillance photographs were produced, and Norris was challenged again. In a silent, attentive chamber he simply replied that he didn't remember. Why would Gary Dobson deny knowing him? He couldn't think why. At the time of the Lawrence murder, Mansfield asked, 'when had you last seen your father?' Norris said Clifford had left the family home when he was eleven and he insisted that he never asked his mother, and she never told him, where his father was. 'Can you help about your father's connection with any police officers?' 'That's nonsense.'

Mansfield remained interested in that 1994 fishing trip, which he said involved Norris, Gary Dobson, Danny Caetano and Neil Acourt and took place very close to the date of Cliff Norris's arrest. 'I never remember going there with them group of people.' Mansfield – clearly wanting to connect the boys as a group with Clifford Norris – suggested that the trip had been a cover for a visit to Cliff in his hideaway, but Norris just stonewalled. A certain knowingness had crept into his attitude by this stage, as if he was satisfied he would not be wrongfooted. Mansfield tried relationships: he was related to the Acourts, was he not?

NORRIS: No.
MANSFIELD: I would be grateful if there were, as it were, no indications from the gallery as to what he might say. I am very concerned just having witnessed it. Are you looking at your mother?
NORRIS: I have been looking at you ever since I've been sitting

here. I don't even know where my mother is in this room.

TRACEY NORRIS (*raising her arm*): I'm here, Dave.

NORRIS: All right, mum.

Mrs Norris, a petite figure with scraped-back, bleach-blonde hair, was sitting, dressed in a dark blue trouser suit, in the front row of a group of half a dozen seats reserved for the inquiry staff, between the public seating and the press. It is very unlikely that Dave did not know exactly where she was, although she may have been partly obscured from him by a pillar. Neville Lawrence turned to look at her and appeared both angry and shocked. He changed seats with Doreen so that he could stare at her, without a break, for the remaining fifteen minutes or so of Dave's testimony. He said later that he merely wished to keep an eye on her to prevent her from sending further signals to her son.

Mansfield pressed on, but it was useless. Norris remembered nothing of the whole Benefield case unless Mansfield himself supplied the information. As to the suspicions of jury-nobbling (of which Mansfield gave a long account), 'It was allegedly it happened.' Mansfield sat down. Ian Macdonald tried to wind Norris up, remarking: 'Still got this general amnesia, have you?' He put to him some of the video transcript and asked if he had any black friends. 'How can I have black friends after all of this?' Would he call someone a Paki? 'I might have done, yes. I've also called a white person a white bastard.' The audience, previously dead still, became restless at this, and when Norris left the chamber there were a few shouts of 'murderer' and 'scum'. Tracey Norris, following her son out, called back: 'We're not scum.'

Luke Knight is more thickset than the others, with thick, black, tousled hair. He was wearing a black suit in a large cut, with an open-necked white shirt. His mother, another blonde, entered the chamber behind him. Luke did not recognize the word 'affirm' on the card and had to be prompted. Questioned by Lawson, he said he was at home on the night of the murder and slept at the front of his house, but heard nothing. He had not visited the Acourt house that night, he said, and Mrs Acourt must have been mistaken when she suggested to police that he had. He had never seen the Acourts with knives and the sword they kept at home was merely an ornament, usually kept on the wall. Other allegations about the group, such as racism and the idea that they called themselves the Krays, were untrue and the first he heard of them was when he read them in the newspapers. On the videotape, he could not remember what he meant when he used the word 'macaroon'. Other remarks on the tapes were 'a bad thing to say', 'just silliness, it didn't mean anything', or 'I just spoke out of anger, I suppose, for what's happened to me.' Mansfield said that Luke had been filmed only the previous night outside the inquiry shouting 'black bastards', and he denied it – 'We were spat on, thrown things at.' As for his words in 1994, 'I've got a lot older.' Mansfield tried to fluster him with a lot of questions in quick succession, but failed. Luke Knight spent just forty minutes in the box and then left with his mother.

There were murmurs as Gary Dobson entered. He is bigger than the others, probably tending to fat and with a receding hairline. He wore black trousers and a black waistcoat with a white shirt and tie, but with his top button undone. He read the affirmation fluently and proved a confident and relaxed witness. He was at home on the night, he said, but went to the Acourts' at about 11.45 p.m., without noticing any police activity, returning home by midnight. He was there when Witness K came and told them of the murder, though he was not at the door. When arrested, he did not mention Norris because he didn't want him arrested too. About the red-handled knife that had turned up in the home of his girlfriend, Gaynor:

DOBSON: I don't recall it being in her bedroom, but it must have just ended up in there.
MANSFIELD: Who put it in the bedroom?
DOBSON: I just said to you, I can't quite remember.
MANSFIELD: You cannot quite remember?
DOBSON: No, I cannot remember.
MANSFIELD: Try a bit harder, will you?
DOBSON: I am trying my hardest. I can't quite remember. It is five years ago. It is a long time.

Then Mansfield asked him why he told Mellish: 'I put it there.'

DOBSON: What? In her bedroom?
MANSFIELD: Yes.
DOBSON: God knows.

MANSFIELD: What?

DOBSON: God knows.

Then Mansfield showed a page from Dobson's diary from 1991 and pointed to squiggly lines at the side of the page.

MANSFIELD: You explained to police that S refers to sex.

DOBSON: No. I can't quite remember that.

MANSFIELD: No?

MOBSON: I don't know. (*Laughs*) I must have been a bit lucky if that was happening every day of the week.

MANSFIELD: Do you regard this as being a particularly amusing experience?

DOBSON: No, I don't. But it's quite embarrassing what you have said just there.

Like others, at the time of the tape he was angry and upset. 'I was young and stupid at this time.' Mansfield had one last try at the heart of the matter, building up eventually to the question of whether, when Gary went to 102 Bournbrook Road that night, the Acourts were washing blood off their hands. The chairman intervened. Mansfield took a step back, but then turned to Dobson's original interview with police, in which he talked about who was in the house. Dobson was unruffled. Altogether, he was relaxed and in control, addressing Mansfield by name as if there were nothing more natural. His answers were more conversational, although not necessarily more revealing than his friends'; he relied less on memory failure and less on monosyllables. He even corrected Mansfield on his geography: 'Can I just tell you, Frant Lakes is in Kent, not Sussex . . . If you get a map, you will see that it is in Kent and not Sussex.'

MANSFIELD: Have you carried a knife and threatened anybody?

DOBSON: No, definitely not.

MANSFIELD: Definitely not?

DOBSON: No. I haven't threatened anybody with a knife.

MANSFIELD: A Stanley knife, for example?

DOBSON: Go on. Carry on.

MANSFIELD: No, no. I am sorry. I am not giving the evidence. You are. You are treating this as a joke, are you not?

DOBSON: No, I'm not treating this as a joke. Finish the question.

MANSFIELD: I am not going to finish the question. You finish the answer. What is it about a Stanley knife?

This led to a story told on the videotape, which Dobson now dismissed as 'a muckabout argument'. When he went round to the Acourt house just after being interviewed by the house-to-house team on the Sunday night, was that to tip them off? 'I can't remember. It is not a thing I can remember. Of course I am going to say the police have been around to see me. It is not that I am tipping anyone off. I have gone around to have a chat to them as you usually do – as friends do.' Was there any reason why Michelle Casserley should have had it in for him? 'I was a bit of a bastard to her.' This was leading nowhere. As Dobson left the chamber a cry of 'Murderer. Murderer' was heard. It was 1.35 p.m.

The suspects had left everyone exhausted and depressed. They had come and one by one they had fenced, obstructed and prevaricated. For the most part they had been better at this than anyone expected. Not once did Mansfield seriously unsettle them. They supplied virtually no new information and had only grudgingly confirmed what was put to them. They were efficiently consistent in their explanation of the video, which was one of the very few things they could be challenged about, and Dobson, who had the most to explain, seemed the best equipped to do it. Of course the constraints on questioning had made all the difference, but they were inevitable. The five had lied cynically and systematically, as they were always likely to, but they also lied transparently, which seemed a mark of contempt. And their behaviour outside the witness box, particularly on Monday evening, clearly fed the hatred felt towards them. Around Hannibal House there was a widespread determination, in terms once used by Doreen, to wipe the smiles off their faces.

At 2.30 p.m. the inquiry resumed before a virtually empty chamber, with readings of CPS statements. The bishop was among the absentees, for by then he was down on the street outside the building trying to prevent a riot. A crowd of around 300 people had spilled into the road and blocked the carriageway closest to the shopping centre. This was at the bottom of the ramp by which the five had left the previous day. The police were very cautious, and although a few punches were thrown there were no arrests, only talk and a little gentle movement. Traffic was blocked in both directions, but the police were anxious to keep a way open for the suspects' van. Everybody was waiting.

Inside the building, as in a military operation, the five were preparing to leave. They were in a fourth-floor room behind the inquiry chamber and with them were Gary Dobson's father and Bradley and Scott Lamb, the Acourts' half-brothers. They also had a police escort of four or five officers but relations with them were not comfortable. The suspects had not yet seen the crowd outside but they had been told about it, and they had also been told that no other exit route from the building was available to them. They would have to run the gauntlet. Using the inquiry panel's private stairs, this large group dropped down to the third floor and rushed along the corridor that formed the spine of the building. Now they were at the lifts, pumped-up and nervous. As they waited someone suggested that they would need two lifts, but a voice shouted: 'No! We're going down together!' A bell rang, a door opened and they all got in, a dozen or more. The air was thick with adrenalin.

Below, the crowd was ready and the police had formed cordons at the bottom of the ramp, covering the twenty or so yards to the van. Outside the cordons, the crowd was pressing in. The five, and their escorts, emerged once again from the glass doors of Hannibal House into the flickering brilliance of the press cameras and the clamour of protest. More nervous and hurried this time, they turned out into the open air towards to the head of the ramp. As they reached it Norris was struck from the side and turned to swing back, while a sudden swell of noise rose from the crowd below. The five did not want to run. They attempted to walk down the ramp with some show of the confidence they had worn the previous evening, but suddenly they found themselves in a hail of missiles – plastic water bottles, oranges, eggs, glass bottles. Norris was hit by a water bottle, fell flat and picked himself up, and they all started to run, in single file. As they approached the foot of the ramp they were no longer above the crowd and people were leaning over the side of the barrier trying to reach them. By now the five were splattered with mess, and in ragged order. Bradley was at the front, trying to shelter Neil and Luke. Behind them were Dave and Jamie, and behind them

Scott. Gary and his father, conspicuously, were ten yards behind that. At the front, a young black man in a pale grey sweatshirt vaulted the fence and took a swing, apparently aimed at Neil. Bradley, the older and bigger half-brother, intervened, lowering his shoulder to barge through. Behind him Jamie, his face contorted, swung a punch. Before they could reach their van they had to make their way through the channel formed by policemen with linked arms, but the crowd, now roaring, had been encouraged by the sight of contact. They surged inward, narrowing the channel to a couple of feet, and bringing all the suspects' group within reach. So it was through a hail of fists and a tangle of pulling, tearing hands that Bradley led them. Neil and Jamie were hitting back; it was a scrum. Finally, battered and splattered, they reached the clearing around the minibus and began to board, Neil with a hand over his bleeding nose, when another man stepped up to swing at Norris. Norris retaliated, and with a little help pushed the man to the ground and punched him. Then they were inside and away.

It was a moment of pure anger, and the police played their part. They did the minimum required of them and no more. They gave no personal protection to the group as they made their way out – no covering shields, no moving wall of police bodies. These suspects who had caused the Met so much trouble were left as clear targets for the crowd. But though missiles and punches flew, the police lines held and the five got away. If they had not, they would in all likelihood have been lynched. Up in the chamber the chairman learned 'with regret' of the disturbance outside and adjourned the session for the day. It was 3.15 p.m.

By that time the suspects had circulated their first-ever statement.

> In 1993 we were all arrested for the murder of Stephen Lawrence, which we all vehemently deny. We do sympathise with Mr and Mrs Lawrence and the tragic loss of their son. We understand their quest to discover what happened to their son and why no one has been convicted of his murder. We have no knowledge of this murder. We were not involved. We did not kill Stephen Lawrence.

They complained that they had been persecuted for years and dragged through the courts, even though no real case had ever been made against them, and in all that time had never been able to put their own point of view 'without fear of our words being manipulated or distorted for the media's sensationalism'. Despite having been acquitted, they said, they continued to be portrayed as guilty men. And they concluded: 'It is time for us to say, "Enough is enough – we are innocent."' These sentiments, so difficult to reconcile with the conduct of the writers both inside and outside the inquiry chamber, were greeted with general contempt.

Chapter Twenty-five **Verdict**

In September the public inquiry heard closing submissions for part one, relating directly to the Lawrence case, and late the following month it completed the dozen or so hearings in part two, which dealt with wider matters of policing and the ethnic minorities. In mid-February 1999 Sir William Macpherson delivered the final report to the Home Secretary, Jack Straw, who made it public later the same month. By that time, five years and ten months after Stephen Lawrence met his death, it was widely recognized that this would be a document whose repercussions would be felt for years to come. The reporting of the inquiry proceedings over the months had removed many doubts for the British public, and confirmed many suspicions. Most people now accepted that the Metropolitan Police had failed catastrophically, with even the Met itself agreeing there may have been a 'systemic breakdown'. And almost everyone recognized that Neville and Doreen Lawrence had been the victims of a terrible and tragic injustice, with the result that they had come to command great public sympathy. Neville received a standing ovation after a speech at the annual conference of the Trades Union Congress in Blackpool, an emotional occasion which was generously covered on national television news broadcasts. Doreen Lawrence was the subject of one of the paintings by Chris Ofili which won him the year's Turner Prize. As 1998 drew to a close she and Neville won a number of 'woman of the year' and 'man of the year' awards, and at Christmas they were invited to broadcast their own message to the nation on Channel Four. In the new year a play opened in London, based on transcripts from the inquiry, and proved an instant success. A series of television documentaries examined various aspects of the case, including two that dwelt on Neville's work promoting racial awareness and highlighting racial injustices. I TV screened a two-hour drama telling the family's story from the murder to the inquiry. Belatedly and perhaps a little guiltily, the wider Britain was embracing the Lawrences.

Long before the report was published many of its conclusions could be taken for granted, either because they were, to use Sir William's word, 'palpable', or because he had dropped heavy hints from the chair about them. It was clear, for example, that the report would criticize the police over first aid, scene management, contact at the hospital and family liaison. There had never been any doubt, since the Kent report, that it would find that the police had been incompetent, and Sir William himself had savaged the Barker review at the inquiry. The panel's views on a number of other issues, however, remained unknown or at least uncertain. What would they say about corruption? What had they made of the Crowley affair? Would they criticize the Crown Prosecution Service? And would they take Mansfield and Khan to task for undertaking the private prosecution, which had ultimately placed at least three of the five suspects beyond justice? Two other matters were of pressing political importance. Sir Paul Condon had been under pressure to resign over the affair for some months, but he had taken the position that he would stay unless the Macpherson report found fault with his personal conduct. This was not a matter on which the chairman had dropped any hints, although it had been plain that he was dissatisfied by Sir Paul's conduct when he appeared during part two, so the Metropolitan Police Commissioner's job hung in the balance. Also unknown was the nature of the panel's conclusions about race. They were obviously, after the exchanges with Sir Paul, likely to make a finding of institutionalized racism in some form, but whether they used exactly those words, how they defined the problem and how they detected it in the evidence would be matters of the greatest importance, and certain to prove controversial.

In mid-January a storm blew up around Detective Inspector Ben Bullock when it was suggested that he would escape planned disciplinary action because he was retiring in the spring. There was outrage at this notion, since Bullock was the only officer not already retired whom the Kent PCA investigation had found liable to discipline for neglect of duty. The last chance to punish anyone in the police, it was said, had been allowed to slip away. Bullock's union blamed the Met and the PCA for delaying the proceedings against him, and pointed out that his retirement date had never been a secret and had not been brought forward – it marked his completion of thirty years in the service. The scandal fizzled out after Bullock agreed to defer his departure, but from that time until the publication of the report the Lawrence case remained in the headlines, speculation about the findings jostling with attempts to pre-empt or discredit them. The Police Federation in particular took every opportunity to air its view that the inquiry had been unfair to its members and that its conclusions should be discounted. Even the mothers of the five suspects became involved, appearing together on the BBC's *Today* programme to protest their sons' innocence and claim that they would still sue the *Daily Mail* if they had the money. On the weekend before the publication of the report the *Sunday Telegraph* announced a genuine scoop – it had seen the contents or some of them – but Jack Straw secured an injunction preventing the distribution of the story, an action which precipitated a controversy all its own.

It was, therefore, in an atmosphere charged with emotion and anticipation that Doreen and Neville Lawrence took their seats beneath the public gallery of the House of Commons on the afternoon of 24 February to hear the Home Secretary announce the findings and recommendations of the inquiry. Prime Minister's Questions came before Straw's speech, and Tony Blair took the occasion to pay tribute to the family and to speak about racism. 'The test of our sincerity as law makers,' he told members, 'is not how well we can express sympathy with the Lawrence family, but how [we act] to make sure this kind of thing never happens in our country again.' Doreen, in that moment, would have been forgiven a bitter memory: in the spring of 1993 she had demanded of Peter Bottomley whether the prime minister (then John Major) was aware of her son's death because, as she told him, if he did not know about it he ought to. Now, thanks to her efforts and those of her husband, the attention of the entire political system, prime minister included, was turned upon the case. And when Jack Straw spoke it was immediately clear that he expected the inquiry report to turn a page in British history.

'The very process of the inquiry has opened all our eyes to what it is to be black or Asian in Britain today,' he said. 'And the inquiry process has revealed some fundamental truths about the nature of our society, about our relationships, one with the other. Some truths are uncomfortable, but we have to confront them.' It was a long and depressing report, he said, but he would not summarize it; it deserved to be read in full. At its heart, however, was a new definition and a new recognition of institutionalized racism, which he accepted. This was something that went far beyond the police. 'Any long-

established, white-dominated organization is liable to have procedures, practices and a culture which tend to exclude or
disadvantage non-white people. The police service in this respect is
little different from other parts of the criminal justice system, or
from government departments including the Home Office, and many
other institutions.' The report contained many recommendations
as to how these problems could be tackled and Straw promised to
push them forward with all speed. It should be 'a catalyst for
permanent and irrevocable change' and 'a watershed in our attitudes
to racism'. As to the specific matter of the future of Sir Paul Condon,
the Home Secretary left no doubt that he wanted him to see out
his remaining ten months in office; Sir Paul, he said, had fully
acknowledged the shame of his force and he was the best man to
set in motion the necessary reforms. In conclusion Straw said: 'This
report was born of the determination of Neville and Doreen Lawrence, of their desire to get to the truth of what happened, of their
desire to ensure that their son was never forgotten. This report is a
testament to them. And upon this report we must build a lasting
testament to Stephen.'

Released to the public as the Home Secretary spoke, it was indeed
a powerful document. The findings were unanimous, endorsed in
equal measure by Sir William, Bishop Sentamu, Richard Stone and
Tom Cook, and they were presented in the first person plural. 'We
strongly criticize . . .', 'We cannot understand . . .', 'We reject . . .',
'We deplore . . .' At 335 pages it was succinct by the standards of
such reports (in keeping with the chairman's businesslike style), and
it was trenchant and ground-breaking.

On the incompetence of the investigation it accepted and adopted,
with few variations, the findings of the Kent team. Like them it
identified a central chain of errors: the failure to recognize the
importance of early tip-offs; the failure to make early arrests; the
botched surveillance; the failure to pursue leads swiftly and systematically; the mishandling of the potential witnesses; the poor organization when arrests finally came. Like Kent, the inquiry report
criticized the quality of leadership, of record-keeping, of office management and of coordination. And like Kent it placed the greatest
burden of responsibility on the two senior investigating officers, Ian
Crampton and Brian Weeden. But it did much more. Drawing on
the characters and comments of the witnesses they had seen, the

405

panel described the context in which these failures happened and drew conclusions about why they happened. Of the 'vital and fundamental mistake' made by Crampton – his failure to make early arrests – the report said that it could not accept his explanation that he had made a 'strategic' decision to wait for further information. Such a decision, it noted, was never recorded as it should have been and Weeden's notes of his briefing from Crampton on the Monday made no reference to it. 'In our view this reflects the fact that Mr Crampton in fact did not make any strategic decision, but allowed the investigation to drift until the point at which he handed it over.'

Of Weeden, the report said that he was 'far too ready to accept the situation handed over to him by Mr Crampton', and as a result the drift was allowed to continue. 'It may be that his meticulous nature made it difficult for him to see the wood for the trees.' The four principal personalities in the Fishpool team were revealingly and damningly described. First there was the 'fastidious and meticulous' Weeden, up to his neck in paperwork and accepting rather than challenging what was happening around him. Then came his deputy, Bullock, hard-working but pessimistic and passive, a long-serving officer 'in a position beyond his abilities'. The office manager, D S Flook, was supposed to be doing four jobs at once, but in the view of the inquiry he 'went through the motions' and performed his task only 'to the best of his inadequate ability'. And finally there was John Davidson, variously described as 'a strong, self-opinionated character' and 'a self-willed and abrasive officer' – by implication, and in such low-key company, he dominated the investigation in many respects. While there was confusion and a lack of direction in the incident room, the report indicated, out on the estates Davidson was handling people badly. 'An over-robust senior detective was unlikely to be the best person to obtain information from young and reluctant witnesses,' it said. Davidson 'would be inclined to seek to dominate witnesses in order to obtain information'.

As to the argument that Fishpool was hamstrung by a lack of resources, the inquiry panel gave it short shrift. Yes, it was clear that the investigation and indeed the whole of 3 Area was undermanned, but that could be no excuse for making bad decisions in areas which had nothing to do with manpower – the timing of arrests, for example. Instead, the report turned the argument on its head, suggesting that the resources problems, and in particular the way in which they were not confronted, were symptoms of bad management. The Met in 1993, it found, was an organization which ignored its own guidelines on manning in much the same way that many of its officers had never read their own job descriptions, and for such failures the more senior officers bore responsibility. This was another sense in which the inquiry went beyond Kent: the panel pursued problems far up into the police hierarchy, and they were usually unhappy with what they found. As in the Kent report, Ilsley was roundly criticized, notably because he 'allowed himself to go along with the weak and unenterprising decisions made by Mr Crampton and Mr Weeden in the very early days', but also because of the Barker review. This was denounced as 'flawed and indefensible' but, less predictably, officers senior to Barker were also required to take their share of blame for its effects. 'It appears from the evidence and documentation before us,' said the report, 'that not a single question was raised by any officer receiving the review.' These included not only Ilsley, Crampton and Weeden, but above them Blenkin and Osland and even Sir Paul Condon. The Commissioner, it was revealed, saw the document on 17 November 1993 and endorsed it with the words: 'Seen. Thank you.' According to Osland, who presented it to him, Sir Paul raised no specific questions about it. Osland himself was painted as a man all too eager to accept the reassurances given by Barker; it told him exactly what he wanted to hear. The broad conclusion was that, even though some areas of the review 'generated obvious questions' – and four were suggested – the leadership of 3 Area and of the wider Met did not ask them; they simply 'allowed themselves to be misled'.

Did corruption play a part? No, said the report. 'Mr Weeden's honesty and integrity are not to be impugned.' 'We find no evidence to suggest that Mr Ilsley was anything other than honest and well-intentioned.' Of Bullock, there was 'no evidence at all that he was a dishonest man'. As for Crampton, Mansfield's allegations were closely examined. The case of Sergeant XX and his links with Clifford Norris was 'plainly highly suspect' and the treatment of the officer was 'unduly lenient', but the question was, did Crampton's connection to XX mean that he too was linked to Cliff Norris? Was there any sign of this in his conduct? This was a matter to which the panel devoted 'anxious and careful consideration', and they concluded that Crampton wrote the reference for XX in good faith without knowing that the sergeant had been associating with Norris. They also found that there was no evidence that Crampton himself had had any contact with Clifford Norris. And they believed that, insofar as he knew of Norris's existence through his previous case, this had not affected his conduct of the Lawrence investigation. True, Crampton was responsible for the failure to make early arrests, but this was a matter of misjudgement and error rather than deliberate sabotage. In short, 'we reject any suggestion that Mr Crampton was corrupt'.

Two other matters fell within the allegations of corruption: the tangled affair of the registration of James Grant and the evidence of DS Crowley. On the first, it was 'palpable that in fact there was never any registration of Grant as an informant', because otherwise documentation would have survived in a number of places. Why was it, then, that Budgen and Davidson insisted that they had registered him? The best available explanation was to rely on Budgen's account of events rather than Davidson's, and to accept that the documents went missing 'simply because they were left without any explanation on Mr Owens's desk'. This in itself was 'lax and highly unsatisfactory', but it suggested cock-up rather than conspiracy. The idea that Davidson was deliberately sidelining Grant did not hold water, moreover, because Davidson subsequently sought a reward for Grant, an action that clearly drew attention to the informant and could have alerted somebody to the fact that he had not been properly registered. For the rest, although the panel had many criticisms of his conduct in other aspects of the case, they were 'not convinced that DS Davidson positively tried to thwart the effectiveness of the investigation'.

With Crowley they were more certain. The detective sergeant had been accused by Ian Macdonald of trying to subvert two murder investigations, the Lawrence case and the Rolan Adams case, and he was also the first officer whom Mansfield had implied might have an association with Cliff Norris. In the Adams case, the report said, 'it appears to us that there is little validity in the allegations made'. Crowley was accused of undermining the evidence of a surviving victim of the attack, Rolan's brother Nathan, but the inquiry found that Nathan was not an identifying witness in the case and his evidence was relatively unimportant. Crowley had indeed had dealings with Nathan but he could not be criticized for them and they had no significant or potential bearing on the Adams trial, which resulted in a conviction for murder. In the Lawrence case, where Crowley's dealings with Duwayne Brooks were concerned the report concluded: 'We believe that DS Crowley's evidence was substantially correct.' However, it stressed the 'significant fact' that, when the evidence of Crowley and Brooks was tested at the Old Bailey, the judge was able to reach his conclusions without having to take a view on the disputed matters. What was agreed between the two men, in other words, was what counted. As for the notion that Crowley might have had a connection with Cliff Norris, there was no evidence of it.

Race was a different matter, and here the conclusions of the inquiry team were radical. Not only did they state unequivocally that institutional racism existed within the Metropolitan Police, but on the basis of evidence in part two they concluded that it existed in other police forces and in other institutions across the country. Even more dramatically, perhaps, they were prepared to identify specific moments, actions, events and comments in the case of Stephen Lawrence which they believed were manifestations of institutional racism at work. They defined the phenomenon as follows:

> The collective failure of an organisation to provide an appropriate
> and professional service to people because of their colour, culture or
> ethnic origin. It can be seen or detected in processes, attitudes and
> behaviour which amount to discrimination through unwitting
> prejudice, ignorance, thoughtlessness and racist stereotyping which
> disadvantage minority ethnic people.

The first evidence of this force at work, said the report, was to be found on Well Hall Road in the minutes after Stephen's collapse. On first aid it summarized the facts: the proper course of action on finding a bleeding body was to find the wound and staunch the flow of blood, but even though they had received training and retraining in first aid, none of the early officers at the scene did this. The inquiry did not endorse Doreen Lawrence's opinion that this was because the officers did not want to dirty their hands with a black man's blood; instead it said simply that these young constables had failed to use their training and had relied too much on the expectation that the ambulance would soon arrive. But it did not stop there, for it took a quite different view of the actions of Inspector Steven Groves, the officer with the clipboard who arrived at the scene by van and, by his own account, took charge. In a series of withering findings, the inquiry team concluded that Groves had comprehensively failed in his duty to take control of the scene and to set in motion a proper police operation. He arrived believing for some unknown reason that there had been a fight; he did not establish Stephen's condition; he did not find out what had really happened and he failed to extract any useful information either from Duwayne Brooks or from the officers present. Instead he sent the van on a pointless tour of local streets while he himself left the scene and walked off in the wrong direction – to the Welcome Inn – to ask questions of people who could have known nothing. This was described as extraordinary. Yet in the witness box at the inquiry Groves (whose 'verbal fencing' with Mansfield proved 'unwise') professed himself 'perfectly satisfied that he had acted with efficiency and thoroughness'. His general demeanour, moreover, and his dogged defence of the word 'coloured', did not impress. This was the report's verdict on Groves:

> We are forced to the conclusion that his attitude and his dismissive conduct were contributed to, if not wholly caused, by unwitting but clear racism. He saw a young man lying injured, and an obviously stressed and agitated young black man on the pavement nearby. It is plain to all of us that he was deflected by what he saw and by his wholly wrong conclusion, and that his whole approach to what had happened was thus undermined by racist stereotyping. We conclude that in this case it must be said that he reacted as he did simply because of what he saw, and that he would not have been similarly dismissive if the two young men involved had been white.

On the treatment of Duwayne Brooks at the scene and on some occasions afterwards, there was a similar verdict, this time of 'unwitting and collective racism':

> We are driven to the conclusion that Mr Brooks was stereotyped as a young black man exhibiting unpleasant hostility and agitation, who could not be expected to help and whose condition and status simply did not need further examination or understanding. We believe that

410

Mr Brooks's colour and such stereotyping played their part in the
collective failure of those involved to treat him according to his needs.

The scene management and the conduct of officers there over the
first two hours were found gravely wanting, a verdict at odds with
Kent's. There was, the report said, a lack of coordination and control
and a failure to grapple with the demands of the situation and to
show energy and imagination, and for this almost every senior
policeman present was required to take a share of the blame. The
image once conjured up by PC Bethel, of officers standing around
with their hands on their hips, was ruefully recalled.

The report attempted to disentangle events at the hospital. On
the disputed identification of the body it found in PC Gleason's
favour: Neville Lawrence and he 'probably did attend the resuscitation room' together, but 'wholly understandably' Stephen's father
had forgotten the incident. When it came to Acting Inspector Ian
Little, however, there was sharp criticism. Little insisted that it was
he who asked Neville to identify the body, but the inquiry team had
doubts. And even if it was true, his own account of the conversation
– 'We've got a young lad in there, he is dead, we don't know who
he is but we would like to clarify that point' – was 'grossly insensitive'.
Moreover Little appeared to have made no proper arrangement for
further contact with the family and did not even ask whether they
would need a lift home.

> His lack of sensitivity and his inaction, particularly at the hospital,
> betrayed conduct which demonstrates inability to deal properly with
> bereaved people, and particularly those bereaved as a result of a
> terrible racist attack. He failed to deal with the family appropriately
> and professionally. This was unwitting racism at work.

Given this approach by the inquiry team, it was inevitable that
the family liaison arrangements should have received the most critical
scrutiny, and so it proved. The complaints by the liaison officers,
Bevan and Holden, that the house was full of 'hangers on', the failure
to respond to or even discuss the family's requests for information,
the poor handling of the matter of the woollen gloves and the dismay
of officers at the arrival on the scene of Imran Khan were all of a one,
the inquiry found. The officers did not recognize that 'the family of

Stephen Lawrence had to be taken as they were found, and as they chose to behave. They were entitled to demand to be dealt with as they were and according to their needs.' There had been a woeful lack of training, sensitivity and preparedness to adapt. This was the conclusion:

> DS Bevan and DC Holden will forever deny that they are racist or that the colour, culture and ethnic origin of the Lawrence family played any part in the failure of family liaison. We are bound to say that the conclusion which we reach is inescapable. Inappropriate behaviour and patronising attitudes towards this black family were a manifestation of unwitting racism at work. Coupled with the failure of the senior officers to see Mr and Mrs Lawrence and to sort out the family liaison [in the first two weeks] we see here a clear example of the collective failure of the investigating team to treat Mr and Mrs Lawrence appropriately and professionally, because of their colour, culture and ethnic origin.

Of Brian Weeden the report said: 'He too readily allowed himself, as his own briefing notes show, to become involved in the negative and hostile stereotyping of the family and Mr Khan. He must be said to have been infected by unwitting racism in this regard.'

The inquiry noted that Bevan and Holden were among those officers who had disputed in the witness box the notion that the murder was racially motivated. This issue more than any other in the race category exercised the inquiry team. The attitude of this group of officers – who also included Davidson, Budgen and perhaps as many as half the Fishpool team – was 'obdurate' and 'untenable' and 'understandably anathema' to the black community. It gave rise, moreover, to the suspicion in the minds of the Lawrences that proper concentration was not brought to bear on the murder of their son. The inability of these officers to accept the racial motive, the report found, 'is a manifestation of their own flawed approach and their own unwitting collective racism'.

The verdict of institutional racism was unequivocal, but the inquiry team were anxious that it should not be misunderstood. They were not saying that the first Fishpool investigation failed because of racism – 'We do not accept that.' Nor were they saying that policies of the Met were racist – 'The contrary is true. It is in the implementation of policies and in the words and actions of officers acting together that racism may become apparent.' Nor were they saying or implying that every officer was a racist. 'No such sweeping suggestion can or should be made. The Commissioner's fears are in this respect wholly unfounded.' The essence of the inquiry's view of the problem was distilled in paragraph 6.17:

> Unwitting racism can arise because of lack of understanding, ignorance or mistaken beliefs. It can arise from well-intentioned but patronising words or actions. It can arise from unfamiliarity with the behaviour or cultural traditions of people or families from minority ethnic communities. It can arise from racist stereotyping of black people as potential criminals or troublemakers. Often this arises out of uncritical self-understanding born out of an inflexible police ethos of the 'traditional' way of doing things. Furthermore, such attitudes can thrive in a tightly-knit community, so that there can be a collective failure to detect and to outlaw this breed of racism. The police canteen can too easily be its breeding ground.

In reaching this view the panel drew not only on the evidence relating to the murder of Stephen Lawrence and its aftermath, but on the many submissions received in part two of the inquiry from academics, police forces, pressure groups and other interested parties, and on the public hearings in part two held in London and other cities. In this evidence too, they found many signs of unwitting, collective and institutional racism.

The report made many recommendations for change to address these problems, some of them simple and practical and some – such as a requirement for thorough auditing and inspection of police performance in matters of race, and a transformation of the police discipline regime – implying a substantial cultural shift. But before all else, it stressed, 'there must be an unequivocal acceptance of the problem of institutional racism and its nature', for only then could it be dealt with effectively. Once that had been achieved, perhaps through the 'catharsis' of the inquiry, the report appealed to the police to reach out to the ethnic minority communities and to those communities not to reject them. That would permit 'the start of the beginning of change'.

Elsewhere, by contrast, the report was notable for its gentleness. The Crown Prosecution Service was found to have discharged its duties properly and to have reached its difficult conclusions about the Lawrence case logically and fairly. Howard Youngerwood (who testified at the inquiry and proved a handful even for Michael Mansfield) 'reached careful and reasoned conclusions and . . . defended his decisions roundly and satisfactorily and conclusively in the witness box'. In the prosecution of Duwayne Brooks the CPS could not be criticized over the questionnaires 'since they emerged as a result of the defence which was being raised by Mr Brooks'. There was 'perhaps some irony' in the fact that the case against Brooks was pursued while the case against Neil Acourt and Luke Knight was dropped, but the logic of the two decisions was evident on close examination. Despite this, and although such decisions are not easy, 'in the end we feel that it would have been better if the prosecution of Mr Brooks had been abandoned early on'.

Assistant Commissioner Ian Johnston was forgiven his poor performance in the witness box, and even his use of the word 'coloured', as part of a general expression of satisfaction with the second investigation. Perry Nove and Bill Mellish were praised and their efforts were held up as examples of sensitive and intelligent police management and dynamic detective work. Michael Mansfield and Imran Khan were nowhere criticized for undertaking the private prosecution, even though the report made clear that this was doomed from the start and that Mr Justice Curtis had made exactly the right decisions. Khan was not criticized, either, over his part in family liaison troubles, although his letters to the incident room were described as 'somewhat peremptory'. However, his dealings with Duwayne Brooks, and particularly the meeting of 2 May 1993, were regarded as unsatisfactory – Khan, said the report, should have informed the police about the encounter. And since Khan insisted that Duwayne was for a time his client, he had to take a share of the blame, along with the police, for the failure to ensure that he was properly cared for. On the whole, however, Khan's role was defended; the police should have been ready to take the family as they found them, and if that meant that a solicitor was involved then so be it.

Finally, the five suspects were discussed. At the inquiry their evidence was 'vague and evasive', they all relied on 'alleged lack of memory' and they showed themselves to be 'arrogant and dismissive'. The videotape revealed violent racism at its worst and the few quotations given in the body of the report were said to 'sully the paper upon which they have been recorded'. But the view of the inquiry panel was that, so far as their evidence from the witness box was concerned, they could not be proved to have perjured themselves. As to their guilt or innocence of the murder:

These men are not proved to have been the murderers of Stephen Lawrence. We are unable to reach any such conclusion upon the evidence, and no fresh evidence is likely to emerge against them now. They remain, however, prime suspects. And the nature of them in 1994, and indeed during their limited testimony in 1998, must surely make us all determined that by education, family and community influence, proper policing and all available means, society does all it can to ensure that the minds of present and future generations are not allowed to become violent and maliciously prejudiced. If these suspects were not involved there must have been five or six almost identical young thugs at large on the night of 22 April 1993 to commit this terrible racist crime. We must all see to it that such crimes do not and cannot happen again.

This report was greeted at first with shock and shame. The message of Jack Straw and Tony Blair struck home, and the idea that British society must reflect and change appeared to be widely accepted. The House of Commons was subdued after Straw's speech and no dissenting voice was heard except that of the black MP Bernie Grant, who demanded Sir Paul Condon's resignation. The airwaves, meanwhile, were thick with resolutions by the great and the good that Britain must try harder and do better, and the newspapers went to press that night with front pages of unusual sombreness. As far as the media were concerned, perhaps inevitably, this mood did not last long, and they soon found other stories to chase. On the night when the report was published white paint was splashed across the commemorative plaque at the spot where Stephen fell on Well Hall Road, and the police were later obliged to admit that the surveillance camera that was supposed to be observing the scene was a dummy. On the following day it emerged that the inquiry team had, by an oversight, included in the appendices to the published report an uncensored list, compiled in 1997 by Kent police, which gave the names and addresses of those, apart from James Grant, who supplied information to the police in the first days after the murder. It was a serious mistake and it was greeted with outrage (although much of the concern was based on a misconception, since the suspects had long known the names of the main potential witnesses), and it was said that Sir William was a worse bungler than the police officers whom he had denounced in his report. By the weekend the conservative press – including the *Daily Mail* – was of one mind: the report was flawed and unbalanced and the idea that all police officers or all white British people were racist was wrong and unjust. Many critics portrayed it as an exercise in political correctness which would make it impossible for the police to uphold the law where black people were concerned. Others, and notably many black people, expressed anger that Sir Paul Condon had been allowed to survive. They noted that other leading public figures, such as Glenn Hoddle and Peter Mandelson, had recently been forced to bow to public pressure and resign but Sir Paul, who had run the Met throughout the whole Lawrence affair, remained in position. The Lawrences were quiet on this issue. Doreen, reading a statement in response to the report, expressed mixed feelings about the outcome of the family's long struggle. 'It has only scratched the surface and not gone to the heart of the problem,' she said, but none the less it represented 'an opportunity not to be missed by society'.

The debate about race in Britain will never end, but it has been transformed by the case of Stephen Lawrence. Ideas such as unconscious or institutional racism have been thrust into the mainstream while notions that were easier to live with, such as the bad apple theory, have lost much of their authority. It is now less widely accepted that all people should be treated equally and more widely accepted that people should be treated according to their needs. More people see that the need to respect others should not be dismissed as 'political correctness'. Such changes were doubtless happening already, but the Lawrence case and the inquiry have been powerful accelerating factors. And as the debate moves forward, so surely will the everyday practice of institutions and individuals, so that it seems reasonable to hope that over time more will be done to prevent and correct racial injustice in Britain. Doreen Lawrence once spoke of Stephen 'bridging the gap between black and white'; perhaps he will.

The case is not over; given its long and tortured history it would be a foolish person who ever said it was. The killers remain at large and the Metropolitan Police never tire of declaring their determination to bring them to justice, although it is hard to see how that could be done. The five suspects still live in southeast London, although they have moved from the homes they occupied at the time of the murder. Their mothers, in their radio interview, complained that the case had ruined the lives of their sons. It is certain that their social lives and their prospects of work and of advancement have been damaged, and the continual public and police attention will have frustrated those of them who might have expected to make a living as criminals. But in the eyes of the many people who are convinced of their guilt that is hardly punishment enough. The victims of the crime, for their part, have paid a high price. Stephen was robbed of a life full of hope at eighteen. Duwayne was left deeply scarred, and endured years of suffering while he did what he could to find justice for his friend. As for the Lawrences, their lives have been changed for ever. The quiet, earnest family of spring 1993 has gone, and perhaps the shattering blow of the murder alone would have done that. But the long struggle, the unimaginable days and nights of anxiety, fear, frustration and anger, following each other relentlessly over six years, have settled it; the couple were driven apart and the marriage was over by the time the inquiry began. It should have been no surprise that the report brought them little satisfaction, for Stephen was dead, his killers were free and for the most part the police officers who failed the family were beyond punishment. Yes, they had been largely vindicated, but so late in the day that it could be little comfort.

What was it, people asked in February 1999, that had made the case of Stephen Lawrence special? Why did this, rather than another unsolved racial murder, become a test of policing, of justice and of racial attitudes? There are many answers. The murder had about it a terrible purity: the victim was a young man of impeccable character; the attack was unprovoked; the racial motive was, or should have been, beyond question. It was impossible for anyone to take refuge in the idea that the victim was to blame. The character and judgement of Stephen's parents were all-important. They made a shrewd early assessment of the first investigation and from then they were single-minded in pursuing justice and truth, prepared to take risks and suffer setbacks so long as the objective was clear. They were well advised: Imran Khan, Michael Mansfield and others helped them to use the law to achieve their ends, even when no legal remedy was apparent. The character and behaviour of the suspects certainly helped to define the case as special; they have inspired an unusual degree of hatred. As for public opinion and the media, they played their parts in the story, but their contribution was belated and perhaps a little shamefaced – this case was driven by campaigning parents, not campaigning journalists, and white Britain was slow at best to recognize the merits of the Lawrences' argument. The Labour government deserves credit for establishing and supporting the inquiry, although it may be that even a Conservative home secretary would have had to act once the Kent investigation's findings were known. In the end, however, the case was special because of the great accumulation of wrongs, large and small, that it comprised, and because the Lawrences, in trying to put at least some of them right, never took no for an answer.

It is not over, and there will be more headlines. But the long story of the case of Stephen Lawrence surely reached its climax in the House of Commons on that afternoon in February 1999 when a prime minister and a home secretary, in the presence of Doreen and Neville, swore to build a lasting testament to their son.

Index